Lincoln Christian College

D1074403

THE NATURE OF RELIGION

"That religion necessarily springs up of itself from the inner experience of every noble soul, that it possesses a province of its own within the human heart, a province of which it is absolute master, that it is worthy, because of its innermost power, to move the noblest and most perfect human beings and to be known by them in its own deepest nature, this it is that I affirm."—SCHLEIER-MACHER.

"Two things inspire the mind with ever new and continually increasing awe and reverence, the more frequently and consecutively they are thought about: the starry heavens above and the moral law within."—KANT.

"God is one in whom we should see all that is good and in whom we should take refuge in every need; therefore, to have a God is nothing else than to trust and to believe in him with our whole heart, as I have indeed often said that the trusting and believing of the heart makes both God and idol."—LUTHER.

J. Wobbermin.

The NATURE *of* RELIGION

BY

GEORG WOBBERMIN
University of Göttingen

Translated by
THEOPHIL MENZEL
Eden Theological Seminary

and

DANIEL SOMMER ROBINSON
Indiana University

With an Introduction by
DOUGLAS CLYDE MACINTOSH
Yale University

THOMAS Y. CROWELL COMPANY
PUBLISHERS :: :: :: NEW YORK

COPYRIGHT, 1933

BY DANIEL SOMMER ROBINSON
AND THEOPHIL MENZEL

All rights reserved

*No part of this book may be repro-
duced in any form without permission in writing from the publisher*

Printed in the United States of America

INTRODUCTION

Dr. Georg Wobbermin, who was born in Stettin (Germany) in 1869, has been well and favorably known to theological teachers and students in the English-speaking world for almost a generation. More than twenty-five years ago he was brought to the Yale Divinity School to deliver the Nathaniel W. Taylor Lectures on Theology. His theme on that occasion was the Theology of Albrecht Ritschl. He represented at that time what may be regarded as the first or the second wave of the movement away from Ritschlianism, according as his former teacher, Julius Kaftan, is or is not regarded as a member of the Ritschlian school. With his somewhat older contemporary, the late Ernst Troeltsch, he may be said to have started, from within the range of Ritschl's deeply penetrating influence, the movement away from a theology which notoriously admitted only so much of philosophy as was needed in order to get rid of philosophy. It was a movement toward a system of faith and thought which, without ceasing to be based upon an appreciation of religious values, was to be frankly philosophical in its eventual procedure and metaphysically defensible in its final results.

At the University of Berlin the young Wobbermin had studied philosophy under Dilthey and theology under Kaftan. Both teachers were Kantian enough to regard metaphysical knowledge as impossible, but Dilthey's *Weltanschauungslehre,* according to which the most defensible world-view was that which gave most appropriate and reasonable expression to the highest human values, must have seemed to the young theologian to accord very well with the teaching of Kaftan, which was to the effect that Christian theology, although a system of theoretical judgments about transcendent Reality, was to be defended by pointing out the validity of the religious value-judgments upon which these theoretical judgments were based. Wobbermin made the obvious identification of Christian theol-

v

ogy with the metaphysical world-view most defensible from a practical point of view. The central thesis of his doctor's dissertation was that Christian theology, as the statement of a world-view, is already in the metaphysical field; that consequently "theology without metaphysics is impossible." But he went on to take the next step also, namely, that theology, involving metaphysical claims as it does, must not be shielded in Ritschlian fashion from scientific and philosophical criticism; rather must it come out into the arena of metaphysical discussion and make good its claim to being rationally permissible as well as practically valid. The doctor's dissertation was followed after a few years by a little book in which a good beginning was made toward putting into practice the recommended program of showing an essentially Christian world-view to be defensible on philosophical grounds. This little book, which is still useful, is available in English, thanks to Professor Robinson's translation of some years ago, under the title, *Christian Belief in God* (Yale University Press).

Professor Wobbermin, who after an apprenticeship as Privatdocent at Berlin was made Professor of Theology in the University of Breslau, was called from there to succeed Troeltsch at Heidelberg and has now been for many years the successor of Arthur Titius in the Chair of Systematic Theology in Göttingen. It is a matter of interest to students on this side of the Atlantic that he was one of the first to introduce to German readers what was then an almost exclusively American study, namely, the (empirical) psychology of religion. Not only did he make William James' *Varieties of Religious Experience* available in German translation; he discussed the problems of religious psychology and began definitely to develop in his theology, partly as supplementing but partly in opposition to the more exclusively "religio-historical" method of Troeltsch, what he calls the "religio-psychological" or "James-Schleiermacher" method. Beginning as William James does, with a survey of the varieties of religious experience, we are led, according to Wobbermin, to the discovery that religion is always and everywhere *a tendency toward the transcendent,* always interested therefore in the *truth* of its ideas about the transcendent, especially in the truth of its idea of God. If man is to continue to be positively religious he must have ideas which he can believe to be true to guide him in his religious quest and adjustment. At this point, then, man to become or remain religious must go beyond any mere external survey of the varieties of religious experience. He must enter into or fall back upon the religious experience and conviction of faith mediated to him by the vitally religious community of which he is or comes to be a member. In other words he must go on beyond the point of view of William James to that of Schleiermacher. But having thus begun again with shared religious feeling and conviction, the theologian, if he is to serve the religious needs of the religious community in our modern age, must go on to interpret his religious conviction and vindicate its truth by bringing it into contact and co-ordination with the assured results of scientific investigation in a metaphysical philosophy at once thoroughly rational and soundly religious.

There is nothing sensational or spectacular about Professor Wobbermin's philosophical theology. He has remained always open-minded to the discoveries of science, sensitive to the suggestions of constructive philosophy, and devoted therewithal to the conservation of the tested and approved values of a vital Christian experience and faith. As in his earlier days he fought the battles of an essentially Christian theism against Haeckel and the naturalistic Left, so in recent years he has withstood the extravagances and irrationalism of Barth and the reactionary Right. One does not have to agree with his philosophy at every point to be able to recognize the wholesomeness and essential soundness of his religious insight.

The work now presented in English translation by two of Professor Wobbermin's former American students has been happily chosen. It represents the author's mature conclusions as to the essential nature and validity of the religious consciousness, and has valuable contributions to make both to the psychology and to the philosophy of religion. Professors Robinson and Menzel are to be thanked for their enterprise and industry in making more widely accessible the contents of this valuable book.

DOUGLAS C. MACINTOSH.

YALE UNIVERSITY DIVINITY SCHOOL.

AUTHOR'S PREFACE TO THE AMERICAN EDITION

To the excellent translation of my book, which Professors Menzel and Robinson have prepared, I will add a brief statement for the English-speaking reader.

The question of the nature of religion is the fundamental question for all science of religion. For unbiased thought it will always remain the fundamental question. Consequently this question unites philosophy (that is, the philosophy of religion) and theology. In scientific religious research both must be developed and expounded in reciprocal dependence upon each other.

This position, which is demanded by the facts themselves, was taken both in the first (1921) and in the second (1925) editions of this book, and it will continue to be the author's position. For it is proven to be the soundest position exactly by the most recent discussions. Today from two opposite starting points this true position is endangered by one-sided views which control their author's sense for absolute reality. On the one hand, this is true of the so-called crisis theology of Karl Barth and Emil Brunner. They would separate the Christian Religion from the other historical religions, and accordingly they would completely isolate the scientific study of it and deal with Christianity entirely by itself. The ultimate conclusion, which not only would follow logically but which actually does follow in their writings, is that Christianity is treated and defined so that it is not a "religion" at all. Such a conclusion reduces the position of Barth and Brunner to absurdity. Objectively there are two ways in which this appears in their writings. . . . In the first place, the concept "religion," with which they work, is not clear, but, on the contrary, is highly equivocal and ambiguous. And because of this ambiguity the distinction between religion on the one hand and magic and mythology on the other hand is not sharply and clearly made.   Indeed religion and magic are often simply treated alike, religion is then interchanged with magic, and magic is unjustifiably and erroneously identified with religion.   This is the double error underlying all of the writings of Barth and Brunner.   It not only makes difficult but actually prevents any complete clarification of the decisive problem.

The other one-sided view is of an opposite character.   It overlooks the uniqueness of the Christian Religion, either by failing to raise the question of its uniqueness at all, that is to say, the question of the specific ingredients of Christianity as Christian, or, in any case, by not allowing this uniqueness full scope and even by restricting and minimizing it from the outset.   This defect dominates the position of Rudolph Otto, as set forth in his *The Idea of the Holy* in a logically careful manner that makes it all the more dangerous in its effects.

This volume deliberately and as a matter of principle aims to correct both of these one-sided views that are so widespread today, in order to make possible, in the full sense of religion's reality, a truly scientific discussion of the agitated question of religion, which is doubly important in this age of anti-religious movements.

G. WOBBERMIN.

GÖTTINGEN, *January,* 1933.

AUTHOR'S PREFACE TO THE
GERMAN EDITION

The publication of this volume, dealing with the nature of religion, has been very much delayed by the World War and by the events which followed it.

However, I may claim a symbolical significance for the fact that in the first edition the year 1921 appeared on the title-page. Exactly one hundred years ago Schleiermacher's chief theological and philosophical work on religion was first published. It is the chief purpose of my volume to take up again the basic tendency permeating Schleiermacher's scientific investigation of religion, and to carry it through more completely than was possible in his day. His theory of a feeling of absolute dependence, and his thesis that statements of belief are verbal expressions of the emotional states of feeling of the pious, seem to me to be the decisive elements in that basic tendency. To be sure it is my opinion that both need correction: the first in the sense of a complement demanded especially by the consideration of the history of religion in general; the other, in order to exclude a psychological shift, which Schleiermacher himself made possible and even partly furthered.

The point of view which overlaps and combines these two elements is the assertion on principle of religious experience as the ultimate court of appeal for all scientific study of religion. If I gratefully acknowledge the contribution which William James made to the clarification of this basic principle and in this sense even speak of a Schleiermacher-Jamesian position, it must here be especially emphasized that this has absolutely nothing to do with the pragmatic philosophy which James advocated. It was purely a misunderstanding on the part of Wilhelm Wundt, which, to be sure, is rooted in the insufficiency of his own scientific principles of religion, when he in his *"Problemen der Völkerpsychologie,"* raised the objection of acceptance of the philosophy of religion of pragmatism both against Ernst Troeltsch and against me. I have in the meantime written a thorough debate with Wundt in the introduction to the later editions of my German translation of James' *Varieties of Religious Experience.* Moreover I have written a critical exposition entitled *Methoden der religions-psychologischen Arbeit* for Emil Abderhalden's encyclopedic work on biological methods, which in its new edition, also takes the related branches of the social sciences into consideration. This article is now obtainable in separate form from Urban & Schwarzenberg (Berlin).

My motto for the religio-psychological method is exclusively this: *Back to Schleiermacher and from Schleiermacher forward!*

This motto does not aim to discard the fruits of the work done in systematic theology and the philosophy of religion since Schleiermacher, nor to minimize in any way their significance. On the contrary, I attach an extremely high value to them—both to those of Albrecht Ritschl and his disciples, especially Julius Kaftan, Wilhelm Hermann and Theodor Häring, and to those of the other more important schools of theology and philosophy of religion. Nevertheless I think that the valuable insights which have been gained in this way are intrinsic parts of the above-mentioned cardinal principle of the religio-psychological method, which is deliberately based upon Schleiermacher.

The close connection between the religio-psychological method and the methodological principles of the so-called "Phenomenology" of Edmund Husserl, has been pointed out already, not only by me, but by various other investigators. A penetrating investigation of the questions herein involved, which simultaneously illumine their relation to the philosophy of value of Heinrich Rickert, is given by Robert Winkler in his *Phänomenologie und Religion* (Tübingen). In another direction the religio-psychological method is related to the "psychology of the understanding" expounded by Karl Jaspers in his *"Psychologie der Weltanschauungen."*

So far as the objections to the religio-psychological method which have been offered by theologians are concerned, I may mention as the most important and capable representatives Friedrich Traub in one direction, and Ludwig Ihmels in the opposite direction.   I have repeatedly considered these objections, and the consideration of them has enabled me to eliminate many former obscurities and to strengthen my position as a whole.   For this I am very grateful to these critics.   In a similar way the practical pedagogical test of the religio-psychological method in religious education and pastoral work has been effective, and for this my gratitude is especially due to Kurt Kesseler and Friedrich Niebergall.

The arrangement of this volume is determined by the method.   It will first treat the question of the nature of religion, without reference to the question of its truth, and then the question of its truth in the light of the question of its nature.

The discussion is such as to make this volume of my *Systematische Theologie* an independent whole.   Its comprehension is therefore not dependent upon Volume One, which deals with the question of the principles of systematic theology in the light of its history during the last hundred years.   Volume Three will have as its subject-matter the nature and truth of Christianity.

GEORG WOBBERMIN.

TRANSLATORS' PREFACE

Anyone reading this book from cover to cover will be impressed with the wealth of material which it contains, and many such readers will agree with the translators in thinking that there is probably no book available in English from which one can learn as much about religion as he can by carefully studying this monumental work. In the absence of an analytical table of contents it will be an aid to cataloguers, and to others having special interests, if we indicate here where certain significant original discussions may be found.

Psychologists will find an important analysis of religious experience at the end of Chapter I, and penetrating criticisms of Professor Leuba's psychology of religion in Chapter XI, Sec. 4. Anthropologists will be especially interested in the critique of Frazer's theory of magic in Chapter IX and in the original material, nowhere else available in English, on the religion of the Australian tribes in Appendix II. Those who are following the controversy between humanists and theists will find Professor Wobbermin's discussions of Natorp's theory of religion unusually suggestive (pp. 146 ff. and 301 ff.). Professor Wobbermin is recognized as one of the greatest living authorities on Schleiermacher, and Chapters III-IV and Appendix I contain one of the best discussions of Schleiermacher's theory of religion available in English. There is an intensely interesting discussion of the Freudian theory of religion in Chapter XI, of mysticism, pp. 186 ff., of Christian Science, Theosophy, and Steiner's Anthroposophy, pp. 68 ff., of primitive monotheism in Appendix II, of totemism in Chapter XI and Appendix III, of Haeckel and Ostwald in Chapter XII, of Feuerbach, of Vaihinger's philosophy of "as if," and of the Marxian theory of religion in Chapter XI, and of the Barthian theology in Appendix I. Professor Wobbermin has spent years studying the religions of India and his discussions of the *Rig-Veda,* pp. 173 ff., the *Upanishads,* pp. 103 ff., the *Bhagavad-*

Gita, pp. 199 ff., and Buddhism, pp. 214 ff., are especially significant.   Perhaps the most original contribution in the book is the exposition of the religio-psychological method in Chapter II, and the application of this method to the definition of religion.   (See especially pp. 181 ff.)

In making this translation our aim has been to rewrite the book into English rather than to give a literal verbal translation.   We have omitted a number of footnotes which would be of slight interest to English readers.   Professor Wobbermin has read our manuscript and has added numerous references to recent literature.   We are deeply grateful to him for his coöperation.

We are much indebted to Professor Douglas C. Macintosh for constant encouragement, and for the excellent special introduction which we are sure our readers will especially appreciate.

THEOPHIL MENZEL,
D. S. ROBINSON.

June, 1933.

CONTENTS

PART ONE

THE QUESTION OF THE NATURE OF RELIGION WITHOUT REFERENCE TO THE QUESTION OF ITS TRUTH

PART TWO

THE QUESTION OF THE TRUTH OF RELIGION IN THE LIGHT OF THE QUESTION OF ITS NATURE

Contents

PART ONE

The Question of the Nature of Religion without Reference to the Question of its Truth

In the pure bosom doth a yearning float,
    Unto a holier, purer, unknown Being
Its grateful aspirations to devote,
    The Ever-Nameless then unriddled seeing;
We call it: Piety!—

———

Dem Herrlichsten was auch der Geist emfangen,
Drängt immer fremd und fremder Stoff sich an.

GOETHE.

THE NATURE OF RELIGION

CHAPTER I

THE QUESTIONS OF THE NATURE AND OF THE TRUTH OF RELIGION AND OF CHRISTIANITY

I

From the point of view of the religio-psychological method the whole task of systematic theology is subsumed under the two cardinal questions: What is the nature of religion? and What is the nature of Christianity? This division of the task is therefore determined by the method. But, on the other hand, it claims to correspond most closely to the subject in question and to be the most serviceable division. Whether this is really true can only be learned after our investigation is completed. Here at the beginning the interrelation which exists between the method and this division of the task must be made clear. For this purpose it is necessary to sketch very briefly the character of the religio-psychological method, and to safeguard it against misunderstandings and misinterpretations.

The religio-psychological method of *systematic theology* is under consideration. But we can substitute for the idea of systematic theology that of *systematic science of religion.* For we view the task of theology primarily from the standpoint of the science of religion. The task of theology is not to be identified with or displaced by that of the science of religion in general, but nevertheless it is to be attacked and carried out from the standpoint of the science of religion. This follows immediately and with imperative necessity from the religio-psychological method. For as a religio-psychological method it refers definitely to religion as such; that is, to religion as a whole and in all its manifestations. The religio-psychological method is concerned above everything else with the question of the specifically religious. It asks, therefore, what is the truly and specifically religious in the data which are empirically called religion, in other words what is it that justifies our referring to these data as religion or as religious. To this end this method attempts to start out from the external manifestations of religious life and from these to penetrate to its ultimate and deepest motives, then to separate those from such elements as have been due to other kinds of motives, thus determining exactly what the pure and specifically religious element in them is.

For if, to use Schleiermacher's famous expression, millions have played with the trappings in which religion has permitted itself to be wrapped, then naturally the chief and the most important task for all scientific religious research is to recognize those trappings as such, and to penetrate beneath them to religion *in its unique essence as religion.*

And this task remains precisely the same for all phenomena which bear the name religion. Therefore the religio-psychological method demands that theological work, and in particular the work of systematic theology, be treated from the standpoint of the science of religion in general. But it does not advocate an identification of theological work with that of the science of religion in general. Entirely the contrary, for the religio-psychological method must sharply oppose every such identification.

For that task, which is fundamental for the religio-psychological method, can only reach its fulfillment through the instrumentality of one's own religious experience. Indeed this is the second important insight which Schleiermacher had attained in his very first work, *Reden über die Religion,* and to which he gave the following expression near the beginning of the first address: "In respect of other human virtues, characteristics, and properties I know that not much is proven before your judgment seat, ye wise and understanding of the people, by saying how one possesses them. They can be known by description, by observation of others, or, as all virtues are known, from the ancient and general legends of their existence. But religion is of such a sort and is so rare, that whoever utters anything concerning it, must necessarily have had it, for nowhere could he have heard it. And to that man who has not himself experienced it, would it not be an annoyance and a folly?"

Thus Schleiermacher deliberately validates that basic idea of Luther, which determined and guided all his work in the Reformation, but which, it goes without saying, was almost entirely lost sight of by his followers, and especially was as good as entirely forgotten in scientific religious research. For this insight of Schleiermacher gives methodological and technical expression to the idea which Luther had so often and so strongly emphasized by referring to the necessity of a personal and inner religious experience. In this respect Schleiermacher has drawn the conclusion of the position of the Reformation for the field of religion just as Kant drew it for the field of rational epistemology. In so far Schleiermacher and Kant belong together. And their belonging together is independent both of Schleiermacher's own scholarly attempts in epistemology [1] and of Kant's theory of religion as presented in his religious work; *Religion innerhalb der Grenzen der blossen Vernunft.* Schleiermacher's epistemology is not entirely consistent with the standpoint of Kant's epistemology. And Kant's theory of religion is the exact opposite of the point of view maintained by Schleiermacher. But Kant's epistemology and

[1] Schleiermacher's epistemology is now best presented in the remarkable discussion of G. Wehrung, entitled: *Die Dialektik Schleiermachers,* Tübingen 1920. Wehrung shows that truly noteworthy initial steps to an inductive and critical procedure are present in the different drafts of the *Dialektik;* but that, nevertheless, the speculative and deductive type of thought dominates; and that religion is buried beneath the speculative philosophy of identity which represents that mode of thought, so that the programmatical standpoint of Schleiermacher's *Reden über die Religion* does not come into its own.

Wehrung's conclusion is entirely in accord with my own judgment of the *Dialektik.* Only I think two things should be added. (1). The unique significance of Schleiermacher, speaking generally, does not lie in the direction of his speculative philosophy, but rather in his analytical and scientific religious research. (2). For Schleiermacher's position as a whole the basic tendency which lies in the direction of his *Reden über die Religion* is ultimately decisive, as is shown from the close relationship of the two most important paragraphs of the *Glaubenslehre*—4 & 15. See the second edition.

For the general controversy over Schleiermacher initiated by the representatives of the socalled dialectical theology (especially by Karl Barth and Emil Brunner) see my article *Schleiermacher* in the encyclopedia: *Die Religion in Geschichte und Gegenwart,* 2nd ed., Vol. V, pp. 170 ff. See also the article reprinted below as Appendix I.

Schleiermacher's religious philosophy are fully analogous to each other. The *new* attitude of consciousness, which was gained in the Reformation and which is due especially to Luther, is at work in both, only in different directions.

Now if it is true, as Luther and Schleiermacher both emphasize, that any understanding of religious phenomena must always be based upon one's own inner religious experience, then there follows from this a further important conclusion binding upon all systematic science of religion. Namely this, that the possibility of a religious investigator reaching a genuinely profound understanding can hold only for that religion in which he is fully at home *by virtue of his own religious experience*. For this reason systematic science of religion must always place that religion in which the investigator is at home at the center of its investigation, and must differentiate it from other religions under consideration. A universal science of religion which deals with all manifestations and forms of religion in exactly the same way is possible in the field of the history of religion alone. From this point of view a purely historical study of religion only is possible, and that means such a study as restricts its ultimate conclusions and evaluations entirely to the framework of purely historical principles and criteria. The moment the systematizing effort is undertaken, the moment the investigator begins to deal with the essence of religion as such, and tries to reveal the unique meaning and to evaluate the religious content, then it becomes necessary to differentiate between the religions, and not simply for practical, but also for objective theoretical reasons.

Consequently in the sphere of Christian culture, the idea of culture being used here in that most general sense which includes religion, next to the question of the specifically religious must be asked the other question of the specifically Christian. The special science of the Christian religion, Christian Theology, can not be replaced by a general science of religion, at least not in the field of systematic theology. But it goes without saying that Christian Theology must be pursued from the point of view of the science of religion, if it is to take the religio-psychological method seriously. That means that the Christian religion itself must be investigated in its relation to other religions and in its significance for the religious life in general. In this respect the religio-psychological method is like the socalled religio-historical method (of Troeltsch). But it differs from that method by taking as fundamental, both as a general methodological principle and as one applicable in all particular investigations and researches, the demand for a unique personal religious experience in the sense in which that demand was validated by Luther and Schleiermacher. Moreover it wants to make that demand methodically fruitful in the most concrete way. Consequently the religio-psychological method must hold that the religio-historical method as such is satisfactory for the historical part of religious knowledge alone, but that, strictly interpreted, it is insufficient for systematic theology.

Now this confirms what was said, namely, that the task of systematic theology has to be differentiated from that of the science of religion, and this in turn makes necessary, at least for our circle of culture, a Christian Science of Religion or Christian Theology. Thus the religio-psychological method shares with the socalled religio-historical method a broad and unprejudiced point of view. Yet, on the other hand, it repudiates the substitution of a general science of religion for theology as the Christian Science of Religion from the very outset, whereas the socalled religio-historical method for a long time did appear to culminate necessarily in such a substitution[2] and today it continues to lean toward this position for practical reasons, although no longer for theoretical reasons.

2

If now we return to the basic characterization of the religio-psychological method, which we began above, it is now almost self-evident that the more exact formulation of it is to be reached through the ideas "religio-psychological circle"

[2] Ad. v. Harnack's position on the question of a general science of religion can only be understood in this way. See his frequently quoted Rektoratsrede: *Die Aufgabe der theologischen Fakultäten und die allgemeine Religionswissenschaft* (Giessen, 1901). See also *"Reden und Aufsätze,"* Vol. II, pp. 159 ff. For the present situation in German theology on this important question see my *Richtlinien evangelischer Theologie zur Überwindung der gegenwärtigen Krisis,* Chaps. I and II (Göttingen, 1929).

and "productive empathy." For it is a matter of understanding alien religious spiritual life from one's own religious experience, thus sharpening the eye for the peculiarities of the specifically religious, and returning to the observation of one's own religious consciousness with this keener insight. And it is a matter of continually extending and of more and more intensively and inwardly shaping this process of reciprocal advancement by grasping, comprehending, and interpreting one's own and alien forms of expression of the religious life in order, in this way, to bring to light in its purest possible form the specifically religious element in the total historical complex of the religious life.

This procedure may appropriately be described by the phrase *"religio-psychological circle."* But since the *feeling-into-process,* which constitutes the very basis of this circle, exactly speaking, reveals itself as a creative continuation or rebirth of experience it must be characterized as productive empathy. In the religio-psychological method of the science of religion and of systematic theology, the religio-psychological circle is dependent upon this productive empathy as its unique instrument. Only with the aid of productive empathy can the religio-psychological circle draw nearer and nearer to its goal as just sketched.[3]

Now this proves conclusively that the religio-psychological objective, so far as systematic theology is concerned, is not realizable by means of *empirical psychology.* Unquestionably the method of empirical psychology is useful in the field of religious knowledge.[4] And since terminology can be used as one likes, one can speak of the psychology of religion and

[3] In volume I the idea *psycho-transcendental* was used to describe this relationship. But since this idea gave rise to many misunderstandings, I have dropped it. Purely technically considered, the process here in question is closely related to the methodological principle of the *Phenomenology* of Husserl. See Robert Winkler's *Phänomenologie und Religion* (Tübingen).

[4] For my part I have never opposed the use of the method of empirical psychology, but on the contrary I have often strongly emphasized the need of it. Any assertion to the contrary is a pure fabrication. Very profound discussions of this matter have recently been offered by Kurt Kesseler in his essays and treatises on the philosophy of religion and religious education. See also the opinion of Fried. Heiler: *Das Gebet. Eine religionsgeschichtliche und religionspsychologische Untersuchung.* Munich, 1918.

even of religio-psychological method in this sense. But however one may estimate the significance and value of empirical psychology, in any event it does not measure up to the task of the systematic science of religion. Indeed how could it, since the task of the systematic science of religion consists primarily in the work of bringing up from the depths of the empirical phenomena or entities designated religion or religious, the specifically religious elements and motives? It goes without saying that one can not do this by means of empirical psychology, since the function of empirical psychology is definitely restricted to describing the actual empirical facts of psychical life and to exhibiting their empirically demonstrable orderliness. *But what in, and which among, these actual facts are the specifically religious can never be discovered by means of empirical psychology.*

Schleiermacher clearly apprehended and concisely expressed for the field of religion what is true in general, namely, that a purely empirical interpretation has "no measure nor formula for distinguishing the essential and the permanent from the changing and the accidental." And still less is it possible for empirical psychology to comprehend the essentially religious in its specifically religious character. Although the opposite assertion is still continually being advocated, and even by such keen and penetrating investigators as Friedrich Traub, Hermann Faber and Wilhelm Stählin, it nevertheless remains self-deception.

This self-deception probably springs primarily from the easily understood and well-meant intention of establishing on a purely empirical basis, and therewith in an unassailable manner, all religio-scientific research in its widest possible extent. But in the first place this intention itself is determined by hypotheses of a positivistic habit of thought. Justifiable in it, as in all positivistic thinking, is the "sense of reality," the insistence upon the unprejudiced evaluation of the actual facts, and for the science of religion this means the actual facts of religious experience. The emphasis upon

English translation by Samuel McComb (Oxford Press, 1932). Cf. my article "Religionspsychologie" in the encyclopedia *Religion in Geschichte und Gegenwart,* 2nd ed., Vol. IV (1930), pp. 1921 ff.

religious experience is the element of truth in that conception, and on this point it agrees with the religio-psychological point of view and method which is here defended. However, the transformation of this empirical interest in reality into a critical faculty of judgment is unjustifiable. At this point the whole procedure usually turns into its opposite. And this is the second important objection to this theory. For a "normative" critique of religion, the criteria of which are drawn from an entirely different viewpoint, and that, too, from a viewpoint which has nothing whatever to do with the empirical religious psychology which they advocate, accompanies the "empirical psychology of religion" of these thinkers. This throws the doors wide open again to dogmatism; at least in principle and in general procedure, even though a particular investigator may succeed in avoiding it for himself.

In Traub and Faber this error is unmistakable inasmuch as they divide the systematic science of religion into two fields of work. It is not so obvious in Stählin because he usually restricts himself to the circle of interest of empirical psychology. But the moment he begins to deal with the overlapping basic questions of the science of religion, the defect in question is very clearly seen in Stählin's writings, and it is all the more obvious because of his accepting without question the position advocated by Traub and Faber.

3

It is, and remains, then, a self-deception in these thinkers when they say that they can answer the question of the specifically religious by means of empirical psychology, and when they in consequence demand that the work of the psychology of religion be restricted to the field of empirical psychology. But how far the effects of this self-deception extend is shown most clearly by certain representatives of the socalled American psychology of religion. This is not true of William James, at least not in any definite way. He occupies after all a unique position among American psychologists of religion. We Germans have not sufficiently recognized this fact. James' psychology of religion, looked at as a whole, stands in closest relation to the methodological postulates of Schleiermacher's science of religion.[5]

To be sure James himself occasionally referred to his investigations in religious psychology as purely empirical. However this is a peculiar use of the word *empirical,* and hence it cannot be considered absolutely decisive in reaching an objective judgment in the matter. For James' use of this expression is strictly determined by his philosophical position, the socalled *pragmatism.* Hence his use of the word *empirical* is evidence of an unjustifiable introduction of a predetermined theory of philosophy into religio-psychological research. At the same time it shows a lack of methodological clarity. In fact James also talks of a "purely empirical philosophy" and he regards his pragmatism as being such a philosophy. Now this idea of a purely empirical philosophy, which, in the strict sense of the word, is absolutely contradictory, nevertheless does make clear what James intended to express in both contexts by the word *empirical.* With this idea he is insisting upon a fundamental return to experience. And when applied to religion this basic principle means a return to inner religious experience.

Now it was precisely in reference to this basic principle that Schleiermacher occasionally described his own research in his *Glaubenslehre* as purely empirical.[6]

Leaving out of consideration the pragmatism influencing James, the same lack of clearness, but also the same aim, comes to expression in both James' and Schleiermacher's use of this word. Looking at the essential fact, James takes up exactly the same position to the problem as Schleiermacher: *the investigation of the unique meaning of the forms of expression of religious life by returning to inner religious experience.* According to James' own declaration, he intends to direct us to the discovery "of the unique nature of religious experience which is ultimately conclusive in respect to the judgment as

---

[5] See my remarks in the Preface to the first and second editions of my German translation of James' *"Varieties of Religious Experience."* See also my essay in Abderhalden's voluminous work on Method, referred to above. (See the Preface to the German edition.)

[6] See the first letter to Dr. Lücke. *Gesammelte Werke,* Part one, Volume II, p. 593.

to what religion in general is." Now this is not a possible objective of empirical psychology.

Hence our critique of American psychologists of religion does not apply to James. But others offer conspicuous examples of the self-deception already mentioned as to the possibility of being able to deal with and to answer the ultimate questions of the science of religion by means of a purely empirical psychological investigation. This is true above all of Starbuck and Leuba, and quite particularly of the latter.[7] The guiding principles with which Leuba attempts to clarify and to establish his own methodological position really characterize this position best, whatever one may think of his proof of these principles.

1. The religious belief in God or in gods rests upon inductions drawn from inner life.
2. Religious experience as an inner experience is subject exclusively to empirical psychology.
3. Since the gods of religion are empirical entities, they are subject to the competency of science, especially of empirical psychology.

By grouping together these theses, Leuba is able to draw the conclusion that empirical psychology, as the determining scientific discipline, proves religious belief in God to be an absolute illusion. In any case the full consequence of giving to empirical psychology the right to answer the question of the specifically religious is here drawn. For it goes without saying that from the viewpoint of empirical psychology inner religious experience is only a definite phase of human psychical life. And since, in a general way, religious experience is focused in the belief in God, it follows that this belief in God is also only a definite phase of human psychical life. And thus the objective content of belief in God is unmasked as illusion. Leuba thus plays the part of a modern Feuerbach. Indeed he developed the theory of illusionism far more rigidly and consequentially than did Feuerbach. (See below, Chap. XI.)

Now looking at the fact itself Leuba's whole argument

[7] *A Psychological Study of Religion, its Origin, Function and Future.* New York, 1912.

is, of course, a mere begging of the question. The conclusion which is finally reached at the end of a complicated exposition is in fact already implicit in the preliminary statement. Religious experience is looked upon as merely a phase of human psychical life. Now within its own limits empirical psychology certainly has a perfect right to this view, only the unique meaning of the religious conviction as determined by the standard of inner religious experience is thereby left entirely out of consideration.

The chief objective of the science of religion is to bring to light the unique meaning of the religious conviction itself. To this end the very greatest emphasis must be laid upon the fact that inner religious experience has the character of a relationship, and always includes in its objective content a thought of an object. The religious belief in God in the sense of the religious conviction does not rest upon an induction drawn from the inner religious life, but on the contrary that belief is a necessary element in the inner religious experience itself, without which the latter absolutely would and could not exist as a real inner religious experience. Saying this does not make the inner religious experience valid. But of course neither does empirical psychology have any right to deny its validity. Leuba's whole argument, being built upon two false theses, is a pure fallacy. As Leuba understands, and would have these theses interpreted, they are valid only for the point of view of empirical psychology, and the first thesis especially already contains an interpretation which has been perfected from this point of view.

Judging the matter as a whole, then, the conclusion is contained in the preliminary statement. And the underlying fallacy of this argument is to be found in the assumption that empirical psychology is competent to answer the question of the specifically religious. Thus purely empirical religious psychology works itself out to its logical conclusion in Leuba. In him we by no means have a narrow and unjustifiable radical exaggeration of this viewpoint, such as Stählin for example maintains, but on the contrary a thorough-going logical development of the methodological principles underlying it. (See the discussion of Leuba's theses in Chap. XI, pp. 296 ff.)

4

All the more, then, must the religio-psychological method of the systematic science of religion be formulated as the *method of the religio-psychological circle.* And the religio-psychological circle, which is here under consideration, is more accurately defined as that which follows from a productive empathy, according to the measure of the psychological and logical structure of the religious consciousness.

It is due to the great service of Schleiermacher that the *psychological structure* of the religious consciousness has been established as the methodological principle of systematic and scientific religious research. We are here dealing with the underlying insight of Schleiermacher, which runs like a red thread through all of his works from the very first edition of his *Reden über die Religion,* but which receives its relatively clearest formulation in the second edition of the *Glaubenslehre.* The youthful religious "orator's" recognition that all conceptual forms of expression of religion, its dogmas and its creeds, are of a secondary order and that they can only be rightly understood from the basic inner religious experience, and that means understood in their *uniqueness,* leads directly to the chief methodological principle of the *Glaubenslehre,* that (christian) doctrines are verbal descriptions of the states of feeling of the pious (christian). I have put the word christian in parentheses because the restriction to the Christian Religion is determined solely by the purpose of the *Glaubenslehre.* For according to Schleiermacher, the basic and decisive methodological principle is equally applicable to all religious belief whatsoever.

To be sure even in Schleiermacher's writings this chief methodological principle of the *Glaubenslehre* undergoes a psychological shift. Later I shall deal with this in greater detail. But the basic methodological tendency itself gives no occasion for such a shift and it may, therefore, be regarded as being quite free from it. Subject to this one qualification it is and remains justifiable precisely because it corresponds to the psychological structure of the religious consciousness. In this respect and to this extent a return to Schleiermacher simply must be demanded. But the position of Schleiermacher certainly is in need of supplementation and at the same time, by means of this supplementation it will be deepened. For the psychological structure of religious consciousness is more complicated than appears at first sight. Exact analysis reveals a larger number of strata than just the two which Schleiermacher recognized. *Indeed, if we would completely describe the psychological structure of the religious consciousness, we must differentiate four or, since the fourth must itself be subdivided, five strata.* They are the following:

1. Religious experience. (The inner religious life in the sense of personal religious experience.)
2. The religious conviction or assurance.
3. The conceptual expression of the religious conviction or assurance.
4. The set of religious images of the primary type.
5. The set of religious images of the secondary type.

The supporting substratum is that of inner religious experience, personal religious experience, for it is in the sense of personal that the word *experience* is here used. All genuine religious conviction or assurance is based upon inner religious experience, regardless of how, looked at genetically, it may have first come into existence. For granted the widest possible differences of origin, nevertheless every religious conviction, which is not just the passing-on by authority of purely traditional ideas, is continually growing anew out of the inner religious experience of the religious person.

This religious conviction is then intellectually crystallized. It seeks a conceptual expression. For only so can it continue and consistently influence behavior. Indeed this purpose essentially and indefeasibly characterizes the inner religious experience, because it has as its basic postulate a relationship between the religious person, as the bearer of the religious conviction, and the objective content of this person's underlying religious experience. Therefore, no matter what form it may take, the intellectual expression is at least always present when religious conviction grows out of inner religious experience. Originally and uniquely, this intellectual expression will clarify and also establish nothing but the religious conviction as that is determined by the inner religious experience which underlies it. A corruption of the religious intellectualizing process is therefore involved whenever, along with the religious experience, other interests and motives influence and, under certain circumstances, even decisively determine it. The practical and magical type of motive, the motive of rationally explaining the world, and the motive of the æsthetical view of the world are often especially likely to seek expression in this way.

But the actual situation is even more complicated. For the intellectual expression of the religious conviction enters the world of appearance in the form of definite particular images or as a set of such images. To a certain extent these images are the stones for the building of the religious intellectual world. Strictly speaking they are the essential means to this end. Their justification and utility should really be measured solely by this basic principle. But it goes without saying that the selection and arrangement of these images can give new occasions for the infection and dislocation of the religious intellectualizing process. And not only that, for on the other hand these images can also independently produce still other images, which have absolutely nothing to do directly with the conviction determined by the personal religious experience simply because they are only occasioned by various analogies and associations of the imagination. And yet they are now taken up into, or at least influence, the intellectual expression of the religious conviction.

Thus analysis reveals four or even five strata to the psychological structure of the religious consciousness: the substratum of the inner religious experience, above that the layer of the religious conviction, and then the layer of the intellectual expression of the religious conviction, and finally the layer, or more exactly, the double layer of the religious images.

Moreover, as has already been emphasized, the *logical structure* of the religious consciousness must be taken into consideration as well as its psychological structure.

In this connection an especially important service has been rendered to religio-psychological research by Heinrich Maier,

in his masterly work on the psychology of affective thinking.[8]
And here we find that there are, above all others, two characteristics which are significant. First, Maier describes the
creations of religious faith as *fancy-images* of the affective
type. He uses the term *fancy-images,* without implying any
secondary meaning of illusionism, to refer to all images which
are not based upon sense experience. This is shown by the
fact that he further differentiates between *cognitive fancy-images,* or those rooted in the rational intelligence, and *affective fancy-images,* or those having an affective volitional
origin. The second significant characteristic is Maier's emphasis on the logical aspect of the creations of religious faith.
The irrefragable certainty by which the religious fancy-images
differentiate themselves most decidedly on the one hand from
the cognitive and on the other hand from the æsthetic fancy-images characterizes this logical aspect of religious fancy-images.

The appropriateness of Maier's unique terminology shall
not here be considered. But the two characteristics just mentioned are as independent of this terminology as they are from
Maier's whole original and profound speculative and philosophical position. On the other hand, I fully concur with
Maier in the opinion that the logical structure of the religious
consciousness is dominated by the *truth-interest.* Religious
conviction wishes to offer truth, and indeed, ultimate and
highest truth. *This assumption of a uniquely valid truth must
be granted, if we would rightly comprehend the unique meaning of the religious consciousness.*

It goes without saying that this claim to valid truth must
not be forthwith confused or identified with the investigator's
own attitude toward the question of the truth regarding religious conviction. At this point the religio-psychological
method stands juxtaposed to two errors which repeatedly recur
from two different points of view. One of these errors is the
failure to take the truth-interest of the religious consciousness
into consideration, in the formation of the religio-psychologi-

---

[8] Heinrich Maier: *Psychologie des emotionalen Denkens,* Tübingen, 1908.
Maier has recently been called to Berlin. The thinking which he calls
"emotional" is somewhat like the existential thinking, so called by Martin
Heidegger and others who follow Kirkegaard.

cal method in general. The other error is the failure to distinguish *truth-interest* and *truth-claim* from *truth-belief*. How great the obscurity in this respect still is may perhaps best be indicated by the fact that I myself have occasionally been reproached for this identification, in spite of the fact that the standpoint which I represent is deliberately based upon a denial of these two alternatives, and hence necessitates the above-named juxtaposition.

To be sure William James has furthered this confusion in so far as pragmatism, which he introduced into religio-psychological research, carries with it the danger of simply identifying the truth-claim of religion with truth-belief, in the service of and for the purpose of establishing a hasty apologetic. For this reason I have constantly and emphatically opposed the introduction of pragmatic philosophy into religio-psychological research. But just as emphatically, on the other hand, must the fact be emphasized that in formulating the religio-psychological method of the science of religion the interest of the religious consciousness in truth must be recognized.

In fact, a proper regard for the psychological and logical structure of the religious consciousness leads to the following demand: From the given historical data, which are either called religion or are frequently referred to with the ideas and terminology of religion, must, by means of productive empathy, be elicited every specifically religious content which can claim to be a valid intellectual expression of religious conviction and which is determined by the underlying religious life. From this it also follows that all the ideas of traditional religion are rooted in an underlying essential motive and tendency which has to be separated from other types of motive, if these ideas are to be grasped in their utmost purity, that is to say, in their specifically religious character. To this end there must be perfected a way of alternating between the historical data and those of personal experience, and by this alternation a progressive clarification of each will be attained. Hence the cardinal and most characteristic principle of the religio-psychological method of the science of religion is the religio-psychological circle which encompasses both the objective historical data of the religious consciousness in general and the data of personal religious experience. That is why this method can be exactly defined as the method of the religio-psychological circle moved by productive empathy.

In this method are combined, then, the valid elements of the procedures of two of the ablest students of the psychology of religion, while at the same time it avoids the limitations and the sources of error in each procedure. The method of William James and that of Wilhelm Wundt are combined in the method of the religio-psychological circle, with the chaff of each removed.

The basic methodological principle of James' work in the psychology of religion is that of selecting extreme cases. This principle rests upon the distinction between *institutional* and *personal religion*. The validity of this distinction, which James rediscovered after it had previously been discovered by Schleiermacher, is indubitable. But James was wrong in isolating and setting the two realms of religion in opposition to each other. On the contrary they are always interrelated and interworking. Frequently institutional religion originates in personal religion. But, on the other hand, the religion of each individual is always determined by institutional religion. Indeed, the very essence of religious institutions is incorporated in the religious creeds. Consequently the interrelation between the traditional conceptions of faith and the personal religion of individuals is of the utmost significance to the student of the latter. For in the creeds of a religious tradition the religious experience of whole generations of men is conserved. James' principle of extreme cases does not do justice to this fact.

The one-sidedness of Wundt's procedure is exactly the opposite. Wundt himself referred to the method of his work in the psychology of religion as that of folk-psychology. And the principle of folk-psychology is then more specifically characterized as historical and genetic. His conception of this folk-psychological or genetic method is concisely summarized in the statement: Religion is through and through a problem of folk-psychology and not a problem of individual psychology. But this statement is false, since the disjunctive premise on which it rests is defective. Hence we must substitute for this statement another: Religion presents both a problem of folk-psychology and one of individual psychology. Only this proposition adequately expresses the real facts. And it is just for this reason that we must insist on having a method which does justice to both points of view and brings into relation both ways of formulating the problem. For then only will it be possible to grasp in its deepest import the problem of method in the psychology of religion. This deepest import lies at the point of intersection of the two ways of stating the problem, and both James and Wundt go around this point, the one in one direction and the other in the opposite. The method of the religio-psychological circle is directed precisely at this point of intersection, and, departing from it, this method is defined by the fact that it works by means of productive empathy according to the inner pattern of the psychological and logical structure of the religious consciousness.

5

This makes it clear why and to what extent the problem of the nature of religion is, for the religio-psychological method, the central problem of all theological research and of all science of religion whatsoever. But this inquiry into the nature of religion has as its specific corollary an inquiry into the nature of Christianity. And in both cases the question of truth has to be subordinated to that of nature.

However, the idea of subordination which is here introduced must not be misunderstood. It relates only to the scientific method of approaching the problem. Hence this subordination does not exclude, but rather assumes, that from other points of view the question of nature is subordinate to that of truth. From the point of view of the theory of value, as well as from that of epistemology, this is the case. But in the work of the science of religion in general, which can be determined by the religio-psychological method, the question of truth is subordinate to that of nature.

Briefly stated, this means two things. (1) In dealing with the questions of the nature of religion and of Christianity we must not introduce the question of truth prematurely. In both cases the question of nature must be dealt with, deliberately and as far as possible, without any reference to the question of the truth of religion or of Christianity. The necessity and the meaning of this restriction will be explained later. (2) The questions of the truth of religion and of Christianity are to be dealt with in the light of the results reached in dealing with the questions of nature. That is to say, they must be divorced from every attempt at an a priori or speculative solution of the problem of truth.

CHAPTER II

I

If, now, we approach the question of the nature of religion, a further consideration of method must precede. How can the nature of religion be determined at all? In what way and by what means is the problem to be grasped and treated scientifically? We are now concerned with methodology in the special context of the concrete question of the nature of religion. Here the religio-psychological method must stand its first practical test. And this first test is of fundamental importance, for the question at stake is precisely the basic problem of the whole science of religion. A method which fails in the search for the nature of religion is entirely worthless as a method of the science of religion. Conversely, a method which is successful in the search for the nature of religion is all the more likely to be the best method in all other respects for every scientific treatment of religion.

This sounds like a truism. Indeed, precisely taken, it is a truism. But it is nevertheless very necessary to refer to this fact with the greatest emphasis, for heretofore it has so little come into its rights that only the least beginnings have been made. And this is especially true of the most important subsidiary problem which arises, the problem of the treatment of Christian doctrine. The method of what is called in academic parlance "Dogmatics," that is, precisely, Christian doctrine, is not, even today, the same as the method for the discovery of the essential nature of religion. The beginning of such a method of treatment, which Schleiermacher made a matter of principle, has not been followed through directly; it has rather recently been discontinued. Schleiermacher's beginning, so far as method is concerned, comes to light from a comparison of sections 4 and 15 of his *"Glaubenslehre."* Section 4 contains the famous definition of religion as "the feeling of absolute dependence." In order to understand this definition correctly it must be remembered that Schleiermacher had previously defined "feeling" as "immediate self-consciousness." Section 15 presents the methodological canon for the *Glaubenslehre:* "Christian doctrines are verbal expressions of the states of feeling of the pious Christian." The "feeling of absolute dependence" of section 4 corresponds to the "states of feeling of the pious Christian" of section 15. So the similarity which exists here for Schleiermacher is obvious. And it is equally obvious that this similarity is based on a way of looking at things which, insofar as one considers the basic determining tendency, must either be described as specifically religio-psychological, or as lying in the direction of the religio-psychological method.

Concretely stated, this methodological similarity between sections 4 and 15 indicates a methodological resemblance between the treatment of the general problem of religion and that of Christian doctrine. Yet this methodological fact, which is of fundamental importance for Schleiermacher's masterpiece, has not been clearly recognized, and still less has it been utilized in further research. Of course it has often been stated, and lamented, that Schleiermacher's earlier conception of religion contains in germ the whole argument of his *Glaubenslehre.* Indeed, for that very reason the latter has been denied all independent value. Nevertheless, this judgment, with its exaggerated generalization of a misgiving which in itself is justified, does not apply to the methodological structure of Schleiermacher's work, but rather to the speculative construction which he introduced into his work, contrary to its own methodological structure. As far as section 15 is concerned, his fundamental tendency of making the Christian religious experience the decisive element in the formulation of Christian doctrines, is overlooked even today because of the exclusive emphasis upon the psychological shift, which Schleiermacher, to be sure, partly encouraged. This shift consists in substituting reflection upon the psychical processes involved in religious experience for the task of discussing the essence of the religious conviction itself.

Consequently Schleiermacher's insight has been lost. This is partly due to his lack of clarity, of which we have spoken. But it is also due to the after-effects of the dogma of verbal inspiration, as that dogma was developed, in the sharpest opposition to the original principles of Luther and the Reformation, by the older orthodox Protestant theologians. Of this, and of the possibility of permanently checking these after-effects, more will be said later on.

2

However, we must reach out still farther, if we would make the way to discover the nature of religion perfectly clear.

The very statement of the problem, the nature of religion, stands in the most intimate relation to the question of method. It is precisely for this reason that the problem of method is here of such vital importance. And here again the fact is note-worthy and instructive that this statement of the problem in the scientific investigation of religion goes back to Schleiermacher. It is due to him that the problem of the nature of religion has become the fundamental problem of all science of religion—of all philosophy of religion and of all exclusively theological research. In 1799 Schleiermacher gave to the second of his *Addresses on Religion* the title, "Concerning the nature of religion." He begins this address with the remarkable words: "You know how old Simonides, by oft-repeated and prolonged silence quieted the one who had pestered him with the question: 'What are the Gods?' Confronted with the much greater and more inclusive question of what religion is, I would gladly begin with a similar hesitancy."

These sentences of Schleiermacher, and the discussion which follows them, made the question of the nature of religion the basic problem of the scientific study of religion. It still remains the basic problem, and it always will remain so in the future.

It goes without saying that the predecessors of Schleiermacher prepared the way for his statement of the problem. Foremost among these predecessors were the theologians and philosophers of the Enlightenment. And from them again connecting threads lead back to Spinoza, on the one hand, and to Leibniz and the English deists on the other hand. Nevertheless these predecessors lacked the necessary clearness and they were uncertain of their goal, and hence they took the false track which led to "natural religion." For just this conception as it was used during the Enlightenment, indicates —although not exclusively, as is usually supposed, but still essentially—the substitution of a form of philosophical and intellectual abstraction for vital religion. By this conception, then, the question which needed attention as a problem was again suppressed or relegated to the background. Kant's *Religion Within the Bounds of Pure Reason* is the classical example of this suppression of the problem. Hence it is important, from the point of view of the history of the problem of the nature of religion which now occupies us, that Schleiermacher combated "natural religion" sharply and unflinchingly in his *Reden über die Religion.* The whole argument of the fifth address is determined by this attack on natural religion. "The so-called natural religion is usually so polished and has such philosophic and moralistic manners that she permits little of the unique character of religion to shine through; she knows how to behave so well, is so reserved and adaptable that she is tolerated everywhere; whereas every positive religion has such strong and pronounced features that in every movement which she makes, in every glance which one casts upon her she inevitably reminds one of what she really is." (1st. ed., pp. 243 ff.)

And all of Schleiermacher's reasons for rejecting natural religion, which he worked out in detail, reduce to this, that such religion is not rooted in and makes no use of religious experience. His argument against natural religion is, therefore, in the most emphatic manner, of a religio-psychological character. Here again, then, the connection between the method and the statement of the problem is manifest.

However, as far as the history of the statement of the

problem is concerned, our previous discussion needs still another important supplement. Schleiermacher is to be regarded as the orginator of this statement of the problem, if we have in mind the strictly scientific formulation. However, the motives which led him to this formulation go back to the Reformation. For these motives are all rooted in the necessity of personal religious experience as the presupposition of an adequate understanding of what religion is. "Religion is of such a nature that whoever makes a statement concerning it must necessarily have had it. To him, who has not himself experienced it, would it not be a stumbling-block or a folly?" (*Ibid.*, p. 15.) It is from this viewpoint that the definition of religion must be interpreted which Schleiermacher gives in the first edition of the "Addresses," that "religion is the perception of and the feeling for the universe," and just with special emphasis upon perception. The meaning of the word *universe* in this formula does not concern us here. But this double conception *perception and feeling* is put there to emphasize the experiential character of religion. That is shown unequivocally by Schleiermacher's more detailed discussion in which he makes religious perception analogous to sense perception. (*Ibid.*, p. 55.) And in this experiential character of religion he also finds the reason why the dogmas and tenets, which are "commonly passed off as the content of religion," do not belong at all to the "unique" nature of religion. (*Ibid.*, pp. 155 ff.)

The contrast to the Catholic conception stands out clearly in these statements, but the following sentences express that contrast even more pointedly. "Believing, commonly designated as such, acceptance of what another has done, to want to feel after and think over that which someone else has thought and felt is a difficult and unworthy service, and instead of being the highest in religion, as is supposed, it must be forthwith abandoned by everyone who wishes to penetrate into the inner sanctuary of religion. To have, and to wish to retain this proves that one is incapable of religion; to demand it of others shows that one does not understand religion. You wish to stand on your own feet at all times and to travel your own road, but may this worthy desire not frighten you away from religion. Religion is no slavery and no captivity; here too you must belong to yourselves, yes, this is even the only condition upon which you can partake of it." The spirit of Luther speaks through these words. They express the most unique and genuine attitude of the Reformation.[1]

This throws a flood of light on the relation of the problem of the nature of religion to the Reformation. This way of stating the problem must be attributed to the Reformation, since it is entirely conditioned by it. On the basis of Catholicism this formulation is not possible and would never have been reached.[2]

Due to its inherent nature, Catholicism excludes the search for the nature of religion in the sense of the fundamental problem of all science of religion and theology. The Catholic conception of the Church implies the exclusion of such a question. Ever since the principle of *extra ecclesiam nulla salus* has gained the upper hand in Catholicism, the problem of the nature of religion has lost its genuine significance for the Catholic mind. For such a principle includes the other: *extra ecclesiam nulla religio*—outside of the Catholic Church there is no real religion.

By abandoning this claim of Catholicism the Reformation laid the foundation for the question which Schleiermacher later stated clearly and decisively, and which it is our business today to carry out confidently and many-sidedly. That in using this statement we are really allowing the historical reality to speak for itself can be shown precisely by the chief Reformation writings of Luther. For example, in the larger Catechism he classifies the pagan religions, along with Christianity, under one uniform and inclusive conception of religion. In his commentary on the first commandment he begins his discussion with the question: "What does it mean to have a God?" This shows that he took the God-idea to be the most universal and basic conception of religion. Whether this is an entirely justifiable assumption must be left for later consideration. At any rate this assumption must be kept in mind, if we would understand Luther.

[1] See my essay: *Gibt es eine Linie Luther-Schleiermacher?* in the Zeitschrift für Theologie und Kirche, 1931, pp. 258 ff.
[2] This is especially true of Roman Catholicism; but it also applies generally to Eastern (Greek-Russian) Catholicism.

The question "What does it mean to have a God?" is followed by his famous answer. "A God is one in whom we should see all that is good and in whom we should take refuge in every need; therefore, to have a God is nothing else than to trust and to believe in him with our whole heart." To justify this view he then appeals also to the "heathen." After exemplifying this with various concrete illustrations he sums it up literally: therefore, that actually, according to all heathen opinion also, to have a God means to trust and to believe.[3] However, he adds, the heathen hypostatised their own fancies and dreamt of God as an idol. Hence they depended upon a mere fiction. But Luther also passes exactly the same judgment upon the worship of saints [4] and the service of mere works [5] under the papacy. Here, therefore, entirely as a matter of principle, he subjects to the same criticism the conceptions of religion of paganism and of Christianity and to exactly the same degree. The conclusion to such a position, which of course Luther did not draw, clearly forces one to the statement of the problem which we find in Schleiermacher under the caption, "the nature of religion."

3

In his *Reden über die Religion* Schleiermacher did not give precise enough directions for determining the nature of religion, to make possible a far-reaching and coherent scientific treatment of the problem. He confined himself to describing, with keen insight, the understanding of religion which he himself had won from his own religious experience. Nor has this gap in his work been adequately filled out in the *Glaubens-*

---

[3] "As namely the heathen who put their trust in force and dominion set up their Jupiter as the highest God; the others who sought wealth, fortune or pleasure and prosperity, set up Hercules, Mercury, Venus, or others," etc.

[4] "In like manner, think of what we have heretofore done in blindness under the papacy. If a tooth hurt a man he fasted and praised St. Appolonia; if he feared conflagration he made St. Lawrence his helper; if he feared pestilence he made a vow to St. Sebastian or Rocho," etc.

[5] "Concerning this there exists also a false worship and the worst idolatry which we have yet practiced, and which still dominates the world, upon which all clerical orders are based, which is really, however, an affair of the conscience, but which seeks help, comfort and salvation in one's own works and attempts to wrest heaven away from God," etc.

lehre. To be sure, the introduction to this masterpiece presents methodological observations of importance. However, no matter how one might estimate these remarks in other respects, they are not clear and unequivocal enough to satisfy our purpose. Hence they did not, in fact, fulfill this purpose for his own or for subsequent ages. The later decades of the nineteenth century reveal the most diverse and varied attempts to determine the real nature of religion. The need of coming to a common understanding, at least in regard to methodology, was usually not recognized at all; and where it was recognized it was not at all satisfied. Purely speculative constructions stood over against the strictly empirical attempts—whether of an historical or of a psychological nature. And between these extremes were methodological hybrids of all shades and combinations.

Not until the seventies of the last century did serious scientific reflection upon the question of the method for determining the nature of religion begin. But even up to the present this movement has not led to the formulation of a unified and dependable method. Nevertheless the situation has been considerably clarified by this movement, and today there are three chief methods of treatment which stand in contrast to each other. Only these three among the previous methods can still claim scientific standing.

1. *The Genetic Method.* This method rests upon the assumption that nothing can reveal the nature of religion to us better than the investigation of its origin. If we knew how religion originated, what causes produced it, then—so it is argued—we would be in a position to study its nature. So far as its methodological principles are concerned, the modern reconstruction of the old euhemeristic theory belongs to this type of method. Likewise the animistic theory belongs here. It enjoyed great favor for a long time, and, with certain modifications, it has recently been defended by Wilhelm Wundt with strong emphasis and breadth of learning. The ancestor-worship theory and the totemistic theory are also closely related to the animistic theory. The latter has been given an original interpretation in the so-called psycho-analytic explanation of the Freudian school. Here the origin and nature of

religion are carried back to the very beginnings of humanity, and it is supposed that the father of the first horde was killed and devoured by his growing sons, they being dominated by incestuous passions, but he was then, by an ambivalence of feelings, replaced by the totem animal. In historical connection with the animistic theory, but standing in partial contrast to it there has lately been developed the pre-animistic theory, which—in various forms—relates religion to the idea of mana and to magic, and thereby seeks light on the origin and nature of religion from its relation to magic.

Even this brief summary shows that within the limits of this method, any real coöperation is out of the question. Likewise this method fails to foster coöperative research. That is one argument against it, but the deciding arguments are questions of principle. These may be traced back to two chief objections, for this method rests upon two unwarranted assumptions. In the first place, in the sphere of spiritual life the matter of origin does not forthwith solve the question of the real nature of the phenomena. The genetic problem of the manner of origin simply cannot be substituted for the problem of the essential nature of religion. The other unjustified assumption is that we can know the prehistoric age of the human species, into which the beginnings of religion must be placed, sufficiently well to find out something definite about its origin. But this assumption is not justified. We know nothing definite about this age. Here we stand on shaky ground and for the most part we are restricted to guesses. Therefore this method must be objected to on principle. In fact, so far as method is concerned, to follow this theory actually means that we turn things topsy turvy. The origin of religion is not a fact open to observation. Rather, it is religion in its historical forms that is an observable phenomenon. Hence, the method of trying to grasp the nature of religion by tracing it to its origin means making that which is poorly known the basis for understanding that which is better known.

But in spite of this criticism the valid element of truth in the genetic method should not be ignored. Even if the problem of origin cannot be simply switched over into the problem of the nature of religion, it still has a close relation to the latter and is therefore of the utmost importance for it. It is more exact to divide the question of the origin of religion into two questions: (1) the question of the first one-time-existent origin of religion, and (2) the question of the primitive beginnings of religious life. Now this second statement of the question has much more scientific value than the former. And precisely this is of great importance to the problem of the nature of religion. For the investigation of the primitive beginnings of religion should also throw light upon special problems of religion's nature. Schleiermacher wanted—according to the express remark in the introduction to the second Address—to take his readers "for the purpose of illustration, back to those child-like days when, being in a more undeveloped state, everything was much more isolated and detached." Of course the reason which Schleiermacher gives here is wrong. For recent research shows with increasing clearness that, instead of everything being isolated and detached, the reverse is true of primitive life, all factors of the spiritual life being interwoven. Nevertheless, underlying Schleiermacher's mistaken formulation is the true insight that the comparison of more highly developed with primitive conditions of religion is bound to be helpful to the understanding of its nature. The anthropologists are wrong in trying to deduce the nature of religion from primitive conditions alone; but, on the other hand, the theologians do not usually allow the study of primitive religion to come to its rights. Edvard Lehmann and Nathan Söderblom [6] deserve credit for having especially emphasized this double-sided situation. It will be shown that we must agree with them without reserve, precisely from the religio-psychological point of view.

2. *The religio-historical method.* This method attempts to discover the nature of religion by comparing historical religions. Hence, it demands a study of the whole historical growth of religion, with the idea of discovering the sum total

---

[6] Edvard Lehmann, *Die Anfänge der Religion und die Religion der Naturvölker.* In Hinneberg's *Kultur der Gegenwart*, Part 1, Section III, 2nd ed., 1913. *Erscheinungswelt der Religion. Die Religion in Geschichte und Gegenwart*, Vol. II, pp. 497 ff. See also van der Leew: *Erscheinungs und Ideenwelt der Religion* in *Religion in Geschichte und Gegenwart*, 2nd ed., Vol. IV (1930), pp. 1860 ff. and Nathan Söderblom: *Das Werden des Gottesglaubens*, Leipsic, 1916.

of characteristics common to all the world's religions. This totality of common features of the historical religions is then held to constitute the essential nature of religion. Characteristic of this method is the insistence upon absolute objectivity. The objective data must simply be exhibited and recognized as normative. All more or less subjectively conditioned hypotheses concerning the origin of religion, and likewise all personal judgments concerning the particular value of certain special forms of religion, must be excluded when dealing with the problem of the nature of religion. Only the objective facts presented by the history of religion can be considered. In this sense the sum-total of common characteristics of the historical religions must be decisive in answering the question of religion's essential nature.

The advantage of this method over the preceding one is obvious. The emphatic demand for the most sincere and unprejudiced consideration of the entire history of religion, of all the facts which history presents to us, is the great service rendered by this method. Its insistence upon (greatest possible) objectivity deserves unreserved assent. However, inasmuch as the qualification "greatest possible" has involuntarily crept into our approval of this demand, therein consists also the justification of an objection. For when we try to exhibit the common characteristics of religions by comparing historical religions, a peculiar difficulty at once arises. The religions observable to us in history present, each in its own way, a great complex of variously interconnected elements. How then shall we judge what it is that is specifically religious in such a complexity? Yes, the difficulty goes still farther. How shall we decide at all in a definite individual case whether the phenomenon in question, even though it has traditionally been called religion, is really religion? In a particular case that may be doubtful. For example, is animism really religion? How important the answer to this question must be in determining the nature of religion is at once made clear by the animistic theory of religion of which we have spoken. And what about Buddhism, especially the primitive "atheistic" Buddhism? For when, as is usually the case, the conceptions of "religion" and "belief in God" are simply identified, this question undoubtedly becomes of crucial importance in determining the nature of religion. The problem arises, then: How can we decide at all, what in the history of the socalled religions is the specifically religious? The religio-historical method gives no answer to this fundamental question. It does not even suggest a way by which we might hope to find an answer to it. It is at this point that the third of the methods mentioned above enters.

3. *The method of the normative standard.* This method holds that as a basis for determining the nature of religion, one must deliberately restrict himself exclusively to that form of religion which he thinks is the valid or true religion. For Christian investigators this is of course the Christian Religion. The other religions are then to be criticised and evaluated from this point of view. This really means treating other religions as preliminary stages of the Christian Religion. The true nature of religion is only what other religions have in common with the Christian Religion. The measure of their nearness to Christianity is at the same time the measure of their truth, or more precisely stated, the measure of their truth-content. But just for this reason Christianity alone can be normative. It alone must be considered the deciding norm for determining the nature of religion.

Now this quite evidently sets up an out-spoken begging of the question as the criterion for the whole scientific study of the problem of religion. From the point of view of the scientific investigation of religion, this assumption signifies precisely such a begging of the question. However, the representatives of this theory deserve credit for having pointed out the unique difficulty in which the religio-historical method is involved. And, closely connected with this, they also deserve credit for having stressed the fact that one's own religious convictions have a just claim to be considered when one is dealing with this question. For the religious convictions of the investigator cannot be entirely excluded from the whole treatment of the problem, even though otherwise the demand for strict objectivity has been taken seriously. It indicates self-deception and lack of self-criticism when this fact is continually contested or even ignored. In deciding the question of the nature of religion, the student of religion would have to exclude himself, if his own religious convictions were eliminated.

It follows, then, that none of these three methods which have resulted from the methodological reflection upon the problem of the nature of religion of the last fifty years offers a satisfactory solution. To be sure, each of these methods contains valid and significant elements of truth. But strong objections may also be made to each method. Moreover, a synthesis of these three methods into a uniform methodological program is not possible, for they mutually exclude each other. If, as we have seen, these methods taken separately do not make possible a uniform plan of action, it follows that they will not make possible a uniform plan of action when taken together.

The question with which we are now confronted is this: Does the religio-psychological method carry us through these difficulties and does it, at the same time, guarantee the uniform technique which is so necessary? This uniform program is of course not to be regarded a priori as a uniformity of results, but rather as a supplementation and a reciprocal self-advancement of the separate investigations.

We must again recall the general character of the religio-psychological method in order to be able to test its application to the individual case in question, which, to be sure, is of such fundamental importance. To interpret alien religious soul-life in the light of one's own religious experience, thereby sharpening the vision for the peculiarities of the specifically religious; to return with increased understanding to the observation of one's own religious consciousness, and to expand still more and to form more intensely and intimately this process of reciprocal advancement in grasping, understanding, and interpreting one's own and alien forms of expression of the religious life, thereby revealing the specifically religious motives of all historical religious life in their greatest possible purity—that is the religio-psychological circle. It operates by means of productive empathy, and it concretely summarizes the religio-psychological method, and by so doing it is able to operate in a particular case in accordance with the psychological and logical structure of the religious consciousness.

This method, applied to the problem of the nature of religion, combines within itself the elements of truth which were brought to light by the critical analysis of the three methods just discussed.

Thus, on the basis of the foundation laid by Schleiermacher, the religio-psychological method measures up in every respect to the problem of the nature of religion as shown by the present status of the question.

4

The judgment just expressed must be confirmed still further, however. For this purpose it is necessary to take up the most important stages of the methodological movement of the last fifty years which is often mentioned.

There are three names which characterize these stages : Julius Kaftan, Max Reischle, and Ernst Troeltsch, but this does not mean that these names correspond to the three methods discussed above. Here we are rather concerned with the methodological discussion of the problem of the nature of religion taken as a whole.

In his book on the nature of the Christian religion, which first appeared in 1881, Kaftan brought the necessary clarity and precision into the discussion, which had been opened up by Albrecht Ritschl in his principal work, published at the beginning of the seventies. In his introduction Kaftan refers to the methodological uncertainty which dominated the discussions of that day on the questions of the nature of religion and of Christianity. From this he concludes that it is necessary first of all to make method itself the object of detailed investigation. In the course of this investigation he formulates the following conclusions :

I. The treatment of the question of the nature of religion must proceed without regard to the ideal conception of religion.

II. It must be kept free from all philosophical presuppositions.

III. It must not be confused with the problem of the origin of religion.

IV. The whole investigation must be based exclusively upon history.

V. The nature of religion must be determined by the general conception of religion extracted from the historical religions and must combine those characteristics which are common to all historical religions. In this way the determination of the nature of religion must follow from a comparison of the historical religions.

The theses I-IV form in a negative (I-III) and positive (IV) sense the presuppositions for the main thesis V.

Historically regarded the importance of Kaftan's position can hardly be over-estimated. In contrast to the caprice which dominated the discussions of the problem in preceding centuries, a program was here set up which sought to throw light upon the task on the basis of the subject itself. The strictest objectivity is the aim of the demands made in theses I-IV. And one may say that these theses were justified in the sense in which Kaftan understood them, and are still justified today. Every capricious construction should be made absolutely impossible. However, although agreeing with the main tendencies of the theses, we must object to the details, for they are open to misunderstanding and they contain erroneous ideas. To the first thesis the reservation must be made that one's own religious experience must not be entirely excluded, but on the contrary that it has a just claim for consideration. To the second thesis it must be said that the task of determining the nature of religion includes epistemological presuppositions which are conditioned by the peculiarity of historico-scientific knowledge.

The concept of value is fundamental to all historico-scientific knowledge. And in such an inclusive task as that of determining the nature of a wholly spiritual phenomenon this concept of value necessarily approaches closely to an evaluation, to the assertion and proof of that which is in question, which in this case is religious value. But that means that the task borders on the work of the philosophy of history.

The reservations which are to be made in regard to theses III and IV were sufficiently explained above in the criticism of the religio-historical method.

The objections which are to be made to thesis V follow from these qualifications of the other theses. A purely historical comparison of religions cannot hope to be equal to the task. For in the phenomena which it calls religious history itself does not offer any criterion for the discovery of that which we know as specifically religious. The nature of religion cannot be constituted by any concept reached by abstraction.

Reischle attempted to preserve the methodological position taken by Albrecht Ritschl [7] in regard to the question of the nature of religion. He did this with appropriate and profound investigations which are very noteworthy even today, both theologically and philosophically. Ritschl's position completely reverses Schleiermacher's basic thesis. For it would show how to grasp the nature of religion by first determining the nature of Christianity. The criticism of the religio-historical method of determining religion's nature, with which Reischle begins, lies to a considerable extent in the direction of the fundamental critical objections raised above. But on the basis of these objections Reischle then attempts to prove the necessity of the method of the normative standard. He does this by the following line of argument. All understanding of spiritual-historical phenomena is conditioned, to begin with, by hypothetical sympathy (Nacherleben), that is, by identifying one's self with the thinking and feeling of the persons or of the groups of persons in question. But this sympathy and imitation must always at definite points be further formed into an independent reconstruction on the basis of one's own experience, because only in this way can a connection be made between the separate elements of a tradition. And to these two activities a third must finally be added, a "comparing" with similar phenomena in one's own life. In this sense Reischle speaks of a three-fold treatment of the transmitted material, *an interpretative, an intuitive,* and a *comparative treatment.* So far this presentation of Reischle is certainly to the point. However, his making the comparative treatment of equal value to the other two is to be challenged. In reality

[7] Max Reischle, *Die Frage nach dem Wesen der Religion. Grundlegung zu einer Methodologie der Religionsphilosophie.* Freiburg, I. B., 1889. Albrecht Ritschl: *Die christliche Lehre von der Rechtfertigung und Versöhnung.* Vol. III, 1st ed., 1874, pp. 170 ff.; 3rd ed., 1888, pp. 184 ff.

it is always included in the other two. There is no justification or occasion for attributing to it special importance apart from the others, as long as we are concerned only with the interpretation of definite historical phenomena.

But Reischle's further argument comes in just at this point. The data before us force us to demand for the discovery of the nature of religion a comparing or a measuring standard rather than an abstract idea. But this conclusion is really unjustifiable. It stands and falls with the making of the comparative treatment independent. For the understanding of historical traditions a comparison of the type Reischle mentions is of course always necessary, but not a special standard of comparison. And a standard of measurement is necessary only for one's own measuring, that is, in our case, for the evaluation of the various forms of religion in their relation to each other, but it is not necessary for the understanding of alien religious life in general.

Just at this point Reischle makes the final leap. As the normative standard of measurement he brings in the ideal standard of his own religion. But therewith the question of the nature of religion is transposed into the other question of the highest or ideal form of religious life. Such a transposition is methodologically not permissible; it is entirely unmethodical. And this conclusion is confirmed by the further consideration that the method of the normative standard, instead of solving the difficulties of the question of the nature of religion which are before us, only leads us into further difficulties. For even the nature of Christianity is not self-evident and unambiguous. On the contrary, just in regard to method, the nature of Christianity itself presents a very difficult and an exceedingly complicated problem, even though this is most bitterly contested.

Troeltsch's discussion of our problem [8] may well claim to represent the apex of all previous methodological discussion. Troeltsch made the leading idea of the religio-historical method still more a matter of principle and developed it more many-

[8] Ernst Troeltsch, *Wesen der Religion und Religionswissenschaft. Kultur der Gegenwart*, Part I, 4. 1st ed., p. 461 ff.; 2nd ed., 1909. Vol. II, pp. 1 ff. *Gesammelte Schriften*, Vol. II, *Zur religiösen Lage, Religionsphilosophie und Ethik*. 1913, pp. 452 ff.

sidedly than Kaftan had done, and, at the same time, he
sharpened and deepened the insights which Reischle had
reached in the working out of his method of the normative
standard. However, he too has failed to achieve from this
position a uniform method of determining the nature of
religion. He thinks that the difficulties which the critical
analysis of the positions of these two methods reveal, can
only be adequately dealt with by separating into four subsidiary tasks the whole undertaking traditionally summed up
in the conception of the nature of religion. He labels these
four subsidiary tasks *psychology, epistemology, philosophy of
history* and *philosophy of religion.* So the apparently unified
statement of the problem of the nature of religion is to be
broken up into a number of problems which are very different,
but closely connected with each other. He thinks that the old
idea that the nature of religion can be expressed in a scientific
definition of religion, and that all of the questions which arise
in this definition can be answered together is misleading. All
scholasticism, which, even today, still works with such a
definition, is antiquated. As far as this statement of Troeltsch
is concerned, we are compelled to agree unreservedly with him
that in fact even today the treatment of the problem of religion's nature almost always ends in scholasticism, and that
we must avoid such scholasticism at all costs. Nevertheless,
the actual effect of Troeltsch's position would be the complete
abandonment of every possibility of ever arriving at a unified
and unequivocal way of determining the nature of religion.
But is this abandonment really demanded by the facts? Can
it be accomplished at all without affecting, undermining in
advance, and invalidating, the undertaking which Troeltsch
also supports?

Of course, in the nature of the case, the problem of the
nature of religion involves both psychological and epistemological investigations. That is due to the inner structure of the
problem itself. For it demands finding a valid criterion which
will justify designating certain definite psychical data by the
terms "religion" and "religious." Just this fact shows, however, that at this point the inner structure of the problem
requires still more than finding a criterion. It demands, evi-

dently, a coördination of the psychological and epistemological way of looking at things. For it is only in this way that the dual character of the points of view which characterize this inner structure can be dealt with at all adequately.

The philosophy of the history of religion has a claim for consideration in the problem of the nature of religion only in regard to the fundamental problems of all historical research in general. In discussing Rickert's great and epoch-making work on the methods of historical science, I have previously defined my position on these questions.[9] On the other hand, any set of postulates of a complete philosophy of the history of religion implies an answer to the question of the nature of religion. And therefore a metaphysic of religion can only be constructed on the foundation of a critical determination of the nature of religion if it is to be insured at the start, and as a matter of principle, against the dogmatic-scholastic metaphysic, in other words if it is to be a real metaphysic "of religion."

Hence, in his attitude to the problem, Troeltsch demands partly too little and partly too much. But his abandonment of a unified method of treating the question is determined precisely by this fact. And since the reasons for this abandonment have been shown to be unjustified in both directions we must hold fast to the possibility of such a unified method.

This brings us back to the religio-psychological method, with its religio-psychological circle which operates with productive empathy, according to the psychological and logical structure of the religious consciousness. Does the religio-psychological method meet all of the requirements which have emerged out of the methodological discussion of the last fifty years? We must answer this question in the affirmative. For, to begin with, the religio-psychological method conserves all of the valuable features of the methodological positions represented by Kaftan and Reischle. And in reference to Troeltsch, the religio-psychological method justifies the valid elements of his argument even more than his own position does. For unlike Troeltsch's position, this method is not satisfied with a mere juxtaposition or a sucession of the psy-

[9] See G. Wobbermin: *Systematische Theologie,* Vol. I, Ch. I.

chological and the epistemological aspects of the problem, but makes possible their coördination. Moreover, the religio-psychological method excludes on principle the hasty acceptance of constructions of metaphysics and the philosophy of history, whereas Troeltsch's position is not only open to this danger, but even encourages it. At least this is the tendency of its principle.

The religio-psychological method may claim to bring to a provisional conclusion the methodological discussion of the question of the nature of religion of the past five decades, the basic principle of which was originated by Schleiermacher. Of course the qualification must be made that new research will always be necessary on the details, in order to deepen the method and to make it more definite. But to go back of the religio-psychological method, with its religio-psychological circle and its productive empathy, will not be possible.

5

The fruitfulness of the religio-psychological method for the problem of the nature of religion is first shown by the fact that it makes possible greater clarity and precision. We have already made it clear that the first investigation of the problem, which was controlled by strict scientific objectivity, resulted in the assumption that the nature of religion must be found in the sum of the characteristics common to the historical religions. However, as we have seen, this assumption is inadequate. And it is at the same time misleading; or, at least, it can be misleading. For a determination of the nature of religion must give us the specifically religious; it must permit us to see what is the unique and the essential religious characteristic of the historical religions and of religious phenomena. However, the sum-total of the common characteristics of the historical religions does not give us this. For a characteristic might be common to all historical religions without being constitutive of the very nature of religion. It could be exclusively peripheral and proceed from motives which are non-religious and which have only an external relation to religion.

The religio-psychological method, with its religio-psychological circle, teaches us to bear this difficulty in mind at the very start in order to avoid, as much as possible, the errors to which it would lead. Positively this means that we can only accept as the essential nature of religion what is specifically religious. Accordingly the task may be stated thus: *the nature of religion must be that fundamental underlying motive of religious life common to all forms of religious expression.*

But have we not now come in a round about way to a slightly different formulation of the program of the religio-historical method? Are we not now really endeavoring to find the nature of religion in the sum-total of its common characteristics? No—absolutely not. For the fundamental motive of religious life common to all forms of religious expression is here interpreted in the sense of the religio-psychological circle. It is therefore not to be determined according to historical criteria. That is why we insisted that an historically proven common characteristic of all historical religions may not constitute the essential nature of religion. For example, when Kaftan, agreeing on this point with Feuerbach, assumes that the striving for natural goods (*i.e.,* the goods of this life) may be shown historically to be a characteristic of all historical religions, then that by no means justifies identifying this striving for natural goods with the essential nature of religion, nor does it even justify including it in the essence of religion. Indeed, the use of the religio-psychological circle as the decisive method forbids such a conclusion. For before the bar of one's own religious experience it is evident that the striving for natural goods does not belong essentially to the religious life, no matter how often and how much it attempts to crowd itself into it. On the contrary it is clear that the reverse is true. The striving for natural goods works against the fundamental motive of religion, and either blocks it or corrupts it. And once an insight into this fact has been gained by introspection, the eye which has thus been sharpened may also recognize the same fact in history.

It can be shown in passing that this way of using the religio-psychological circle was employed by Schleiermacher, and that this expression "religio-psychological circle" is only a technical description of the process which he used in his treatment of the problem of the nature of religion. This process is already observable in the *Reden über die Religion*. He begins his discussion of the nature of religion in the second Address by demarcating religion from (rational) metaphysics and morality, and then he allows the reader to raise the objection that all the literature of religion "from the beautiful poetry of the Greeks to the Holy Scriptures of the Christians" contradicts his view. For in all this literature one learns what is the nature of the gods and what their will is, and everywhere the votary is praised who knows the former and does the latter. Schleiermacher's answer is worded entirely in the sense of the religio-psychological circle: "But that is exactly what I have told you, that religion never appears in a pure state; those are all merely the foreign elements which cling to it, and it is just our business to free religion from them." [10]

This process was later developed much more definitely and precisely by Schleiermacher in the *Glaubenslehre*. It comes to expression in section 4 which is so important for the entire position of the work because it is so fundamental. The first statement of the famous theory of absolute dependence reveals it in a unique, and precisely because of this uniqueness, in an unequivocal way. "The common element of all expressions of piety, regardless of their differences, that by which they are distinguished from all other feelings is this, that we are conscious of ourselves as being absolutely dependent, or to say the same thing, that we are conscious of ourselves as being in a relation to God." As far as I know attention has never been called to the literary defects in this statement. "The common element—is this, that we are—conscious of ourselves."

---

[10] *Op. cit.*, pp. 47 ff. Compare also the more detailed discussion of this attitude, pp. 56 ff. "So it was religion when the ancients, disregarding the limitations of space and time, regarded all the different species of living organisms in the world as the creation and domain of an omnipresent being; they had seen a unique manner of action of the universe as a unity, and had given expression to their vision. It was religion when, for every helpful fact wherein the eternal laws of the universe were strikingly revealed in the finite they built temples to the god to whom they belonged and gave his name to them, they had grasped an act of the universe and so characterized its individuality and character," etc.

Ordinarily Schleiermacher never used such a crude and jarring construction. Since he did use this form in just this fundamental sentence it cannot be accidental. It must have been due to the fact that this way of putting it characterized especially well the uniqueness of the process which he had in mind. The inter-relation of the objective and of the subjective factor in the process is made clear in this statement. So far as its methodological character is concerned, therefore, the theory that the feeling of absolute dependence is the essential nature of religion lies in the direction of the religio-psychological circle.

If, however, the nature of religion is to be seen in the common underlying motive of all forms of expression of the religious life, then there follows from this insight still another conclusion in regard to the general treatment of the problem of the nature of religion. Namely this, that the final determination of the nature of religion can only be reached after the whole realm of the forms of expression of the religious life have been discussed and brought into relation to the underlying motive in question. A realization of this fact makes the task seem doubly complicated. For behind this fact is another to which we previously called attention. It is that the investigator of religion can only be sure of understanding, in the fullest sense of the word, the innermost depths of that religion which produced his own religious experience. For the Christian student of religion, this means that he can hope adequately to fulfill the demand just made of bringing all the forms of expression of the religious life into relation with the fundamental religious experience only so far as the Christian religion is concerned. Consequently determining the nature of religion is completed for him when he has treated the total faith-content of Christianity from the point of view of the religio-psychological circle. And for every student of religion who is of another faith—a Jewish or Mohammendan, or Buddhistic student, etc.—the situation is accordingly exactly the same. So here the religio-psychological circle again validates itself. And it follows from this that a conclusion can be reached only after the faith-content of Christianity has been unfolded.

And this fact was also surmised and alluded to by Schleiermacher. It lies at the basis of the evaluation of Christianity in the fifth Address where it is said that religion has nowhere been so completely idealized as in Christianity and in its original conception, or where it is stated that Christianity in its most characteristic attitude usually prefers to see in religion and its history the whole universe, that it remakes religion itself into the material for religion, and is thus at the same time a potentially higher form of it. (See 1st ed., pp. 293 ff.) And this is especially true of the general position of the *Glaubenslehre,* as Schleiermacher's explanations in the letters to Dr. Lücke unmistakably show. For in these letters, in spite of the universal significance of the theory of the feeling of absolute dependence, he protests against the opinion that he would absorb the specifically Christian into a universal religious knowledge, on the ground that for him such knowledge could be nothing else than an abstraction from the Christian.[11] And he characterizes the ideal which remains before him thus, so that it may become clear to his readers that the verse, John I, 14, is the text at the basis of all his theology (p. 611). Now this verse concerning the incarnation of the Logos forms precisely the connecting link between the history of religion in general and Christianity in its religious uniqueness. That was also known to the early Christians, and came to expression in their idea of the λόγος σπερμάτικος.

It follows as an unavoidable conclusion from the facts just discussed, that putting the problem of determining the nature of religion before that of determining the nature of Christianity can only be provisional. Later on it will be necessary to state this more accurately.

Moreover, there is also a conclusion to be drawn from these facts which bears on the provisional treatment and affects our solution of the problem of the nature of religion. In dealing with this problem, if the common underlying motive of all the forms of expression of the religious life must be decisive, and if the underlying religious motive can be grasped unquestionably only by means of the underlying religious ex-

[11] Schleiermacher, *Sendschreiben an Lücke, Werke,* Part I, Vol. II, p. 602.

perience, then the psychological structure of religious experience must be clarified before any headway can be made. This leads us back to the path which was opened up with such intuitive insight by Schleiermacher.[12]

---

[12] Karl Barth and Emil Brunner have taken a position which leads in exactly the opposite direction from that expounded above. However their position is already broken asunder. See Wilhelm Barthelheimer, *Schleiermacher und die gegenwärtige Schleiermacherkritik*, Leipsic, 1931. See my paper in the *Theologische Zeitung*, 1932, No. 9, and Appendix I below (pp. 343 ff.).

CHAPTER III

FORMAL-PSYCHOLOGICAL PROLEGOMENA TO DETERMINING THE NATURE OF RELIGION

I

"Piety, taken in itself, is neither knowledge nor action, but a distinct kind of feeling or of immediate self-consciousness." (See section 3 of the second edition of Schleiermacher's *Glaubenslehre*.)

In this sentence Schleiermacher summarizes his conception of the psychological structure of original religious experience. The purpose of this summary is to lay a foundation for a discussion of the question of the nature of religion, which then begins in section 4. It is an old and an ever-recurring misunderstanding—even in the scientific study of Schleiermacher—to try to find in section 3 a determination of the content of the nature of religion. But that clearly contradicts Schleiermacher's obvious train of thought. The theory of the feeling of absolute dependence is not presented until section 4. And in the sense of Schleiermacher, this theory first presents a determination of the content of the nature of religion. Section 4 shows, for the first time, what qualitatively unique or "distinct kind" of feeling constitutes the nature of religion; while section 3 merely decides whether, in general, any—but here as yet indefinite—distinct kind of feeling characterizes the nature of religion. Thus the contention of section 3 is of a purely formal nature; it remains within the bounds of formal psychology.

Schleiermacher is certainly partly to blame for this misunderstanding. Following directly after the sentence which we have quoted he refers to the corresponding discussion in the *Reden über die Religion,* especially to the sections of the second Address in which the demarcation of religion from morality and (rational) metaphysics is established. Now the third section of the *Glaubenslehre* also presents this same demarcation of religion from metaphysics and morality, from cosmology and from moral philosophy. And so the terminology of the *Glaubenslehre* was first employed in the fuller discussion which Schleiermacher presented in those sections of *Reden über die Religion,* beginning with the second edition.[1]

However, the incoherencies in Schleiermacher's underlying principle should not mislead us. This principle concerns the fundamental preparation for the problem of the nature of religion, and not the problem itself. It deals with the relation of knowledge, action, and feeling from the point of view of the existence and functional relations of the human soul. It is the actual existence and not the meaning of the psychical functions which is really involved here. Hence the question is stated from the point of view of empirical psychology. As Schleiermacher emphatically remarks, he is only presenting material "borrowed from psychology." And as the thesis of section 3 seems to assume that there is no fourth function alongside of knowledge, action, and feeling, the question arises whether or not there is in the soul such a fourth function. Now this statement of the question is quite evidently a problem of empirical psychology. Religious experience is here examined from the standpoint of its psychical existence and not from that of its meaning. A problem of being is involved and not a problem of meaning. Therefore, the nature of the content of religion cannot rightly be brought into consideration here.

To be sure the problem of the nature of the content of religion naturally presents a problem of meaning. However, Schleiermacher here only opened up the way for this differentiation. He did not himself carry it through clearly and precisely. That is why there are so many incoherencies and inconsistencies in his presentation.

We must, then, for the time being, keep strictly within the bounds of the task before us. We are concerned here only with the formal psychological preparation for the problem of the nature of religion, and not with the question of its

[1] Compare, for example, pp. 60 ff. of the third edition.

content. But we can learn from Schleiermacher on this problem, too, and hence we will begin our exposition with him.

It is true that in detail, Schleiermacher's formulations concerning the mutual relations of knowledge, action, and feeling are not free from objections. To be challenged is the fact that he designates the functions in question by the words *knowledge, action,* and *feeling,* and then later places feeling in juxtaposition to knowledge and action. However, he is careful enough to consider the affinities and relations which exist between feeling on the one hand, and action and knowledge on the other hand. He does not advocate, then, as has often been and is still repeatedly done, a complete isolation of religious feeling. Yet one must object to the fact that he compares feeling to knowledge and action, whereas the only psychologically valid procedure would be to compare it to the functions underlying knowledge and action, namely, to the functions of knowing and willing. This error was caused by the polemic which forms the background of Schleiermacher's whole discussion, the polemic against the old dogmatic scholastic definition of religion as a way of knowing and worshipping God. Since this traditional definition encourages the transformation of religion into metaphysics and morality, it was bitterly combated by Schleiermacher. Hence his formulation: religion is neither knowing nor acting. To be sure, as the discussion in the second part clearly shows, he includes thinking and willing under knowing and acting. Nevertheless the train of thought as a whole centers around the conceptions of knowledge and action. This explains how it was possible for Schleiermacher to place feeling in a completely analogous relation to both of the other two functions, to thinking and willing. Consequently he neglected the more intimate homogeneity of willing and feeling, of the affections and the will.

However, the decisive and vital point of Schleiermacher's thesis has not yet been touched upon, and what has already been said must be completely subordinated to this vital point. It is *Schleiermacher's identification of the conception of feeling with the idea of "immediate self-consciousness,"* and his obvious treating of religion as a distinct kind of immediate self-consciousness. There can be no doubt that the decisive meaning of his whole formulation lies precisely here. His explanatory remarks bring this out clearly.[2] For this reason, although it is often done, it is wrong to base one's theory of religion on Schleiermacher and then to reject his conception of feeling. It must also be added that, taken objectively, the most important insight of Schleiermacher must be found in his identification of feeling and immediate self-consciousness.

When Schleiermacher places the psychological scene of religion in immediate self-consciousness, his interest is directed toward the immediacy of fundamental religious experience. And the opposite view, which he has in mind and hopes to exclude, is that of rational reflection upon religious experience and its conceptual forms of expression. Fundamental religious experience does not belong to the sphere of speculation, but to that of immediate self-consciousness—the uttermost depth of the spiritual life of men. What Schleiermacher has in mind here is entirely in line with the well known description in the second Address of "that first mysterious moment" of religious experience, the description of which is followed with the words: "I can only show you the attitudes and feeling which develop from these elements. But this must be said: No matter how perfectly you may understand them when you believe that you have them clearly in your consciousness, if you do not know and cannot show that they have originated in you and were originally identical and undifferentiated, do not argue further with me or with yourselves, for it is not so. . . . You may have memory and ability to imitate, but you have not religion."[3]

Thus the general psychological observation underlying Schleiermacher's estimation of the psychological structure of religious experience is his distinction between the subjective and the objective consciousness, and his conception of their relation to each other. But it must be remembered that

[2] The note to section 2 is especially conclusive. Here Schleiermacher censures the theory supported by Baumgarten-Crusius, first the contrasting of feeling and self-consciousness, and then this, that through the use of the term perception, feeling seems to reach over into the territory of objective consciousness. At the same time the way the last-named conception is used by Schleiermacher should be especially noticed.

[3] As given in the first edition. In the later editions the last sentence was altered.

Schleiermacher's distinction differs from a similar distinction made by modern psychology. Schleiermacher conceives of the objective consciousness in the sense of perceptual objectivity. The discovery that there is also a non-perceptual comprehension of objects was made later. Schleiermacher does not reckon at all with any such process. He thought only of perceptual objectivity, more precisely, of the reflective processes of the mind in which it results. It could be held, then, that there is an objective content and an objective relation for the subjective consciousness. Of course, it would have to be of an entirely different type from the objectivity of ordinary acts of perception and thinking.

Schleiermacher expressly observes that his term "feeling" needs to be qualified. Hence he added the qualification "immediate," lest anyone be led to think of a self-consciousness which is more like an objective consciousness or a conception of one's self reached by introspection. By way of explanation, Schleiermacher then continues: "When such a conception of ourselves as we find in a certain moment comes home to us, or when it penetrates the separate functions of our state of mind, then this self-consciousness seems to accompany the state of mind itself." To distinguish this type of self-consciousness from the type which merely accompanies the momentary state of awareness, he then uses the expression "immediate self-consciousness."

The distinction between the subjective and the objective consciousness is interpreted by Schleiermacher so that only the subjective consciousness penetrates into the inmost depths of the human mind. The objective visualizing consciousness, even when it is made an object to the subject, is only secondary to this deeper subjective consciousness.

But another fact is also implied in Schleiermacher's expression "immediate self-consciousness," which can alone reveal to us its full meaning as a unifier and coördinator of the other functions. We refer to "self-consciousness." By "immediate self-consciousness" he means the self, the "I," the personality-forming factor of human mental life. The experiential character of the subjective consciousness in question is further characterized as belonging to self or ego consciousness. A self—an ego—is the bearer of the experience. The relation to the self or the ego is therefore fundamental to the experience. Thus when religion is characterized by Schleiermacher as belonging to immediate self-consciousness, it is at the same time regarded as an affair of our most personal self. Accordingly, religion is always related to or directed toward the self. And religion really is then, a direction of and a relation to the self. That must again be emphasized most emphatically, if Schleiermacher's position is to be properly interpreted. Religion does not belong to the mere manifestations or activities of the self; no! it is a direction of the self, more precisely characterized, it is a way in which the self is directed or finds itself directed. In this conception of "direction" there is implied a reference to an objective counterpole of the condition of religious feeling in Schleiermacher's sense of the word. It is at this point that Schleiermacher then begins to consider the content of the nature of religion, but we cannot take that up until the next chapter.

2

With this conception, Schleiermacher paved the way for an insight which could not be stated in more exact psychological terms and could not be applied until recent times. Disregarding the earlier attempts to formulate this insight, there are three directions and methods of thinking in recent psychological research which cross each other at this point: the underlying thesis of the Külpe-Marbe school of psychology, Heinrich Maier's psychology of emotional thinking, and the psychological position especially represented by Theodor Lipps. That ideas are not the decisive element in thinking, but that, on the contrary, all ideation is determined by the act of thinking; further, that there is a kind of thinking which originates from motives of feeling and will, an emotional thinking parallel to the purely intellectual or cognitive thinking; and finally that the self is to be regarded not in the sense of Hume's ever recurring theory of a bundle of ideas, but as an indissoluble factor which is rooted in experience itself: all of these insights of recent psychological research, which have been reached from varying starting-points, are anticipated in principle in Schleiermacher's position and are already so fully operative there that they may be developed directly from it. If this is true then it is also permissible, as was done above, to interpret or to develop Schleiermacher's position so that these recent psychological movements and views are fully taken into account.

And it is, of course, not accidental that this view or elaboration of Schleiermacher's position is here demanded and championed in the name of the religio-psychological method. Moreover, the fundamental tendency of the religio-psychological method points in this direction. For inasmuch as the methodological character is oriented, not exclusively, but still fundamentally to the psychological structure of the religious consciousness, it must seek to understand the formation of religious ideas by the religious conceptual content back of them, and this in turn from the total religious conviction into which it develops, and the latter again from the underlying religious experience. This methodological approach, then, already includes the relations to the three tendencies of modern psychological research: the first, that of the Külpe-Marbe school; the second, that of Heinrich Maier; and the third, that of Theodor Lipps.

Accordingly, we can summarize the discussion of the formal-psychological preparation of the question of the nature of religion as follows: *Religion is grounded in the subjective consciousness, i.e., in the affective and volitional life of man, and in such a way that it is entirely conditioned by the ego-function, and that its conviction and its conceptual content, including all of the formation of ideas developed therein, must be understood in reference to the underlying religious experience.*

Naturally the psychological investigations as such were and are decisive for this formal-psychological prolegomenon to the determination of the nature of religion. The religio-psychological circle itself cannot yet come directly into play at this point. But later on it must be shown that this conclusion can stand in the face of the history of religion, indeed, it must even be shown that it is confirmed by the history of religion, so far as that is possible in the nature of the case.

This is most evident in Christianity, especially in Protestantism, so far as it was determined by the factors of the Reformation. In his conflict with Roman Catholicism, Luther took his stand on the Scriptures as the Word of God. But in his interpretation of the word of God, this principle was decisive: "No man can understand God's Word unless he receives it directly from the Holy Spirit. But no man receives it from the Holy Spirit unless he experiences, tries, and feels it, and in this same experience, the Holy Spirit instructs as in His own school, outside of which nothing else is taught except falsehood and chatter." [4]

In the Catholic forms of Christianity the same principle is operative, although in an entirely different way. This is apparent especially in the form of worship, particularly in the Mass. A Protestant, who has witnessed the celebration of the Mass in an Eastern-Orthodox Catholic Church, recognizes this much easier than one who has seen the Mass celebrated only in a Roman Catholic Church. For there the sharp contrast between the hierarchical and the magical elements of the cultus disappears, thus facilitating a temporary disregarding of these elements. And when one has learned to disregard these factors, it must be admitted that then the immediate impression of the cultus, especially of the liturgy, upon the emotions is extraordinarily strong. When the priest and the deacon pass through the place of worship, in the short and the long processional, first bearing the Holy Scriptures and then the elements of the Sacrament, a clearly discernible holy terror passes through the congregation.

Now when we contrast the religion of the culturally backward races and nations, the socalled primitive peoples, with the various sects of the Christian Religion, the fact in question can also be proved with adequate certainty. This can be done first of all by answering the question: What individuals in such races are regarded as being especially religious? that is: Who are the official representatives of religion, and in what manner are they distinguished? For we find that everywhere among primitive people medicine-men, fetish-priests, Shamans,

---

[4] This especially pregnant formulation is found in the preface of Luther's writing entitled: *The Magnificat, Translated and Interpreted,* 1521.

Angakuts, or however else they may be called, have the reputation of being especially religious. Think, too, of the religious raptures and ecstasies, which are the tokens of religious leaders, and which occur among the backward races of all parts of the world. It is evident that we must classify them with similar phenomena found among more advanced races; e.g., with the wild ravings of the ecstatic fakirs mentioned in the *Rig-Veda,*[5] with the religious revels of the devotees of the Thracian Dionysos, with the exercises of the Dervishes, both the singing and the dancing Dervishes, and with the religious ecstasies of the Old Testament prophets. In view of these facts it cannot be doubted that for such races the characteristic mark of religion really consists of such states of rapturous excitement.

In the second place, think of the specifically religious ceremonies in the life of these races, *i.e.,* the more specific conditions under which their religion is practised. It is significant that these ceremonies are held preferably in such places and under such conditions as are apt, in a special degree, to influence the emotions of men and to produce in everyone a condition of suspense and excitement. The seasons of full moon or new moon are quite generally the preferred religious seasons, while mountain tops and mysteriously dark and densely covered groves are the preferred places of worship.

In the religion of the Vedas, with its strongly developed sacrificial cult, the nights of full moon and new moon play an important rôle, as is shown by the significance attached to the full and new moon sacrifices.[6] The recognition of this fact is independent of the acceptance or rejection of Hillebrandt's Soma-moon theory. With respect to that side of the Vedic religion in which we are here interested, the view expressed incidentally by one of the Vedic authors is quite conclusive: "Mighty is worship. I will incline myself towards

[5] *Rig-Veda* X, 136, 1 f., speaks of "long-haired ecstatics clothed in yellow garments who follow the movements of the wind when the gods have entered into them." H. Oldenberg (*Die Religion des Veda,* second edition, p. 404) aptly observes that this hymn describes the orgiastic ravings of the ancient Vedic world, which is still unrefined by the thirst after salvation that motivated the ascetics of Buddhist times, and that it is still bound to the crude forms of wild shamanism.

[6] Alfred Hillebrandt, *Das Altind. Neu-und Vollmondsopfer in seiner einfachsten Form,* 1880.

worship. Worship supports Heaven and Earth. Worship
the Gods! Worship rules over them!" (*Rig-Veda* VI, 51, 8.)
That in this last sentence worship is placed even above the gods
is a characteristic which is peculiar to this passage and is rarely
ever found in the *Rig-Veda.* Disregarding this fact we find
depicted here that significant power which determines the
universe and which is so familiar to the Vedic devotee.

The position of Buddhism is especially important for the
immediate preliminary question, as well as for the entire task
of discovering the nature of religion. Buddhism seeks to bring
to its devotees knowledge and enlightenment. "Those beings
which proceed from one source, their source is taught by the
Exalted One and also the end which they take: this is the
teaching of the great ascetic." As a brief Buddhist creed this
saying is found inscribed upon many monuments.[7] And a
Buddhist legend tells us that the ascetic, Gotama Sakyamuni,
attained a knowledge of the chain of causes and effects, and
of how to suspend the chain (Karma), under the sacred tree
of enlightenment, and that thereupon he became the Buddha,
the Enlightened One, who, after some hesitation, decided to
proclaim this knowledge to the world. Here everything seems
to be based on logical and rational knowledge. To state the
problem which arises clearly and in the terminology favored
by modern philosophy, religious validity seems to be included
in and subsumed under logical and theoretical validity.

However, this does not completely and accurately characterize the situation. For the knowledge itself which is here
in question exists throughout under "emotional" conditions.
Buddha intentionally teaches his disciples only that which "pro-
motes the way of holiness, that which leads to the withdrawing
from worldly things, to the extinction of desire and to the
cessation of that which is transitory."[8] Moreover, not simply
all speculative, but in general, all purely theoretical knowledge
is rejected and is even branded as "a path of opinions, full of

[7] Compare T. W. Rhys Davids, *"Buddhism, American Lectures,"* second
edition, 1904, p. 42.

[8] This is especially evident in the story of the conversation of Buddha
with his disciples at Kosambi in the Sinsapâ forest. (Samyûtta Nikâya,
V, pp. 437 f.)   Compare H. Oldenberg, *"Buddha, sein Leben, seine Lehre,
seine Gemeinde,"* 6th edition, 1914, pp. 230 f. Compare also, Hermann Beckh,
Buddhismus (Sammlung Göschen), Vol. II, pp. 7 ff.

suffering, corruption, excitement, and torture." [9]   The knowledge proclaimed is exclusively that which helps to save from
suffering.   Hence salvation is the ultimate and deciding factor.
It actually dominates the whole argument and imagination of
Buddhism.   As the oft-quoted saying which tradition ascribes
to Buddha himself has it: "As the great ocean, my disciples,
is permeated by only one savor, the savor of salt, so my
teaching is permeated by only one savor, the savor of salvation." [10]

One of the previously mentioned factors has not yet been
discussed expressly, and, therefore, needs to be considered
now: the significance of the ego-relation and the ego-function
for original religious experience.   This factor is most clearly
discernible in prayer.   For prayer is conditioned wholly by
the function of the self.   And since prayer is of fundamental
importance for all vital religion—for Luther faith is nothing
else than pure prayer, and according to Schleiermacher's judgment, "to be pious and to pray are really one and the same
thing"—the importance of the ego-function for religious experience follows unquestionably.

In the voluminous and valuable anthology of prayer, which
Friedrich Heiler has compiled, this fact is quite evident.   This
can perhaps be characterized most sharply and accurately by
referring to the statement of Plotinus, the Neo-platonic mystic,
that in prayer a man stands "the one to the one" before his
God.[11]   In general the mysticism of Plotinus tends strongly
toward allowing the self to be absorbed and lost in the pantheistically conceived deity.   Hence, when even this mystic
Plotinus coined this phrase, he perforce is a particularly indubitable witness to the irrefragability of this conclusion.   So
far as Christianity is concerned, it will suffice here to refer to
the Lord's Prayer in the New Testament, which serves as the
model prayer for all Christian bodies, since it especially assumes the child-father relationship in its opening words as

---

[9] *Majjhima Nikâya* I, p. 485.   Compare Oldenberg, *op. cit.*
[10] I will refer also to the especially lucid story of the conversation of
Buddha with Mâlunkyâputta.   (*Majjhima Nikâya* I, p. 426.)   Compare
Oldenberg, *op. cit.*, p. 315.
[11] See Plotinus: *The Enneads,* V, 1, 6, and VI, 9, 11.

well as in all of its separate parts, and particularly in the fifth petition.

In reference to primitive religion, two things must be mentioned. First, that here, too, the religious child-father relationship is developed to quite an extent, at least in embryo. Religio-psychologically interpreted, this fact means that even among primitive people the kinship relation to the deity is claimed quite generally, and that the deity is preferably referred to expressly as "Father" or "Our Father." [12]   And it is especially noteworthy that the name of "father" is used with great frequency, indeed almost regularly, for the "great Gods," or "exalted beings" which play such a unique and important rôle among primitive people, especially among races of the most backward culture.   In fact, it was just for this reason, that the Scottish anthropologist, Andrew Lang, who was the first to call attention to this fact with the greatest emphasis, developed his theory of primitive monotheism.   The designation of these gods as "father"—Lang calls them "high Gods" —seemed to him to be a complete analogy to the Biblical, and especially to the New Testament belief in a Father God. Lang's estimate of the situation is untenable. Nevertheless, the actual facts are extraordinarily significant for the history of religion. Among the tribes of Southeast Australia, which stand in the foreground of interest in the latest research into primitive religion, the designation of father occurs again and again. Among the tribes of southwestern Victoria, the highest being is called *Pirnmeheeal,* which means the same as our word "father."   The words *Mami-ngata* and *Mami-ngorak,* by which others of these tribes designate their high god, has the same meaning. And likewise, *Mungan-ngaua* also means "our father" among the Kurnai.[13]   But this custom is by no means re-

[12] But other relationships are also used, such as the child-mother relationship and the grandchild-grandfather relationship. Occasionally, several of these relationships are simultaneously utilized. This means that not all of these relationships are to be understood in the narrowest physiological sense, but in the more general and transferred sense. This also applies to the name of Father. Among primitives the name of father is very often used quite generally to designate a position of authority and honor. But, on the other hand, this does not exclude the fact that the religious use of the name of father also echoes the actual child-father relation.

[13] A. W. Howitt, *The Native Tribes of South-east Australia,* London, 1904, pp. 488 ff. Compare also my work: *Die Frage nach den Anfängen*

stricted to the Australian tribes. Similar practices exist among primitive people all over the world.

For illustration, I will give just a few examples. Routledge reports concerning the Akikuyu in British East Africa that they call their highest god *Ngai,* their first father.[14] In West Africa *Nzambi* or *Nyambi, i.e.,* ruler, is invoked as "our father" in times of threatening danger.[15] The Kubushmen call upon *Ho'we,* their high god as *Ba, i.e.,* "father." The village elder offers a prayer to him at the time of the onion harvest, according to H. Vedder's report, in this set wording: "Father I come to Thee, I entreat Thee, give me food and all things so that I may live." [16] Of the Indian tribes, the Delawares, for example, call their highest god *Nanaboush* and *Naskaboush, i.e.,* "original father of beings" and "original father of things." [17] The Mosquito Indians when passing dangerous rapids, turn to *Davan Eisi, i.e.,* "Master-Father." [18] Among the Bahan tribes of Central Borneo, the highest being is called *Tamai Tingei,* "our high Father." [19]

And of *Shang-ti,* the "highest ruler" of ancient Chinese religion, who occupies an entirely separated position from the ancestor-worship which dominates in daily life, it is occasionally said that he is called "our father and mother." [20] Moreover, it must be considered that since the earliest times, the Chinese emperor has been called the "son of heaven." Here we must consider two things. Firstly, that *Heaven-Tien* is used wholly as a substitute name for Shang-ti, and as the most frequent and popular. Secondly, that the privilege of ceremonial worship of the "highest ruler" is reserved ex-

der Religion in Religionspsychologischer Beleuchtung, Zeitschrift für angewandte Psychologie, 1915, pp. 361 ff. See below, Appendix II.

[14] Routledge: *With a Prehistoric People,* London, 1910, p. 226.

[15] R. E. Dennet: *At the Back of the Black Man's Mind,* p. 142. Compare Söderblom: *Das Werden des Gottesglaubens,* p. 165.

[16] H. Vedder in the *Zeitschrift für Kolonialsprachen,* I, 6. Compare Söderblom, *op. cit.,* p. 144.

[17] Lang: *Making of Religion,* pp. 233 ff.

[18] K. Sapper: *Mittelamerikanische Reisen und Studien,* 1902, p. 267.

[19] Compare W. Schmidt: *Grundlinien einer Vergleichung der Religionen und Mythologien der Austronesischen Völker* (Denkschriften der Kaiserl. Phil. Akademie der Wissenschaften in Wien, 1910, 63).

[20] In the Shi-King, the book of songs (II, 5, IV, 1). According to the treatise of the former Chinese Minister of Culture, Yuen beh Ts'ai, on the names of the gods in the classical annals of China which Söderblom reprints in *Das Werden des Gottesglaubens,* pp. 242 ff.

clusively for the emperor, who is at times expressly designated "son of Shang-ti." This worship is carried out in the great sacrificial festival at the time of the winter solstice on the "altar of heaven," south of Peking, the largest place of worship in the world.

In this connection, finally, we must also refer to Max Müller's famous comparison of the words for deity in the Indogermanic languages: Dyaus pitâ = Zeùs πατήρ = Jupiter. In spite of the misuse that has been made of this formula, even by Max Müller himself, it is a valid and conclusive proof that the child-father relation of a worshipper to the supreme beings is widespread. (See Max Müller's *Hibbert Lectures*.)

It is true that these great gods play a comparatively minor rôle in the life of primitive people, and especially in their worship. It has been thought, therefore, that one must deny them all religious significance and regard them as purely mythological creations, in the sense of religiously indifferent mythological poetry.[21] However, this inference cannot even be seriously considered in a religio-psychologically orientated investigation. It is only possible for that type of thinking which disregards every religio-psychological approach as a matter of principle. It can in no way do justice to the facts. For even though the worship of the great gods is relatively submerged in primitive life, it is not entirely absent, and often it emerges into view in critical situations. Even the examples cited above show this clearly. Then, too, it is not merely the inner psychological probability which indicates that the practical repression of the great gods has been a gradual process. Tradition also partly proves this emphatically. And the general picture which Chinese religion presents to us can only be understood under this presupposition. So the child-father relation, which is expressed in the belief in the great gods, is of great importance for a general estimate of these religions.[22]

[21] For example. W. W. Skeat-Bladgen: *"Pagan Races of the Malay Peninsula,"* London, 1905, I, 173. Still more as a matter of principle, Paul Ehrenreich: *Allgemeine Mythologie,* Leipsic, 1910, pp. 78 f.

[22] Friedrich Heiler's position is closely related to the one supported above; however, it differs from it in this respect: He tries to find the origin of prayer fundamentally and without exception in the God-father belief (*op. cit.,* pp. 129 ff.). This solution of the historical and genetic phase of the entire problem does not seem to me to be sufficiently proven.

But this child-father relation has as its presupposition and conditioning factor the ego-relation. And in order to point out the function and relation of the self, it must be recognized that to the greatest extent primitive prayer is kept within the *do ut des* formula. This can be shown best by calling to mind some especially typical examples of this type.

"O Lord, dost thou love me at all? Lead the Gnu into my path"—so prays the bushman who has had bad luck in the hunt.

"I pray thee, give me long life"—a prayer reported of the Sioux Indians.[23]

An Ewe prays: "O full-moon, save me on my journey. Take care of me so that I may return safely to my home."[24] The prayer of a Wa-nyika who is on a journey is similar: "Mulungu on high! See, I am making a journey. Have pity on me, that I may return safe and sound."[25] Spieth reports the following prayer for the consecration of a Mawu-priest among the Ewe tribes: "God, here is thy food, in order that thou mightest bless, from now on, the work of thy priest. I have come at thy command to wash away the sins of thy priest by which he has besmirched himself. I will do this to thy child, with whom thou, O God, remainest. So, grant, O God, that his days may be many."[26] K. Th. Preuss had dictated to him a Cora Indian shaman's prayer for the cure of sickness: "God, who art my mother, my father, on thy account I remember a very sad happening. . . . Do thou it, for I am not able to do it. . . . I cannot do it. And I am afraid. So do thou it, God, thou who art my mother."[27]

Finally we shall give several prayers of the more highly

Moreover, Heiler's emphasis upon this solution, in my opinion, exaggerates the importance of the historic-genetic problem. From the religio-psychological point of view no such importance can be attached to that problem.

[23] Friedrich Heiler: *Das Gebet,* pp. 60, 61 (English translation).

[24] J. Spieth: *Die Religion der Eweer* (Quellen der Religionsgeschichte, Group 10). 1911, pp. 52 f.

[25] Le Roy: *La Religion des Primitifs,* Paris, 1911, p. 301. (According to Dr. L. Krapf; with original text.)

[26] J. Spieth: *Die Religion der Eweer,* 1911, p. 19.—Mawu is the highest god of the Ewe tribes, although the pair of gods Mawu-Sogble (male) and Mawu-Sodza (female) as well as Mawu Sowlui stand next to him as servants of God. The trowo (tro, plural trowo) are "special gods"; they are children of God and gods of the earth who are near to men and bring their affairs to God.

[27] Konr. Theodor Preuss: *Die Religion der Cora-Indianer* (Die Nayarit-Expedition, Vol. I, 1912, pp. 264 f. (with original text).

advanced, although still illiterate, Galla in Abyssinia.[28] Here monotheistic influence, from either a Jewish or a Christian or a Mohammedan source is possible. However, this does not affect their religio-psychological value. Rather, the fact that they were capable of being so influenced, and such influence as may have taken place, would itself be significant and instructive.

"God of the earth, my Lord, thou art above me, I am under thee. As the tree keeps the sun away from me, so keep thou misfortune from me, if misfortune threatens me; be thou my shade! I entreat thee by day, I call to thee by night. . . . If I do not pray to thee with all my heart, thou wilt not hear me, but I entreat thee with all my heart, so thou knowest it and art gracious unto me." And a morning prayer: "O God, thou hast permitted me to pass the night in peace, so let me also pass the day in peace. . . . Calling to thee, O lord, who hath no other lord above thee, I begin this day." And an evening prayer: "O God, thou has permitted me to pass the day in peace, permit me also to pass the night in peace. . . . In thy hand I pass the day, in thy hand I pass the night, thou art my mother, thou art my father."

It cannot be denied that in such prayers the prayer-atmosphere of the Psalms is attained. This is not only true of the last-mentioned prayers of the Galla, in which either directly or indirectly, Biblical influence is perhaps at work, but it is also true of the previous examples. And how strong and lively the relation of the self is in the prayer-atmosphere of the Psalms, needs only to be mentioned. It is true that it has been maintained that the self in the Psalms is never individualistic, but must be taken throughout collectively and generally, that is, as applying to the congregation or nation. But, in the first place, this theory is disputable. And besides, even if it were wholly true, it would constitute no real objection to the emphasis upon the relation of the self. *For even then the individual-personal function of the self of the worshipper would be operative in every practical concrete case in the original collective or social self.*

---

[28] According to Carl Meinhof: *Religion der Schriftlosen Völker Afrikas* (Einzelausgabe aus Bertholets Religionsgeschichtl. Lesebuch.) Tübingen, 1913, pp. 39 ff.

In this connection, Buddhism requires special consideration. For Buddhism, at least the original Buddhism which is
uniquely important for the history of religion, knows no
prayer. In it, meditation takes the place of prayer. Now
meditation, of course, also includes the personal relation.
However, Buddhist meditation seems inclined to exclude the
personal relation, allowing the self to empty and to de-
personalize itself in meditation.

Hence, the personal relation is of fundamental importance
for the general status of Buddhism. In not a few passages
in the Buddhist canon the reality of the self seems to be denied
directly, and Hume's idea of the self as a bundle of ideas,
seems to be presupposed in its most radical form, e.g., in the
dialogue between the nun, Vajirâ and Mâra, the tempter.[29]

"What, in your opinion, is a person, Mâra?"

"Only a heap of changeable forms (sankhâra; sanskrit;
samskāra). A person cannot be grasped. . . . It is only suffering which comes into being, suffering is that which exists
and passes away; nothing else but suffering comes into being,
nothing but suffering passes away again."

And then Vajirâ explains this observation with the illustration of the wagon: just as one uses the term wagon when
the parts of a wagon are put together, so also, whenever the
five groups (of elements comprising our earthly being [30]) exist,
there is a person. In the story of the Javanese king Milinda,[31]
which belongs to the post-canonical literature, this illustration
is carried out in minute detail. The king asks the saint Nâgasena who he is. The saint answers: "I am called Nâgasena,
O great king. But Nâgasena, great king, is only a name, a
label, a sign, an expression, a mere word. A subject cannot be
grasped therein." And then this is proved by using and applying in detail the illustration of the wagon.

In the light of these passages it seems all the more signifi-

[29] *Samyutta Nikâya* II, p. 135. Comp. Ernst Windisch, *Mâra und
Buddha*, pp. 146 ff.; Oldenberg, *op. cit.*, pp. 295 ff.

[30] According to Oldenberg's translation they are: corporeality, feelings,
ideas, forms, and knowledge; but the terminology of Max Walleser is more
exact (*Die Philosoph. Grundlage des Älteren Buddhismus,* 1904); Form,
feeling, perception, imaginative power, and consciousness.

[31] *Milindapañha*, pp. 25 ff. Compare R. Garbe: *Beiträge zur indischen
Kulturgeschichte,* 1903, pp. 95 ff.; Oldenberg, *op. cit.*, pp. 291 ff.

cant and instructive that Buddhism nevertheless did not draw the seemingly necessary conclusion and deny absolutely the existence of a self. *This whole problem is of special significance in Buddhist thought from the point of view of the problem of eternal life.* And since the interest here is directed chiefly toward the personality of Buddha himself, the idea of eternal life is primarily applied to him. That is why the problem is discussed in Buddhist literature, not only with the concepts *satta* and *attâ,* but also with the concept tathâgata. The word *satta,* e.g., appears in the conversation of the nun, Vajirâ with Mâra, to which we have referred. It corresponds to our "person." Attâ is the Pâli form of the Sanskrit word *Atman,* which plays such an important rôle in Brahmanic speculation. It really denotes "the self" or "the ego." Tathâgata, the "perfect one" [32] is a self-designation, a designation of Buddha in his Buddha-quality.

When one asks about the content of this satta, attâ or tathâgata, the orthodox answer is evasive. Buddha himself was asked by the itinerant monk Vacchagotta: [33] "How is it, esteemed Gotama: does the self exist?" To this question, tradition says, the Blessed One remained silent. But he also remained silent when the itinerant monk immediately asked the counter-question: "Is the self non-existent?" And then after both refusals to answer, Buddha reveals to his favorite disciple Ananda that either a negative or an affirmative answer would only have confused the questioner all the more. King Pasenadi, of Kosala, asks the nun Khemâ, whether existence can be ascribed to the Tathâgata beyond death. Upon receiving the answer that the Blessed One has not revealed this he tries to ask every possible question, but he always receives the same answer. And so the disciple of Buddha concludes the lesson in these words: "That the Perfect One is beyond death, is not true; that the Perfect One is not beyond death is also not true; that the Perfect One at the same time is and is not beyond death is also not true; that the Perfect One neither is

---

[32] Tathâgata denotes literally "he who has conducted himself thus," *i.e.,* he who has taken the right path which leads to Buddhahood. Compare Otto Franke in the appendix to his German edition of the *Dîghanikâya,* pp. 287 ff. (Quellen zur Religionsgeschichte, Group 8, 1913.)

[33] *Samyutta Nikâya* IV, p. 400. Compare Oldenberg, *op. cit.,* pp. 313 f.

nor is not beyond death, is also not true." And this answer does not leave the king dissatisfied, rather it satisfies him to the highest degree: "But Pasenadi, the king of Kosala, received the words of Khemâ, the nun, with joy and approval, rose from his seat, bowed in reverence before her, walked around her and went away." [34] Sâriputta, foremost among the disciples of Buddha, rejects as heresy the teaching of the monk, Yamaka, that the tathâgata has no existence beyond death. Sâriputta convinces him by showing that even in the visible world Yamaka was unable to apprehend in truth the self of the Perfect One.[35]

A self is not to be grasped; that remains the last word in the orthodox doctrine. What does this conclusion mean, what sense has it? Does it imply a radical negation of the self, or does it leave open a positive attitude? To begin with it must be said that this question cannot be assuredly and unequivocally answered. And this uncertainty is characteristic of Buddhism. However, to a certain extent the possibility of giving a positive answer at least exists in the Buddhist system of thought. The conversation of Sâriputta with the monk, Yamaka, to which we have referred, points entirely in this direction. The world of the Sankhara is, of course, a world of continual change from becoming to disintegration. But that this world represents the only and ultimate reality is nowhere stated. On the contrary it is even presupposed that there is a completely different reality,[36] which surpasses all human comprehension, and in which, then, the problem of the self must be answered differently, namely, in a strictly positive way. And if one repeatedly thinks over the whole situation with this consideration in mind, the conviction becomes stronger and stronger that this is the correct interpretation. For only this interpretation can give us a completely har-

---

[34] *Samyutta Nikâya* IV, pp. 374 ff. Compare H. Oldenberg, *op. cit.*, pp. 319 ff.

[35] *Samyutta Nikâya* III, pp. 109 f. Compare H. Oldenberg, *op. cit.*, pp. 322 ff. From this statement Franke *Dîghanikâya* (p. 296) tries to deduce the conclusion that nothing but the verbal concept remains of the soul. But this reasoning is based upon a false disjunction.

[36] Here the Nirvana problem touches on the whole train of thought. Compare below.

monious view of the whole of Buddhism which can be reconciled with even the harshest negations.

It is extremely instructive to consider how the most distinguished Indologists stand on this question. Among them all possible interpretations are represented. Especially significant is the sharp contrast between the positions of H. Oldenberg, on the one hand, and of L. de la Vallée Poussin on the other.[37] The latter defends with the utmost possible conviction, the completely negative interpretation, and for this reason he cannot do justice to any passages which exhibit the least trace of a positive answer. Contrariwise, Oldenberg seriously attempts to make the positive passages also really understandable. Hence he concludes that the desire to rescue the hope in a reality which surpasses all comprehension, retreats behind the veil of mystery, in order to avoid that type of thinking which hesitates to accept an eternal reality as conceivable.

From the religio-psychological point of view, there can be no doubt as to which of these two views we must accept. Religio-psychologically the passages in question can only be interpreted as Oldenberg interprets them. Indeed, to a certain extent Oldenberg's own interpretation is religio-psychologically conditioned. To be sure he was not conscious of this. But that it is true can be shown clearly from his own reasoning. And this will also prove that the religio-psychological point of view is demanded by the facts themselves. The other attitude toward Buddhism, which Oldenberg combats, would force us, in dealing with the problem of Nirvana which will be discussed later, to deny absolutely and unconditionally every religious character to (primitive) Buddhism; and it would also compel us to evaluate primitive Buddhism exclusively as a philosophy and as a philosophical school, to separate it completely from the field of religious validity and to relegate it unreservedly to the field of logical-theoretical validity. But that is a conclusion which clearly would not do justice to the phenomenon which primitive Buddhism presents, and this has also been recently recognized more and more generally by spe-

---

[37] La Vallée Poussin, Louis de, *Dogmatique Bouddhique; La négation de l'âme et la doctrine de l'acte,* Journal Asiatique, IX, 2, pp. 237 ff.; X, 2, pp. 357 ff. *Bouddhisme: Opinions sur l'histoire de la Dogmatique,* Paris, 1909, p. 172. Hermann Oldenberg, *op. cit.,* pp. 319 ff.

cialists in Buddhist research.   But in any case, such a general
conclusion cannot be based upon the claim that the facts at
hand prove conclusively the specific negative attitude to the
problem of the self, which is the point now under consideration.
Buddhism, then, can certainly be included in the formula
at which we have arrived for the formal-psychological preparation for the problem of the nature of religion : the underlying
emotional character of the religious consciousness is conditioned by the ego-function; the religious conceptual content
and its set of ideas, can only be rightly interpreted by the
underlying religious experience which has been determined
by this ego-function.

It should at least be mentioned here that this judgment applies especially to Buddhism in its later historical development
and as it is today.   For example, in modern Japanese Buddhism prayer to Buddha Amitâbha (Amida Buddha) plays a
very important rôle in just the two most wide-spread and influential sects—the Jodo-shu and the Jodo-Shin-shu.   Meditation, as well as moral teaching and the quest for wisdom,
recede completely behind the appeal to the name of Buddha
(Namu Amida Butsu).   It is true that this prayer to Buddha
contains a strong magical element.   Yet, on the other hand,
it is still deliberately practiced as an expression of trusting
surrender.   This is clear from one of the classical writings
(Sai-yo-sho) of the Jodo-shu : "In the last analysis the prayer
Namu Amida Butsu signifies nothing else but this : 'Save us,
O Buddha Amida'!   And such a petition, often repeated, is
then nothing more than just a real profound longing for the
assistance of a saviour, a longing for the power of another.
And no matter how often we pray, how could anything ever
be produced which we might attribute to our own strength?" [38]

Now this quotation shows that all doubt concerning the
personal existence of Buddha has been dropped.   The goal of
faith is to enter, with Buddha's help, into the "Pure Land"
(Jo-do), after which the two sects are named "sect of the
Pure Land" (Jodo-shu) and the "true sect of the Pure Land"

[38] Compare the splendidly instructive description of Hans Haas: *Amida
Buddha, Unsere Zuflucht.* Göttingen and Leipsic, 1910 (Quellen der
Religionsgeschichte, Group 8), p. 99.

(Jodo-Shin-shu). But the "Pure Land" is the "World in the West," where Buddha lives, the Sukhavati-world. And the entrance into this world or being reborn in it is designated quite generally in the sacred texts as an "entrance into life." "How wonderful it is that they shall now come to life in the Pure Land, from which they need not return to Samsâra (the alternation between birth and death)," says a famous letter of Hohen Shonin,[39] the founder of the Jodo sect. Here, then, the personal eternal existence of the faithful is no more doubted than that of Buddha himself. And between Buddha and his followers there exists "a close relation inasmuch as if a man turns his mind toward Buddha, Buddha, on his part, remembers him" (p. 98). We have here in the most explicit way an I-you relation and such a relation presupposes the validity of the I-relation.

3

Finally let us take a first look at two phenomena of modern European-American cultural life, concerning which some might doubt whether they are to be regarded as "religious," or at least, what their relation to religion is. Of course, both of them claim most emphatically to be friendly to, and to promote religion. Indeed they even desire to surpass and in the end to supplant the Christian religion in all of its sectarian forms. I refer to the so-called "prayer-healing" (more correctly "thought-healing") cult, on the one hand, and to the theosophical and anthroposophical movement on the other hand. And the grouping of these two phenomena together also shows the close connection that exists between them, which has, as far as I am aware, not heretofore been recognized. We are dealing in both cases with total attitudes which emphasize logical and rational knowledge so strongly and place it so far in the foreground, that upon critical examination one at first gets the impression that they both belong entirely to the field of logical-theoretical validity, and not to the field of special religious validity. The ideas which they advance, and even the individual images in which they clothe these

[39] Compare Hans Haas, *op. cit.,* p. 40.

ideas, claim to embody in themselves immediate knowledge of reality, but they are not ways of expressing an emotionally conditioned conviction. And so the ego-relation also seems to be either completely excluded or at least to be excludable from this system of ideas.

Rudolf Steiner claims to be able to read from the so-called *Akasha Chronicle* the story of the birth of the universe and the periods in the history of human culture. It is true that this story corresponds to a shocking extent with the phantasies of Madame Blavatsky, who has frequently been exposed as a swindler. But according to Steiner it is strictly objective cosmological and anthropological and ethnological knowledge. And when Mrs. Eddy's Christian Science is taken literally and consistently the human self must be denied all independent existence. For man is a ray, emanating from the eternal divine spirit, and "should only act as God acts." God is the only real existence. Everything which exists is Divine Spirit.[40]

However, assertions like these clearly involve the representatives of both systems in self-deceptions, and in self-contradictions. Upon closer examination it becomes quite clear that these systems do have an emotional character and are conditioned by feeling and wishing. Of course, Rudolf Steiner repeatedly insists that the wisdom which he propounds is intelligible to every one who thinks logically. Yet according to his own teaching, an understanding of his system can only be gained by those possessing a spiritual condition due to more profound causes in human nature than can be reached by logical-rational knowledge. And Christian Science attempts to heal sickness by means of the mental insistence that there is no sickness. Nevertheless the healing power of the method depends upon a ready acceptance of this idea and upon voluntary concentration.

Hence the significance of the ego-function for both systems is already implied in what we have just said. And viewed externally, this ego-function is already strongly ap-

[40] *Science and Health with Key to the Scriptures* (with German translation), Boston, 1913, e.g., pp. 263 ff., pp. 302 ff. Compare Karl Beth: *Gesunddenken und Gesundbeten, Eine Beurteilung des Scientismus*, Vienna, 1918.

parent to every observer in the repulsive worship of personalities which is equally present in both movements. And in this respect, there is just as little difference between the two branches of Theosophy; the Anglo-Indian Theosophy of Madame Blavatsky and Mrs. Besant on one side, and the German Anthroposophical Theosophy of Rudolf Steiner on the other;[41] as there is between the entire theosophical movement and the Christian Science founded by Mrs. Eddy.

Of course it might seem as if a fundamental difference between Christian Science and Theosophy could still be established at this point, purely in reference to our subject of the self, inasmuch as the former must, at least if it is to be consistent with its basic principle, completely deny the ego-relation, whereas Theosophy, on the contrary, due to its doctrine of rebirth, or Karma, which it has borrowed from Hinduism, makes the ego or the self the basic principle of its worldview. However, this is not the actual situation and the truth is that the difference is not so great. For in both cults there exists such deep-lying uncertainty and unclearness that in the end the two positions strongly resemble each other. As far as the doctrine of rebirth of Theosophy is concerned, it must be remembered, to begin with, that Buddhism has also accepted and championed that doctrine.[42] Moreover it is the primitive Buddhism which, as we have seen, officially, at least, rejects every definite position in regard to the problem of the self, and thereby actually proclaims also that every relation to the self may be entirely ignored which champions the doctrine of Karma. And within the theosophical movement itself, Madame Blavatsky and Colonel Olcott, the founders of the first Theosophical Society (1875), have defended the Buddhist interpretation.

And in the teachings of Rudolf Steiner the indefiniteness has not actually been removed. Of course the "ego" or the self plays a very important rôle in his anthropology and psy-

---

[41] See Lehman-Tessel: *Theosophie nebst Anthroposophie und Christengemeinschaft* (Göschen, vol. 971).

[42] The Karma doctrine, although consistent with the Vedas, is found for the first time in the religio-philosophical literature of India in the *Brihad Aranyaka-Upanishad* 4, 4. 6.

chology.[43] For he describes the self precisely as the "actual being" or as the "true being" of man. Indeed, he teaches that the eternal truth is united with the self to form one being and that it is by this union that the self attains eternity. However, we are left entirely in the dark as to the sense in which the idea *eternity* is here used, whether in a specifically religious sense or in the religiously neutral sense of an endless existence. Moreover the unity of the self is later endangered by the separation of the "spiritual being" of man into three parts: the spirit self (the higher Manas), the life spirit (buddhi), and the spiritual man (atma).[44] Hence it is not surprising that the indefiniteness of Steiner's theory becomes all the more evident when concrete individual doctrines are considered. This applies especially to Steiner's Christology.[45]

Think, for example, of Steiner's teaching that at the baptism by John, the solar-ego of Christ united with the man Jesus to form Christ-Jesus, and that on Golgotha, when the blood flowed from the wounds of Jesus, the Christ-ego passed into the earth and is now seen by the initiated in the spirit-center of the earth. Think, too, of Steiner's account of the childhood of Jesus. According to him the Christ-child of Matthew's Gospel is not identical with the one of Luke's Gospel. The former is the reincarnated Zarathustra, and the latter is the reincarnated Krishna of the *Bhagavad-Gita*. Both of them were then united into one person in the twelve-year-old Jesus. The reincarnated Krishna returned to the spirit realm but Zarathustra passed into the body of Krishna by resigning his own body to death.

It cannot be denied that such fancies presuppose a total lack of clearness as to the significance of the ego-function.

[43] Rud. Steiner: *Theosophie, Einführung in übersinnliche Welterkenntnis und Menschenbestimmung,* 13-18 edition. Leipsic, 1920, pp. 33 ff.—*Die Geheimwissenschaft im Umriss,* 3rd edition, 1910, pp. 35 ff.—*Ein Weg zur Erkenntnis des Menschen, in 8 Meditationen,* 2-5 edition, 1918, pp. 67 ff. And in many other passages of Steiner's other writings, many of which are available in English.

[44] This pigeon-hole analysis came originally from Hinduism. Its psychology is determined chiefly by the Saṃkya philosophy. Compare Richard Garbe: *Die Saṃkya-Philosophie, Eine Darstellung des indischen Rationalismus,* Leipsic, 1894, 2nd edition, Ch. IV: *The Doctrine of the Soul.*

[45] Compare the writings of Steiner: *Das Christentum als mystische Tatsache; Die Geistige Führung des Menschen und der Menschheit; Weihnacht, eine Betrachtung aus der Lebensweisheit.*

But precisely the same unclearness also characterizes Christian Science.

In the light of the formal psychological point of view with which we are here concerned we can say of these two movements in conclusion that they are unmistakably similar to religion, but that they partly convert the religious factors into their opposites and also that they partly misconstrue their significance and true meaning. With these two important reservations, from the formal psychological point of view the claim of both of these phenomenon to religious validity must be recognized. In saying this nothing is said about the contentual aspect of the problem. For our formal psychological statement of the problem does not yet consider the nature of the content of religion.

Thus both of these cults show a formal analogy to religion just as magic and mythology—reserving all further judgment —probably reveal a formal similarity to religion. And to the mind which has become expert in the religio-psychological method, the question may well arise at this point, whether Christian Science and Theosophy are not best classified under magic and mythology; whether Christian Science does not represent a kind of modern magic, and Theosophy a type of modern mythology.

CHAPTER IV

SCHLEIERMACHER'S CONCEPTION OF THE NATURE OF RELIGION

I

In turning, now to the task of defining the intrinsic nature of religion we must again depart from Schleiermacher. He defined the nature of religion as the feeling of dependence. In the fourth paragraph of the *Glaubenslehre,* as we have already learned, he stated more exactly that the nature of piety is the individual's consciousness of being absolutely dependent upon God, or, what amounts to the same thing, of being in relation to God. We have already referred to the peculiar grammatical form of this statement, which is so very important for Schleiermacher's whole theological and religio-scientific position. Here we are concerned only with the meaning of the statement.

And first of all it is necessary to note the relation of these two characterizations to each other. To say that we are conscious of being in relation to God is asserted to be identical with saying that we are conscious of our absolute dependence. The consciousness of absolute dependence, the feeling of absolute dependence, as Schleiermacher later also expresses it, is the uniquely determining idea. The other characterization, which uses the idea of God, merely aims to connect this uniquely determining idea with traditional terminology.

This fact is of the very greatest importance. It shows that Schleiermacher knew that the customary attempts to define the nature of religion are, strictly speaking, really empty tautologies. Over against such verbal definitions, his formulation marks the beginning of a real factual definition of religion. When the nature of religion is defined with the idea of God, the actually decisive problem lies precisely in this idea of God. And this inevitably leads to mental confusion. "God" is just the traditional linguistic term for the conceptual object of religion. The whole problem of the nature of religion is included in the question of the conceptual object of "religion." For that can only be "religious" which contains the nature of religion. Hence all traditional definitions of religion either leave the decisive question of the nature of religion entirely undetermined, or they assume it in their formulation in the form of a *petitio principii* or a begging of the question. The former is the case when the idea of God itself is conceived in a purely formal way, and on the other hand, the latter is true when a definite idea of God is meant by the word *God*. And ordinarily this alternative, not being kept clearly in mind, is not decided.

The dogmatic scholastic definition of religion as the "knowledge and worship of God" (*modus deum cognoscendi et colendi*) is the clearest illustration of this. But in the last analysis that is also true of quite recent attempts to define religion with the idea of the "holy" (Windelband, Söderblom, Rudolph Otto), or with the idea of the "numinous" (Rudolph Otto, Friedrich Heiler). The idea of the holy and of the numinous are verbal definitions of the religious conceptual object. But these writers make no attempt to give a real definition of that object. At least they make no straightforward attempt, and hence they fail to give a clear and precise definition of it.

Schleiermacher saw through this vicious circle (*circulus vitiosus*). Indeed his point of view is deliberately intended to escape it. For in the sense in which Schleiermacher understands it, the idea of the feeling of absolute dependence constitutes a real definition of the religious conceptual object. Not only is his idea of religion not purely subjective, but his main interest is directed precisely toward grasping the content of the religious object. The purely subjective interpretation of Schleiermacher's conception of religion is a complete misunderstanding of his position.

Before proving this fact by expounding the *Glaubenslehre,* we must first call attention to the *Reden über die Religion.* For it is upon them that the widespread subjective misinterpretation is chiefly based. Yet it goes without saying that in reaching a full understanding of Schleiermacher it is absolutely unjustifiable to subordinate the *Glaubenslehre* to the *Reden über die Religion,* as, for example, even Natorp does. The *Reden über die Religion* must rather be subordinated to the *Glaubenslehre.* For on the whole the *Glaubenslehre* presents Schleiermacher's position in its clearest and most mature form.

Nevertheless the idea of religion in the *Reden* lies precisely in the direction of the position taken in the *Glaubenslehre.* When Schleiermacher in the first edition of the *Reden* describes religion as the perception and feeling of the universe, and then, in the later editions, more and more subordinates the idea of perception to that of feeling, there already lies in this fact the germ of the theory of the feeling of absolute dependence. Actually, then, an interest in the religious conceptual object is strongly at work even in the idea of religion of the *Reden,* and indeed, even in the very first edition.

That this has so often been and still is overlooked is due primarily to a misunderstanding of the relation of Schleiermacher to Spinoza. To be sure, in the second Address he says: "Offer with me reverently a tribute to the manes of the holy rejected Spinoza. The high World-Spirit pervaded him; the Infinite was his beginning and his end; the Universe was his only and his everlasting love." [1] Now this tribute to Spinoza is not, as is usually said, a reference to the pantheism of Spinoza, at least not primarily and in its basic purpose. Unquestionably the idea of immanence which runs through the *Reden* is pantheistic. But the decisive religious interest of Schleiermacher does not stick throughout to this pantheistic wrapping. And this is also true of his relation to Spinoza. Schleiermacher rests back on Spinoza over against the radical subjectivism of Fichte, who ultimately derived the human Ego solely from himself. Only religion can successfully combat such a perfect idealism and meet it with a higher realism. It is this higher realism with which Schleiermacher is concerned. He praises Spinoza because to him the Universe was the highest and ultimate reality.

Schleiermacher's definition of the nature of religion as the

---

[1] F. Schleiermacher: *Addresses on Religion* (John Oman's translation), p. 40. Translator's note.

"perception and feeling of the Universe" has to be interpreted from this point of view. Only then does the argument of the Second Address become clear. External nature—so Schleiermacher begins—which so many take to be the holy of holies of religion, is really only its outermost court. Neither the fear of the powers of nature, nor the awe of nature's quantitative Infinitude, nor the happy enjoyment of her beauties leads one into the unique depth of religion. The outer world is always primarily to be interpreted by the inner. Consequently it is quite peculiarly to the affections of the mind to which religion is related. "In order for man to have religion he must first have discovered human nature, and he finds that only in and through love." Human nature, then, transmits the true substance of religion, that is to say, human nature with her spiritual life—so we must interpret Schleiermacher —constitutes a limitation on all human perceptual and conceptual interpretations of external nature. And to that extent human nature does not exclude, but rather includes, the whole of nature which can come within man's ken. Yet human nature is composed of an infinite diversity of all kinds of particular individuals, each one of whom embodies it in his own unique way. Consequently religion embraces the whole being of human nature, not just the entirety of mankind at a given epoch, but the entire existence of humanity for all time, human nature in its complete historical evolution. "History in the most unique sense of the word is the highest object of religion. Religion rises and falls with history."

Nevertheless—so Schleiermacher continues—we are not yet on the border of religion. For human nature also, taking it in the sense already mentioned so as to include in it external nature in its entirety, does not yet constitute the totality of the universe. "Rather human nature in this sense is related to this totality of the universe as particular men are related to human nature, . . . and there must be found a still higher character in man than his humanity, if we are to identify him and his appearance with the universe." And then Schleiermacher concludes this whole line of thought with the judgment which really pervades it from the beginning: "All religion expresses itself in such an awareness of something outside and beyond nature." It is primarily in the light of this statement that full clearness and inner consistency can be given to the passages already quoted.

Perception and feeling of the Universe means, then, the awareness of a reality outside and beyond human nature, using the expression human nature in the theoretically and epistemologically widened sense which has just been stated. Hence the very idea of the Universe refers to a reality of a higher order, a reality which stands behind and transcends the whole empirical spatio-temporal world, and which limits and supports that world in its entire being and evolution.

2

It is only a step, and to be sure, a step in exactly the same direction, from the perception and the feeling of the Universe to the feeling of absolute dependence of the *Glaubenslehre*.

For the theory of the feeling of absolute dependence brings into still clearer relief and into sharper expression the interest in the content of the religious object. What is the exact meaning of this idea of a feeling of absolute dependence which dominates the whole *Glaubenslehre?* According to Schleiermacher's own unequivocal statement, we can best comprehend this idea by distinguishing the feeling of absolute dependence from feelings of dependence which are not absolute but which are only relative feelings of dependence. Such relative feelings of dependence stand in a correlative relation to relative feelings of freedom. In distinction from the relative feelings of dependence the feeling of absolute dependence is that in which every phase of consciousness, no matter what its specific content may be, is ultimately experienced as dependent. Accordingly every thought of dependence on "something else" is subordinated to this. But a full understanding of this idea requires a more detailed exposition of Schleiermacher. Ordinarily there is and can be no feeling of absolute dependence on the entire domain of the phenomenal world. In varying degrees we always possess independence and freedom over against the existence and the phenomena of the finite world. Consequently within the realms of the phenomenal world, as we ordinarily conceive it, only relative feelings of dependence and of freedom are possible. The combinations of these two feelings are extraordinarily diverse. Between the two extremes of a maximum of feeling of freedom and a minimum of feeling of dependence on the one side and a minimum of feeling of freedom and a maximum of feeling of dependence on the other side, may be found all degrees and types of combinations. But both types of feeling are always intermingled. Now the feeling of absolute dependence "never arises within this sphere."

The feeling of absolute dependence, on the contrary, takes us beyond the phenomenal world in its entirety and in its widest possible conception. It brings us in relation to a reality on which the finite world as a whole is dependent. That "Other, presupposed" in the feeling of absolute dependence by the relation of dependence is neither a special aspect of the phenomenal world nor the totality of all its phenomena; no! it is a reality which transcends the entire phenomenal world, and upon which that world is itself just as dependent as is the particular consciousness which has the feeling of dependence.

Consequently, when Schleiermacher characterizes the nature of religion as a feeling of absolute dependence, this proves that he thinks that the decisive and essential feature of religion lies in the relation of man to a reality of a higher order, to which the whole phenomenal world is subordinated and by which it is limited.[2] And when he then immediately uses the word *God* to define the objective content of the religious consciousness, this must mean, as he himself remarks, that this word is taken as expressing first of all what in that feeling is the "determining agency" (the objective being over against the one who has the feeling of dependence). And he expressly adds that every other content of the idea of God must first be developed out of this essential content. That feeling is for Schleiermacher the "basic form of all piety." Hence, in order to sharpen his opposition to Hegel, he stresses the fact that

[2] This fact is stated with the greatest precision at the beginning of paragraph 5 of the *Glaubenslehre*, where Schleiermacher summarizes the argument of paragraph 4. Here the feeling of absolute dependence is set over against that of self-consciousness "which, in its relation to the perceptual, finite world splits itself into a relative feeling of dependence and a relative feeling of freedom."

the feeling of absolute dependence is not determined by any previous knowledge of God. *But an objective content and an objective relation are certainly included in the feeling of absolute dependence. Indeed, this objective content is precisely the highest reality determining all finite existence.*

Let us now call attention to and especially stress an aspect of Schleiermacher's line of thought which is usually either overlooked or misunderstood. For in a special way, a genuine understanding of the whole theory depends upon it.

Speaking quite generally, how did Schleiermacher reach this conception of a feeling of absolute dependence? To use his own words, if that self-consciousness which expresses the relations of the self to the perceptual finite world splits itself into a relative feeling of dependence and a relative feeling of freedom, then manifestly it is of far-reaching importance to ask how under these conditions the feeling of *absolute* dependence can nevertheless arise and persist. Indeed, Schleiermacher himself expressly states that in this situation the feeling of absolute freedom is utterly impossible for us (that is to say, for us human beings, for us finite creatures). Then why is not the same conclusion to be drawn with regard to the feeling of absolute dependence? Why must we not also say that the feeling of absolute dependence is for us an impossibility? How did Schleiermacher avoid drawing this conclusion? How did he reach the feeling of absolute dependence?

He reached it from religious experience and only and exclusively from religious experience. The feeling of absolute dependence is affirmed because of his religious experience. And, furthermore, only that interpretation which expresses the basic conviction of religious experience as a feeling of absolute dependence is then expounded. In the decisive part of his exposition Schleiermacher writes: "If, now, our theory, looked at from the other side, demands a feeling of absolute dependence, it follows that such a feeling can never be produced by an object in any way presented to us, (that is to say) by an object belonging to the spatio-temporal world." [3] The idea of

[3] Schleiermacher did not deny that the feeling of absolute dependence always has an object. He only denied that it has an object "in any way presented," and in Schleiermacher's terminology that means an empirical object, one belonging to the spatio-temporal world.

a feeling of absolute dependence follows, then, as a demand of the basic principle. But this basic principle speaks in the name of piety and of religious experience. For it aims to express precisely the common element in all the quite distinct forms of piety. Accordingly, the exposition of the content of the feeling of absolute dependence, which follows the passage quoted above, is likewise in the name of religious experience. It is the final development of what the feeling of absolute dependence means in the sense of piety. And in this sense it means man's being limited by a reality which transcends the entire finite world, and it refers to man's relation to this transcendent reality.

Thus the whole theory of the feeling of absolute dependence rests throughout upon religious experience. It aims only to give conceptual expression to the basic religious conviction which is rooted in all religious experience. It intends to give a more precise definition of the "basic form of all piety."

At least this is the meaning of the reasoning which was ultimately most decisive for Schleiermacher himself. The discussion in paragraph 4 of the *Glaubenslehre* leaves no doubt on this matter. This fact also confirms the position given to the feeling of absolute dependence in the *Glaubenslehre*. Indeed, on this point the letters to Dr. Lücke give us authentic information as to Schleiermacher's purpose and general plan. To be sure, he developed the theory of the feeling of absolute dependence, not in the body of the *Glaubenslehre,* but in the exposition of his philosophy of religion in the introduction, and he himself sharply and definitely emphasized this fact.[4] Yet this in no way alters the fact that the theory of the feeling of absolute dependence is fundamental for the entire content of the *Glaubenslehre* and, again speaking for Schleiermacher, it ought to be fundamental. Consequently no exposition of his theory of religion can be considered conclusive which does not rest upon the clear line of interpretation of the *Glaubenslehre* as a whole which is indicated by him in his letters to Dr. Lücke.

[4] By philosophy of religion I here have in mind the broad, purely factual meaning of the term and not the narrower sense of Schleiermacher's terminology, which restricts it to that critical discipline which seeks to analyze the central meaning of each of the various historical religions.

3

This interpretation, however, was never completely developed by Schleiermacher. Rather it is corrupted and interfered with by another speculative and deductive interpretation. This is most evident in the philosophical writings of Schleiermacher, especially in his *Dialektik,* where various objections—in different degrees, but nevertheless all of them to a certain extent—are utilized to make a deductive and rational derivation of the religious feeling. Now this rational and speculative line of thought is also present in the *Glaubenslehre.* And it interferes with the unified development of the central thesis of that work to which we have been referring. This is especially true of the important discussion of the theory of the feeling of absolute dependence in paragraph 4, for Schleiermacher there tries to prove that the feeling of absolute dependence is the highest stage of human self-consciousness. Such an attempt amounts to a turning of the whole interpretation in the direction of rational deduction. Rightly Schleiermacher should have limited his interpretation by calling the judgment in question a judgment of belief, that is to say, by treating it as an assertion of religion about itself, thereby giving philosophy the task of investigating how the religious judgment fits in with the philosophical interpretation of human spiritual life. Instead of doing this Schleiermacher anticipates the value-judgment of philosophy and thereby endangers the specific meaning of the judgment of religion itself. In truth he endangers also the understanding of the underlying determination of the nature of religion which is implied in the judgment of religion.

This explains the numerous misunderstandings of Schleiermacher's position, against which he was already so strenuously contending in the letters to Dr. Lücke, but which, even today, continue to find new defenders. We will make our conception of the basic theory of religion of Schleiermacher clear by discussing those misunderstandings which are of special significance today. In so doing we will deal first with the philosophers Wilhelm Wundt, and Leuba, and then with Natorp, and then we will deal with the theologians Schäder, Dunkmann, and Rudolph Otto.

We are here interested in Wundt's [5] whole conception of Schleiermacher, the fundamental essence of which must be abstracted from his general point of view. The dual thesis that Schleiermacher's attitude toward religion itself cannot be identified with his philosophy of religion, inasmuch as the latter is grounded throughout in metaphysics and dialectics is the basic and decisive assumption of Wundt. It was his falling back on this assumption that caused him to object to our linking Schleiermacher and James together. (See above, pp. 11 f.) Similarly an elaboration of this dual thesis can be used as an argument against our interpretation of Schleiermacher's theory of religion.

However, this dual thesis itself has to be rejected, and, indeed both parts of it. Moreover, the accompanying explanation, which Wundt appends to and thinks of as implied in the dual thesis, must also be rejected. Certainly when taken by itself the first part of this dual thesis is justifiable, and just because of its perfectly self-evident validity, it is necessary expressly to emphasize this fact. Indeed it is always important to keep this fact in mind, if we want to understand Schleiermacher. His philosophy of religion as a whole does not adequately and clearly express his attitude towards religion. But, on the other hand, the specific meaning of Schleiermacher's philosophy of religion rests precisely upon the fact that in it he deliberately tries to give a scientific statement of his attitude toward religion itself. The independence and the factual significance of the first thesis is best assured by giving special attention to this fact. Yet this is just what Wundt does not do. Hence his second thesis is not only inadequate but directly erroneous. For that Schleiermacher's philosophy of religion is based upon metaphysics and dialectics is not true, at least not in the concise factual sense in which Wundt means it. The statement is true only in a formal sense. As a matter of actual fact Schleiermacher's philosophy of religion is primarily based upon just his "position to religion itself," that is to say, on his understanding "of the religious states of feeling of the pious," to use his own words.

[5] Wilhelm Wundt: *Probleme der Völkerpsychologie*, Leipsic, 1911, pp. 102 ff. There is an English translation of this work by E. L. Schaub.

When taken separately Wundt's two statements may thus be justified. But the explanation with which Wundt defends the dual thesis is so exaggerated that it points in exactly the opposite direction to what Wundt intends. An understanding of Schleiermacher's "position toward religion itself" is the underlying prerequisite to a correct evaluation of his philosophy of religion. Indeed, Schleiermacher gave a systematic, consistent, and comprehensive exposition of his philosophy of religion only in the *Glaubenslehre*. The section of the *Dialektik* which deals with this subject is incoherent and fragmentary. This criticism holds of every one of the separate objections of the *Dialektik* taken singly, but in a special sense it applies to these objections taken as a whole. On the other hand, the *Glaubenslehre* presents a unified and unequivocal position. That this work exhibits a speculative tendency, and rests upon a speculative foundation, Schleiermacher describes as precisely "the worst and grossest misunderstanding." [6] And he who takes into consideration Schleiermacher's entire life-work, must agree with his own judgment here, at least so far as it refers to the ultimate and decisive basic tendency of the *Glaubenslehre*.

Leuba shares with Wundt the view that any attempt to find in Schleiermacher a position that is oriented to the psychology of religion is mistaken.[7] But he expresses this opinion especially in his evaluation of the theory of the feeling of absolute dependence. Indeed, it cannot be denied that just this attitude toward that theory of Schleiermacher is crucial to his entire well-knit theory. Consequently a refutation of Leuba's interpretation of Schleiermacher's theory of religion will provide us with a criterion for the evaluation of his theory as a whole. Moreover this criterion shows that view to be thoroughly fallacious. In no way does Leuba's interpretation do justice to Schleiermacher's theory of religion. He completely misunderstands precisely his basic insight. Indeed, at the very outset he makes the mistake of treating Schleiermacher as the chief representative of what is usually called the "feeling theory of the nature of religion." This shows that he entirely over-

[6] See the second *Sendschreiben an Lücke,* W. W. Part I, Book II, p. 609.
[7] James H. Leuba: *A Psychological Study of Religion, its origin, function and future,* New York, 1911, pp. 32 ff.

looked the fact that Schleiermacher's idea of feeling has to be sharply distinguished from the popular idea, and that one cannot understand what his idea of feeling means except by relating it to his idea of "immediate self-consciousness." Hence the critique which Leuba directs against all "feeling theories" is not at all valid against Schleiermacher. For in his theory of religion he had no intention of setting "feeling" over against the other basic psychical functions.

Moreover, the argument which Leuba directs especially at Schleiermacher is just as far from the real facts. Leuba says that the feeling of dependence is no better suited to determining the nature of religion than any other feeling. For "these feelings are all met with in secular life as well. They cannot, therefore, be a means of unequivocal discrimination between the religious and non-religious experience." [8] The exposition of Schleiermacher's view which was given above makes it absolutely clear that this line of reasoning is simply false. "The feeling of absolute dependence (in Schleiermacher's sense) never is found in this whole secular realm." Leuba's argument is valid only of that region of human psychical life which Schleiermacher describes as "sensuous feeling," using this term in its widest sense.[9]

Just at this point Leuba belatedly remembers, and also reminds the reader, that Schleiermacher does not define the nature of religion in terms of the feeling of dependence in general, but only in terms of a special kind of feeling of dependence. Here, then, one at last expects Leuba to analyze the "feeling of absolute dependence" of Schleiermacher. But, no! he again disappoints us. For even here he makes no attempt whatever to explain the meaning of the feeling of absolute dependence. On the contrary he now jumps over to the terminology of the *Reden* and discusses the ideas of the Universe and the Infinite, yet without ever explaining these ideas in the special sense in which Schleiermacher used them.[10] All that is valid in this

[8] *Loco citato*, p. 35.
[9] Compare Schleiermacher's own express statement: "So that we also regard as sensuous the social and moral feelings no less than the self-regarding sentiments." *Der Christliche Glaube*, etc., 2nd ed., paragraph 5, sec. I.
[10] *Loco citato*, p. 36. "To hold that the larger power upon which one feels dependent is—in the case of religion—necessarily infinite, is to mis-

discussion is the reminder that in Schleiermacher's theory the development of the religious consciousness and also that of the lower religions has too often been overlooked.

On the other hand, in concluding the argument which has just been sketched, Leuba makes a very significant statement; namely, that the difference between the various feelings of dependence is rooted in the difference between the corresponding objects, this being asserted of every feeling of dependence.[11] *But this statement is not against, but is rather favorable to Schleiermacher. For exactly this idea underlies Schleiermacher's whole theory of religion as its decisive and prime motive. The theory of the feeling of absolute dependence, as Schleiermacher conceives it, can only rightly be interpreted, when one looks at it from the basic viewpoint of the object to which it is related and grasps the meaning of this object.*

Over against a condemnation of Schleiermacher's theory of religion as a whole, Schäder [12] is to be commended for having recognized and emphasized the religio-psychological aspect of his position. *He thinks that Schleiermacher is entitled to the honor of being the originator and founder of the religio-psychological statement of the problem for all scientific religious and theological research.* Moreover, Schäder rightly recognizes that the theory of religion of Schleiermacher is the cornerstone of his religio-psychological statement and investigation of the problem. Accordingly, so Schäder thinks, the modern psychology of religion has in Schleiermacher a "precursor of the

interpret ordinary experience. In his religious moments, man is not ... usually (!) conscious of dealing with the unlimited. His transactions take place between himself and a greater power, the degree of greatness of which he does not usually (!) consider." Here it is quite obvious that Leuba is prevented from understanding the unique meaning of the theory he is criticising by his purely empirical psychology. Schleiermacher could entirely agree with this statement. He would only add that this does not settle the question, indeed, it does not even touch the central point at issue. For the real interest of Schleiermacher is just this, that such expressions of alien religiosity belong with personal religious experience, and must be understood in relation to it. See the conclusion of paragraph 4 of the 2nd edition of the Glaubenslehre, and our discussion above, pp. 47 ff.

[11] *Loco citato.* p. 36. "If, as a matter of fact, we discriminate without hesitation, between the feeling of dependence upon Wall Street, upon a father, upon Yahweh, upon a mistress, upon the absolute, it is not because the feeling is in each case qualitatively different, but because the objects are clearly distinguishable."

[12] Erich Schäder: *Theozentrische Theologie. Eine Untersuchung zur dogmatischen Prinzipienlehre.* Part I, 3rd ed., 1925.

grand style." He is that because of his profound analysis of religion and also because of his interpretation of the psychologically basic essence of religion, which is implicit in the theory of the feeling of absolute dependence. Yet just this means to Schäder not the strength but the weakness of and the error in the theory. He regards this as the root of Schleiermacher's "anthropo-centric fallacy," which, in the last analysis, makes him a mere religious psychologist and deprives him of the title of "theologian" in the precise sense. For his socalled theology is through and through anthropo-centric, instead of being theo-centric, as every theology has to be. Precisely upon the basis of this evaluation of Schleiermacher's theory of religion, Schäder builds and defends the disjunction between theo-centric and anthropo-centric theologies. He treats Schleiermacher as the originator of the false anthropo-centric theology, over against which must be placed the modern and true theo-centric theology. "In fact, by turning theology which must point to God, away from its proper object, the great man is the chief thorn in the flesh of theology. For he tied it up with religion, and, more than that, with the human aspect of religion." [13] Precisely this fact is the very heart of Schleiermacher's theory of religion and from there it has worked out its wider consequences.

He who reads such statements, after having made an extensive study of Schleiermacher's writings, will unconsciously scratch his head and ask himself the question: "How in the world are such judgments possible?" Schleiermacher makes the central purpose of theological research the investigation of the human aspect of religion! Unquestionably he makes this human aspect of religion the point of departure for the work of the theologian, as a matter of method, and this is what makes him the father of Protestant Theology and of all modern critical science of religion within Protestant Theology. But does he make the human aspect of religion the central goal of theology? As we shall presently see, Schäder attempts to base this interpretation on the *Glaubenslehre*. Now, in any case, this means that Schleiermacher would have had to have abandoned completely the point of view of the *Reden über die*

[13] *Loco citato*, p. 19.

Religion. For there he made the Universe, and not humanity, the central goal of the religious life and also of theological research. Indeed, he there described the essence of religion as "the perception and feeling of the Universe." And immediately after introducing this term, he again used it to differentiate religion from metaphysics and ethics. "Religion sees humanity only as a focus of all relations in the entire Universe . . . , she sees in humanity, no less than in all other particular and finite entities, the Infinite, of which humanity is a copy, a symbol." [14] Is this anthropo-centric? No! *On the contrary it is obviously the strongest possible denial of every anthropo-centric viewpoint.*

Now let us consider the *Glaubenslehre.* This is supposed by Schäder to embody Schleiermacher's anthropo-centric position. Moreover, he thinks that it is precisely the general theory of religion of the *Glaubenslehre* which does this most. The conception of the feeling of absolute dependence embodies throughout an anthropo-centric character, since this feeling is an ego-feeling. And being a feeling of the ego, in the end it is only an ego-experience. *In the concepts of "ego-feeling" and "ego-experience" Schäder's whole argument is concentrated.* This makes it all the more noteworthy that he does not give a more accurate and unequivocal definition of these two concepts. For in and of themselves they are far from being exact scientific ideas. On the one hand, every experience of man is an ego-experience insofar as it is just an experience belonging to himself. On the other hand, it is at least questionable whether there is, speaking generally, a pure ego-experience, that is to say, an experience in which the individual's own self is an object of experience. And, in any case, Schleiermacher himself denies just this. Indeed, to justify this denial, he begins the discussion of the basic thesis of a feeling of absolute dependence with a

[14] *Reden über die Religion,* 1st ed., p. 51. Compare also especially the discussion on p. 80. "To love the World-Spirit and to rejoice in his works, that is the goal of our religion, and fear is not in love. It is not otherwise with those beauties of the earth, which the sympathetic man appreciates with such ardent love. What is that bright play of color . . . ? What is it, not in your eyes, but in and for the Universe? For so you must always ask when your religion is involved." No one could find a sharper and clearer opposition to the anthropo-centric standpoint as defined by Schäder.

sharp opposition to Fichte.[15]   Then, too, the idea of an ego-experience must first be distinguished from the view which Schleiermacher founded and defended, if it is to be used as a polemic against his theory of religion.   Instead of doing this, Schäder contents himself with giving his own interpretation of the idea of an ego-experience.   In an experience of himself man is "ruled by himself," he is "held fast by himself" (pp. 7 ff.). And it is in this sense that the feeling of absolute dependence of Schleiermacher's theory of religion is an ego-feeling or an ego-experience.

In my opinion a more forced interpretation, or one more sharply in contrast with the basic intention of Schleiermacher, is inconceivable.   For he expressly stated in his chief work that the feeling of absolute dependence is identical with the consciousness of "being in relation to God."   Schäder's interpretation would force us to infer that this statement is a deliberate deception of the reader.   For on this point and in this connection it is simply out of the question that Schleiermacher was self-deceived.   When one holds fast to his feeling of absolute dependence, as Schleiermacher himself did, then he cannot deceive himself into thinking that precisely this feeling of absolute dependence brings him into relation with God.   In scientific research there is simply no sense in speaking of a self-deception where the author is supposed to have said exactly the opposite of what he meant.   For it is with the essential meaning of Schleiermacher's statement that Schäder is concerned and not with an implication of it.   Hence there remains only the supposition that Schleiermacher's statement was deliberately intended to deceive the reader.   But even though Schäder were to adopt this supposition, that would not be all.   This opinion would have to be supported by an examination of Schleiermacher's whole intellectual development.   For Schleiermacher's statement is through and through but a precise formulation of his whole theory.   At least this is true, when the choice of the word

---

[15] "In every consciousness of self there are two elements, one—so to speak—an ego-element and the other a non-ego element; the latter presupposes for all consciousness of self something other outside of the ego, by which the ego is determined and without which consciousness of self would not be what it is at all." *Glaubenslehre,* 2nd ed., paragraph 4, section I.

"God" is disregarded. And since this term is used quite generally as a description of the objective counterpart (the objective, opposite pole) of the religious relation, we should not give it any special meaning other than this, as Schleiermacher himself expressly stated.[16] Moreover, this is consistent with the facts. For Schleiermacher really was concerned with a general theory of religion, which would comprise all stages in and all varieties of religious experience.[17] That is just the reason why we have to think of this formula of Schleiermacher as the basic expression of his whole theory. But it is just this fact that Schäder must attack. He claims that the theory as a whole makes the feeling of absolute dependence appear as a feeling or an experience of the self. But this is an erroneous assertion. It overlooks what Schleiermacher considered absolutely essential; indeed, what he regarded as ultimately the decisive factor, namely, the relation to a "co-ordering Other" (mitgesetze Andere) in the feeling of absolute dependence, elsewhere also called the "co-determining Other" (mitbestimmende Andere). From the religious viewpoint this co-ordering and co-determining Other is an absolutely transcendent reality, exalted above the whole phenomenal world. That is the central idea in Schleiermacher's whole conception.

The only really intelligible attempt of Schäder to establish this fact, over against his own exposition, is his reference to a sentence of Schleiermacher, which certainly is not unequivocal when torn out of its context and taken by itself. In identifying absolute dependence and relation with God Schleiermacher says that this means that the source of our existence and of every self-conscious experience of our impressionable and self-active existence is best described by the term "God," and that this is for us the original and true meaning of all such experiences.

---

[16] *Loco citato.* Paragraph 4, Section 4. "So that God only means for us first of all that which is the determining factor in this feeling, and, although we suppress this in our consciousness, nevertheless every further content of this idea must first be evolved out of this given and basic content."

[17] Since Schäder never considers this fact, he cannot understand Schleiermacher. From the start he formulates his criticism from the viewpoint of the Christian idea of God; more exactly, from the viewpoint of a definite dogmatic statement of the Christian idea of God. See Otto Hofmann's *Der Begriff der religiösen Erfahrung in seiner Bedeutung für die Prinzipienfragen der Religionsphilosophie.* Leipsic, 1921.

Schäder interprets this to mean that the application of the casual viewpoint to God and the thinking of him as an efficient cause must be deduced from the feeling of absolute dependence. But then we should have an illogical and irrational conclusion. To use Schäder's own words, we would actually have to speak of a "Schleiermacherian derivation of God from the unlimited feeling of dependence." [18] But this is a false interpretation. The ambiguous expression "the source of our existence" has to be made consistent with Schleiermacher's whole doctrine, and to do this, it must be interpreted to mean the "co-ordering and co-determining Other" involved in the feeling of absolute dependence. Logically, this inference is implied in the statement quoted. But it is borne out by a careful examination of its entire context. Indeed, Schleiermacher is not speaking of the source of the feeling of absolute dependence, as Schäder assumes, but of the source implicit in our whole existence. Furthermore this inference is also borne out by Schleiermacher's comments following the passage quoted, where we find him so identifying God-consciousness and self-consciousness that neither can be separated from the other. And again, this inference is made still clearer by his statement that man is endowed not only with the feeling of absolute dependence which he always retains, but also with an immediate consciousness of himself which develops into a consciousness of God.

It is now important to bring Dunkmann into our discussion, since he has attempted in a noticeable and very effective way to hold to a position in the philosophy of religion far removed from that of Schleiermacher on the whole, and yet one that is in the closest possible touch with Schleiermacher.[19] To be sure he has not succeeded, so far as his theory of religion is concerned. For, like Schäder, he has misunderstood the profoundest meaning of Schleiermacher's idea of a feeling of absolute dependence. Dunkmann thinks that two lines of thought must be distinguished in the exposition of this theory, one psychological and the other dialectical. Now it so happens that the psychological analysis proves the impossibility of a

---

[18] *Loco citato,* p. 43.
[19] Karl Dunkmann: *Religionsphilosophie. Kritik der religiösen Erfahrung als Grundlegung christl. Theologie,* Gütersl. 1917, pp. 270 ff.

feeling of absolute dependence, while, on the other hand, the dialectical argument is opposed to the psychological analysis in that it seeks to establish deductively and dialectically the reality of the feeling of absolute dependence.

However, on both points this criticism implies a misunderstanding of Schleiermacher's view. Never did he assert the complete impossibility of a feeling of absolute dependence. He asserted its impossibility only for the systems of relations of men in the phenomenal world. On the other hand, Schleiermacher did not reach the feeling of absolute dependence by the method of dialectical reasoning—at least not primarily—, but as an expression of his religious experience. Not until he had thus reached it did he ask what this feeling of absolute dependence means from the standpoint of human knowledge as a whole. To be sure in answering this question the speculative standpoint of dialectics was at once introduced. But the feeling of absolute dependence itself, including its immediateness and its uniqueness, was not deduced by Schleiermacher; on the contrary, it was induced from religious experience. He thought that the feeling of absolute dependence is the common character of all the various forms of piety. Consequently it is the basic form of all piety and the basic religious relationship in which all others are contained.

Rudolph Otto is unquestionably one of the ablest authorities on Schleiermacher of the present day. This makes it especially important to point out that his interpretation of Schleiermacher's theory of religion is also not entirely free from error. Perhaps this is due to the fact that Otto, as he freely admits,[20] introduces into the religio-psychological point of view ideas which are taken from his neo-Frisean type of thought. This makes him overestimate the speculative and dialectical element, which actually functions in the exposition of Schleiermacher's theory of religion, and prevents him from holding fast to the central thread of the theory.

[20] Rudolph Otto, *Das Heilige. Uber das Irrationale in der Idee des Göttlichen und sein Verhältnis zum Rationalen.* English Translation by John W. Harvey, *The Idea of the Holy,* Oxford Press, 1923, p. 8. "It is not easy to discuss questions of religious psychology with one who can recollect emotions of his adolescence, the discomforts of indigestion, or, say, social feelings, but cannot recall any intrinsically religious feelings."

Consequently Otto's interpretation remains at a higher level of the same general viewpoint, yet with some of the error of Schäder on the one hand and with some of that of Leuba on the other.

Otto nevertheless begins his discussion of Schleiermacher's theory of the feeling of absolute dependence with the deliberate recognition that this was a significant discovery which fortunately revealed a very important aspect of underlying religious experience. However, he at once adds that there are two things to be presupposed about this discovery. First, that Schleiermacher distinguished the religious feeling of dependence from other feelings of dependence only in degree and not in kind. Now this statement is disputable. According to Schleiermacher there is not simply a difference of degree, but a thorough difference of quality between the feeling of absolute dependence and ordinary feelings of dependence. A difference of degree does exist between the various ordinary feelings of dependence, depending upon whether they are more or less feelings of dependence or feelings of freedom. But the feeling of absolute dependence is to be sharply distinguished from this whole sphere in its entirety, as altogether different in quality.

When Schleiermacher distinguishes three stages of self-consciousness: the confused animal-like consciousness; the sensuous consciousness in that widest sense of the word which includes the social and the moral feelings; and the feeling of absolute dependence, it obviously follows that the third stage is qualitatively just as different from the second as the second is from the first.[21] Moreover, the feeling of absolute dependence alone transcends the "contradiction" existing between all finite entities, and as Schleiermacher expressly emphasizes, "this character" belongs ultimately to it alone.[22] *For him this characteristic difference is not, as Otto says, a mere difference of degree, but a qualitative difference.*[23]

[21] See *Der Christliche Glaube,* 2nd ed., paragraph 5.
[22] *Loco citato,* Section 2, conclusion.
[23] Compare also *Loco citato,* Sec. I, middle: "In the feeling, which is here described as wholly sensuous, there is something co-ordering and co-determining therein, although we suppress the awareness that naturally accompanies this inter-working, and whether we are conscious of being relatively dependent or relatively free, there is a sense in which we stand over against and are like this something, and, indeed, so much so that

The other mistake which Otto has made in dealing with Schleiermacher's theory of religion is his thinking that the feeling of absolute dependence is immediately only a *feeling of the self* for which one has, *primarily by a process of inference,* to think of a source, which is then taken to be the divine self. To a certain extent Otto here shares Schäder's misunderstanding which we have already discussed. But it is especially noteworthy that Otto's misunderstanding here is based upon the error just discussed of treating the feeling of absolute dependence as one of the "natural" feelings of dependence. To this extent this entire position of Otto supplements that of Schäder. And the criticism of the view of one is at the same time a test of the validity of that directed against the other. In the last analysis both interpretations involve misunderstandings of Schleiermacher.

we as individuals or as members of a whole (for example, in the love of country) find ourselves opposed to another individual. In this respect this kind of feeling is to be distinguished from the feeling of absolute dependence in the most definite way." In this passage Schleiermacher clearly states the qualitative uniqueness of the feeling of absolute dependence. To illustrate the religious feeling of absolute dependence, which he admits is "still more and something different than feelings of dependence," Otto refers to Abraham's saying in his conversation with Jahweh: "I have taken upon me to speak unto the Lord, who am but dust and ashes." (Genesis, XVIII, 27.) Although this does indicate a significant aspect, which needs to be considered, it hardly brings out the total character of the feeling of absolute dependence. To indicate this it would perhaps be better to refer to a mental state like that of the prophets Jeremiah or second Isaiah, as expressed in the words that Jahweh makes them utter: "Can the clay say to the potter: 'What dost thou?'" (Isa. XVIII, 9.) "As the clay in the potter's hand, so are ye in my hand." (Jer. XVIII, 6.) And we must also bear in mind the use which Paul and Luther made of this idea.

CHAPTER V

THE RECASTING OF SCHLEIERMACHER'S THEORY OF RELIGION

I

What follows, then, for our own task, from our clarification of Schleiermacher's theory of religion? Two things follow. The first is that, in order to determine the nature of religion ourselves, we must begin with Schleiermacher's theory. For it takes us into the inmost recesses of religion. But the second result at once follows, that a further development and a recasting of Schleiermacher's theory of religion is necessary. In its original form this theory is inadequate, since it is exposed to numerous misunderstandings for modern men, even on the part of such keen and learned scholars as those to whom we have referred. And in our opinion, just as surely as these are ultimately misunderstandings, just so surely must the blame for their existence be laid to the theory.

Still this opinion does not alter the fact that Schleiermacher's theory really does take us into the actual and ultimate depths of religion. Consequently we must hold fast to the insight gained therefrom as the foundation of our own further investigation.

It will suffice here to refer to some especially conclusive reasons for taking this position. When Goethe described the religious contemplation of his old age in the language of the theory of reverence of his *Wanderjahre,* and when he put the reverence for that which is above us at the head of the three types of reverence, he was essentially only giving another name to that state of feeling which Schleiermacher called the feeling of absolute dependence.

In his treatment of the *Wanderjahre,* Friedrich Gundelfinger (Gundolf), the latest interpreter of Goethe, has hardly touched upon his theory of reverence, although it occupies a dominating and central position in the total world-view which Goethe defended in that work. To be sure, in his introduction Gundelfinger incorrectly sketches the theory, doing violence to the facts. Consequently he is misleading. Nevertheless even he writes in this very same introduction: "The original tendency of man, which underlies all ritual and all mythology, is the reverence for that upon which he is absolutely dependent." [1]

William James conducted his religio-psychological studies with the emphatic purpose of exhibiting the varieties of religious experience. In his one-sided emphasis upon this point of view, he was even misled into making the statement that the student of religion must actually abandon the hope of finding any uniform interpretation of the nature of religion. Yet James also sums up the results of his survey of the whole field in these words: "That personal attitude which the individual feels himself impelled to take toward what he apprehends to be the divine—and you will remember that this was our definition—will prove to be both a helpless and a sacrificial attitude." And to explain the sense in which he uses these words, James adds: "For when all is said and done, we are in the end absolutely dependent on the universe." [2]

Back to Schleiermacher and forward from Schleiermacher! This, then, is the motto for our further investigation.

2

But in this formulation of the problem we approach closely to the formulation supported by Paul Natorp in his *Religion innerhalb der Grenzen der Humanität.*" [3] The title of this work at once suggests that Natorp tries to adopt and to develop Kant's theory of religion. Yet in doing this Natorp

---

[1] Friedrich Gundolf: *Goethe,* Berlin, 1918, p. 39.
[2] *The Varieties of Religious Experience,* p. 51.
[3] 2nd ed., Tübingen, 1908.—Kurt Kesseler offers valuable criticism of Natorp in his writings: *Das Problem der Religion in der Gegenwartsphilosophie,* 2nd ed., Leipsic, 1920; *Kritik der neukantischen Religionsphilosophie der Gegenwart,* Leipsic, 1920. *Religionsphilosophie,* 1927.— The analysis of Natorp's position which Friedr. Karl Schumann offers from the point of view of Rehmke's philosophy is also noteworthy: *Religion und Wirklichkeit; Kritische Prolegomena zu einer Religionsphilosophie,* Leipsic, 1913. See also Schumann's book: *Der Gottesgedanke und der Zerfall der Moderne,* 1929.

deliberately tries to utilize Schleiermacher's insights and to establish a connection with them. Indeed, he attempts nothing more nor less than to develop logically the decisive start made in Schleiermacher's theory of religion. Consequently he claims that his religio-philosophical investigation represents the logical application of that method which Schleiermacher was the first to originate. Now it must be said in advance that the science of religion can never be thankful enough to Natorp for his thorough-going attempt to discover the nature of religion. And we in particular must count it to his great credit that he so emphatically returned to Schleiermacher for his method. Yet we cannot accept his conception of Schleiermacher's theory of religion.

However, in order better to understand what follows, it must be remembered that Natorp eliminates completely the transcendental character of religion, indeed it is a matter of principle with him not to regard a transcendental claim, *i.e.,* a claim of being in relation to a transcendental reality, as belonging to the nature of religion. On the contrary he represents a completely subjective theory of religion, inasmuch as he places religious experience in the realm of the object-less consciousness. And he distinguishes this object-less consciousness most sharply from the objectifying consciousness, with its three separate spheres, of knowledge, of the moral activity of the will, and of the creative æsthetic imagination. It is true that the object-less consciousness is the common basis of these three objectifying spheres or functions of consciousness, and that all three repeatedly draw renewed strength from it, but that consciousness itself is truly object-less and a purely immanent subjectivity. And religion belongs to this sphere.

For this view of religion Natorp appeals to Schleiermacher. This is assumed to be the only logical development of his starting point. In referring to feeling as the foundation of religion in the human consciousness, Schleiermacher opened the way which leads directly to Natorp's position. For in the human consciousness feeling represents precisely pure subjectivity, the inner nature of the spiritual life *per se,* the self-existence of the soul *per se.* But although this insight is implied in Schleiermacher's starting point, yet he did not always retain it and he failed to carry it to a conclusion, but abandoned and turned away from it. That is to say, Schleiermacher erroneously transformed infinity of feeling, in the sense of uncertainty and formlessness, into a feeling of the Infinite, thus restoring again to feeling the object-relation which his original premise excluded. However, if we think of feeling in the sense of his original premise, as being strictly and definitely a boundless and a formless feeling preceding every formation of objects, then we must exclude from it every objective relation and treat *this feeling precisely in its indefiniteness, in its boundlessness and in its formlessness as the very essence of religion.* Natorp admits that Schleiermacher's feeling of the infinite obscures this fact, but so little that we need only to draw away a veil to recognize the infinity of feeling as the actual object of the feeling of the infinite.

Now we are not as yet concerned with Natorp's proof of his position. Here only *the connection with Schleiermacher* is to be considered. The question can, therefore, be asked: Is Natorp justified in appealing to Schleiermacher for the general tendency of his theory? Does the logic of Schleiermacher's premise really carry us in the direction in which Natorp is looking? If so, no matter what we might think of Natorp's theory in detail, we would also have to undertake the recasting and the extension of Schleiermacher's theory of religion, which we have demanded, in this same direction.

However, these questions must be answered in the negative. They must be denied absolutely and unconditionally. Natorp does not show us the right way to recast Schleiermacher's theory, and he cannot rightly appeal to him in support of his own views.

Which form of Schleiermacher's theory of religion does Natorp hold? And, in view of his own general theory, what does he think of the relation of these various forms to each other? We get no answer to these questions from Natorp. Since his position is entirely uncertain and vacillating in this two-fold respect, it is groundless.

Natorp might appeal to the *Reden über die Religion* in

their earliest form with a semblance of justification. For the subjective element is most pronounced in them. But, first of all, a definite path leads from this earliest form of the *Reden* to the theory of absolute dependence of the *Glaubenslehre,* so that Natorp would also have had to take a stand on the latter. However, he deliberately avoids referring to Schleiermacher's earliest view that religion is the "perception and feeling of the Universe." Naturally, for this emphasis upon "perception" can never be made to harmonize with Natorp's theory. And still less can the theory of the feeling of absolute dependence be harmonized with it. *The two theories do not correspond at any point, indeed they are actually contradictory in every essential respect.*

Natorp begins with the formal psychological foundation upon which Schleiermacher built his theory. According to the latter, religion is not mere theoretical knowledge about God, neither rational nor historical; nor is it just a peculiar direction of the will nor a kind of imaginative creation. Religion includes all of these, and cannot be severed from them: yet they are its forms of expression rather than its essence, they are by-products and symbols rather than the throbbing heart of the religious consciousness. The heart of religion is feeling. And out of religious feeling first emerges the characteristically religious type of knowledge, morality, and art. Consequently Schleiermacher does not regard feeling as a new and separate sphere of consciousness, alongside of the intellect, the will, and creative imagination, but as the fundamental psychical driving power *per se.*

To this extent Natorp's reasoning does actually correspond with that of Schleiermacher. But from this point on they move in absolutely opposite directions. Even in a formal way, this is true. Precisely taken, the line of thought which has been thus far described, is Natorp's whole theory of religion. Everything else is for him only an interpretation of this line of thought. For him the formal-psychological treatment of the problem of religion also constitutes the determination of the nature of the content of religion. For Schleiermacher, however, we have only made a formal beginning toward the determination of the nature of the content of religion when we have described its emotional character. Thus for him the nature of religion consists in the certainty of feeling, and not, as with Natorp, in its uncertainty. And this certainty of feeling, which is the essential characteristic of religion, takes us so completely out of the sphere of mere subjectivity and pure inwardness that it can be characterized in its uniqueness only by the object-relation which belongs to it. And finally: the "object" of this object-relation, instead of being of a merely inner-psychical nature, does not even belong to the realm of "temporal" or "finite" existence at all.[4]

In conclusion, Natorp has not followed the direction of Schleiermacher's religio-psychological position; he has rather abandoned it and made it ineffective. In the end he uses Schleiermacher's formal-psychological foundation merely as a starting point, and he reads into its terminology his own previously established speculative and moralistic world-view, which does not take religious experience into account primarily, but only gives a purely deductive and speculative treatment of it. Instead of correcting Schleiermacher's main error, Natorp only increases and extends it. So we can learn nothing for our task from Natorp's attempt to recast Schleiermacher's theory of religion, unless it be that he only understands the very beginning of that theory.

3

If, now, we begin the attempt to complete Schleiermacher's theory of religion upon its religio-psychological foundation, we must be careful at the very beginning to avoid Schleiermacher's errors. As we have seen, there are two of these errors. One is an inadequate consideration of the history of religion, especially of the lower forms of religion. The other is the premature introduction of the speculative and dialectical problems of philosophy into the science of religion. The religio-psychological method must completely exclude any such procedure. And it must deliberately attempt to remedy the

[4] *Der christliche Glaube*, etc., 2nd ed., chap. 4, sec. 4: "Here we must be reminded that this 'Whence' is not the world in the sense of the totality of temporal existence and still less any one particular part of it."

first error, since its main purpose is to establish a balance between history and religious experience with the help of the religio-psychological circle which operates by means of productive empathy. Hence our first positive task will be to reveal more definitely and clearly the religio-psychological direction observable in Schleiermacher's theory of religion, thus insuring it against false interpretations. Religio-psychologically considered, the main tendency of the theory of the feeling of absolute dependence is this: to express the relationship of man to a reality which transcends the whole finite space-time universe, and to assert his dependence upon that reality.

This results, first of all, in the following recasting of Schleiermacher's view. *The nature of religion is to be found in the relationship of man to an "over-world" in which he believes and which he intuits by faith, and upon which he feels himself to be dependent.* This definition must be further supplemented and elaborated later on. For the time being we intentionally restrict ourselves to the task of recasting the theory. This inverts the relation of the two main elements of Schleiermacher's thesis to each other, putting man's relationship, which he had put last, to the front, and letting his statement about the feeling of absolute dependence follow in the second place.[5]

This two-fold change, and the double-sided recasting which it involves, is required by the religio-psychological point of view. For in determining the nature of religion, the relationship itself is the primary factor. The feeling of absolute dependence is a resultant of and a reaction to this relationship. The testimony of one's own religious experience leaves no doubt about this, and without exception a religio-psychologically interpreted history of religion confirms it. Prayer, the most important mode of expression of all piety, aims expressly to establish or to maintain and to cultivate such a relationship.

Even in primitive religion this is clearly the purpose of prayer, as is shown by its forms: supplication and conversa-

[5] Here our recasting coincides completely with that of Rud. Otto, and this is the element of truth in Otto's position toward Schleiermacher's theory of religion which we criticized above (p. 91 ff.).

39834

tion (to use Heiler's fitting terminology).[6] It is shown further by the various types of prayer postures and prayer ges-
tures, which are all closely analogous to the customs of
greeting and of homage of the social order; and it may be
seen, finally, in the practice of prayer, especially in the frequent use of expressions denoting political and also [7] social
relationships in addressing the spirits and gods. In this connection we must again point out that the use of the name of
father is of cardinal importance. Especially characteristic
also, is the not infrequent duplication of kinship terms, as in
the prayer to Isis, of the Isis cult: "Oh my father, my brother,
my mother Isis." [8] For in such cases it is especially evident
that precisely the element of close and intimate relationship
is the deciding factor. Then too, it should be mentioned that
in the ancient Chinese language the word-picture for prayer
is composed of the signs for divinity, mouth, and man, which
denotes the conversation between man and the divinity.[9] And
when sacrifice is considered along with prayer, here also the
conservation or the reëstablishment of a kinship relation is
clearly the decisive factor. For example, the saying of a
Kafir priest during the offering of a sacrifice is very characteristic: "Here you (spirits) have your sacrifice, for we
do not want to keep anything from you, for we receive everything from you which we need." [10] And the highest offering
in the Vedic worship, the Soma, not only gives to the Gods
necessary nourishment, but also creates a state of intoxication
in which the devotee also shares: "We drank the Soma, we
became immortal, we came to the light, we found the gods.
What enmity can now harm us, or what craftiness of men,

[6] Cf. Heiler: *Das Gebet,* 2nd ed., pp. 51 ff. This conversational prayer,
which is carried on by frequent repetitions, deserves special attention, since
in prayer conversation serves, as H. Schurtz (*Urgeschichte der Kultur,*
Leipsic-Wien, 1900, p. 483) rightly observes, to establish a feeling of
together-ness.

[7] Among these the relationship of lord, chief, king, and ruler should be
named, but also that of friend.

[8] E. A. Wallis Budge, *Egyptian Magic* (Books on Egypt and Chaldea
II), 1901, p. 49. Cf. Fr. Heiler: *Das Gebet,* 2nd ed., p. 143. Compare
also the examples already mentioned in Chap. III above.

[9] W. Grube: *Religion und Kultur der Chinesen,* 1910, p. 40. Compare
also Fr. Heiler, *op. cit.,* p. 516.

[10] A. Kropf, *Das Volk der Xosa-Kaffern, im östlichen Südafrika nach
seiner Geschichte, Eigenart, Verfassung und Religion,* Berlin, 1906, pp. 188 ff.

Lincoln Christian College

Immortal One! King Soma, save us by thy grace! Know thou that we have entered into a covenant with thee. Power and courage arise! Deliver us not according to thy fancy unto an enemy."

The extent to which sacrifice is regarded from the point of view of the kinship relation in the Vedic religion can be illustrated by another verse of a hymn to Indra: "The sacrifice became, O Indra, thy strength, and the feast of pressed Soma, thy joy. For the sake of the offering, help us; thou who art worthy of it, give aid to this offering. This offering has aided thy thunder-bolt in the battle against Vritra." (*Rig-Veda* VIII, 48, 3, 8.)

The Barhis, which is of fundamental importance in the Vedic sanctuary and its ritual, also deserves special attention. The Barhis is the sacrificial couch, *i.e.*, the grass bed which is made ready so that the Gods may sit upon it and participate in the sacrificial feast. "Strew well the grass for the sacrifice! As the children come from here and there to their mother, so shall the gods seat themselves upon the sacrificial couch." [11] Thus we read in one of the many passages of the *Rig-Veda* where the Barhis is mentioned.[12] The fire-god Agni, who, as a personification of the sacrificial fire, supervises communications between men and the gods, is summoned to call the gods to the sacrificial feast: "We choose Agni as the messenger of our feast. Agni the all-knowing Hotar,[13] the clever one. Again and again, Agni, the lord of the district, the much beloved leader of the sacrifice is summoned in their petitions. As soon as they have been born, bring hither the gods, O Agni, for him who has preferred the sacrificial couch; thou art our Hotar who is worthy of adoration. Awaken the hungry (gods), O Agni, and when thou hast

[11] *Rig-Veda* III, 32, 12. The combat of Indra with the dragon Vritra is extolled in the *Rig-Veda* as the most glorious deed of the heroic God. Indra's weapon in this combat was the Vajra, the thunder-bolt.

[12] *Rig-Veda* VII, 43, 2 f.—The Barhis itself is also addressed: "Spread thyself out as soft as the clouds, the songs have been sounded; give us success, thou beautiful bed of grass." V, 5, 4. Compare Oldenberg, *op. cit.*, pp. 342 ff.

[13] In the highly developed Vedic sacrificial ritual the Hotar is the sacrificing priest who chants the hymns in which the gods are praised and invited to the sacrifice. In the *Rig-Veda* Agni always appears as the Hotar of the gods.

delivered thy messages, seat thyself, together with the gods, upon the sacrificial couch." (*Rig-Veda* I, 12, 1 ff.) Beside the Barhis burns the sacrificial fire, to which are consigned the sacrificial offerings, and which is therefore often called the "Mouth of the gods" in the *Rig-Veda*.[14]

And insofar as Buddhism really is a religion, whose original form even lacks not only the element of sacrifice but also that of prayer, we may speak of a *relationship to Nirvana which is to be reached by meditation.*

In one of his last publications Oldenberg explained the relation between the doctrine of the *Upanishads* and the beginnings of Buddhism. He pointed out that the atmosphere of Nirvana in Buddhism can hardly be distinguished from that spirit which is expressed in the prayer salutation of the *Brihad-Āranyaka-Upanishad:*

> Out of non-existence lead me unto the real,
> Out of darkness lead me unto light,
> Out of death lead me unto deliverance from death.[15]

In the last line quoted the original says "unto immortality" but the word "immortality" is used here in the sense in which it is also recognized by Buddhism. Thus Buddha himself begins his first discourse with the saying, "Open your ears, ye monks. Immortality hath been found."

Moreover, there is in this *Brihad-Āranyaka-Upanishad* a dual version of the famous conversation of Yājñavalkya with Maitreyī concerning immortality.[16] When he is about to leave his household to live as a hermit and is desirous of dividing his possessions between his two wives, Maitreyī asks her husband concerning immortality: "What are those possessions to me by which I cannot become immortal? Give to me, O exalted One, the knowledge which you possess." Then

[14] Oldenberg, *op. cit.,* pp. 103 ff., p. 342, pp. 457 ff.
[15] *Brihad-Āranyaka-Upanishad* I, 3, 38. Compare Paul Deussen: *Sechzig Upanishads des Veda.* 2nd ed. 1905, p. 390. This Upanishad belongs to the group of the oldest Upanishads, where the doctrine of the *Upanishads* is found in its purest form. Cf. M. Winternitz: *Geschichte der indischen Literatur,* Vol. I, 1909, pp. 196 ff. See R. E. Hume: *The Thirteen Principal Upanishads.*
[16] *Brihad-Āranyaka-Upanishad* II, 4, and in more extended form IV, 5. Cf. Paul Deussen, *op. cit.,* pp. 416 ff., pp. 481 ff.

Yājñavalkya speaks to her of the "self," the Ātman which permeates all being as the salt permeates the water of the sea, which alone gives value unto all things of value, even unto the gods and which is by nature unchangeable, and indestructible.[17] To enter into absolute one-ness with this Ātman, beyond the world of duality and consciousness—that is immortality.

And as surely as the relation of the worshipper to the Brahman-Ātman of the *Upanishads* is an actual relationship, just so surely is the relation of the worshipper to Nirvana in Buddhist teaching also experienced as an actual relationship.

Of course this relationship in the *Upanishads,* and especially in Buddhism, has its own peculiarities. And so we must add an immediate qualification to our conclusion. The tendency toward a religious relationship, which is undeniably present in these religions, does not come to full fruition, but is prematurely withered and shriveled. Maitreyī is perfectly right when she remarks to her husband, after he has expounded to her the teaching concerning Ātman and has concluded with the statement that after death there is no consciousness, that she finds herself unsatisfied and confused. And Yājñavalkya's answer to her objection is even more unsatisfying. He violently suppresses the objection with a purely theoretical and rational speculation and with an utter disregard of religious motives. Entirely aside from the fact that the proof for this theoretical and rational speculation (it may be summed up in the question: how can one perceive the perceiver?) [18] is quite vulnerable, the complete elimination of religious elements, in the face of the Brahman-Ātman teach-

[17] This latter saying concerning the indestructibility of the Ātman belongs to the expanded revision of the dialogue which is even more extended; but it may also be found in three other places in the Yājñavalkya-passages (*op. cit.,* III, 9, 26; IV, 2, 4; IV, 4, 22).
[18] This is true of both versions of the story. Epistemologically considered the (in itself correct) epistemological reflection, which, however, only applies to the relational human perceptive faculty as such, is without further ado converted into a metaphysical ontological judgment and is thereby transformed into its opposite, *i.e.,* into a speculative assumption. Deussen's interpretation of the teaching of the *Upanishads* (cf. also in addition to the previously named monograph, his *Allgemeine Geschichte der Philosophie mit besonderer Berücksichtigung der Religionen,* Vol. I, Leipsic, 1906, 2nd part, pp. 36 ff.) intensifies the one-sided attitude of the

ing which on the whole is religiously conditioned throughout, is unjustified and unsatisfying.

Maitreyī, versed in sacred knowledge, is in the right as against her illustrious husband.[19] For judging by this rationalistic argument and the criteria therein validated, his whole doctrine of Ātman would become untenable, and unjustifiable, and would therefore collapse. This argument would make it entirely meaningless to espouse the worship of the Ātman and to teach : "The self, indeed, we should see, and hear and understand, and meditate upon, O Maitreyī; indeed, He by whom the Self is seen, heard, understood, and recognized, by Him this whole world is known." [20] Without question the fundamental principle of Yājñavalkya, which is also the fundamental principle of the whole doctrine of the *Upanishads,* denotes *a relationship between the finite and the infinite self.* Why this relationship may not attain to "eternal duration" (to use Goethe's phrase), if it can ever be possible at all, is in fact not made clear. For the Ātman is itself supposed to be eternal ("unchangeable and indestructible being"). Herein lies the confusion of the *Upanishads.* And it becomes still greater the more intimate we take the relationship of the finite self to the infinite to be, according to the formula *tat twam asi,* "that art thou" (that is, your self is the Ātman). For it is evident that this formula does not mean complete identity in the external and literal sense, since in that case there could be no plurality of finite egos or selves.

To the extent to which man comes to God, he shares in His eternal life. "He that believeth (that is, he who is in living fellowship with God) hath eternal life." (John VI :47.)

4

At this point the question concerning mysticism naturally arises. Can mysticism be included in a theory which takes

Upanishads, inasmuch as Deussen first turns the view of the *Upanishads* in the direction of the illusionistic Maya theory, and then does violence to the views of Kant which he identifies with the latter.

[19] According to the account, *op. cit.,* IV, 5, 1, she understands the discussion about the Brahma, whereas Kātyāyani, the other wife of Yājñavalkya, knows "only what women know."

[20] This sentence is also identical in both versions.

the religious relationship as crucial for the determination of the nature of religion? Obviously this question is closely related to the whole problem and evaluation of mysticism. However, we do not want to raise the question of mysticism here in its entire scope, but we will rather restrict our discussion to the specific question with which we are immediately concerned. Moreover, for the time being we purposely restrict it to Christian mysticism. Above, in order not to anticipate in advance, we did not designate either the doctrine of the *Upanishads* or that of Buddhism as mysticism. Later this double restriction will have to be removed, but here it will help us to clarify the complicated perplexities of the problem.

Friedrich Heiler, who has lately earned the greatest distinction for the contributions he has made to the study of mysticism, defines it as "that form of communion with God" in which the world and the self are radically negated, in which the human personality is dissolved, submerged, and engulfed in the infinite one-ness of the divinity.[21] For Heiler this is the all-inclusive definition of mysticism which comprises all of its individual forms and nuances. Even Christian mysticism, with its many representatives and types, is to be included in this definition. At the same time Heiler merely points out as a reservation, that mysticism is often not developed purely and consistently, but is sometimes permeated and restricted by motives of a different nature, especially by motives belonging either to prophetic or to revealed religion, these being the other two main types of piety. However, the actual fundamental tendency of mysticism is that stated in the above definition. Heiler expressly emphasizes the fact that even that more personal type of mysticism originating out of prophetic piety, still coincides with consistent mysticism in that its *ultimate aim* is the striving for salvation.

If Heiler's theory were correct, then the determination of the nature of religion which we have supported would be wrong at its very starting point. It would then have to be given up, or at least radically revised. At least this would hold insofar as mysticism is religion (which Heiler certainly

[21] Friedrich Heiler; *Das Gebet,* 2nd ed., p. 249.

claims). If this presupposition is not at once granted, then we face the alternative: either mysticism is not religion at all, or our conception of religion is wrong at the very beginning. *For mysticism, in Heiler's sense of the term, cannot be classified as a relationship.* Of course when Heiler begins his thesis with the words, mysticism is a "form of communion with God" it does seem that the idea of a relationship is included and therefore presupposed in this definition. One might even think that the idea of "communion with God" denotes precisely the religious relationship, and that this is only a more concrete name for it. However, a reconciliation cannot be reached in this way. Heiler's idea of "communion with God" can obviously not be taken strictly; it must be taken in the most general and in a very vague sense. The precise formulation of that which Heiler wishes to say begins with the relative clause, "in which the world and the self are radically negated." For Heiler communion with God is a metaphysical attitude. His thesis is unequivocal only when thus interpreted. On any other interpretation it would be self-contradictory, a pure *contradictio in adjecto*. Heiler's view is that mysticism is that metaphysical attitude of man in which the world and the self are radically renounced. And even if the full consequence of this metaphysical position is seldom carried out, nevertheless the fundamental tendency of mysticism —of all mysticism—is radically to negate the world and the self. This fundamental tendency corresponds with the ultimate aim of all mystical striving for salvation, which is to dissolve the human personality into the infinite one-ness of deity.

However, Heiler's evaluation of mysticism must be challenged, especially when applied to Christian mysticism. Here he has not sufficiently applied the religio-psychological method of observation, toward which he leans and which he employs to a considerable extent. He clings too much to and is too strongly influenced by verbal and thought-forms.

This applies, first of all, to his statement that in its fundamental tendency mysticism radically negates the world and the self. *This identification and complete equalization of the*

*world and the self, under the comprehensive point of view of
the purpose of radical negation, does not do justice to mysticism and especially not to the fundamental tendency of mysticism.* Of course the world and the self are frequently placed
along side of each other and are apparently equally condemned
by the mystics. But to a more deeply penetrating eye, made
keen by the religio-psychological method, it appears that even
then a definite differentiation has to be made. Heiler himself
begins the defense of his position with a "characterization of
the elementary psychical experience" of mysticism. And as
an example of the "retreat from the world into the self" in
mysticism, he first quotes the following lines of Tersteegen:

> I am so weary of strange things,
> So tired of multiplicities
> Which bring me nothing but torment;
> This suffocating finity!
> I perish nigh, Eternity,
> O let my spirit breathe in thee!
> Should I consume my time and strength
> With things which cannot comfort give?
> My spirit to that source must turn
> For which it hath been made to live.
> Away with nature, dreams and show!
> For One alone I fain would live.

Do these lines exemplify a radical negation of the world
and the self? Evidently not. "Away with nature . . . I
live for One alone." These lines express the basic attitude
and it actually excludes the equalization of the world and the
self. And the more this attitude is emphasized the more this
equalization is excluded.

Neither can one argue, as Heiler's reasoning might naturally suggest, that in these lines only one element is emphasized, and that since they refer only to the "retreat from the
world into the self" the other element, the radical negation
of the self, is to be discussed and exemplified further elsewhere. But if the basic tendency of mysticism really were
two-sided, as Heiler claims, then it would actually have to be
exemplified as such, that is, in its duality. So far as the lines

quoted above are concerned, they exemplify this duality so little that they rather exclude it.

Precisely for this reason Heiler also fails when, in the next section, he tries to find in Tersteegen's writings an example of the radical negation of the self. Here is the example which he quotes:

> Flesh, the reason, sense and nature,
> All are destined unto death.
> Would that I from life were taken,
> And of striving were bereft.

Do these lines signify a radical negation of the self according to Tersteegen? Absolutely not. When judged by his whole style of writing they signify only a negation of the worldly passions and tendencies of the self. These Tersteegen certainly does negate, but not the self in itself and as such. Consequently in regard to the hope of eternal life, the conclusion that the human personality will be dissolved, either in the common pantheistic or in the extreme Buddhist sense, does not necessarily follow. And the correctness of this view can be proven even more extensively and emphatically. And the linking of the world and the self under the viewpoint of negation, which is missing in the examples already given, can also be exemplified in Tersteegen. And just these examples are especially valuable in clarifying his position. They do not support but rather argue against Heiler. For example, in the closing verse of the hymn, "O Gott, O Geist, O Licht des Lebens," we find the words "I would forget the world and the self." This looks like a completely identical evaluation of the world and of the self. The two-fold tendency which Heiler's thesis asserts, seems to be indisputably proved. But it only seems so. On closer examination the semblance disappears. The verse reads:

> To Thee I give myself and stay
> Far from all else, to Thee so near.
> I would forget this world and self
> Believing firmly: God is here!
> O God, O Spirit, Light of Life,
> No man in vain hath sought Thy sight.

Here the forgetting of the self not only does not exclude, but is rather regarded as the condition under which the self "remains near" to God.

It follows that we must also interpret in the same way those passages which appear to demand a negation of the self in an even more radical fashion than "the forgetting of the self." In the fifth verse of the hymn "Gott ist gegenwärtig" we find the expression, "let me wholly vanish." It would seem that the tendency toward complete negation of the self could hardly be expressed more definitely. And yet this is again only semblance. This must be our conclusion, even when we entirely disregard the verses which follow, with their further explanation of the main thought, and consider only the fifth verse:

> Air, which filleth every thing
> In which we mortals hover,
> Source from which all life doth spring
> Sea, which is boundless ever,
> Wonder of all wonders
> In Thee would I sink under.
> I in Thee,
> Thou in me,
> Let me vanish wholly,
> To see and find Thee only.

The words which immediately precede "let me vanish wholly," as well as those which immediately follow, leave no doubt concerning the real meaning. Here again the phrase "let me vanish wholly" does not mean a radical negation of the self as such, but only of that self which is constituted by a worldly love of finite existence. Therefore this idea when taken *sub specie æternitatis,* does not necessarily lead to a dissolution of the ego, but, on the contrary, to a most intimate living fellowship with God. And the "give and take" relationship is in no sense excluded, but is expressly presupposed: "I in Thee," and "Thou in me."

That this whole way of thinking involves the possibility, and therefore, also the danger of being turned in the direction mentioned by Heiler, should certainly not be denied, but should constantly be kept in mind. However, the fundamental tendency of Tersteegen's mysticism is not the dual one mentioned by Heiler. It can be much better expressed in the words of the first Epistle of John: "And the world passeth away and the lust thereof; but he that doeth the will of God abideth forever." (I John II, 17.) The only question is whether Tersteegen takes this will of God entirely in the sense of the New Testament and whether he places enough emphasis upon the "doing" of this will. For another saying from the Gospel of John is closely related to the one just quoted: "If any man willeth to do his will, he alone shall know of the teaching, whether it is of God." (John VII, 17.)

However, even for Heiler, Tersteegen is not a representative of consistent mysticism, but only of the inconsistent type. Hence consistent mysticism might still refute our approach to the determination of the nature of religion. Consequently we must discuss a representative of consistent mysticism in order to clarify the situation. Heiler thinks that Eckhart is a consistent mystic. Let us, then, consider him. However, two things must first be stated with regard to Heiler's *distinction between consistent and inconsistent mysticism*. In the first place, we must emphasize the fact that this distinction applies only to the *working out of the fundamental tendency and not to the fundamental tendency as such*. For even the most inconsistent mysticism would have to reveal the fundamental tendency of mysticism as such. If, therefore, Heiler's dual tendency, which we have already discussed, cannot be accepted as the fundamental tendency of inconsistent mysticism, neither can it be the fundamental tendency of all mysticism.

This proves that we would have to make another kind of distinction between the various forms of mysticism, one which would make possible a qualitatively different characterization. And in the second place, Heiler himself has not reached an entirely unified and unequivocal conception of mysticism. On the one hand, he thinks that mysticism is to be found in its full consistency in the *Upanishads,* in the *Vedanta* of Shankara, in Hinayana Buddhism, in Plotinus, the Areopagite, Eckhart, Tauler, Angelus Silesius and Molinos. Yet, on the other hand, he sometimes names (primitive) Buddhism as the only really

consistent form of mysticism.   Now it is just because he
selects atheistic Buddhism as the only real example of consistent
mysticism that the error in his whole attitude toward mysticism
has a greater significance than would be attributed to it if it
were merely a matter of distinguishing a relative from an
absolute consistency.   For this makes atheistic Buddhism the
criterion of all mysticism.   Now even though the term "atheistic" may require a more exact definition, nevertheless a judgment is hereby pronounced in advance upon all Christian
mysticism.   However, this will be taken up later.   In the meantime we will confine ourselves to Heiler's original terminology,
and will discuss Eckhart as a representative of consistent
mysticism.

Can Eckhart be included in the formula which says that
mysticism radically negates the world and the self?

Undoubtedly the tendency to negate the world is carried out
with greater assurance and bluntness by Eckhart than by Tersteegen.   This is asserted with the greatest imaginable direct-
ness and pointedness.   In the papal bull *"in agro Dominico,"*
promulgated in the year 1329, soon after Eckhart's death, some
of his teachings are branded as being heretical, and others as
suspected of being heretical.   At the end of the second group
of sayings we find this: "All creatures are simply nothing; I do
not say that they are not much, or only something, but that
they are a mere nothing." [22]   Although this idea is often found
in Eckhart's sermons, this particular sentence is taken verbatim
from his sermon on John I, 17. "All creatures are simply
nothing, I do not say that they are not much, or only something, but that they are a mere nothing." [23]   According to Eckhart creatures are "a mere nothing" insofar as they are taken
by themselves and are thought to depend upon themselves.
What Eckhart aims to say is that they owe their existence
solely to God; and that in themselves they are nothing. [24]   To

[22] Denifle: *Archiv für Literatur-und Kirchengeschichte des Mittelalters,*
II, 1886, pp. 636 ff.
[23] Fr. Pfeiffer, *Deutsche Mystiker des 14 Jahrhunderts,* Anastatic reprint of the edition of 1827, Vol. II, Sermon XL, p. 136.   (In Walter Lehmann, *Die Klassiker der Religion,* Vol. 14-15, Göttingen, 1919, p. 199.)
[24] Compare the sentence in this same sermon which follows the one
just quoted. "That which has no being is nothing.   All creatures have no
being, for their being depends upon the being (presence) of God.   If God

be sure, in this sense we are here confronted with the most radical negation of the world. However, we must not overlook the reservation expressed in the phrase—"in this sense." For it means that the tendency toward negation which is present here, despite all its pointedness and bluntness, does not carry us in the direction of Buddhist scepticism and indifference. On the contrary, Eckhart unites with this evaluation the highest possible evaluation of nature: "If one were only able to understand nature, he would not need to listen to any sermon. Every creature is a book and is full of God." [25] However, in the sense mentioned above, Eckhart's mysticism does lean toward the radical negation of the world.

Does he also deny the reality of the self? This would have to be regarded as entirely unlikely, simply because of the strict differentiation which Eckhart makes between the soul and (other) creatures. For example, in the same sermon from which the paradoxical saying about the pure nothingness of creatures was quoted, he says: "When God created all creatures they were so worthless and so small that he could not mingle with them. But he made the soul so similar to and so much like himself that he could give himself to it, since everything else that he might otherwise give to it, it would regard as nothing." [26] In the sermon on Matthew II, 2, he proclaims as the central teaching of his mysticism that the birth of God takes place in the nature and "ground" of the soul, and then he puts with this teaching a discussion of what characteristics, for this in-dwelling of God, the soul possesses that other creatures in which God also exists do not possess. He introduces this discussion with the expressly emphasized admonition: "Consider now the difference." And then he explains that God is of course by nature in all things as the working and sustaining power, but he exists creatively only in the soul. Other creatures are the foot-prints of God, but the soul is by

were to disappear for one moment, they would vanish into nothingness. I have often said, and it is true: He who would take the whole world with God would have no more than if he had God alone. Without God all creatures mean no more than if one had a mosquito without God—it would be all the same, no more and no less."

[25] In the sermon on *Ecclesiastes* 50, 6. In Pfeiffer, *op. cit.* Sermon XXXIV, p. 271.

[26] Cf. Pfeiffer, *op. cit.*, p. 136.

nature created in the image of God. This image of God must be realized and made perfect by this birth, and no creature is capable of this except the soul.[27]

At this point in Eckhart's teaching the elaboration of his central teaching begins, and this is rightly usually regarded as the most important characteristic of his mysticism. This central thought is the identification of the inner "ground" or "spark" of the soul, with God himself. "That is the spark which is so close to God that it is a single undifferentiated 'one' with him." [28]

In developing this idea Eckhart involves himself in the same difficulties and contradictions to which attention was called in the discussion of the Ātman theory of the *Upanishads*.[29] However, when one examines Eckhart's speculation from the religio-psychological point of view it is not difficult to uncover his ultimate underlying motive. For it is noticeable everywhere in his explanations, and within his reasoning it stands in the very closest relation to his speculative theory, without, however, itself being in any way conditioned by or dependent upon it. This ultimate motive is the striving for the greatest possible nearness to God, for the most intimate fellowship with God that is possible. As far as the practical life of man is concerned Eckhart sets up the principle that that type of human conduct is the best which brings man nearer to God.[30] And this

[27] Cf. Pfeiffer, *op. cit.*, pp. 10 ff.

[28] Sermon on Luke 1 :28, Pfeiffer, *op. cit.*, p. 286.

[29] From the religio-psychological point of view the similarity between Eckhart's doctrine of the spark and the Ātman speculation of the *Upanishads* is indisputable. As the innermost nucleus of the spiritual life Eckhart's spark corresponds exactly with the Ātman. This is shown very clearly, e.g., in the famous passage of the *Chandogya Upanishad* (III 14- Deussen, p. 109) where in a fundamental way the identity of the Brahman with the Ātman is proclaimed as the doctrine of the Candilya, and it becomes especially evident in the paralleled text of the *Catapatha-Brahmana* X 6: 3: "Worship the Ātman! His nature is thought, his body is breath, his form light, his self is eternal. As small as a grain of rice or barley or millet, so this spirit dwells in the self. He is as golden as the light that is devoid of smoke. Greater than heaven, greater than the other, greater than this earth, greater than all creatures. He is the self of breath, he is my self. And when I depart from hence, I shall unite myself with this Ātman. He who has this shall truly never have any doubts. Thus spake Candilya." Comp. Oldenberg: *Die Lehren der Upanishaden,* etc., pp. 57 ff. In this text of the *Chandogya Upanishad* the Ātman is thrice designated as "existing in the inner heart." Comp. *Deussen, op. cit.*, p. 110.

[30] In the sermon on Luke II: 49 Pfeiffer, pp. 16 ff. Compare p. 23.

he designates as the truly decisive criterion for the certainty of
eternal life, that man trusts completely in God and is certain of
him because of love and intimate communion.

For Eckhart this practical religious interest is first completely satisfied by the speculative theory discussed above. But
he overlooks the fact that this theory also contains a factor
which works against this practical interest. If the idea of
identity is taken strictly logically and is carried to its conclusion,
there can be no such thing as "nearness" or "fellowship." No
doubt this interest is for him the deciding factor. And precisely this interest is also operative in all of his precepts, which
demand a "becoming free," a "stripping of the self from the
self," a "going outside of one's self," a "giving up of the self,"
a "disappearing," and sometimes even a "destruction of the
self." [31]

Let us restrict our discussion to the argument in which he
employs this very strongest expression, "self-destruction." [32]
Here, Eckhart says, one task is ours, namely, the destruction
of the self, and then he adds immediately that if this is to be
complete, God must accomplish it in us. But in developing this
idea, he immediately substitutes for the idea of self-destruction
the ideas of self-deprecation and self-humiliation. Then the
meaning of these terms is illustrated with the words of the
Gospel, "Whosoever shall humble himself shall be exalted."
"He that is greatest among you shall be your servant." And a
little further on Eckhart continues: "And because we keep
ourselves free, empty and bare of things that are in heaven—,
and because I abandon myself for his sake, therefore God will
be completely my own with all that he is and can do; just as
much my own as his, neither more nor any less." Quite similarly we also find in the frequently mentioned sermon on James
1:17 that he who would completely receive God must have
entirely given up himself and must have denied himself; such
a man then receives from God all that God has and in the
same way that God possesses it. For—and here Eckhart himself places, immediately preceding, the leading motive of his
reasoning—God must give himself to me to be my own, just

[31] In the *Table-talks*, Pfeiffer, p. 559.
[32] In the *Table-talks*, Pfeiffer, p. 574.

as he himself is his own, or there is nothing at all that is my own.[33]   Thus ultimately the important thing to Eckhart is that God "becomes my own."   Obviously this fundamental tendency of Eckhart's mysticism does not signify a radical negation of the self of the same kind that is required in the negation of the "world."   For if the self were radically negated, then nothing more could be my own.   *When considered in the light of its religious motive, Eckhart's mysticism rather means the striving for the most intimate relationship that is possible between the soul and God.*   But, of course, the danger of a shifting of this fundamental tendency, which we have already mentioned in the case of Tersteegen, exists also for Eckhart.   And the danger is all the greater for him because his leaning toward theoretical speculation is stronger.   However, the rôle which religious interest and speculative leanings play in mysticism, as well as the type of speculative leanings which operate in it, will be discussed later.   Here we must be satisfied with the conclusion that mysticism also, at least when taken in its widest sense, confirms that determination of the nature of religion which puts the relationship aspect into the prominent foreground.   And the widest sense of the word mysticism is precisely determined by the extent to which the mystic keeps the religious interest in the foreground.

5

That modern poetry also, insofar as it is at all religious, thinks of religion as a relationship, or at least reveals an awareness of this fact, has been shown by Wilhelm Knevels in his very noteworthy discussions.   His opinion of the nature of religion, which he has approached entirely from the background of modern poetry, he formulates in the following sentences: "A 'religion' without a relationship always stands apart from real religion and cannot be brought into an organic connection with it through any artifice.   With some people it may take the place which religion occupies in others, or which it once previously occupied in themselves: it may release the same psychical functions and have a similar meaning within the spiritual life:

[33] Pfeiffer, p. 136.

but it will never be possible to find an assignable content for a
conception which tries to include two such different things as
religion which is a relationship, and 'religion' which is not a
relationship.[34]   To the examples which Knevels has gathered
I will add only one.   In Rainer Maria Rilke's *Stundenbuch*
(p. 9) we read:

> "Thou, Neighbor God, if oft in the long night
> I disturb thee with loud knocking,—
> It is because I seldom hear thee breathe
> And know: thou art alone in the room
> And if thou needest aught, there is none
> To reach thy groping hand a drink.
> I am always listening.   Give me a little sign,
> I am quite near."

Whatever one may think of the appropriateness of the expression "Neighbor God," in any case it characterizes religion
as a relationship.   Of all modern authors, Ingeborg Maria Sick
has expressed this characteristic nature of religion most emphatically.   In "Hochlandspfarrer" she describes the preaching
of the pastor of Li (*Idem,* pp. 36 ff.).   She has him say: "I
came up here to help souls, even though it be but one single
soul, to get into touch with God.   I did not come primarily to
help them find a God, for most of them have done that.   I came
to help them find the living God and to enter into intimate
fellowship with Him."

This thought, the author adds, was the dominant note of
all of the pastor's preaching.   And then with a few additional
strokes she sketches his argument in detail.

Again and again she especially emphasizes the establishment
of a real relationship to God.   "Your relationship to him is
what is involved.   The relationship is there, so you cannot evade
it in any way.   But unless you accept it for yourself, it will
not only become a non-entity for you, but something worse, a
mere opinion.   The relationship to God is developed in the
same manner as all the personal relationships of life—you give

[34] Wilhelm Knevels: *Simmels Religionstheorie. Ein Beitrag zum religiösen Problem der Gegenwart,* Leipsic, 1920, p. 16.—See also his *Brücken
zum Ewigen* (1927), 1931.

yourself up to it. But since this relationship goes deeper than the most profound human relationship of which you are a part, you have to surrender yourself to it much more completely."

These sentences express an understanding of the innermost nature of religion which gives great satisfaction to the investigator who holds the religio-psychological point of view. It should be expressly emphasized that the results of poetic intuition here completely coincide with those of a penetrating religio-psychological analysis.

6

The nature of religion, we have said, is to be found in the relationship of man to an "over-world" in which he believes, which he intuits by faith, and upon which he feels himself dependent. *We must now turn our attention to the object-content, or objective counter-pole of the religious relationship.* Our definition calls this an "over-world." This terminology aims to describe a higher reality transcending the world of the senses. And this "over" is to be taken in that two-fold sense which naturally follows from the religio-psychological point of view, for it points both to the existence and to the value of the "over-world." *For the religious conviction that toward which the religious relationship is directed is an "over-world," both in its existence and in its value.* Of course the value-content stands in the foreground for the religious consciousness. But it is also a self-evident presupposition that this value-content is rooted in the nature of the over-world itself, in its actual existential nature. The fundamental religious judgment, corresponding to the religious conviction rooted in religious experience, is from the first, not only a value-judgment, but a value-judgment and an existential judgment in one. To the extent that Ritschl's theory of the value-judgment overlooked this religio-psychologically undeniable fact, it not only gave occasion to many misunderstandings, but it was also frequently misleading, although this was the opposite of Ritschl's intention. On the other hand, the idea of the "over-world" must be restricted to value and existence, if it is to correspond to the universal and fundamental religious motive inherent in all the

various forms of religion. As we are here using the term
over-world, other characteristics, especially spatial form, do not
essentially belong to it.[35] The "over" of the religious "over-
world" signifies only existence and value, and not a spatially
localized being. For if it included the latter, at least the
higher religions, and especially Christianity, could not be
brought under this conception. The "Kingdom of God" of
the Christian thought-world is exalted above all spatial as
well as above all temporal limitations. It is supra-temporal
as well as supra-spatial.

But there are strong objections to our formulation. Two
criticisms are involved which originate from entirely different
starting-points and which aim in opposite directions. One of
these criticisms holds that this definition says too little, while
the other that it says too much.

The first criticism claims that the idea of God is indispensable for the determination of the nature of religion and
objects to our leaving it out of the definition. To meet this
objection we must first of all refer back to our previous discussion of formal terminology. When the word "God" is
employed universally to designate the object-content of religious experience, then we get an empty tautology. Hence
the objection is significant only when one advocates a contentual demarcation of the idea of God, and in the end this
involves a personalistic formulation of the idea of God. Then
the question becomes: Does the idea of an "over-world" have
to be given a personalistic sense in determining the nature of
religion? Concretely stated, this would mean that the idea
of an "over-world" would have to be restricted to monotheism

[35] Formerly (see *Christian Belief in God*, translated by D. S. Robinson,
Yale Press) I used the idea of the "world beyond" in this same sense. That
expression intentionally avoided the phrase "the other world," and since it
most decidedly emphasizes the purely qualitative aspect of its content, I
thought I had guarded against every misunderstanding. But since Nietzsche's idea of the superman has come to be generally used, I prefer the
term *over-world* because it corresponds exactly to Nietzsche's concept.
Wilhelm Knevels (*Simmels Religionstheorie*, Leipsic, 1920, pp. 38 ff.) advocated using the term "transcendental reality of values." This unites
very precisely all of the decisive factors of the religio-psychological point
of view. But I doubt whether it is wise to tie one's self down to such
technical philosophical terminology. But technically Knevels is entirely
correct. The "over-world" of religious faith actually is "a transcendental
reality of values." The German term is *Überwelt*.

and polytheism. A very important consequence of such a restriction would then be that all pantheism would have to be eliminated at the start from the field of that which passes as religion. But since this is today a very much debated question, and since it is also of such great importance for the entire evaluation of our modern spiritual life, it is not advisable to begin with it. If we were to take up this question now we would inevitably get into a vicious circle in the treatment of our present problem. In the interest of the most unrestricted method of treatment, and of one which would not prove to be premature for later decisions, it is methodologically advisable to leave the question of pantheism aside for the present. But the fact that this decision is technically necessary needs to be expressly emphasized. For it is customary to make just this exclusion of pantheism the criterion of the whole treatment of the problem. From a religio-psychological standpoint this is undoubtedly a begging of the question, and it involves, as was said, a vicious circle.

From a religio-psychological point of view the question of how we are to decide this matter demands the most careful and unprejudiced thought. For it is here that the demand for a personalistic conception of God appears. Since the religio-psychological position requires making the personal relationship the fundamental element in determining the nature of religion, it would seem to be logical and necessary *to conceive of the counter-pole of this relationship personalistically as well.* However, deeper consideration compels us to use greater caution. At least in a rudimentary form, a personal relationship is possible, not only to a personal being, but also to impersonal entities. For example, one may have a personal relationship to his native country. And even though a personalistic factor is involved here, inasmuch as all of one's countrymen are included in the idea of native land, even this cannot be said of pure ideas such as Science or Art. Yet we can attain a personal relationship to them. Hence we must leave open the possibility of a corresponding relationship in the field of religion. Consequently we are not justified in demanding arbitrarily a personalistic conception of the object of the religious relationship, when we use the religio-psychological approach. But at the same time it is true, of course, that the religious relationship can attain complete satisfaction only through the relationship to a living and personal God. *The tendency toward a personalistic conception of the object of the religious relationship is actually inherent in the elementary form of all religious conviction which is based upon religious experience.* Yet historical facts demand that we be satisfied with this much, and that we do not count the fulfillment of this tendency as essential to the nature of religion. Among these historical facts we should probably include some from primitive religion, and then, above all, those of Buddhism in its original (Hinayana) form.

The religion of primitive peoples would of course not come into question here if one were to regard as adequate the animistic theory, which has enjoyed such popularity recently and which Wilhelm Wundt has greatly elaborated. As late as 1896 Otto Pfleiderer, in the third edition of his *Philosophy of Religion,* advanced the principle that animism is the practically undisputed basis upon which the still "debatable questions concerning the beginnings of religion must be kept" (3rd ed., p. 16). In fact Tylor's theory of animism, first advocated in 1867 and then elaborated in his book *Primitive Culture,* which immediately became famous, dominated almost absolutely and indisputably the treatment and evaluation of primitive religion for a period of nearly four decades.

However, in recent years matters have changed considerably. A new tendency began with the twentieth century but it has wielded its strongest influence since about the year 1910, especially as a result of the tireless researches which J. G. Frazer has carried out and published in *The Golden Bough.*

Frazer's researches have given us two new insights which have exercised a decisive influence. First, he showed that the whole idea of animism as Tylor used it, did not connote a single and uniform meaning, but rather unjustifiably confused phenomena which are different in nature. By animism Tylor meant, on the one hand, the idea of an animation of the objects of nature, in other words, that either all or some natural objects are animated in the sense of having a spirit or soul in them; but he also meant, on the other hand, that there are souls and spirits which are not bound to any natural objects but whose existence is independent of such objects. Now in any case these two meanings are not necessarily identical, and just how they are related to each other is not made clear in Tylor's theory.   As a result the idea of the fetish and the whole idea of fetish worship or *fetishism,* has been used confusedly and ambiguously. Moreover, this ambiguity has caused theories of ancestor worship and of hero worship to be championed in a most one-sided fashion.

But along with this insight into the vagueness and ambiguity of Tylor's concept of animism there goes another which is even more far-reaching and pervasive in its consequences. It is not true, as Tylor claims, that primitive people think of natural objects as being *animated,* that is, that they think of them as having special spirits residing in them. Of course they think of them as being *alive;* for they are thought of in analogy to living beings and this means that they are conceived of as being really alive.   At least in certain circumstances or on special occasions natural objects—sun, moon, and stars, clouds and winds, mountains and hills, trees and flowers, springs, ponds, and rivers, etc.—are thought of as alive, as living creatures. But being alive is not necessarily the same as being animated (by a spirit).   Natural objects can be thought of as alive or as living creatures without being thought of as the bearers or dwelling places of special spirit beings. This is also shown by the psychology of childhood. The child thinks of its doll and many other objects, whether they be household objects or objects of nature, as alive, and accordingly treats them as living beings. But this does not cause him to think of them as being in any way possessed by a spirit. Natural objects can be thought of as alive before any conception of a spirit has even developed.

Tylor did not observe this. He used the idea of *alive* and *spirit-filled* as interchangeable, and then developed his theory of possession by spirits so as to imply the presence in primitive mentality of an actual spirit-idea and spirit-theory.   And thus he read into primitive thought something which is not there. It is for this reason that we differentiate today between *animatism* and *animism,* using animatism in the general and broader sense, and animism in the narrower sense of an actual spirit-theory.[36]   Animatism is, then, the theory that objects of nature are merely animated, whereas animism treats them as being spirit-filled, that is, as being the bearers or dwelling places of special spirit-beings.   Animatism is thought to be prior to animism, and it is in this sense that we speak of a pre-animistic stage in the development of culture.   And now the following must be added.   Recent studies indicate that primitive peoples often think of vitality as a power or force which expresses itself in different objects in various unfoldings of power, in diverse forms or degrees of the development of power.   Now this power or force is thought of as being concentrated to a special degree in certain places : in certain separate things, natural objects or human implements or even in certain individual human beings.   Hence there is in them a special concentration of power, and from such centers a special unfolding or manifestation of power may emanate.

This whole manner of thinking was first carefully studied among the Melanesians, who call this power or force *mana.*[37] For this reason the expression *mana* or *the theory of mana* is often used to designate this type of thought wherever it occurs.   Other primitive people use other expressions; for example : *orenda, manitu, wakanda,* et cetera.

Such a power or force plays an important rôle in the life of primitive people.   It underlies their whole system of magic, their magical ideas and customs, and magic dominates to the greatest extent the life of primitive peoples.   The purpose of magic is to get a control with the aid of this power which cannot be obtained by ordinary human means.   For example : by means of this power primitive man seeks to gain control over other men to make them friendly or harmless, or even to bring them to a mysterious death : but he also seeks to gain

[36] The best account is given by Nathan Söderblom: *Das Werden des Gottesglaubens.   Untersuchungen über die Anfänge der Religion.*   Leipsic, 1926, pp. 19 ff.

[37] The basic studies were made by R. H. Codrington: *The Melanesians. Studies in their Anthropology and Folk-Lore,* Oxford, 1891.   See especially pp. 118 ff.

influence over animals, especially game, or over the phenomena of nature, the weather, rains, et cetera.

The idea of *tabu* is closely related to this idea of mana. Tabu is whatever cannot be touched by men, or at least only under very special precautions, or it is that which has been withdrawn from ordinary use.

Both ideas have an inner relationship to each other; anything that has mana is therefore tabu. For example, any utensil which contains mana is tabu, and similarly a man who has mana is tabu.

The idea of tabu pervades the field of primitive religion, but its influences are also to be found in many of the historical religions that are far beyond the primitive stage. The clearest example of this is in the Old Testament. The idea of holiness in the Old Testament still contains in unmistakable terms the element of tabu. Everything which is "holy" becomes untouchable for man and, in case of accidental contact, it will destroy him.

In view of the connection between the ideas of mana and tabu, the questions arise whether the idea of mana does not also pervade the field of religion and what importance it assumes in religion. As we have seen the mana idea is the basis of all magic. But magic, which throughout the whole history of religion is always attaining a new relationship to religion, stands in the closest relationship to primitive religion. Even the Vedic Religion reveals to the widest extent a continual over-lapping of religious and magical ideas.

In view of this fact the importance of the idea of mana for primitive religion is an extremely difficult problem. For in particular cases it is always debatable whether the religious or the magical factor is decisive. Nevertheless it seems to me that on the whole it must be admitted that even religion may and occasionally does develop from the idea of mana. If this is true then we would have primitive religions in which this impersonal vague power alone would constitute the objective counter-pole of the religious relationship, and for which a divine being of a personal nature would be excluded.

Among the old reports of the Jesuit missionaries of their mission work among the Algonquins we find the following

statement of Father Allouez: "They call everything which
seems advantageous or injurious to them 'manitu,' and insti-
tute a ritual or offer to these things worship such as we offer
only to the true God." [38] Concerning this statement Söderblom says that Manitu's nature has never been better described in the reports of missionaries than in this passage.
"The power is indifferent. But whether it brings destruction
or aid, it does not leave man untouched but rather becomes
the occasion for practices which become a part of the system
of sacred worship." [39] This judgment of Söderblom must,
however, be qualified, for it applies to extreme cases and does
not characterize the general situation. For the statement of
Father Allouez concerning evidences of a worship and ritual
directed toward the impersonal "power," applies not only
to the very rare exceptional cases reported by the Jesuits, but
in general only to the exceptional cases in all of the literature
of primitive religion.

Similarly the argument which Söderblom, from his Brahmanism background, advances in favor of a Mana-religion
must also be qualified. He tries to prove that we must actually
recognize a real Mana-religion by treating Brahmanism as one
of the possible developments of this Mana-religion. For in its
original meaning, Brahma, the fundamental principle of
Brahmanism, is, the mana of primitive peoples, the mysterious source of power of all super-human processes. This
judgment can certainly not be disputed, for it strikes at the
heart of the matter. Brahma is originally the mysterious power
which is inherent in the Vedic Scripture and like-wise in the
Brahman who knows and administers it.[40] This can be
illustrated with exceptional clarity from the *Atharva-Veda,*[41]
but also with adequate certainty from the three chief *Vedas,*
inclusive of the *Rig-Veda.*[42] Yet, on the other hand, the doctrine of Brahma has grown out of the religious system of

---

[38] R. G. Thwaites, *Jesuit Relations and Allied Documents,* Cleveland,
1896, p. 284.

[39] Nathan Söderblom. *Das Werden des Gottesglaubens.* Leipsic, 1926,
p. 60.

[40] Compare H. Oldenberg, *Die Religion des Veda,* 2nd ed., p. 65, pp.
475 ff.

[41] Compare the examples collected by N. Söderblom, *op. cit.,* p. 272 ff.

[42] Compare H. Oldenberg, *op. cit.,* pp. 476 ff.

Vedic polytheism. And it is quite impossible to conceive of the existence in this system of an underlying stratum or a parallel stratum of Mana-religion, of such a nature that it would have remained free of all polytheistic influence. Here we come back to the confusing interlacing of religion and magic, and we must accordingly restrict the validity of the Brahma doctrine for the Mana-religion to the exceptional or mixed cases. Whether it is correct to speak of a Mana-religion of primitive peoples aside from such cases, is at least doubtful, and in my opinion it is improbable in the light of the available evidence.

However, on the question of whether the counter-pole of the religious relationship is a personal being Buddhism is of much greater importance than primitive religion, that is, Buddhism in its original form. The cautious consideration necessary toward this form of Buddhism prohibits us from including in the general determination of the nature of religion a personalistic conception of the object of the religious relationship. For the justification of this argument a two-fold assumption is of course decisive, that original Buddhism is "atheistic" and that it must, on the other hand, nevertheless be treated as a religion.

Both assumptions require explanation. We will begin with the last one. The difficulty which Buddhism presents to the student of religion would of course be most easily and completely removed if its religious character and, correspondingly, its validity as a religion, could be denied altogether. Hence it can easily be understood why this has often been done, and is still, to a certain extent, popular in theological study. We even find theologians who show an outspoken interest in the general history of religion making this denial. Thus B. C. Schaarschmidt, in his outline of the history of religion, reaches the conclusion that "apparently Buddhism does not belong to the field of religion at all.[43] But inasmuch as he also expressly states the reason why he holds this view, namely, that otherwise the definition of religion which he gave at the beginning of his book would not be tenable, he gives away his whole

[43] C. B. Schaarschmidt. *Die Religion. Einführung in ihre Entwicklungsgeschichte*, Leipsic, 1907, pp. 230 ff.

method and, at the same time, illustrates perfectly the actual state of affairs.[44]

The difficulty which is herewith presented is of course not to be under-estimated in the least. The religious character of Buddhism is actually tremendously problematical. Nevertheless, it seems to me that there can be no doubt whatever that we, along with theologians like H. Hackmann, Edv. Lehmann and Nath. Söderblom, must attribute such a religious character to Buddhism.[45] Yet there can certainly be no doubt that Buddhism is not a pure religion, but a religion which has been strongly influenced and permeated by philosophy. Nor should we be misled by the fact that Buddhism deliberately and emphatically renounces all metaphysical speculation. For although it has no speculative leanings, Buddhism has a very strong leaning toward and capacity for rational dialectics. And this leads to a rationalization of religion, which reacts upon the whole field of religious life, and invariably impedes and distorts the specifically religious motives. Neither can one prove Buddhism to be a religion by stressing the preponderance in it of the practical interests of life. For the practical interests of life need not necessarily take on religious form; and a philosophy of life based upon these interests may remain entirely within the bounds of rational and metaphysical reasoning.

However, that which makes Buddhism a religion is the expressed and, indeed, entirely dominant *striving for salvation from the spatio-temporal conditions of existence or from the kind of existence which "the world" has.* Reference has already been made in another connection to the well-known saying of Buddha, which must again be considered here: "As

---

[44] In contrast, the argument which Otto Hofmann presented recently against over-valuing the religious content of Buddhism is of an entirely different nature: *"Der Begriff der religiösen Erfahrung in Seiner Bedeutung für die Prinzipienfragen der Religionsphilosophie.* Leipsic, 1921, pp. 90 ff. The objections which Hofmann raises and supports with very logical reasons are really extremely important.

[45] H. Hackmann, *Der Buddhismus,* Tübingen, 1906. Edv. Lehmann. *Der Buddhismus als indische Sekte—als Weltreligion.* Tübingen, 1911. Nathan Söderblom: *Das Werden des Gottesglaubens,* 1926, pp. 211 ff. Among the Indologists, Herm. Beckh especially has recently adopted this position in his splendidly informative presentation of Buddhism (Sammlung Göschen, 2 volumes).

the great ocean, oh my disciples, has only one savor, the savor of salt, so my doctrine has only one savor, the savor of salvation." In fact, this saying provides the best key to the understanding of the entire historical phenomenon of Buddhism.

Standing in the most intimate relationship to Brahmanism, the Saṃkhya philosophy, and the Yoga system, Buddhism nevertheless differentiates itself from all of these three systems alike by the attempt to make salvation attainable by everyone. And so the first sermon of Buddha, the famous sermon of Benares, which is typical of all of his other preaching, is dominated completely by the idea of salvation. For the doctrine of the four sacred truths expressed in this sermon: the sacred truth concerning the nature of suffering, the origin of suffering, the removal of suffering, and the means by which suffering may be removed, contains the idea of salvation as the pivotal point around which everything else revolves. And later on it was just here that the process of reconstructing Buddhism began. Even in the case of Mahāyana Buddhism, and all the more in the case of modern sects, the change in original Buddhism is based upon the belief that these sects must demand and are able to furnish a better guarantee for the search for salvation. And throughout all of this the uniqueness of the Buddhist striving for salvation, to which we have already referred, must be kept clearly in mind. The salvation which they seek is salvation from the conditions of worldly existence. Accordingly the thirst for this world is the chief cause of suffering. This world-thirst stands—perhaps not as the final one for the theory—but yet in a practical way as the strongest and, therefore, as the most important cause of suffering. Thus in the *Dhammapada* (verses 335 f.) we read:

> Whom the world-thirst overcometh,
>   Devouring meanly as a poison,
> His troubles grow unceasingly,
>   Spreading like Birana-grass.
> He who this world-thirst overcometh,
>   Low and difficult to check,
> His troubles quickly vanish from him
>   As water from the lotus flower.

But does not a consideration of just this fact lead us to the final and decisive reason against the recognition of Hinayana Buddhism as a religion? Is not the religion which it preaches, *self-salvation?* From the religious point of view this is undoubtedly the weakest point in the Buddhist doctrine. However, we must also caution against a misuse of the term "self-salvation." The self-salvation involved in Buddhism is a peculiar kind of self-salvation.

To begin with, let us look at the person of Buddha as such. Certainly it was Buddha himself who attained saving enlightenment under the Bodhi-tree, and who then resolved to show the rest of mankind, by proclaiming his enlightenment, the way which leads to salvation. But that he gained this knowledge in his last life upon earth, which he lived after having had innumerable other forms of existence, was due, not to his own self-sufficient human powers, but rather to the working of a higher world-order which just at this time allowed the whole series of his former existences to terminate in his life as Buddha. And just this higher world-order remains as the presupposition to and preliminary condition of his whole life-work. It is also the presupposition wherever the similarity between the relation of the disciples and of Buddha himself to salvation is emphasized. This is made especially picturesque in the parable of the one hen and the many chicks, where first one chick and then another picks its way out of the egg-shell.[46]

The situation, then, is this: Buddha teaches men to save themselves as he has also saved himself. But in this two-fold activity he is fulfilling a plan of salvation which has been eternally existent, which belongs to eternity and in which he serves as the means to the end. And if Buddhism did not at this point arbitrarily call a halt to and block the way of reflective thought, then either it would have to express more clearly the teleological character of this plan of salvation and then champion a philosophy of life which permits such a plan of salvation, which means that it would have to conceive of the eternal power which rules over all of reality as a living ethical personal

[46] *Suttavibhanga, Pārājika,* I, 1, 4. Compare Herm. Oldenberg, *Buddha,* 6th ed., p. 373.

God; or it would have to abandon this whole plan of salvation and consequently also the idea of salvation which is based upon it.

It is because Buddhism arbitrarily dodges just this alternative, that it tries to hold fast to the idea of salvation and yet to ignore any idea of divine grace. *That is the "atheism" of Buddhism.* In this sense Buddhism is actually atheistic. Its atheism is based upon the deliberate dodging of a dilemma into which it is led by its own basic position, and from which it is absolutely unable to find an escape.

However, the "atheism" of Buddhism is a term which must be more completely clarified and more definitely determined, if it is not to give occasion to misunderstandings and wrong interpretations. *This Buddhist atheism is in a class by itself.* It is an atheism which in theory strictly renounces monotheism but which does not exclude polytheism, but entirely includes it. And it is not merely a later degeneration or retrogression which permitted the return of polytheistic views, as was the case, for example, when in the Catholic church of Christendom, polytheism again made its entrance in the rise of the cult of the saints. On the contrary, original Buddhism, even with all of its atheistic appearance, is at the same time completely polytheistic. The gods of contemporary Indian religious thought were not excluded from the genuinely Buddhist type of thought, but were taken up by it, and they play a very important rôle in it.

It was especially the polytheistic recasting of the belief in Brahma which strongly determined the Buddhist philosophy of life. As already in the *Upanishads* the impersonal Brahma was recast into the personal God Brahma, in analogy to the ancient belief in the gods, so this Brahma was later further multiplied in a polytheistic fashion and was split up into numerous classes or orders of Brahman divinities. Now Buddhism also reckons at every step with these many classes and this great host of Brahman divinities. It was especially Brahma Sahampati who, according to the oldest traditions, often entered influentially into the life of Buddha. For example, after Sakyamuni had attained to the saving enlightenment under the sacred tree and had thus become the Buddha by this achievement, Brahma Sahampati descended from his Brahman heaven and by unremitting pleas which overcame Buddha's doubts, prevailed upon him not to keep for himself the enlightenment which he had won, and the salvation which it involved, but to go and proclaim this teaching.

"Wide open be the door of immortality to all who have ears to hear. May they receive the Dharma with faith." [47]

So Buddhism did not abandon the idea of gods. *But the gods of which Buddhism speaks belong to the world of perpetual becoming and passing away, to a world which bears the mark of suffering; and salvation from this world is the actual goal of the Buddhist quest.*

After his first sermon Buddha proclaims to the five monks who have heard him that through the understanding of the four holy truths he has "attained to the highest perfect enlightenment in the world of gods and men, in the world of Mara and Brahma, among the race of ascetics and Brahmins, gods and men." The "world of gods and men"—the "race of Gods and men": these expressions are characteristic of the Buddhist philosophy of life. Salvation does not come from the gods. Moreover, the gods need salvation themselves. *Therefore the Buddhist belief in God does not signify a religious relationship.* The Buddhist belief in God is merely mythology. Buddhism overcame mythology in principle, that

---

[47] *Mahâvagga,* I, 5, 2 ff. The beautiful parable of the variedly growing lotus blossoms, which reminds us of the parable of the sower in the New Testament, is found here: "Just as in one lotus pond there are water lilies, blue lotus blossoms and white lotus blossoms which are born in the water, grow in the water, and do not rise above the water but blossom forth in the deeps; and other water lilies, blue lotus blossoms and white which are born in the water, grow in the water and reach up to the surface of the water; and other water lilies, blue lotus blossoms and white which are born in the water, grow up in the water and reach beyond the surface so that the water does not moisten their blossoms; so also, as the Blessed One gazed upon the world with the eyes of a Buddha, he saw creatures whose souls were pure and others whose souls were not pure from the dust of the world, souls with keen senses and with dull senses, noble creatures and mean creatures, good hearers and poor hearers, some who lived in fear of eternity and of sin. And as he beheld this he spoke this saying to Brahma Sahampati:

"Wide open be the door of immortality,
    To all who have ears to hear.
To avoid useless fatigue and trouble
    I have not yet proclaimed the noble word to the world."

is to say, in the ideal of its philosophy of life, as little as it overcame magic. For magic also remained alive within Buddhism. For example, consider the story that belongs to the ancient tradition, that Devadatta, the Judas Iscariot among the disciples of Buddha, turned loose a wild elephant against Buddha in a narrow street. Whereupon Buddha used his power of friendship upon the elephant, who, being affected by this power of friendship, lowered his tusks without doing any harm to the Blessed One.[48] And although the disciples of Buddha must pledge themselves not to glory in super-human accomplishments with a desire for gain,[49] according to Buddhist doctrines by practicing contemplation (Dhyana, Pali: Jhana) they are enabled not only to survey the series of their own existences which forms a part of the wheel of rebirths, but also to attain wondrous magical powers of a different kind, such as: vanishing from sight and reappearing, or multiplying one's own personality.[50]

Mythology and magic, then, remain active in Buddhism. *The Buddhist belief in God (belief in the gods) is completely identical with mythological motives.* For example, one must remember how the previously quoted tradition concerning the first sermon of Buddha concludes. After the wheel of his truth [51] was set rolling by the Blessed One, it is said that the gods of the earth sent forth this cry: "Now has the insurpassable Kingdom of Truth been established by the Blessed One at Benares in the deer park." And then it continues: "When the Cātummahārājika gods heard this shout of the

[48] Cf. Herm. Oldenberg, *Buddha*, p. 363. English translation by W. Hoey.

[49] It is the fourth of the great monastic rules which emphasizes this prohibition. Cf. Oldenberg, *Buddha*, p. 399. That this prohibition involves an important restriction of the use of magic should not be overlooked. One can even speak of a relative animosity toward magic in primitive Buddhism, as Max Weber has done. (*Gesammelte Aufsätze zur Religionssoziologie*, Vol. II, 1921, pp. 217 ff.) But then the relativity of it must be strongly stressed. Max Weber's account tends toward a generalization which would misinterpret the actual facts. This exaggeration is related to his whole approach, which over-emphasizes and over-strains the character of Buddhism as a system of "salvation for intellectuals."

[50] That magic is developed to the highest possible degree in later Buddhism, especially in Māhāyana Buddhism (prayer wheels and prayer flags), needs only to be briefly mentioned here.

[51] This is the standard expression in Buddhist literature for the beginning of Buddha's preaching activity.

gods of the earth, they also proclaimed these words. From the Cātummahārājikā gods it was heard by the Tāvatimsā gods, and from these by the Yāma gods, from these by the Tusita gods, from these by the Nimmānarati gods, from these by the Paranimmitavasavatti gods and from these by the Brahmakāyikā gods. And in that twinkling of an eye, in the very moment, in the second that these words reached the Brahma world, the ten thousand worlds trembled, they shook and tottered and an immeasurably powerful light was seen on the earth which even surpassed the super-natural power of the gods." (*Mahâvagga*, 1, 6, 6.)

This is pure mythology. And if we summarize the previous discussion we arrive at these two conclusions : (1) that a theoretical belief in God is not necessarily the basis of a religious relationship, and therefore cannot be taken as a criterion for the determination of the nature of religion, and (2) that in spite of its practical atheism, a religious character must still be ascribed to Buddhism.

7

We now come to the second objection which may be raised to our definition. If we make the primary characteristic of the nature of religion the relationship of man to an "over-world" in which he believes, then the use of the concept "over-world" might be regarded as saying too much. And even the more specific determination, which we have already set forth, restricting the over-world to existence and value only, also signifies too much. The transcendental element implicit in the idea of an over-world, and since it is actually implied it should be deliberately expressed, does not rightly belong to the nature of religion.

The general position upon which this objection is ordinarily based usually aims to designate the transcendental element, even of the Christian religion, as unjustified and invalid. The Christian religion must be so stated and defined for our modern age as to abandon completely the claim to transcendence. But before we discuss this position we shall glance at the rest of the history of religion. Here again we may use the two phenomena, which were discussed above, to prove our position: primitive religion and Hinayana Buddhism. Here, however, the emphasis must be placed primarily upon the latter.

That the Mana-religion, insofar as we wish to reckon at all directly with it among primitive people, involves a belief in an "over-world" and even depends entirely upon this belief, at once follows from our previous discussions of the Mana-idea. But since we must later on thoroughly discuss the question of the relation between magic and religion,—a question to which, as we have already pointed out, every reference to the Mana-idea leads, we shall not consider it further at this point (see chap. IX and appendix III). Only this should be mentioned in connection with what has already been said, that from the point of view which is now in question, the line of development from Mana to Brahma is quite unmistakably convincing. For this development signifies the highest possible ascendency of the over-worldly character of the other world.

Moreover, it cannot be seriously disputed that, even in its most primitive form, belief in the gods implies belief in an over-world. As the most primitive form of belief in the gods we might take that form which Hermann Usener designates with the term *"occasional gods."* A single specific phenomenon, which particularly provokes and excites the religious consciousness, is momentarily deified. The symbols of success in garden and field, with which Usener illustrates his theory in conjunction with W. Mannhardt's studies in folk-lore, actually present the best and most graphic examples. Especially the dedication and formal worship of the last sheaf of the season, which is found in many countries, reveals the situation clearly: in the cutting of the grain the spirit of the field has been gradually crowded back into this last sheaf. Thus this particular object is actually deified in a most direct fashion, as Usener says, without the mediation of any thought of a generic character, no matter how restricted: "this *one* thing which you see before you, that, and nothing else is the god." [52]

Here we have the clue to an understanding of all fetishism,

[52] Hermann Usener: *Götternamen. Versuch einer Lehre von der religiösen Begriffsbildung.* Bonn, 1896.

a conception so frequently and so thoroughly misunderstood. For in a single flash *the actual meaning of fetishism* becomes clear from this fact. Usener, however, reached his insight into the way occasional gods are formed from his study of the *specialized gods.* For the occasional gods are the preliminary stage of the specialized gods, the latter naturally developing from the former as soon as the particular phenomena which have been deified as occasional gods are thought of as recurring regularly. Thus arise the gods of plowing, sowing, harrowing, reaping, et cetera, in fact "an unlimited series of god-concepts which for the time being have independent validity." [53] In the 14th book of his *Antiquitatis rerum divinarum* M. Terentius Varro assembled from the old *indigitamenta,* the liturgical books of the priests, long lists of such *"die certi,"* to use his expression. Such lists were often used by Latin ecclesiastical writers in their polemics against polytheism. In the Vedic Religion we find such specialized gods in those names which are formed with the suffixes *tar* and *pati.* The suffix tar denotes the doer of some act: so there is a god Dhātar (maker), Trātar (guardian), Savitar (instigator).[54] Pati signifies "Lord." So there are Prajāpati (the Lord of progeny), and Brihaspati or Brahmanaspati (Lord of prayer) and others. These specialized gods are unmistakably occa-

[53] The specialization proceeds much further in part. According to Fabius Pictor the Romans differentiated, in connection with the cultivation of a field, between 12 divinities; and even this statement can be supplemented. Comp. Usener, *op. cit.,* p. 76.

[54] The famous Sāvitrī, the verse of the *Rig-Veda* (III, 62, 10) with which the study of the Veda began, is named after Savitar because in this verse Savitar is implored to stimulate the thoughts. After the consecration of the pupil (upanayana) the pupil (brahmacārin) became a "twice-born" being. The recitation of the Sāvitrī often took place on the third day after the upanayana. Comp. Oldenberg: *Die Religion des Veda.* Second ed., pp. 465 ff.

That Savitar could specifically be developed into the sun god, is also given in the nature of the "instigator." Comp. e.g., *Rig-Veda,* I, 35, II, 38; and also A. Hillebrandt: *Ved. Mythologie* (large edition), III, 113 ff. (small edition), 141 ff.—And for the understanding of the development of Indian religious history, the following is also worthy of notice. The *Svetāsvatara Upanishad,* which belongs to the second of the four groups of Upanishads, following in temporal sequence (Comp. M. Winternitz, *Geschichte der indischen Literatur,* Vol. I, 1909, pp. 205 ff.) is one of the oldest witnesses of the developed Yoga system. The passage in question begins with several lines of the *Yajur-Veda* which appeals to the God Savitar for the strength to exert or harness (Yoga) the spirit. Comp. Paul Deussen, *Sechzig Upanishads,* pp. 294 ff.

sional gods which have been generalized. However, each one of these concepts indicates, for the religious thought of the persons who employ them, *the belief in an over-world which opens itself up to them at the point indicated.* Usener summarizes his opinion of the situation in the words: "Each one of these concepts, insofar as they designate a divine power, is imbued with the attribute of infinity. But this attribute applies to the depth only, and not to the breadth, it applies only to that point or line which is covered by the concept." [55] This conclusion touches the heart of the matter, and it also confirms the correctness of our own position.

To my knowledge it has never been noticed, by the way, in the whole discussion of the question which has followed Usener's discovery, that the insight which he won by his historical and philological research, was already anticipated by Schleiermacher's religio-psychological acumen. Schleiermacher writes in the second of his *Reden:* "It was religion, when the ancients, for every favorable happening in which the eternal laws of the world revealed themselves clearly, worshipped the God to whom the happening was ascribed; attributed a special name to him and built a temple which belonged to him alone; they had grasped an act of the universe and characterized herewith its individuality and its peculiar nature" (p. 57). Obviously this is Usener's fundamental idea.

Finally, that all ancestor worship signifies for the worshiper the cultivation of a relationship to an over-world, hardly needs special mention. In China, the classical land of ancestor-worship, this is clearly revealed in the development of a most reverent subservience which is now shown just as much to the ancestral tablets as it was once shown to the "filial descendant" or ritualistic representative of the ancestors. [56] In the passage of the *Li-ki* summarizing the instructions for the sacrificial ritual, [57] it is said that one can only serve the higher powers

[55] Herm. Usener, *op. cit.,* p. 276.

[56] Ministers, men of high honor, and officials must descend from their carriages when meeting such a ritualistic representative of an ancestor. *Li-ki, Tsengtsze-wen,* II, 26 (according to Wilhelm Grube in Bertholet), *Religionsgeschichtliches Lesebuch,* p. 22.

[57] It is the 22nd book of the *Li-ki* with the name of Tsi-t'ung, summary of sacrifice, coming from the time after the death of Confucius (478 B.C.).

after one has completely paid these respects.[58] And in the Shi-king, the canonical book of songs, we find the following descrip-tion of an ancient sacrifice to the ancestors:

> With pride we go and manner fine
> With steers and perfect rams
> To Fall and Winter sacrifice.
> With hide removed and bones made
>   small,
> These men prepare and those bring in,
> The intercessor offers prayer.
> How brilliant is the sacrifice!
> Ancestors come, with majesty.
> The lines of spirits happy are,
> And bless the grand-sire's piety,
> Rewarding him with fortune great.
> His life shall flourish endlessly.[59]

A real difficulty is presented, however, by Buddhism. *Has Buddhism anything whatever to do with an over-world?* Does not the final goal of Buddhist aspiration and striving signify, rather, Nirvana, the negation of every over-world? The very fact that this question must be raised, coupled with the fact that an unequivocal answer cannot at once be given to it, indi-cates the unique position which Buddhism occupies in the history of religion. It is for this reason that the student is repeatedly tempted to deny Buddhism's religious character. However, he knows that this will involve him in other and even worse difficulties. In discussing the "self-salvation" of Buddhism, we learned that this self-salvation presupposes, and is based upon an eternal plan of salvation, according to which the appearance of Buddhas takes place in the cycle of world-eras. Is not this eternal plan of salvation itself an over-world? Buddhism avoids asking this question. But when the question is raised,—and it is perforce unavoidable for everyone who refuses to surrender to the obstinacy of Buddhist thinking— then it has to be answered in the affirmative. *The final and basic presupposition, then, upon which the whole Buddhist*

[58] *Op. cit.,* XXII, 5. (In Bertholet, p. 30.)
[59] *Shi-king,* II, 6, 5 (Vict. V. Strauss: *Schi-king,* Heidelberg, 1880, in Bertholet, p. 28).

world-view and philosophy of life stands or falls, is the conviction of the existence of an over-world.

This is true entirely aside from the problem of Nirvana and regardless of how one interprets Nirvana. Thus, even though it were taken to be purely and strictly negative, that is, to mean a radical denial of every hope of immortality for man, it would still remain true that Buddhism presupposes an eternal plan of salvation as a real over-world. As a real over-world; for within the framework of the Buddhist philosophy of life, and on the basis of the conditions of finite and transient existence, such a plan of salvation cannot be understood. The cycle of finite existence is absolutely closed, running itself out according to strict causality. The plan of salvation stands above this cycle and makes it possible for those who have fathomed the cycle to escape from it.

Even in the first group of disciples, the lack of a consistent understanding of the idea of Nirvana gave rise to doubts, misunderstandings, and false conclusions. "Nirvana, Nirvana, it is said, friend Sāriputta. But what is Nirvana?"[60] This question shows that the etymology of the word gave no clear explanation of it, even for the Buddhists. And therefore modern interpreters are not justified in appealing to etymology for their radically negative interpretation. The "extinguishing" is not necessarily an extinguishing of all existence as such. It is certain, rather, that, even for the spiritual *milieu* of Buddha, the word Nirvana was simply a name for the highest salvation or the highest bliss, without any more precise designation of the manner of this salvation or bliss, and especially without any tendency toward a purely negative definition of salvation. (See Oldenberg, p. 309.) And considering the whole manner of thinking of Buddhism, the answer to the question of the meaning of this "extinguishing" can only be this, that it is the extinguishing of the "desires" that is meant, the extinguishing of the thirst for more and ever new life in the world of the senses. The sacred truth of the origin of suffering is: "It is thirst which leads from re-birth to re-birth, together with joy, and desire which here and there finds

---

[60] *Anguttara Nikāya*, Vol. V, p. 414 ff. Comp. Herm. Oldenberg, *op. cit.*, pp. 304 f.

its joy, the thirst for lust, the thirst for becoming, the thirst for the transient." And this second of the four sacred truths corresponds then to the third concerning the release from suffering: "The release from this thirst through complete extinction of desire, by letting it go, by divesting one's self of it, by loosening one's self from it, by giving it no habitation." (See Oldenberg, p. 237.) In this manner it is said, in the continually recurring formula in praise of salvation, that rebirth is destroyed and that there is no more return to this world. And the following very picturesque parable also applies to the extinguishing of the thirst for life in the world of the senses. "As if, O disciples, a lamp composed of oil and wick is burning, but if no one poured oil upon it from time to time or tended to the wick, then, O disciples, because the old fuel is consumed and not replenished, the lamp will go out because of lack of fuel; so also, ye disciples, will the thirst be removed in him who remains in the knowledge of the perishability of all the fetters of existence." (*Saṃyutta Nikāya,* vol. II, p. 86.) And according to the chain of cause and effect, as it is described in the twelve-fold formula of causality, this release from thirst would also dissolve the whole realm of suffering.

That is the meaning of the extinguishing which is implied in the basic motives of Buddha's teaching. It should also be remembered what the factors are which Buddha himself regards as the strongest hindrances to his teaching. "For humanity which moves in earthly affairs, which has its habitation in earthly activity and finds pleasure there, this thing will be hard to grasp, the law of causality, the chain of cause and effect; and this also will be hard for it to grasp, the coming to rest of all things, the letting go of all things earthly, the extinguishing of desire, the cessation of all longing, the end, Nirvana." (*Mahāvaga* I, 5, 2 f.)

And so also to the previously quoted question about Nirvana which was put to Sāriputta, the answer is given: "The extinction of desire, the extinction of hate, the extinction of delusion: that, O friend, is called Nirvana."

Now it must be considered, of course, whether the logic of Buddha's teaching does not go still further, and demand a *purely negative definition* of Nirvana. Since Buddha's formula of causality conceives of the cycle of becoming .and passing away as being both strictly closed and entirely self-contained, his doctrine naturally has to demand as a matter of principle the renunciation of every over-world, just as modern neo-Buddhism consistently champions such a renunciation.

Thus far we must accept Oldenberg's thesis that, if the Buddhist philosophy of life is to be logically consistent, nothing can exist outside the cycle of causality, except a vacuum. (See Oldenberg, p. 312). But Oldenberg qualifies this thesis by pointing out that in those passages in which the demand for logical consistency has become intercrossed by motives of a different type, Buddhism does *not* draw this conclusion. And it is on the basis of this qualification that Oldenberg then forms his final conclusion about the Nirvana problem, after a thorough examination of all the pertinent passages of the Pali-canon. He approves Max Müller's attack upon the radically negative interpretation of Nirvana, but he is nevertheless much more careful and reserved in his attitude than Max Müller, who interpreted Nirvana to mean the completion of existence in a realm of eternity. The historical accounts of the primitive Buddhist brotherhood *do not give us a completely uniform picture*. The previously mentioned purely negative interpretation of the basic Buddhist position was partly carried out and supported, but it was also partly rejected. And an examination of the evidence shows that even in the primitive congregation the *positive train of thought* which supported an *affirmative* answer to the problem of the next world and of eternity was predominant.[61]

---

[61] Herm. Oldenberg, *op. cit.*, p. 319. In opposition to this Max Weber claims that the nature of Nirvana was perhaps left problematical in its more definite details by Buddha, but that it was doubtless identified with absolute extinction by the earliest teaching. (*Gesammelte Aufsätze zur Religions-soziologie,* 1921. Bd. II, p. 232.) However, this view of the situation, for which he thinks he offers "sufficient evidence" after the appended note, is not only not proven by Weber, but is finally even self-contradictory. For it is only in the earliest teaching that we find Buddha's own conception. Moreover the whole subsequent historical development of Buddhism into the Hīnayāna and Mahāyāna schools becomes unfathomable, if we accept Weber's view. And he is then compelled to attribute the missionary propaganda of Buddhism, in its final motive, to the material interests of the monks in multiplying the number of those who nourish them, namely, the lay-members (Upāsaka). Comp. *op. cit.*, p. 249. But with this statement Weber carries his own view *ad absurdum*.

Thus in Oldenberg's opinion the logical consistency of the basic Buddhist position became intercrossed at an early stage by motives of a different type, and that position itself was then further recast to accord with these new motives.

We cannot be grateful enough to Oldenberg for the careful sifting and clarification of the material. *But in evaluating the basic position of Buddhism we will have to go further than he went.* The cleavage, which is historically given and which finds expression in ancient and modern mutually exclusive interpretations did not first arise because of the addition of alien elements to the basic position, but it is implicit in the basic position itself. *The religious tendency implied in the quest for salvation of this basic position, excludes the purely negative conception of Nirvana and demands the affirmation of an eternal realm.* The tradition which has come down to us can only be made intelligible in all of its aspects and tendencies when it is so interpreted. In men of such absolute sincerity as Buddha and his disciples the apparent fear of a pure negation which is everywhere evident in the tradition, can only be explained by the religious motive just mentioned, and never by the considerations of mere expediency to which Oldenberg refers.

Sometimes this religious motive is actually expressed. In the previously mentioned conversation between King Pasenadi of Kocala and the nun Khemâ, the king asks why the Blessed One has not revealed whether he would exist beyond death or not. The nun answers with the counter-question of whether the king has an official who is able to count the grains of sand on the shores of the Ganges or to measure the water of the ocean, and then adds: "The Perfect One, great king, is free from the condition of whether his being were able to be counted with the numbers of the realm of the body; he is deep, immeasurable, and as unsearchable as the great ocean." Here it is clearly the idea of eternity, and precisely the genuinely religious idea of eternity; with its distinction between the basic nature of eternity, and all that is contained in it, and the totality of temporal existence; which dominates the answer. And to this elucidation we must also add the closing sentence of Khemâ which we have already discussed in another connection: "That the Perfect One is beyond death is not true; that the Perfect One is not beyond death is also not true; that the Perfect One at the same time is and is not beyond death is also not true; that the Perfect One neither is nor is not beyond death, is also not true."

It is the *totaliter aliter* of eternal existence which finds expression in these words in a characteristically Buddhist form of speech. But the eternal existence as such is presupposed in the *totaliter aliter* and therefore it is affirmed and not denied.

The situation is still clearer in those passages in which the religious motive applies only to basic religious conviction, without directly touching upon faith in "immortality." For this purpose the following Udāna [62] is especially important: "There is, O disciples, a not-born, a not yet come to pass, a not-created, a not-formed. And if, O disciples, there were not this not-born, not yet come to pass, not-created, not-formed, then an escape from the born, that which is come to pass, the created, the formed, could never be known. But because there is now, O disciples, a not-born, a not yet come to pass, a not-created, not-formed, therefore an escape from the born, the come to pass, created, and formed, can be known."

In this saying the Buddhist quest for salvation is revealed in its clear consistency. Longing for salvation and the quest for salvation lose all meaning when the world of natural processes, which originated within time and space, represents the ultimate reality, when it is interpreted as self-contained and as carrying its own meaning and the purpose of its existence within itself. And Buddha's saying gives expression to precisely this conviction. When we disregard the peculiar pattern of ideas conditioned by Buddhist literary usage, then we have here the conceptual formulation of a conviction which is inseparable from a real longing for salvation, because this con-

---

[62] *Udāna VIII*, 3. Udāna signifies: Exhalation, outcry, inspired saying. The writing bearing this name, which belongs to the Pali canon, contains eighty narratives which all end with a Udāna ascribed to Buddha. Note the similarity to the ancient Christian collections of the sayings of the Lord.

Most of the Udānas probably go back to the earliest period. But most of the supplementary narratives are probably of a later origin. Comp. M. Winternitz, *Geschichte der indischen Literatur*, Vol. II, Leipsic, 1913, pp. 65 ff.; Karl Seidenstücker: *Allgemeine Einleitung zum Udāna*, Leipsic, 1913. Seidenstücker has also recently published a German translation of the Udāna, Augsburg, 1920.

viction arises naturally of itself from an experience conditioned by such a longing for salvation. The "not-born, not come to pass, not-created, not-formed," which is sharply differentiated from all that is born, come to pass, created and formed, signifies a higher reality according to its nature and value, lying beyond the world of the senses, and therefore an over-world in the sense in which we have used the term. And when a "knowing" of this over-world is mentioned here, of course an intellectualistic-rationalizing attitude is involved, but what is meant is finally a conviction of the same type as the one expressed in man's need of salvation. The idea of salvation is conditioned by the certainty of an over-world. It becomes meaningless when this certainty is abandoned.

The abandonment of this certainty also makes necessary the abandonment of the idea of salvation. For when the idea of salvation is retained without this certainty, it is robbed of its basic strength and accordingly of its vitality, as is shown in a terrible way in modern neo-Buddhism. For it the highest bliss of no-more-suffering is the condition in which the process of life rushes toward extinction as a flame which receives no more oil; and this is life in a state of dying. "The tremendous 'It is not worthwhile' begins, and calmly and quietly the life process, which supports itself by its lack of any origin, vanishes within itself—it fades out forever." [63]

So Buddhism's quest for salvation works itself out clearly and unhindered, with all definiteness and without any reservation, in that saying which expresses the certainty of an over-world. It is not true, as Oldenberg claims, that it was not until the entrance of alien motives into the basic position of Buddhism that the victory over the radically negative conception of Nirvana was made possible. In this final but still decisive point for the whole evaluation of Buddhism, the purely historical approach of Oldenberg has prevented a complete understanding of the situation. For the quest for salvation belongs to the basic position of Buddhism. If it were to be regarded in any other way, then Oldenberg's own interpretation of Buddhism would be shattered at its foundation.

[63] German edition of the *Dhammapada* of the neo-Buddhist publishing house, Zehlendorf-West near Berlin, 1919. Interpretation of verse 23, p. 89.

If this is true, then we are confronted with the necessity of a still more radical break with Oldenberg. For then the basic position of Buddhism itself has to be evaluated differently. The *inner cleavage* which Oldenberg would explain by the effect of conditions introduced after Buddha's death, is imbedded *already in the basic position* of the Buddhism of Buddha himself. It is due to the fact that along with the certainty of an over-world, which conditions and is above the world of the senses and is consistent with the quest for salvation, there goes a sceptical and rational metaphysic, which strongly endangers this certainty and in any case hinders its complete operation. As a consequence the latter only comparatively rarely comes to clear and definite expression.[64] These two factors, the tendency toward salvation with the belief in an over-world which is implicitly contained in it, and the metaphysics of a rational and sceptical type mutually exclude each other. Buddhism attempts to unite the two, and necessarily one or the other factor must be neglected. That is the inner contradiction in the basic position of Buddhism. But the belief in an over-world cannot be torn out of this basic position without at the same time suspending the tendency toward salvation.

Modern neo-Buddhism strikingly confirms the correctness of this judgment. For in it the longing for salvation and the quest for salvation is "extinct." And in its place there has come the dullest and weakest resignation which praises as its highest goal that "gradual ebbing away" necessarily following from renunciation.[65]

---

[64] The following passage from *Udāna VIII, 1,* is closely related to *Udāna VIII, 3:* "It is, O monks, that realm where there is neither earth nor water, fire nor air, not an infinite realm of space nor an infinite realm of consciousness, not a realm of nothingness, not a realm of perception nor also non-perception, not this world nor another world, (not) both sun and moon. That, O monks, I call neither coming nor going, nor standing, not passing away nor becoming. That is without a point of support, without beginning, without a foundation; just this is the end of suffering." It is impossible not to recognize the relationship between this saying of Buddha and the one discussed in the text. And yet there is also clearly noticeable here, on the other hand, a touch of metaphysical dialectic quite alien to the contrasting religious motives.

[65] Compare in the neo-Buddhistic edition of the *Dhammapada,* which has been mentioned, the explanation of verse 181, p. 110.

8

The history of religion, then, evidently makes impossible every attempt to exclude the transcendental element in determining the nature of religion.   For if neither primitive religion nor Buddhism can be used to support such an attempt, then its main justification has thereby been removed.   But this conclusion is finally also substantiated by the rôle which the *idea of miracle* plays in the history of religion.   We do not intend to discuss here the miracle problem in the modern sense of the word, since it will be treated when we take up the nature of Christianity.[66]   But it is necessary here to clarify the meaning of the religious conception of miracle.   For precisely the situation which we have just discussed provides the frame-work into which, from the religio-psychological approach, the significance of the religious conception of miracle belongs.   This idea of miracle is the concrete form and specific manifestation of the *ineffable character* necessarily attributed to the object-content of religion.   The over-world by its very nature is free from the conditions of space-time reality, and consequently also from the conditions of rational knowledge.   It is the "wholly other" to which we have already referred.[67]   This is enough to prove that *a violation of natural law can in no wise be reckoned as a part of the vital content of the religious idea of miracle.*   The religious idea of miracle simply signifies the religious evaluation of an empirical process, namely, the correlation of that process with the over-world.   But the basic religious miracle is man's relationship to the over-world *per se.*   And when taken strictly that relationship in no way excludes, but rather involves the conclusion that a conception of miracle that is alien to religion can seriously endanger religion.

However, the view exactly opposite to this is also championed by scholars who have seriously busied themselves with

[66] For the time being I would refer to my little volume, *Der Christliche Gottesglaube in Seinem Verhältnis zur Heutigen Philosophie und Naturwissenschaft,* 3rd ed., p. 62 ff.   Translated by D. S. Robinson under the title: *Christian Belief in God* (Yale Press).

[67] Rud. Otto has admirably expounded this conception of the *Totaliter aliter* in his work, *Das Heilige,* 1931, and I unreservedly agree with him. (English translation, *The Idea of the Holy,* Oxford, University Press, 1923.)

the nature of religion.   Paul Natorp is the most important and influential champion of this position.   He takes the bull by the horns.   He uses the Biblical-Christian religion itself as evidence, and passes over the rest of the history of religion.   And it is particularly Schleiermacher, whose leadership we have so far followed, who is to point out the way to Natorp's conception of religion.   For he aims to apply Schleiermacher's theory of religion in a pertinent and logical manner.   That this aim is based upon a serious error, we have already seen.   So we are here concerned only with Natorp's argument for his own position.

As was just stated, Natorp refers to the history of religion only as far as it affects the Biblical-Christian religion.   He attempts to prove the correctness of his interpretation of the Biblical-Christian religion at three important points of its development.

First of all he mentions second Isaiah.   For its author religion consists primarily and exclusively in faith in the ethical ideal of humanity, in the final victory of goodness.   This faith can certainly be called religion if ever anything deserved the name, and yet it is evidently only the enthusiastic expression of faith in absolute reality, in unconquerable power, and consequently in the inevitable victory of the ethical ideal of humanity.[68]

In this argument Natorp neglects precisely that element which is the decisive factor for the author of second Isaiah. He overlooks the fact that, according to the conviction of the prophet, this victory of goodness is not accomplished by a humanity which is dependent upon itself, but by the overworldly and providential rule of Jahweh.

Natorp next refers to primitive Christianity which not only coöperated in elevating the ethical ideal of humanity, but actually succeeded in elevating a large portion of humanity. Nothing else was so characteristic of primitive Christianity as the desire to establish the Kingdom of God upon earth.   However, this last phrase is so emphasized by Natorp as to misinterpret the situation.   Of course it was the aim and purpose

---

[68] Paul Natorp: *Religion innerhalb der Grenzen der Humanität,* 2nd ed., Tübingen, 1908, pp. 15 f.

of primitive Christianity to establish upon earth the Kingdom
of God and precisely in that ethical and social sense emphasized
by Natorp with a highly sensitive insight into this aspect of the
idea; but the fact is that its *dominant interest* was directed toward the Kingdom of God as that transcendental reality which
stands in contrast to all that is mundane and finite. Natorp
says that to establish just this Kingdom of God upon earth,
in the hearts of men, in the love of man to man, was the lofty
meaning of Christianity, and that this idea was compelled by
religious logic to express itself in the idea of the divine-
humanity of its Saviour, while he, in turn, was regarded as the
example who was to elevate humanity itself to the level of the
divine. All this is certainly very pertinent and indisputable.
But does it really annul transcendence, as Natorp claims?
Absolutely not; for transcendence abides as the presupposition
and condition of that side of the religious conviction which
Natorp has emphasized.[69] Natorp can only deny this because he
does not at all grasp the transcendental idea in its religious
purity, and in its freedom from all alien motives and additions,
but conceives of it at the very start in terms of a *mythological
formulation*. Hence he then rejects, along with this latter
which he rightly criticizes, the first also, which is in no way
affected by his criticism. Later on we shall discuss the question
of how the idea of transcendence and the idea of immanence
in Christianity mutually supplement and circumscribe each other.
But even then we shall find that the idea of transcendence as
such is not abolished, but that it is only thereby more definitely
formulated and insured against mythological misinterpretation.

In the third place Natorp refers to Luther. The German

---

[69] However, Natorp's polemic against one-sided exaggerations in the
one direction or the other is absolutely justified. "To accuse a religion
which finds it possible to define its God straightforwardly by means of
fellowship, indeed, by means of a fellowship which we know only in terms
of fellowship between men and in terms of no other fellowship than that
which we human beings have with each other; to accuse such a religion of
abolishing the fellowship of man with man and of restricting everything to
the individual is certainly not just. And to blame such a religion, in distinction from others, for its genuine transcendence is also not just."

We can unreservedly approve these statements. Moreover we also find
unmistakably in them the beginnings of a religio-psychological method of
approach. However, this approach is not utilized by Natorp.

reformer is said to have restored the pure and original meaning of the Christian faith in that he conceived of it, not as a mere historical-factual acceptance of a truth, and not as an acceptance of ecclesiastical doctrines on authority, nor even as a theoretical science of the super-sensual, but as a conviction which is drawn immediately from the depths of the moral consciousness, and which is, therefore, absolutely subjectively founded. Accordingly, on all questions of religion the final authority for Luther was "what he calls conscience." This rediscovery of the genuine source of all faith in conscience, interpreted as the innermost tap-root of human self-consciousness, is to be regarded as the real achievement of Luther. This explains the reformer's honest evaluation of the earthly duties of man. And it also explains his free and pure evaluation of marriage, of the family, of the state, and his active enthusiasm for the training and instruction of the young, not only of the higher classes, but of the whole nation down to the lowest classes. And this rediscovery of the "original moral and humanitarian meaning of religion" also made it possible for men of the Enlightenment, such as Lessing, Kant, Fichte, and even Goethe and Schiller, to retain a positive relationship to religion in spite of their alienation from the letter of the traditional creeds. Under the surface this "original moral and humanitarian meaning" of religion is still working mightily in the Protestant world, and it must now be given again a position of complete domination.

Natorp's arguments reveal a thorough-going understanding of Luther and the Reformation. But at the point which is decisive for us here, that is, on the problem of the transcendental element in religion, first of all he does not define it clearly and unequivocally enough, and then, finally, he directly shifts it out of its place. For Luther, the final authority in matters of religion, as also in all questions of a world-view or a philosophy of life, is not conscience in the sense of a morality based upon the merely natural powers of man, but rather conscience thought of as arising from God, that is, as emerging *out of religious experience*. Now this is an *ethical and religious* court of appeal of such a type that the transcendental idea is directly presupposed by and consequently is implied in it. "And if the judge and everyone else must acquit you, God will still not acquit you, for he sees the mischievous heart and the deceitfulness of the world which, when you give an inch, will take a yard in addition, so that open injustice and violence results. . . . For God desires first of all a clean heart, although we, as long as we live here, cannot bring it so far that even one commandment remains, not to speak of the others also, and this continually convicts us and reveals how pious we are in the sight of God." So Luther writes in the larger catechism in explanation of the 9th and 10th commandments. And in the "conclusion" to the commandments, he adds, that no man can succeed in keeping even one of the commandments as it should be kept because they "are too high for anyone to succeed through human strength." For this reason Luther always emphasizes that the first commandment is the "greatest" from which all others should proceed. When the heart is directed toward God as the first commandment demands, that heart, Luther says, "has fulfilled this and all other commandments."

Ricarda Huch has recently expressed a one-sided opinion of Luther, which goes in the opposite direction, and a discussion of her evaluation will make our attitude to Natorp's position clearer.

She formulates her opinion in the thesis that Luther's lifework consisted in opposing morality. But this paradoxical thesis is correct only when the conception of morality is strictly identified with the idea of righteousness by works. But not only is this contrary to the accepted use of the term, it is not even consistently held by Ricarda Huch in her letters about Luther's faith. She passes from this first thesis to another, namely, that all consciously ethical activity is subordinated by Luther to unconscious and purely instinctive behavior. This statement does violence to the innermost intention of Luther, as certainly as it rightly recognizes and emphasizes one of its elements. When we start from Kant's statement of the problem, with its sharp distinction between inclination and duty, there is no doubt but what Luther on the whole would side with Kant. He only differs from Kant in that he does not share with him the exaggerated rigorousness which Schiller has castigated in his well-known epigram.[70]   For Luther had reached the insight that duty itself may develop into inclination.   And he won this insight just by placing, as a matter of principle, the ethical consciousness in relation to the religious consciousness. The direction of the heart toward God, which the first commandment demands, fulfills that and all other commandments: this statement of Luther is the most concise formulation of his whole ethics.

Natorp's attempt to prove a theory of religion which would completely eliminate the idea of transcendence, by sketching the development of the Biblical-Christian religion, is therefore a failure.   Despite the great importance which Natorp attaches to this historico-philosophical construction, for that is what this attempt is when it is precisely taken, the actual working foundation of his theory is not this, but is rather the epistemological-psychological understructure upon which Natorp has built this construction.   When the Marburg philosopher, in order to preserve his position, asks that the relation of these two sides of his theory be regarded in the opposite way (see p. 90), we may condone this self-deception, but for our own position we cannot take this view.

For we must continue to consider this epistemological-psychological understructure.   We designate it as epistemological-psychological in order to state its character quite generally for the time being.   How this is to be more closely determined, must be reserved for later discussion.   But this understructure, which Natorp simply designates as psychological, is for us all the more important because from the way in which Natorp appeals to Schleiermacher, and wishes to have his position regarded as the continuation of Schleiermacher's theory of re-

----

[70] Schiller's epigram is as follows:

> The friends whom I love I gladly would serve,
> But to this inclination incites me;
> And so I am forced from virtue to swerve
> Since my act, through affection, delights me.

From Kant's standpoint the only answer possible is:

> The friends whom thou lov'st, thou must first seek to scorn,
> For to no other way can I guide thee;
> 'Tis alone with disgust thou canst rightly perform
> The acts to which duty would lead thee.

ligion, it seems to be like our religio-psychological point of view.

In relegating religion to the realm of feeling, Schleiermacher was and still remains correct. But Schleiermacher was wrong in that he transposed the *infinity of feeling* into a *feeling of infinity,* and thus won for religion an objective content. If the nature of feeling were more correctly determined, the right determination of the nature of religion would at once follow naturally. *It is not the certainty, but it is the uncertainty of feeling that determines the nature of religion, because this uncertainty belongs to the nature of feeling itself, insofar namely, as feeling is given without an object.* For *object-lessness* is the actual characteristic of feeling by which it is differentiated from all other aspects of consciousness. If, then, the nature of religion is to be found in feeling, it follows that uncertainty and object-lessness have to be essential to religion.

Even this brief sketch shows, before entering into details, that Natorp's theory can correctly pass neither as epistemological nor as psychological, that it moreover confuses both methods of approach, and finally that, on the whole, it contains an absolutely vicious circle. The object-lessness of religion, in consequence of which the transcendental element in religion is treated as non-essential, is not actually proven, but is violently projected into the facts and is asserted so as to beg the question.

The whole construction, and again we are dealing here with a construction, is based upon the distinction between the objectifying and the object-less consciousness. Natorp uses this distinction to relegate religion to the realm of the object-less consciousness and to deny it every object-content. . . . How is this distinction to be evaluated? Natorp so applies it that the objectifying consciousness unfolds itself in three directions, as knowledge, will, and artistic imagination, and in contrast to this trisected objectifying consciousness, he treats feeling as the object-less aspect of consciousness. For feeling is not, like knowledge, will, and æsthetic imagination, a peculiar type of objectification, but it is the subjective counter-part to them. So far Natorp's argument is only epistemologically oriented. The conception of feeling used here is peculiar and this peculiarity needs to be more strongly emphasized. Feeling is a name for the *common point of relationship of the various functions of consciousness,* a name, then, for the purely formal relationship to the self. At the same time it must also be pointed out that Natorp defines the conception of the objectifying consciousness in a peculiar way, and so as to presuppose without further proof a certain epistemological judgment. With a neo-Kantian exaggeration of the critical point of view, this *objectification* is thought of as *creating the object,* and that is why knowing and willing, to which the creative imagination is also added, are all included in the conception of objectification. Instead of such a construction, a more unprejudiced view would speak of a perceptual object in the realm of knowledge and of an attitude toward objects in the realm of the will, for this would leave a free scope for the various possible epistemological points of view that can be critically formed.

However, Natorp himself fails to stick to his purely epistemologically oriented conception which defines feeling as the formal relationship to the self. When he designates his whole treatment of this problem as psychological, he actually does introduce a psychological characterization of feeling into the discussion. And it is only this fact that makes it possible for him to approach the problem of the nature of religion from this basis. For in itself epistemological reflection has directly nothing at all to do with this question. This shift in the meaning of the term feeling, as well as in his whole line of reasoning, which is characteristic of Natorp, becomes especially evident in those passages in which he states that feeling represents the unapproachable depths of inwardness, the actual alive-ness, the ceaseless activity of the psychic life. (See p. 35.) *For this is an entirely different conception of feeling from that which was previously discussed.* In this sense feeling is in a most intimate relationship to the will, and together with the will it constitutes the emotional aspect of consciousness. But just for this reason the possibility must also be left open for feeling, in this lastnamed sense of the word, to include a relation to an object. Psychological analysis also completely confirms this fact. Nor is this merely primarily or exclusively true in the field of religion. In other experiences also the relation to an object is very often essential for the emotional life. What would a feeling of friendship or a feeling of love be without a relation to an object? And so the relation to an object inalienably belongs to religious feeling because it belongs to the very nature of all feeling.

But Natorp uses this term feeling in two senses so that he can deny to feeling in general, and also to religious feeling, any relation to an object, so that he can characterize feeling as object-less by nature. Religious feeling, and thereby religion itself, then becomes a merely formal and structural state of consciousness. In order to exclude the transcendental idea from the nature of religion Natorp misuses the conceptions of religion and of religious feeling by making them mean nothing more than the formal relationship to the self. Such a view is simply a flagrant denial of the real nature of religious feeling. Logically it would necessarily result in the complete abandonment of the conception of religious feeling. *For such a view is entirely incapable of furnishing a criterion for the differentiation between religious and non-religious feelings.* And it is especially incapable of recognizing differences and gradations of a qualitative sort, or even of intensity within the sphere of religious feeling. William James has greatly advanced the understanding of the religious consciousness by his title calling attention to the *varieties of religious experience.* And as we have seen, at this point he comes into intimate contact with Schleiermacher's religious and religio-scientific method of approach. According to Natorp this statement of the problem by Schleiermacher and James would have to be regarded a failure and as absurd. For Natorp's theory concludes in advance that varieties of religious experience do not exist and are even impossible, just because it is a consequence of his theory that they are not permissible. The justified validity of religion, according to Natorp's theory, is to be restricted to the recognition of the formal structural state of consciousness.

This leads us to a final fact which has to be considered in evaluating Natorp's theory of religion. Abandoning the transcendental element in religion as a matter of principle, his theory, *from the beginning, emphatically proceeds from the point of view of the problem of the validity or truth of religion.* The problems of the nature and of the truth of religion are methodologically so little separated that they are in fact com-

bined at the very beginning. From the point of view of the
task of determining the nature of religion, this means that the
determination of its nature is adapted to the philosopher's pre-
established opinion as to its claim to validity or its truth-content.
This turns topsy turvy the only procedure that is methodologically permissible. Such a begging of the question makes an
unprejudiced treatment of the problem of the nature of religion
entirely impossible for Natorp.

We must postpone until later Natorp's treatment of the problem of religious truth. For the time being we are contented
to have established that his attempt to exclude from the determination of the nature of religion the relation to an over-world,
although containing many discussions which are fruitful and profitable in themselves,[71] has to be regarded as being,
on the whole, a complete failure.

We return then to the result at which we had already arrived in our discussion of Schleiermacher: The nature of religion is to be found in the relationship of man to an over-world
in which he believes, which he intuits by faith, and upon which
he feels himself to be dependent. Let us designate this result
as the recasting of Schleiermacher's theory. It adds no factors which were not included in Schleiermacher's formulation,
but it presents those that were in a new arrangement, and in
a different relation to each other. And as a result of this re-
arrangement, a new shade of meaning is given to his theory.
But this recasting must now be still further supplemented by
an actual addition. For religious feeling does not exhaust itself in the feeling of absolute dependence.

[71] The merits and accomplishments of Natorp's work in the philosophy
of religion, concerning which we had no occasion to speak in more detail
in connection with our discussion, are of a four-fold nature. 1. The strict
application of the method of critical thought in the Kantian sense. 2. The
energetic demand to take up again and apply the principles of Schleiermacher's treatment of religion. 3. The rejection of all theories which
attempt to relegate the nature of religion to some single psychic function.
4. The realization that religion must be regarded and evaluated as the
whole unified attitude of man. For these factors see the very noteworthy
discussions of Hans Schlemmer: *Die religiöse Persönlichkeit in der Erzie
hung. Eine religionsphilosophisch-pädagogische Untersuchung.* (Philosophische Bibliothek, Vol. 3), Charlottenburg, 1920. The treatise of Helene
Sacken is also noteworthy: *Zur Frage des Religionsbegriffs im System der
Philosophie,* Marburg, 1919.

CHAPTER VI

SCHLEIERMACHER'S THEORY OF RELIGION SUPPLEMENTED

I

It has often been argued that Schleiermacher made the feeling of dependence central in religion, whereas in fact the feeling of dependence and the feeling of freedom are so equally involved that the latter must be placed on a par with the former, the nature of religion being found only in a combination or an interworking of both of these feelings. However, instead of improving Schleiermacher's theory, such an attempt to perfect it really corrupts it. The religious feeling of dependence cannot tolerate a feeling of freedom that is put on a basis of absolute equality with it. Schleiermacher saw this quite correctly; and that is precisely the permanently valid element in his conception of a feeling of "absolute" dependence. A feeling of freedom which claims to be equal to or even to compete with the feeling of dependence affects the purity and assurance of the religious consciousness; instead of being religious it is of a magical nature, and it leads, not to religion, but to magic. Any feeling of freedom, which really becomes a part of religion, has to be subordinated to the feeling of dependence. This even applies to the feeling of ethical freedom, a feeling that is entirely compatible with the religious consciousness and, upon certain levels of religious development, is an essential ingredient in it. For religious conviction ethical freedom is also a component element of that reality which, in its totality, is taken to be dependent. No more trustworthy witness for this fact than Goethe could be found: "It is not our refusal to acknowledge anything that is above us which makes us free, but rather that we actually revere something which is above us. For in our reverence for it we draw ourselves up to it."

Yet at least this is true: the conception of the feeling of dependence *does not exhaust* the content of religious feeling.

For the whole nature of religious experience is not embodied in the feeling of dependence. The basic religious experience is a state of tension, characterized by the experience of being overwhelmed and by the experience of being elevated standing juxtaposed to each other. This is reflected in reverence, which also essentially includes both factors, as the German term (*Ehrfurcht*) shows: reverence for something which frightens or humiliates us and yet which makes us happy and exalts us. And in the term *religion* also, the etymology of which is still uncertain and disputed, usage reveals unmistakably this characteristic of tension. Awe and reverence are the two kinds of sentiments belonging to the sphere of religion. Now this characteristic of tension is not, or at least is not sufficiently expressed in the feeling of dependence. Therefore to remedy this defect a supplement to Schleiermacher's theory is necessary.[1]

However, it must again be emphasized in advance that we are concerned only with a *supplement*. The feeling of dependence as such really is the *basic religious feeling*. On this point Schleiermacher is right over against his critics, including even the most recent. The original and basic feeling of religious experience is the feeling of dependence. This is most clear and evident in the Psalms of the Old Testament. Throughout the Psalms the feeling of dependence is the foundation and presupposition of all other religious assertions. This is expressed with unsurpassable vividness and unequalled emphasis in the wonderful verses of the 139th Psalm:

"Thou hast beset me, behind and before,
And laid thy hand upon me.
Such knowledge is too wonderful for me;
It is high, I cannot attain unto it.
Whither shall I go from thy spirit?
Or whither shall I flee from thy presence?

[1] In the following discussion my reasoning coincides in part with the position defended by Carl Stange on the one hand, and with that of Georg Mehlis on the other hand. Comp. Carl Stange: *Christentum und Moderne Weltanschauung*, 1911 (2nd ed., 1913); *Religion als Erfahrung*, 1919, *Studien zur Theologie Luthers;* 1928. Georg Melhis: *Einführung in ein System der Religionsphilosophie*, 1917.

> If I ascend up into heaven, thou art there;
> If I make my bed in Sheol, behold, thou art
>   there.
> If I take the wings of the morning
> And dwell in the uttermost parts of the sea;
> Even there shall thy hand lead me,
> And thy right hand shall hold me."

The two series of pictures with which the psalmist portrays his belief, describe most impressively the inescapable nature of his dependence.[2]

In the Psalms the basic religious feeling of dependence is quite often expressed by referring to the earth which supports all human life:

> "The earth is the Lord's, and the fulness thereof; the world,
>   and they that dwell therein.
> For he hath founded it upon the seas, and established it
>   upon the floods."   (Psalm 24, 1 and 2.)

However, on the basis of this feeling of dependence, two additional forms of feeling now come into operation, which are, of course, closely related to it although they are not merely aspects but rather involve new factors. Out of the basic religious experience there is added to the feeling of dependence the *feeling of security* and *the sense of longing*. There is also indisputable evidence of this fact in the Psalms. The feeling of security and the sense of longing do not always appear with equal force; sometimes one dominates, and sometimes the other. But often, and particularly in some of the especially important and historically influential Psalms, the intimate connection between the two is also outwardly expressed by their subordination to and inclusion in the feeling of dependence. Recall, for example, the beginning and end of Psalm 42:

> "As the hart panteth after the water brooks,
>   So panteth my soul after thee, O God.
> My soul thirsteth for God, for the living God:
> When shall I come and appear before God?"

---

[2] Comp. the very fitting remarks of Hans Schmidt, *Psalmen, deutsch, im Rhythmus der Urschrift*, 1917, p. 98.

"Why art thou cast down, O my soul?
And why art thou disquieted within me?
Hope thou in God; for I shall yet praise him,
Who is the help of my countenance, and my
        God."

And in the 22nd Psalm, in contrast to the apparent deser-
tion which is first asserted, the intertwining of the feeling of
security and the sense of longing becomes all the more clearly
evident:

"My God, my God, why hast thou forsaken me?
Why art thou so far from helping me, and from the words
        of my groaning?
O my God, I cry in the daytime, but thou answerest not;
And in the night season, and am not silent."
"Be not far from me; for trouble is near;
For there is none to help."

2

This triad of the feeling of dependence, the feeling of security, and the sense of longing which we have just illustrated
from the Old Testament Psalms, a collection which has not
without justification been called a compendium of the entire
history of religion, may also be found everywhere in the history of religion, and if not always with quite the same
certainty and definiteness, then at least in rudimentary and preliminary stages. That is proven by those phenomena in which
the religious life more or less regularly expresses itself.

Prayer and sacrifice must again be especially mentioned.
In prayer and sacrifice there is revealed a relationship of man
to an over-world upon which he feels himself to be dependent,
in the protection of which he knows himself to be secure, and
which is the object of his longing.

In the prayers and rituals of primitive people, the sense of
longing is of course less prevalent, while the feeling of dependence and the feeling of security dominate the religious atmosphere. So far as these two feelings are concerned it will
suffice to refer to the prayers and the formulas of worship

already cited above.   But that, in addition to these two feelings,
the sense of longing is also necessary to complete the religious
consciousness cannot even be denied, in the light of religio-
psychological research on primitive religion.   In the first place
we may refer to the universally employed prayer-gesture of
turning toward the divinity in making the reverential address,
and then to the no less generally customary salutations of the
prayer and the sacrificial formulas which, as we have seen,
quite unmistakably prefer the terminology of kinship.   Not
always, but in most cases, the especially frequent use of the
name of father involves an element of longing.   And this is
even more true of the use of the name of mother.   Heiler has
made the very apt observation that there is an original religious note sounding out of many of the songs of Mary.[3]   But
it is only necessary to mention how strongly the sense of
longing prevails in most of these songs.

Keeping this in mind, prayers and songs of worship like
the following should be considered:

> "Art thou not our father,
>   The father of the fathers,
>   Thou, Tsuigoa?
>   O that we might praise thee!
>   O that we might repay thee!
>   Thou father of the fathers,
>   Thou O lord,
>   Thou Tsuigoa?"[4]

Along with this prayer of the Khoi-Khoi (Hottentots),
addressed to the heavenly God and original father Tsuigoa, consider this cult song of the Kora Indians:

> "Our Mother in heaven is thinking of her earth,
>   She is thinking of what she shall decide with her thoughts.
>   Our Mother in heaven intends to depart from there on the
>   way to Texmata.
>   Our Mother in heaven is already descending there.
>   Our Mother in heaven comes near to her goal.

[3] Fr. Heiler: *Das Gebet,* 2nd ed., p. 142.   English translation.
[4] Theophilus Hahn: *Tsuni-Goam.   The Supreme Being of the Khoi-Khoi;*
Trübners Oriental Series, London, 1881, p. 59 (with original text).

> Our Mother in heaven is already appearing in the midst
>   of Texmata.
> She is already there in Texmata and is thinking.
> With her staff of feathers she is explaining to the gods
>   in Texmata what she thinks.
> She thrones already above all of the gods and finishes
>   therewith.
> She finishes by explaining her thoughts to them." [5]

Even in prayers of an apparently eudaemonistic type, a trained ear may detect a note of longing. A prayer of the Ewe-speaking peoples will serve as an example: "O Dzake! We thank thee, for thou hast aided us in our labor so that the yam grew to be large. Thou shalt therefore eat before we eat! Here I therefore bring to thee thy portion! We pray thee, grant that this new year which now approaches, may find us safe in order that we may come again and bring to thee something new." [6]

Another prayer of the Ewe-speaking peoples, taken also from the very copious and reliable collection of Spieth, shows us that the sense of longing can be expressed very strongly in the worship of ancestors and of the dead: "Father! Mother! Brother! You have left me here alone, and now I suffer agony. Come, therefore, and lead me also away from here, so that I may find rest with you!"

For the Chinese ancestor-worship this same fact is also attested by the rite of formally recalling the dead.

Thus the higher the level of religion mounts, the more significance and scope is won for the sense of longing, since it is increasingly deepened and turned inward. What religious fervor is voiced in the following lines which are taken from the hymns of the Peruvian Incas:

> "O Creator of the world, O Maker of man,
>   Lord of all lords, To thee alone,
>   With eyes that fail, With longing to know thee,
>   I come to thee, To know thee, To understand
>   thee."

[5] K. Th. Preuss: *Die Religion der Kora-Indianer* (Die Nayarit-Expedition, Vol. I), 1912, p. 29.

[6] J. Spieth: *Die Religion der Eweer* (Quellen der Rel-Geschichte, Group 10), 1911, p. 95. The following example is on p. 245.

> "Come, then, Grand as the heavens,
> Lord over the earth, Creator of all things,
> Creator of man! Ever I adore thee . . ."

> "Thee am I seeking, To look upon thee,
> Like as on a river, Like as on the springs,
> Gasping with thirst." [7]

That this development reaches its climax in Christianity, needs no further elaboration.   Its basic religious conviction, which in turn also dominates its whole philosophy of life, may be summarized by Augustine's saying: "O Lord, Thou hast made us for Thyself; and our hearts are restless, until they find their rest in Thee."   In Him from whom, through whom and toward whom are all things, and who is at the same time a living divine personality, so that He must be regarded as the unified totality of all truly ethical and personal spiritual life, in such a God human longing is able to find true rest.

Although modern poetry is largely only unconsciously or involuntarily under Christian influence, yet Wilhelm Knevels has very strikingly shown that the idea of longing may actually be used as a criterion of its religious or non-religious attitude.[8] Among the examples which he has collected, those taken from the poetry of R. M. Rilke and Stefan George, which might easily be multiplied, are especially instructive.   And the lyric poetry of Rabindranath Tagore could also be considered from this point of view.   I shall select only a few lines: [9]

> "No more sailing from harbour to harbour with this my
>   weather-beaten boat.   The days are long passed when my
>   sport was to be tossed on waves.
> And now I am eager to die into the deathless.
> Into the audience hall, by the fathom-less abyss where
>   swell up the music of toneless strings, I shall take
>   this harp of my life.
> I shall tune it to the notes of forever, and, when it
>   has sobbed out its last utterance, lay down my silent harp
>   at the feet of the silent."

[7] Markham: Hastings' *Encyclopædia of Religion and Ethics*, I, 470 f. Comp. Heiler, p. 188.
[8] Wilh. Knevels, *Simmel's Religionstheorie*, Leipsic, 1920, pp. 39 ff.
[9] Rabindranath Tagore: *Gitanjali*, Nos. 100 and 103.

"Like a flock of homesick cranes flying night and day back
to their mountain nests, let all my life take its voyage
to its eternal home in one salutation to thee."

On this point Buddhism again occupies a unique place in
the whole history of religion.   In Buddhism the feeling of dependence recedes while the feeling of security and the sense of
longing are dominant.   Nirvana, as something anticipated in
contemplation but also as obtainable in this earthly life, presents
the hope of complete security; and hence longing is powerfully
and consciously diverted toward Nirvana, whereas the basic religious feeling, the feeling of dependence, is only faintly and
slightly noticeable.   The dependence upon the causal-mechanism
of the world-process is resisted and, to the extent that one approaches Nirvana, it is overcome.   But there can be no feeling
of dependence of a higher type on Nirvana, for the salvation
which is sought in Nirvana the Buddhist attains by his own
efforts.   To be sure there is a certain reverence for the majesty
of Nirvana, but this finds expression only in the sense of longing and in the feeling of security.

Does this mean that the feeling of dependence is entirely
lacking in Buddhism?   Hardly that.   For the fact that the
feeling of dependence is also operative in Buddhism is what
makes it a religion.   However, since this feeling cannot be
directed toward Nirvana, the inner unity of the religious
emotional life is rent asunder in this religion.   The feeling of
dependence is cut loose from its contact with the feeling of
security and the sense of longing, from which it can alone receive a higher purpose and a religious justification.   And it is
just because of this separation and isolation that it has no
unified unequivocal object to which it is related.   This again
produces another inner contradiction; namely, between theory
and practice.   In consistency with Buddhist theory the feeling
of dependence would have to be directed toward the eternal
order of salvation, which, due to the various eras of the world,
demands the advent from time to time of a Buddha who attains the saving knowledge and then sets "the wheel of the
law" of this knowledge into motion.   For even according to
their own teaching the Buddhists are dependent upon their doc-

trine, no matter how much they may make themselves independent of the personality of the Buddha.

To be sure, the conception of the *Pacceka Buddhas* seems to necessitate another qualification. Solely by his own effort but also purely for himself, a Pacceka Buddha achieves a knowledge of salvation, without receiving, on the one hand, the power and the desire to proclaim this knowledge; and without being in need, on the other hand, of hearing the preaching of a Sammâsam-Buddha, that is, of a universal Buddha. But in any case this conception of the Pacceka Buddhas applies only to very rare and exceptional individuals. The sources prove that it played only a very minor rôle in the earliest Buddhist congregation. And according to later doctrine, the appearance of the Pacceka Buddhas is restricted to those world-eras which have no universal Buddha.

So this possible exception does not apply to "the Buddhists," the followers of Gotama Buddha, who alone come into consideration in this connection. For them the fact that their Buddha achieved and proclaimed saving enlightenment is an absolute condition of their own hopeful striving for salvation. For the classical formula for the saving significance of Buddha states: "He appeared in the world for the salvation of many, because of compassion on the world, for salvation, for joy to gods and men." It is at this point that the theory and the practice of Buddhism have become separated. According to the theory the significance of Buddha is restricted to his having made possible the self-salvation of the men of a certain era. "He, the Exalted One, is he who prepares the unprepared way, who is creator of the uncreated way; however, the followers on the way are the disciples who are now present, following after him." [10] However, in practice Buddha has become an authority to a degree which takes away in advance all of the value of one's own religious experience, or rather, which makes personal religious experience altogether impossible. A further development of the religious consciousness in the direction which is here only alluded to, such as the New Testament claims for Christianity as a matter of

[10] *Majjhima Nikâya*, Vol. III, p. 15.—Comp. Oldenberg, *op. cit.*, 6th ed, p. 373.

principle (John XVI, 13), is likewise absolutely excluded.
Even the earliest congregation consciously and anxiously desired to hold fast and to restrict itself to the real or imagined
doctrines and precepts of Buddha. The resolution ascribed to
the first Buddhist council, which, according to the official tradition, took place shortly after Buddha's death, is as follows:
"The congregation does not determine that which has not
been determined (by Buddha), and does not cancel what he
determined; it accepts the precepts which he has laid down
and remains faithful to them." [11] In other words, "absolute"
dependence, not upon a super-empirical over-world which lies
beyond space and time, but upon something definitely fixed in
time and space! Hence the purely religious feeling of dependence is entirely absent, or at least is practically absent in
Buddhism. Its place has been taken by a dependence upon
tradition which, if it does not presuppose, at least necessarily
results in a very extreme form of belief in authority. In this
respect Buddhism offers a close analogy to Roman Catholicism,
yet it remains far behind Catholicism because it lacks a correc-
tive such as the infallible Pope or formerly the infallible
Council of Romanism which can counter-act the subjection to
tradition. In a very convincing way Oldenberg has shown
that this rigid adherence to tradition explains Buddhism's
incapacity for organization.[12] And even more important than
this is the other insight which results from the religio-
psychological approach; namely, that this belief in authority
indicates an inner disruption in the religious attitude of Buddhism, closely corresponding to that cleavage which was previously pointed out from another angle of approach.

3

And so, in its own way, Buddhism also proves that the
feeling of dependence is the basic religious feeling, and that
it is completed by the feelings of security and longing. In
view of this fact, however, it is now necessary to make a

---

[11] *Cullavagga* XI, 1, 9. Comp. Oldenberg, *op. cit.,* p. 383.
[12] H. Oldenberg, *op. cit.,* pp. 388 ff.—Comp. also the splendid discussions
of Max Weber, *Gesammelte Aufsätze zur Religionssoziologie,* Vol. II, 1921,
pp. 251 ff.

further supplementation of Schleiermacher's theory of religion. Due to their common relation to the religious feeling of dependence, the sense of longing and the feeling of security also have a reciprocal relation to each other. When the feeling of security is connected with the object of longing, there is involved a recognition of the entity toward which the longing is directed as the highest form of life. And inversely; when the sense of longing is related to that power under which one feels one's self to be secure, it results in a striving for the enrichment and the enhancement of life which finally culminates in the quest for salvation. Hence the consciousness of a norm or the sense of obligation on the one hand, and the quest for salvation on the other, belong also to the whole of religious consciousness as it emerges from the basic religious experience.

Moreover, the entire history of religion shows that the sense of obligation and the quest for salvation are constituent elements of religious life. As far as the quest for salvation is concerned, this thesis needs no special proof. For this quest is the starting point for all eudaemonistic and illusionistic theories of religion, the defects of which lie just in the one-sided isolation and exaggeration of this factor. This quest for salvation is in itself not yet religion, nor can it of itself produce religion, unless the concept of a relationship to an over-world (in the sense in which it has already been defined) is also presupposed. Besides, only Hinayana Buddhism can be claimed as an example of a religion without the quest for salvation. But even here such a claim is not justifiable. For the Buddhist striving for Nirvana is unmistakably characterized by a quest for salvation, no matter how much the negatively directed tendency toward freedom from suffering may protrude. This statement has been expressly attributed to Sâriputta, the foremost of Buddha's disciples: "Nirvana is salvation, Nirvana is salvation." [13] And the maxims of wisdom of the *Dhammapada,* which has been correctly termed the "truest mirror" of Buddhist feeling, confirms this judgment, even more by the whole manner of thought and by the atmosphere of feeling which dominates them, than by the separate

[13] *Anguttara Nikâya,* V., pp. 414 f.   Comp. Oldenberg, *op. cit.,* pp. 304 f.

maxims which describe Nirvana as the highest bliss.[14] And referring especially to the *Dhammapada,* although in no wise basing his interpretation exclusively upon it, Oldenberg treats the inner joyousness with which Buddha pursued his goal and which is far removed from all resignation, as an indisputable and well-established fact. To be sure, in this respect also there is an inner contradiction in Buddhism. The striving for bliss is rooted in the will to live, and hence it can only be truly satisfied by the enhancement or deepening of life and of the inmost will to live. But Buddhism considers the will to live exclusively from the point of view of this earthly life of suffering which is bound by space and time. Consequently it is unable to seek a deepening of the will to live in the Christian sense of "more abundant" life in the tenth chapter of the Gospel of John. Or, leaving out of consideration the comparison to Christianity, Buddhism excludes that interpretation of the will to live which Nietzsche expresses in these lines of his *Mitternachtslied:*

> "All desire seeks eternity,
> Seeks deep, profound eternity."

Hence it is all the more unique and also contradictory that Buddhism nevertheless, not only retained the purely mythological theory of an endless cycle of rebirths in the framework of its whole doctrine, but even made it the foundation of its religious and philosophical world-view. This unfounded, meaningless, and evil "eternity" prevents Buddhism from fully grasping and evaluating the true conception of eternity.[15]

---

[14] Compare the lines 23, 203, 204, 368.
Piously and persevering, this high endeavour as their goal
The wise men reach the highest bliss, to Nirvana find their way.
Hunger is the greatest plague, this earthly frame is deepest pain;
Nirvana is the highest bliss to him who has this truth attained—
Highest gain our health may be, contentment is a boon most rare,
The best of kinship may be trust, yet highest bliss Nirvana is.
The Bhikshu practising good-will, and peaceful in the Buddha's truth
Shall reach the peaceful blissful state, where all things come to perfect rest.

[15] Although it cannot be taken into account more fully until later, in connection with the treatment of Christianity, a comparison with Nietzsche is extremely instructive at this point. Nietzsche also places his mythological theory of the continual recurrence of every identical thing in opposition to

In the most crass and one-sided fashion this contradiction reappears in modern neo-Buddhism. It reverts to crass naturalism and materialism. Without any qualification it states that life, regardless of where and how it is lived, is necessarily always the unity of becoming and of passing away. Consequently the idea of "eternal life" is a childish conception. For life, both in its form and in its content, is nothing more than becoming and passing.[16] To make clear to ourselves the absolute superficiality of this "doctrine of life" we must also consider what is stated in another passage about Nirvana: "Nibbana (Pali for Nirvana) is nothing else than the state of freedom from desire which is experienced immediately as the highest bliss. . . . That this state of freedom from desire, of annihilation of the instincts, should after a certain time result also in physical annihilation is inherent in the very nature of life, which has no other anchor and support than desire. Consequently, with the passing of desire, life itself also passes away" (p. 113). The scholastic-dogmatic presumption of this "knowledge" and its claim to infallibility, becomes all the more ridiculous when we remember that neo-Buddhism elsewhere claims to reject all absolutistic thinking in favor of realism. That the doctrines of those who make these assertions are to be exempted from this judgment should at least have been stated occasionally.

The other result of our religio-psychological analysis of the religious feelings, namely, that in addition to the quest for salvation the consciousness of obligation must also be attributed to the nature of religion, leads us into greater difficulty. If this thesis is correct, then the relationship to the ethical sphere, to morality, is essential to religion, and the ethical factor cannot be eliminated from religion without injuring, and finally even destroying, in its essential nature, religion itself. However, this evaluation of the situation is hotly dis-

the Christian belief in eternity. But yet he shows very clearly that he had a true understanding of the actual meaning of the idea of eternity. He is truly a "man with two souls" (ἀνὴρ δίψυχος), to use the phrase of Ernst Bertram (*Nietzsche,* 1919).

[16] Comp. in the *Dhammapada* edition of the neo-Buddhist editors the exegesis of verse 187, p. 110.

puted, although it seems to the scholar who takes the religio-psychological attitude to be necessary and indispensable.

Formerly it was especially those who advocated, as a matter of principle, the idea of a morality without religion, who denied the original and essential connection between religion and morality. But much more significant than this manifestly partisan objection is that which is raised today in a quite objective manner by those who dispute this thesis in order to grasp the nature of religion when it is stripped of all of its accretions. Foremost among the latter is Rudolf Otto. And his conception on this point is all the more important for us not only because his aim is intimately related to our own, but because his discussion embodies a method which is unmistakably analogous to our religio-psychological method.

In characterizing the basic content of religion Otto employs the concept of the *numinous*. As he uses this term it is supposed to designate "the holy minus its moral factor." [17] And precisely this numinous, which, in Otto's own terms, is the residue of the category of the holy after we subtract its moral factor, is just what constitutes the essential nature of religion. Thus according to Otto the moral factor does not of itself belong, either directly or natively, to the nature of religion. Moreover, it can be completely severed from religion without the existence of religion being thereby endangered. Indeed, it is just by means of such a separation that the nucleus of religion can be seen in its purity and clarity. For this nucleus is just what remains after the moral factor is subtracted from the category of the holy. There can be no doubt that Otto deserves credit for having brought absolute clarity and consistency into the discussion by giving this interpretation and by creating the terminology in which it is expounded. And this credit is not minimized in any way by our partially rejecting his theory.

It is also true that Otto has impressed wide circles and has won unqualified approval for his interpretation. However, this shall not mislead us in our judgment. For according to the previously developed religio-psychological analysis, the

[17] Rudolf Otto: *Das Heilige* (1917), 1931, p. 6. English translation *"The Idea of the Holy,"* p. 6.

theory of the numinous is objectionable in one respect. However, before we state what this is, let us note the very significant element of truth in Otto's theory. For there are several respects in which there is truth in it. In the first place, the underlying search for the characteristic feature, or combination of features, which finally constitutes a real criterion for the nature of religion, is valid, since it is a search for the *specifically religious.* At this point our own method coincides completely with that of Otto. And that applies not merely formally, for we also agree with Otto that the customary use of the concept of the holy to determine the nature of religion signifies an *unjustified moralization,* since definite moral ideas —possibly Christian or at least nearly Christian ideas—are thereby read into the essential nature of religion. With just as much emphasis as Otto we reject this false moralization of religion. That is demanded, not only by our criticism of the method and logic of the normative standard (see p. 33 above), but even by the main principle of the religio-psychological point of view, since it aims to grasp the nature of religion as determined by specifically religious experience.

However, while we are able to agree with Otto in rejecting this false moralizing, we cannot admit that the moral element has to be entirely eliminated in order to find the pure nature of religion. In my opinion, there is here a gap in Otto's reasoning which he has never really filled, and which in the end makes it impossible for him to do justice to the situation.

Moreover another circumstance is also involved in his position. In the passage in which he first gives a basic definition of the numinous, and just after he says that the numinous is the holy minus its moral element, he says: "and, as we can now add, minus its 'rational' aspect altogether." This addition indicates the shift which Otto undertakes from another angle and in a new light. For is the moral element unequivocally and necessarily of a rational nature—rational, namely, in the sense of the distinction between the rational and the irrational which is presupposed by the term rational? If this were true, then of course Otto's decision would have to be approved by everyone who wants to guard religion against rationalization. For a critic's failure to approve it would mean that he believed in rationalizing religion. And since the religio-psychological method emphatically forbids any such rationalization of religion (see above, pp. 45 ff.), it especially would have to extend a cordial welcome to Otto's interpretation. But the assumption is false. Morality as such is not rational in the sense of the contrast between the rational and the irrational. *All moral teachings and moral concepts are rational, but the original phenomenon of the moral, which underlies these moral teachings and moral concepts, is not rational in the same sense.* That Otto converts the search for the moral element in religion into a search for the rational element, by subordinating the rational to the moral, seems to me to be due to the influence of neo-Friesianism upon his method of investigation.

Here, to a certain extent, Otto comes into conflict with his own program. In *The Idea of the Holy* he restricts himself to the irrational aspect of religion, and on the other hand, he considers its rational side in his *Kantisch-Friesische Religionsphilosophie*.[18] However, this division of the task leads to difficulties on both sides. According to Otto's own opinion, the irrational is present in all religions as their real inner essence, and without it there "would not be religion at all." Hence it is impossible to understand how his second book, which he admits only takes the rational side of religion into account, can claim to be a philosophy of religion.

On the other hand, his attitude toward the irrational side of religion does not explain his including the moral factor of the holy in the category of the rational, since it can be understood only from the point of view of neo-Friesianism. And since neo-Friesianism is concerned with the problem of the truth of religion, a premature influence of the problem of truth upon the task of determining the nature of religion is involved here, even though it is quite hidden.

However, since it is the emphatic demand of the religio-psychological method to keep the treatment of the problem of the nature of religion free from every premature introduction of the problem of its truth, and since the statement of the problem is from time to time weighed from this point of view, it follows that we must reach a different conclusion from that of

[18] Comp. Rudolf Otto, *op. cit.*, p. 5.

Otto as to the relation of the "moral factor" to the nature of religion. Above all we must then differentiate clearly and distinctly between those specific moral views that are conditioned by historical development, and the original phenomenon or basic principle of morality. Specific moral ideas as they are historically conditioned certainly cannot be included in the universal nature of religion, and especially not those which use the word "holy" to express the *absolute* moral predicate. Yet all moral ideas, no matter how varied they may seem, presuppose the consciousness of obligation or of a norm, the consciousness of being bound by certain norms in one's attitude and conduct, of being obligated to certain actions or abstentions, of having to recognize some kind of rules or principles. It is upon this basis that the moral life of man unfolds in its whole profusion and in its various forms. But no matter how numerous and diverse these forms may be, all of them equally presuppose the sense of obligation, for ultimately they are nothing else but varied forms of the sense of obligation. Hence our thesis, as opposed to that of Otto, claims that wherever religion is enkindled and moves the human heart, there the sense of obligation is also awakened. And this fact is rooted in the innermost and deepest nature of religion as expressing the relationship of man to an over-world, to that which is felt to be an over-world by reason of its nature and value. Mere shuddering before spooks and ghosts is not yet religion. Such an experience is of course partially analogous to religion, but it is not in and of itself religion.

4

In defense of this position we may again appeal to the entire history of religion, and especially to the significance of *prayer and sacrifice* in this history. Even in their most primitive forms, prayer and sacrifice always include recognition and obligation. This fact is clear in the prayers which we have previously cited. And every section of Heiler's comprehensive collection of prayers furnishes additional examples. However, special emphasis must here be placed upon sacrifice. By sacrifice man expresses his obligation to a superior being. In Christianity this involves the surrender of the whole personality to the service of the kingdom of God as the sacrifice. Here the factors of obligation and surrender are most clearly evident. But even in those religions where this is not made so clear, where obligation and surrender are hidden behind the external cult practices and their secondary utilitarian aim, and where they sometimes disappear almost completely, to the trained eye they are nevertheless discernible in the background as the ultimately decisive motives underlying the whole phenomenon of sacrifice and finally, therefore, underlying the idea of sacrifice itself. For in sacrifice we always have to do with surrender, surrender of the values of human existence, surrender of the values of property, or of life, or of personality. Such surrender presupposes the recognition of a higher value or of a system of higher values, and, in addition, the recognition of obligation to that higher value or system of values. *Obligation, recognition, and surrender are the pillars upon which the whole phenomenon of sacrifice rests.*

Thereby we in no wise overlook the fact that originally sacrifice appears everywhere as *petitionary sacrifice,* that is to say, as a petition for help according to the principle of *do ut des*. This fact itself is historically indisputable; and yet it cannot hide the equally important fact that the utilitarian aim cannot itself explain the sacrifice.

Yet just the expression of this opinion gives rise to another objection from the representatives of the most recent scientific investigation of religion, an objection which is apparently more penetrating and which must, therefore, now be considered. That school of investigators chiefly represented by Marett would make the objection that since the original sacrifice was a *magical sacrifice,* the interpretation of sacrifice, both of the historically given phenomena of sacrifice and of the idea of sacrifice which dominates these particular phenomena, must start with magical sacrifice. Just as the prayer incantation at the sacrifice was originally a magical spell, so the most original form of sacrifice must have been the magical sacrifice, and later developments of sacrificial practices and ideas must be approached in the light of this fact. However, this objection must here be rejected as absolutely unjustified. It is based upon a confusion in the statement of the problem which is ultimately due to the absence of a religio-psychological attitude. Upon closer examination the religio-psychological investigator must regard this popular modern interpretation of sacrifice as a pure begging of the question.

We are dealing with sacrifice as a form of expression of the religious life which is attested by the whole of human history. Therefore this attempt, as a matter of principle, to trace sacrifice back to magical sacrifice is equivalent to trying to find the nature of religion in exorcism, in magic. But that this reduction of religion to magic fails to promote the understanding of religion but rather hampers and, in the end, even makes it impossible, is self-evident to anyone who has even begun to think, to investigate, and to study religion with the religio-psychological method. For religious experience emphatically forbids any such identification, and only after a complete side-tracking or elimination of religious experience is it possible. But a method of investigation whose working principle demands the elimination of religious experience deserves the name of a "science of religion" as little as the study of music would deserve its name if it should make the elimination of musical appreciation its working principle.

Magic certainly does have a close relation to primitive religion, both historically and psychologically, yet in itself magic is not religion, but is rather something quite different from all religion, even primitive religion. However, the more precise determination of the relation between religion and magic must here be postponed. Later on it will be taken up in an unprejudiced way with a full discussion of the real situation. But precisely in order that this may be done absolutely objectively, the relation of religion to magic cannot be decided in advance. (See Chapter IX and Appendix III.)

Let us return, then, to our argument. The fact about sacrifice which requires most earnest consideration is not the fact of magical sacrifice, but is rather this, that at the very beginning of religious development *petitionary sacrifice* occupies the dominant and central position in the religious system of sacrifice. In the Vedic cult we find petitionary sacrifice still occupying this dominant position. And for this very reason the Vedic cult proves conclusively that petitionary sacrifice offers no decisive

objection to our evaluation of sacrifice. For although petitionary sacrifice occupies this dominant position in the Vedic cult
whereas the thank-offering recedes completely,[19] while the ex-
piatory sacrifice is absorbed into the system of petitionary sacrifice, and furthermore although magic frequently forces its
way alongside of and sometimes even permeates Vedic sacrifice,
nevertheless there can be no doubt that on the whole Vedic
sacrifice intends to and does express obligation, recognition,
and surrender.

To be sure, the gods from whom help and good will are ex-
pected and petitioned, are supposed to be delighted, satisfied,
and strengthened by the sacrifice, yet these gods are thought
to have a justified claim to this sacrifice, and men are thought
to be *obligated* to render it. That the gods really have this just
claim and that men have this obligation, is the presupposition
that is discernible all through the Vedic sacrificial cult. The
head of every family is to observe this cult scrupulously with
one fire, while the rich man is also obligated to care for the
cult of the three fires. And while the daily morning and evening sacrifice, as well as the full-moon and new-moon sacrifice,
are common to both cult forms, yet each also has special and
strictly observed requirements. Consequently sacrifice appears
ultimately as that event which is by far the most important
concern of human life. This all-surpassing, all-conditioning (of
all other values and all other cult forms) value of sacrifice
may occasionally be so intensified that sacrifice is portrayed as
the highest cosmic potency *per se*. This is the case in the
Purusha-hymn of the *Rig-Veda* [20] which makes the act of
creation a sacrificial act of the gods. The gods sacrificed the
thousand-headed, thousand-eyed and thousand-footed Purusha
(man, original man), and by means of this sacrifice there arose
not only the various parts of the world and the various crea-

[19] Whether thank-offering is completely absent in the Vedic cult or
whether specific sacrifices, such as the sacrifice of the first fruits of the
field or the great horse sacrifice, are to be regarded as thank-offerings, is
still a disputed question among Vedic scholars.

[20] *Rig-Veda*, X, 90. Paul Deussen gives a detailed discussion of this
hymn: *Allgemeine Geschichte der Philosophie mit besonderer Berücksichtigung der Religionen*, I, 1, 2nd ed., 1906, pp. 150 ff.—Comp. also L.
Scherman, *Philos. Hymnen.*

tures, but also the great gods, Indra and Agni.   The hymn concludes with the lines [21] which appear again in another passage of the *Rig-Veda:*

> "Through sacrifice the gods offered sacrifice;
> And these were the first ordinances."

No matter how strange this fantastic speculation may appear to us, in it the significance of the idea of sacrifice, and the imperativeness of the obligation to sacrifice, become most graphic.[22]   If men, if the world in which men live, including all of its creatures and even the chief gods of the Vedic cult, owe their existence to sacrifice alone, how can human beings, on their part, escape the obligation to sacrifice?   How can they expect to prove themselves worthy of life without a sacrificial attitude and a willingness to sacrifice?

Buddhism rejects all cult sacrifice.   Herein it is like Biblical Evangelical Christianity.   Yet Buddhism is distinguished from Evangelical Christianity most decisively by its attitude toward the idea of sacrifice.   The true Christian dedicates his whole personality to the service of the Kingdom of God, that is, to the love of God and of man, and there is no trace of this in Buddhism.   This is not merely because actual belief in God is not found in Buddhism, for even when we disregard the belief in God entirely and only apply the idea of sacrifice to brotherly love alone, the sacrificial attitude is still lacking.

To be sure, the idea of sacrifice is not entirely absent from Buddhism.   On the contrary it is at times emphasized so strongly that an absolute parallel to the Christian conception seems to be implied.   This is true of quite a number of stories of the Buddha's conduct in his previous existence, insofar as the portrayal of the sacrificial life of Buddha is really the dominating purpose of these stories.   The "Story of the Wise Hare"

[21] *Rig-Veda*, I, 164, 50.—We have only quoted the first half of the stanza above.   The second half reads: "These mighty beings ascend to heaven where the gods, the ancient Sadhyas dwell."   Whether this stanza was added to the Purusha-hymn later or not, is here of no consequence.

[22] Another quite different interpretation of this hymn, which, referring to the history of human sacrifice in India, draws an analogy between it and the Abraham-Isaac narrative of the Old Testament, is not taken into consideration here.

is especially graphic.[28]   Buddha says that he once lived as a
hare in a mountain forest and instructed his companions, a
monkey, a jackal and an otter, concerning their duties, and so
he instructed them to have in readiness at the festival days of
the full moon, gifts for those who were worthy of them.   But
then he realized that he had no gift to offer, for he lived only
upon grass, and grass is not a fitting gift.   And so he decided
to offer himself to some worthy being as a gift.   When, therefore, the story continues, the king of the gods, Sakka (Indra)
came to his dwelling place in order to test him, Buddha said,
"Today I will give alms such as I never gave before; and you
will not have broken the precepts by destroying life.   Go, my
friend, and gather wood, and when you have made a bed of
coals, come and tell me.   I will sacrifice my life by jumping
into the bed of live coals.   And as soon as my body is cooked,
do you eat of my flesh, and perform the duties of a monk."
And he then actually carried out this purpose.   "I gave my
whole body with all of its members to the Brahmin."

When we disregard its being clothed in the thought-forms
of the belief in, or rather, in the mythology of Saṃsāra, do we
not have here a formulation and an evaluation of the idea of
sacrifice, which is absolutely identical with the evangelical
Christian idea? No! For, in the first place, we must remember
that in such narratives the idea of sacrificial living is entirely
subordinated to that of portraying the unique preparation of
him who bears the title of Buddha.   And, secondly, it should
be especially noted that the idea of sacrifice is not stated here
in its ethical purity but is given a ritualistic turn and restriction.   In conformity with the ideas of the time and with the
purpose of the narrator, the Brahmin of the story is a Bhikkhu,
the monk whose name expresses the obligation to live the life
of a beggar.   Hence this glorification of the sacrificial system
refers to the relation of the lay-supporters to the mendicant
monks.   And in the main it is restricted to this relationship.
But this is equivalent to a ritualistic exaggeration and restriction.   The very Buddhism which rejects cult sacrifices, nevertheless encourages a ritualism which is just as restricted and

[28] The English version of this story is in H. C. Warren's *Buddhism in
Translation* (Harvard Press), pp. 274 ff.—Translators' note.

exaggerated in its sacrificial practice as is the cult sacrifice of Brahmanism. This is another inner cleavage in the Buddhist doctrine.

However, apart from this relationship of the laity to the monks, the idea of sacrifice as such remains almost completely inactive in Buddhism. In other words, in those relations where it should become active, if it is to have any importance for the history of mankind, it is inactive. In place of, and in peculiar contrast to the restriction which we have mentioned, there appears an expansion which weakens the force of the sacrificial attitude in practical life and even hinders its operation. The following formulation of the readiness to sacrifice, which is found in the *Sutta Nipāta* 149, is quite characteristic and instructive on this point.

> As the mother, even with her own life,
> Guards her only son,
> So for all creatures he awakens
> Within himself boundless feeling.

Oldenberg has called attention to the fact that this analogy does not, as the facts would frankly insist and demand, end in a challenge to imitate the mother's sacrificial courage and her willingness to sacrifice, but that it is violently converted into the commandment to foster boundless feeling toward all creatures. This deadens the vital nerve of the sacrificial idea and cripples its power. And this is all the more true since sympathy with all creatures is used primarily, and even almost exclusively, to nourish a state of mental indifference, and not to preserve an active love of one's neighbour. In verses 210-212 of the *Dhammapada* an emphatic warning is even given to avoid this brotherly love:

> "Seek not that which is dear, nor ever that which is not dear.
> Not to see what is dear brings pain, likewise to see what is not dear.
> Therefore, let nothing be dear to thee! A dear loss is truly hard.
> There are no chains for them who hold nothing dear or not dear.

Pain is born of what is dear, and what is dear gives rise
    to fear;
He knows no care nor any fear if fully freed from what
    is dear."

A truly sacrificial attitude cannot be reconciled with such
principles, because such an attitude requires action, strength,
and positive behavior. Instead of encouraging this, Buddhism
rather inhibits it. And in this respect modern neo-Buddhism
even increases the inadequacy of the Buddhist view of the world
and of life. The neo-Buddhist *Zeitschrift für Angewandten
Buddhismus* declares that the highest pinnacle of wisdom is
not that men should think it important to desire good things,
but that they should rather desire with moderation, and that
there is no better means of attaining this moderation than the
continual conscious meditation upon death which robs all of
our hopes and our desires of their importance.[24] No, my neo-
Buddhist friends, that is not true! Your teaching is rather
the most perverted and miserable nonsense conceivable. If
it were really true then the world would never have honored
(not to mention Jesus Christ at all) either Socrates or Plato,
either Paul or John, either Luther or Kant, either Fichte or
Schleiermacher, nor would it have glorified Dante or Shake-
speare, Goethe or Schiller, Michelangelo or Dürer, Bach or
Beethoven. And Carlyle would have had to leave his book
on *Heroes and Hero Worship* unwritten.

The idea of sacrifice belongs, then, to the nature of religion.
And the consciousness of obligation is imbedded in the idea of
sacrifice. But this same consciousness of obligation is found
in still other forms of religious worship, especially in the
cleansing and propitiation ceremonies of which there are also
numerous forms throughout the whole history of religion.
Since we have just been discussing sacrifice, propitiatory sacrifice constitutes a natural transition to this sphere. Now what
was said above about sacrifice in general especially applies to
propitiatory sacrifice; namely, that magic frequently approaches
and forces its way into it. And this means that the system

---

[24] Comp. in the translation of the *Dhammapada,* the explanation of the
6th stanza, p. 86, published by the publishers of the journal mentioned above
(Neubuddhistischer Verlag, Zehlendorf-West bei Berlin), 1919.

of propitiation ceremonies itself is to a large extent interspersed with, or is even completely fashioned by magic. Defilement and uncleanness are to be removed by magical practices, for example, they are to be washed away by water or burned away by fire. Here again we must reserve our opinion of this fact until we discuss the relationship between religion and magic. However, the close connection between magic and propitiation can in no way blind the religio-psychologically trained scholar to the fact that the rites of cleansing and propitiation belong by their very nature to religion. That this fact has been lost sight of today by numerous investigators and that, in contrast to it, they expound the view that these ceremonies of cleansing and propitiation belong to the sphere of magic, a view, which is technically absolutely inadequate, is caused precisely by a lack of religio-psychological training.

Even Goethe, as a result of his exceptional emotional penetration, incidentally suggested how this relationship, which is rooted in the very nature of religion, is to be viewed.

> In the pure bosom doth a yearning float,
>   Unto a holier, purer, unknown Being
> Its grateful aspirations to devote,
>   The Ever-Nameless then unriddled
>   seeing;
> We call it: Piety!—

We may disregard the monotheistic and Christian colouring of these lines. Yet even then there remains the basic religious mood of dedicating one's self to a holier, purer, unknown power. If the object of the religious relationship, the over-world, no matter how unknown it may be in other respects, is yet "holier and purer," then man in his natural state is not worthy of the religious relationship, and must be cleansed and purified in order to come into contact with God, or more generally, with the over-world.

The history of religion, studied in the light of the psychology of religion, leaves no doubt that ultimately the practices of cleansing and propitiation go back to this motive, which in turn grows out of the basic religious experience. That is evidenced already by the intimate relation, in which the rites of cleansing and propitiation stand to the idea of sacrifice, not merely externally, but in the most completely inward way.

Thus, in the Vedic cult, the preliminary consecration of the sacrificing priest with the so-called *Diksha*[25] was a necessary part of the most important sacrifice, the Soma sacrifice. This consecration was performed in the sacrificial hut where the sacrificing priest, with his head covered, seated himself upon a black antelope skin near the sacrificial fire. In the books of ritual this Diksha ceremony is called a tapas. Tapas, that is, heat, is the standard term for the castigation which prepares man for fellowship with the gods. Accordingly, it is said of this consecration: "If the Diksha-consecrated one becomes thin, then he is ritualistically clean; if his skin clings to his bones, he is ritualistically clean; if there is nothing more in him, he is ritualistically clean; if the black element in his eyes disappears, he is ritualistically clean."[26] Hence, the ceremony of castigation is supposed to make the priest worthy of carrying out his sacrificial duty.

To understand this Diksha ceremony, however, the peculiar observances which are connected with it must be considered. The requirement of closing the last three fingers of both hands and of speaking stammeringly, remind us of similar practices among primitive peoples quite generally, which serve to depict the process of the rebirth of man.[27] Now in the texts of the *Brahmanas* the interpretation of the Diksha as a ceremony of rebirth or new birth is also expressly expounded, and the symbolism is carried out in great detail. The conviction that man must be lifted above his natural state cannot be more emphatically expressed than by the requirement or the symbolic performance of an act of rebirth. In spite of all of its specifically Christian peculiarities, the idea of rebirth in Christianity is a direct continuation from this primitive beginning.

The inherent inner relationship of the rites of propitiation to the religious idea of sacrifice is no less clear. And along

[25] H. Oldenberg: *Die Religion des Veda,* 2nd ed., pp. 397 ff.
[26] Alfr. Hillebrandt: *Ritual Literatur; Vedische Opfer und Zauber* (*Grundriss der indo-arischen Philologie und Altertumskunde*), 1901, p. 126.
[27] This material is in H. Schurtz: *Altersklassen und Männerbünde,* Berlin, 1902; L. Frobenius: *Die Masken und Geheimbünde Afrikas,* Halle, 1898; J. G. Frazer: *The Golden Bough,* 3rd ed.; *Balder the Beautiful,* Vol. II.

with this relationship the consciousness of obligation also expresses itself in these rites in an unmistakable manner. Propitiation presupposes guilt, and that means, more precisely stated, the consciousness of guilt. It is only from a consciousness of guilt that there arises the conviction of being obliged to propitiate.

In the Vedic cult propitiatory sacrifices, and other rites of propitiation, are offered chiefly to Varuna or also to the whole group of deities called the Adityas, to which Varuna, often forming a twin deity with Mitra (sun and moon), belongs. Their mother, the goddess Aditi, is also one of the important Adityas. The central ideas of this whole system of worship are the ideas of sin, guilt, and propitiation. Sin and guilt, however, are measured by Rita, the law or the order of the universe. According to the sense which is here applicable, Rita means the physical and moral world-order, so interpreted that the moral precedes and includes the physical. Now Varuna and Mitra are regarded as the "two lords" or as the "guardians of Rita." Referring to them, a hymn of the *Rig-Veda* (V, 63, 7) says: "Through the sacred law ye rule the whole world." Varuna especially is revered in this way. And it is especially Varuna who punishes unpropitiated sin, and who forgives the guilt of expiated sin:

"Fain to know this my sin, I questioned others: I sought the wise, O Varuna, and asked them. This one and the same answer even the sages gave me: 'Surely this Varuna is angry with thee.' What, Varuna, hath been my chief transgression, that thou shouldst slay the friend who sings thy praises? Tell me, unconquerable lord, and sinless I will quickly approach thee with mine homage." [28]

Let us now summarize the results of this chapter. For us the nature of religion is the relationship of man to an overworld in which he believes and of which he has intimations in his faith, on which he feels himself to be dependent, in whose shelter he knows himself to be secure, and which is the goal of his heart's most ardent yearning. The inmost essence of religion resides, then, in the surmising and believing relationship to a

[28] *Rig-Veda*, VII, 86, 3, 4. Comp. Oldenberg: *Die Religion des Veda*, p. 302.

reality which, in its essential nature and intrinsic value is to be characterized, over against the finite, space-time, sense-world, as an over-world. This relationship reflects itself in the feeling trinity—the feeling of dependence, the feeling of security, and the feeling of ardent yearning. The feeling of dependence is the fundamental religious feeling and it allows itself to be differentiated into the two polar opposite and conflicting feelings of security and ardent yearning, in order that it may overcome this oppositeness. The state of tension which exists between the feeling of security and ardent yearning includes the dual tendency: striving for blessedness and consciousness of duty. To Schleiermacher's theory of religion we have added the last-named factors. To be sure, it could be claimed that these factors are implicit in Schleiermacher's theory, but that they are not clearly stated. The defect in his theory is merely this, that it emphasizes almost exclusively the synthetic unity of the feeling of dependence, and practically disregards the alternation between the feeling of security and the sense of yearning involved in that synthetic unity.

Thus far we have derived this supplementation and completion of Schleiermacher's theory chiefly from a religio-psychological treatment of the data taken from the history of non-Christian religions. How this theory of religion is to be applied to Christianity and to the history of Christianity, cannot here be indicated. That must be reserved until after we have given a full discussion of the question of the nature of Christianity.[29] However, it should now be very briefly mentioned that Christianity also undoubtedly shows this synthesis, when its religious life is understood from the point of view of the basic Christian experience, by perpetually surmounting the contrasting relation of thesis and antithesis within the trinity of feeling constituting all religious experience. For if the over-world of the Christian faith is composed of that God from whom, through whom, and toward whom are all things, (so Paul in an important passage, summarizes his conception of the Christian religion in its relation to the rest of the history of religion) then obviously the subjective trinity of the feelings

[29] See Georg Wobbermin: *Das Wesen und die Wahrheit des Christentums, Systematische Theologie*, Vol. III.—Translator's note.

of dependence, security, and yearning find their objective correspondence in the trinitarian determination of the over-world,
that is, of the divinity itself. From God, through God, toward God are all things: concretely stated, this is the conviction
that the almighty creator and lord of all vitally permeates the
world and history with his self-revelation, and thereby is the
original source and the ultimate goal of all ethical, spiritual,
personal life. In spite of the deviations and confusions through
which the attempts to arrive at a conceptual formulation of this
conviction have passed in the history of the doctrine of the
trinity, this doctrine is in itself the closer determination of all
religious experience as such, and it also grows immediately out
of the basic religious experience of the Christian type.

As we have already said, a more detailed treatment of this
problem belongs elsewhere. Our next task is to complete our
survey of the history of religious life, (which we have constantly kept in mind in determining the nature of religion),
by trying to give a logical classification of the *historical forms
of religion.*

CHAPTER VII

THE NATURE OF RELIGION AND THE MULTIPLICITY OF RELIGIONS

I

The questions now arise: Is the religio-psychological method of investigation applicable to the problem of classifying religions? Can we use it to bring nearer the solution, which is so much needed, of this complicated problem?

We can not expect much help from Schleiermacher in dealing with this problem. In a general discussion of it, we cannot start with him, but must rather begin with those factors which we have called—the recasting and the supplementation of his theory. For it is just in this respect that the theory of the feeling of absolute dependence shows its impracticality. Schleiermacher himself has said [1] that since the feeling of absolute dependence taken by itself and in the strict sense of his theory is very simple, its principle offers no basis for variety. Such a basis, he continues, can only be deduced from the fact that this feeling must first be fused with a perceptible excitement of self-consciousness before any one of its phases can be completed.

But inasmuch as he at once adds the remark that such perceptible excitements are to be regarded as infinitely manifold, he himself thereby nullifies the usefulness of this basis of distinction.

Therefore, if we are to find an actually usable and fitting basis of distinction, we must begin with Schleiermacher's theory of religion as we have recast and supplemented it to make it accord with the actual facts. But we must state in advance that, in discussing this problem in accordance with the general principles of the religio-psychological method, we must try to harmonize the history of religion with our analysis of

[1] *Der Christliche Glaube,* etc., 2nd ed., paragraph 5, section 3.

184

subjective religious experience. To the extent to which we succeed in this the chief factors in the development of our theory of religion will necessarily correspond with those of its actual historical development. In making this assumption we concur, on the basis of the religio-psychological method, with the kernel of truth in Hegel's philosophy of history.

However we are now interested in *finding a principle of classification*. To do this, let us give detailed consideration to the changes we had to make in Schleiermacher's theory. We recast his theory by making the relationship of man to an over-world in which he believes the center of our determination of the nature of religion. Making this relationship the center gives us two points of view which are important in determining a principle of classification: the point of view of revelation and that of the value or the goal of salvation; concretely stated, the idea of revelation and the idea of salvation.

To some extent and in some form all religions and all religious leaders appeal to revelation. That is an historical fact, which has not always been as sufficiently recognized by Christian theologians as it should be. For there is no religion which does not appeal either to an earlier or to a present revelation, or finally, to both forms of revelation at once. Moreover, all religions promise to their adherents some kind of salvation; and all religious leaders either intuit by faith some kind of salvation or hope to attain the goal of salvation. This is the dual fact presented by history. Now a religio-psychological investigation finds that this historical phenomenon is grounded in the nature of religion itself. Being rooted in the basic religious experience, it refers us back to this experience. When the nature of religion consists of the relationship of man to an over-world, the *idea of revelation* and the *idea of salvation* will necessarily follow. These ideas merely bring the two possible phases of this relationship to expression. Somehow the over-world makes itself known to man; it creates an awareness of itself, it reveals itself. Without such a revelation the objective justification of religion's own possibility would be lacking. The religious relationship (in the sense of religious conviction, since the problem of truth is not yet being discussed) would not be objectively possible. Man turns to the over-world on the basis of revelation. He yearns for it, and desires from it what his natural life cannot give him, and he finally seeks, through devotion to it, the satisfaction of the deepest needs of his life. And without a desire for salvation, the subjective justification of religion's possibility would be lacking. As religiosity, religion would become subjectively impossible.

Departing from our recasting of Schleiermacher's theory of religion, which we found to be necessary, we therefore reach the ideas of revelation and salvation as criteria for the principle of classification. Now what additional criteria can we derive from our supplementation of Schleiermacher's theory? We refer to the supplementation of the feeling of dependence by the feelings of security and of ardent yearning. *Since these two feelings presuppose the feeling of dependence, and since they are both based upon it, the reciprocal relationship between them must be made the decisive factor.* As we have seen, this reciprocal relationship produces the *striving for salvation* and the *consciousness of responsibility.* And since the consciousness of responsibility also implies the ethical tendency involved in the associations of men with each other, we may speak of two basic tendencies of religious life. It is appropriate to call these the *mystical* and the *ethical* tendency. The varying relations of these two to each other are those of reciprocal superordination and sub-ordination. Thus the mystical can sometimes almost completely repress the ethical tendency. And conversely the ethical can restrict and almost completely repress the mystical tendency.

In their inner relationship these two pairs of criteria constitute a standard which makes possible a satisfactory classification of religions. Using this standard we reach two dual divisions. The dual criterion of the ideas of revelation and of salvation must first be applied because this criterion originates in the basic religious experience itself. And on the basis of this experience, the ideas of revelation and salvation may be identified, or they may be split-up and divided. *Thus plural and single religions must be distinguished.* In popular terminology this contrast is expressed by the terms polytheism and monotheism. But both of these terms are inexact. Plural religions are not all "polytheistic" in the usual sense of that word, nor are all single religions rightly named monotheistic. The inadequacy of this terminology is obviously closely related to the above-mentioned unfitness of the conception of God to determine the nature of religion.   Yet it should be expressly emphasized that the intention behind the popular terminology is completely justified.   Whether the religious life achieves unity or not does make the greatest difference to its structure. The objection recently made to this conception, and which was formulated especially strongly by Wilh. Wundt, is entirely untenable. His thesis that this distinction is as good as mean- ingless for the religious consciousness and becomes of con- sequence only when philosophical reflection has begun, he did not get from religion itself but, on the contrary, he derived it from a previously accepted philosophical presupposition and then applied it to religion.[2]

Again we can appeal to Schleiermacher, perhaps not to the formulation which he himself gave, but certainly to his suf- ficiently apparent deeper insight, which still shines through and stands in contrast to that formulation. He demanded a dual division of all religions: first, according to differences of type within the same stages of development, and secondly, according to differences of degree or stages of development.[3] Of course this demand is in itself well justified.   The only objection is that Schleiermacher places both principles of division along- side of each other as equally important, whereas the former is actually decisive.   His neglecting this fact avenges itself on Schleiermacher by forcing him to violate his own principle, and just at the very place that is most important for his whole point of view. For he violates his principle when he con- cludes that Christianity is superior to other types of religion belonging to the same line of evolution, Judaism and Islam. (See Paragraph 8, part 4.)   If Judaism, Christianity, and Islam actually belong to the same line of evolution of the religious life, then no one of these religions can be essentially

[2] Wilh. Wundt: *Mythus und Religion* (Völkerpsychologie II), part 3, pp. 742 ff.   English translation by E. L. Schaub.

[3] *Der Christliche Glaube,* 2nd ed., paragraph 7: "Some of the various definitely marked off religious groups occurring in history represent different stages of development and some represent different types of religion."

superior to the other two. Our chief interest, then, is Schleiermacher's principle of gradation. As early as the *Reden über
die Religion* he advocates a triple division. But the fact is—
and this is the peculiar circumstance to which we have already
referred—that in this triple division, the deepest insight which
Schleiermacher won does not get full recognition. Yet the
guiding principle which he stated at the beginning of his discussion lets this insight stand out much more clearly. For
he says that those forms of piety in which all pious states of
feeling express the dependence of all finite beings upon *one*
highest and infinite being, represent the highest stage, and
that all other stages are related to these as lower forms from
which men are destined to pass on to the higher. However,
logically this principle would not lead to a triple but to a
dual division. And this judgment is based upon the clearest
possible realization that the unity or non-unity of the religious
consciousness is the deciding characteristic. Plural religions
and single religions : that is the inclusive classification which
we must employ.

Each of the two main classes must be subdivided on the
basis of the other dual criterion, that of the basic mystical and
ethical tendencies and their relation to each other. For plural
religions and single religions can both allow either the mystical
or the ethical tendency to become dominant. And here again
we can make use of an observation which Schleiermacher has
incorporated in his previously mentioned formulation. For
the differences in type in the highest stage of his triple division he distinguishes by the concepts teleological and æsthetic
piety. (See paragraph 9, part 1.) A profound meaning is
implied in this distinction. However, here again Schleiermacher fails to reach an unequivocal and self-consistent position. In characterizing the difference between these two types
of piety he sometimes employs the contrast between ethical
and natural, but at other times that between active and passive,
or self-active and quietistic. But when we free Schleiermacher's discussion from this confusion, we find that logically
the distinction between the mystical and the ethical basic
tendency of religious life is what he intended.

2

In proceeding now to characterize in greater detail the four groups of the forms of religion so as to accord with the dual division from which they have sprung, we shall use the generally accepted names as far as possible to avoid burdening the discussion with new terms.

But it must be kept in mind that we also intend to define these popular terms more exactly by employing the two criteria of the classification itself.

Within the class of plural religions we distinguish between *primitive religions* and *national religions* (Volksreligionen). In primitive religions the separate manifestations of the over-world or their representations alone are accepted, without their being brought into unity. And for the most part, if not entirely, these manifestations belong to the realm of natural events. Correspondingly the salvation which is hoped for by the worshipers, consists of special benefits which are desired and which are related either to the natural life or to some extension of it. Hence the ethical tendency of the religious life remains quite stunted in primitive religion. The mystical tendency, however, is quite emphatically expressed; but only in the form of a mystical-*magical* religiosity, that is to say, in the form of a mysticism of a magical nature, a mysticism culminating in and reverting to magic. Accordingly, primitive religion is always in the most intimate relationship to magic. Often religion and magic are completely interwoven. Still we can speak of a *mystical*-magical religiosity in the sense that magic here is itself that primitive magic which proceeds from the idea of mana, that is, from the idea of a mysterious sacred source or realm of power. And the mystical tendency operates with and expresses itself in such magic.

In the national religions the revelation of the over-world is no longer found, or at least not exclusively, in isolated facts or events of nature, but along with—or rather predominantly in—the regulations of national life. The moral ideas and legal institutions of national life are thought to be revelations of the over-world. Accordingly the idea of salvation is essentially determined by reference to such social groups as the family, the clan, the village, the city, and the nation. In this stage of religious development the fortune and welfare of such social groups constitute the central and dominant point of the hopes for and of the conceptions of salvation. Hence the ethical tendency, of which there is only the weakest beginnings in primitive religion, comes more to the front here. On the other hand, the mystical tendency, at least in the form of the mystical-magical religiosity of primitive religion is comparatively weakened. However, magic *per se* also retains a very important sphere of activity within the bounds of national religion. But instead of being connected with the original mana idea it is merely an external magic, consisting of stereotyped external practices. Over against this external magic the cultivation of the mystical or the mystical-magical tendency withdraws into special cult-associations, the so-called mystery cults, which are a continuation and a reorganization of the secret societies of primitive peoples.

Proceeding, now, from the plural religions to the single religions, let us first mention the *legalistic religions,* since they are closely related to the national religions. The extension of revelation to ever wider spheres results in the taking of a unified and inclusive code of laws to be the decisive revelation, and salvation is then considered to consist in the possession of this highest code. Obedience to this law guarantees the protection and the aid of the one highest divinity, and as a natural result the other gods are relegated to the background until they finally entirely disappear. In legalistic religions the ethical tendency reaches its most powerful development; but the mystical tendency remains stunted. Judaism and Islam, as well as original Confucianism, are legalistic religions. And to the extent that its dualism—and this is at least the ideal of the theory—is not thought of as ultimate, but is subordinated to the final goal of the victorious reign of the good God Ahura-Mazda, Parseeism is also of this type. And it should also be mentioned that, within the historical development of Christianity, some forms of Roman Catholicism show distinct traces of legalistic religion, and also that so-called deism takes essentially this form.

In contrast to the legalistic religions there are the *con-*

templative religions of salvation. In them, an extensive expansion accompanies an intensive enhancement and a subjective deepening of the idea of revelation. Revelation consists in the fact that the over-world directly reveals itself to man. And salvation is regarded as the elevation of the human soul to the realm of the over-world. The lifting of the soul out of the finite-natural sphere of existence, out of all of its misery and futility and the leading of it to a realm of a higher order, is the goal and purpose of this type of religion. Here, then, the mystical tendency of religious life is strongly developed, but in such a way that the ethical tendency is thereby in danger of being suppressed or cramped in its operation.

To this class of the contemplative religions of salvation belongs, first of all, Buddhism. Insofar as Buddhism is to be treated as a religion at all (see above, pp. 126 f.), it must be taken as a typical example of the contemplative religions of salvation. Further, pantheism also belongs here and thirdly, mysticism, that is, taking these terms to mean only the religious phenomena appearing in history under these names. However, this necessary reservation also proves that in these two cases we find ourselves upon slightly different ground than heretofore. For pantheism and mysticism do not necessarily and always possess a religious character. There is a purely philosophical and speculative pantheism, and there is also a mysticism which is not of a religious nature and which has no direct connection with religion. Along with this situation there is another which must also be noted here. Religious pantheism and religious mysticism, with which we are alone concerned here, appear in the history of religion not as independent movements, but only as off-shoots which grow from the root or trunk of other religions. Disregarding Christianity for the present, the source religions are not only national religions but also legalistic religions. However, the types of religious pantheism and religious mysticism which have developed within the sphere of these two sources must be regarded as contemplative religions of salvation, because of their own general form.

Thus along with Buddhism we regard pantheism and mysticism as contemplative religions of salvation. Does Christianity also belong to this class? For the very fact that we were compelled to say of certain of its special historical degenerated forms, that they were closely related to the legalistic religions, proves that Christianity as a whole and in its essence is not a legalistic religion. Since we cannot even regard these degenerate forms unreservedly as legalistic religions, it follows *a fortiori* that we cannot evaluate Christianity itself and in its pure form as a legalistic religion. Must it then be classified as a religion of salvation, or is it perhaps equi-distant from the religions of salvation and the legalistic religions, harmonizing those factors which upset the balance toward the one type or the other? Here these questions can only be asked, but not yet answered. For an agreement concerning the nature of Christianity is first necessary in order to provide a basis for an answer.

3

However, the results so far attained now compel us to clarify further the problems of pantheism and of mysticism. We have placed pantheism and mysticism alongside of Buddhism as special forms of the contemplative religions of salvation, because both of them share with Buddhism those characteristics which the religio-psychological investigation indicated were the dominant motives for the establishment of the class of contemplative religions of salvation. Now there are two respects in which this conclusion signifies a peculiar point of view. *First of all mysticism, as a special form of religion, is distinguished from the mystical tendency inherent in all religion. And secondly, pantheism and mysticism are not to be identified, but are to be regarded as two distinct forms of contemplative religions of salvation.* Precisely this twofold distinction makes it possible to bring clarity into some complex problems that have heretofore defied all attempts at solution.

Mysticism stands in the center of this problem-complex. Recently various scholars have realized that the confusion which still exists in regard to the problem of mysticism can only be removed by differentiating the various phenomena included under the name of mysticism, and by establishing such unequivocal conceptions as this differentiation would make possible. Nathan Söderblom, Reinhold Seeberg and Theophil Steinmann must be mentioned in this connection. Söderblom distinguishes as a matter of principle between the mysticism of personality and the mysticism of infinity.[4] This distinction he regards as the most important of the entire higher science of religion as such.[5] Seeberg distinguishes between a voluntaristic mysticism, the awareness of what determines us from within—a rationally unfathomable spiritual life-energy, and a speculative and contemplative mysticism, a super-rational yet intellectual comprehension of the transcendent.[6] The voluntaristic mystical experience consists of a rationally unproven, but yet inwardly necessary, subjection of the will to the spiritual life-energy; but in the other type mystical experience is an intuitive knowledge of the absolute ground of the universe. Finally Steinmann recommends a distinction between mysticism in the wider and mysticism in the narrower sense of the word.[7] For him mysticism in the wider sense means those forms of fellowship with God which are historically related to primitive ecstatic experiences, regardless of whether they are of a theistic or of a pantheistic type. But mysticism in the narrower sense is for Steinmann the cultivation of fellowship with the divinity pantheistically conceived. However, he also makes the reservation that perhaps also experiences of the divinity theistically conceived might be termed mystical in the narrower sense.

The three distinctions made by these scholars are in my opinion extraordinarily valuable and helpful. Each of them refers to factors which are justified by the facts and which can, therefore, claim consideration. In line with what was said above we had best begin our own discussion with *the question of the relation of mysticism to pantheism.* Is all mysticism pantheistic? Albrecht Ritschl affirmed this question with em-

[4] Nathan Söderblom: *Religionsproblemet inom Katolicism och Protestantism,* 2 vols., Stockholm, 1910.

[5] According to a personal statement of Söderblom to Wilh. Fresenius. Comp. the very informative work of the latter: *Mystik und geschichtliche Religion,* Göttingen, 1912.

[6] Reinhold Seeberg: *Die Lehre Luthers* (*Lehrbuch der Dogmengeschichte,* Vol. IV, Part I), pp. 310 f.

[7] *Die Religion in Geschichte und Gegenwart,* 1st ed., Vol. IV, pp. 594 ff.; 2nd ed., Vol. IV, pp. 360 ff.

phatic certainty and built his whole conception of mysticism upon this affirmative answer. He ascribes the pantheistic character of mysticism to the influence of neo-Platonism, as it was transmitted through the writings of the Pseudo-Dionysius, the Areopagite. Hence Ritschl thinks that the areopagite's idea of God is the decisive characteristic for mysticism. This makes the problem of mysticism purely a matter of its historical statement. But it is just this purely and exclusively historical statement which fails to do justice to the problem of mysticism. Considering the part which mysticism plays throughout the whole history of religion, this purely historical statement of the problem must certainly be regarded as inadequate. Moreover Ritschl fails completely to place the problem of mysticism into the frame-work of the general science of religion. He treats it as being merely a matter of church and doctrinal history. But in reality the problem which it presents is much more inclusive. Of course it is true that the conception of mysticism belongs primarily to church history and is closely correlated with the idea of scholasticism. Scholasticism and Roman Catholic mysticism condition and mutually supplement each other. Denifle's studies of Eckhart have proven this beyond dispute. No less a man than Harnack, the great master of Protestant church history, agrees with the Roman Catholic theologians on this point and accepts Denifle's argument as "authentic proof." [8]

However, this does not dispose of the matter. For analogies to the phenomenon of mysticism, as revealed in the history of the Christian Church, present themselves to the student of religion so frequently and so insistently that he cannot let them pass unnoticed.

When we began considering the problem of mysticism we purposely first restricted ourselves to Christian mysticism in the interest of methodical clarity. But in the course of our discussion the necessity for a more penetrating religio-historical comparison has already arisen at one point. In the history of Hindu religion we found in the mysticism of the *Upanishads* an unmistakable analogy to the mysticism of the Middle Ages; yes,

[8] *Archiv für Literatur—und Kirchengeschichte*, Vol. II, 1886, pp. 417 ff. Ad. v. Harnack: *Lehrbuch der Dogmengeschichte*, Vol. III, pp. 376 f.

an analogy even to the most central and essential teaching of the foremost exponent of Medieval mysticism: Eckhart. The Ātman of the *Upanishads* corresponds exactly to the "spark" in the great German mystic's theory of the soul. (See above, pp. 114 ff.)

And so the question arises: how are mysticism and pantheism related to each other in the history of Hindu religion? Is that mysticism so intimately connected with pantheism that it must be regarded as pantheistic in its essential nature? If that were true then it would have to be said of Christian mysticism that it is only the influence of the genuinely Christian conception of God which prevents its being completely pantheistic. However, the actual facts do not warrant this conclusion. To be sure they show what must be especially emphasized, namely, that mysticism contains a strong leaning toward pantheism, and accordingly that the pantheistic form of mysticism is preponderant. But still this pantheistic form is not necessary and insurmountable for mysticism. The *tat twam asi* (that art thou) formula, which dominates the thought of the *Upanishads,* is undoubtedly to be taken in the pantheistic sense.

"If men think that by a knowledge of Brahma they will become everything, what then did that Brahma know from whence all this sprang? Verily in the beginning this was Brahma, that Brahma knew (its) Self only, saying 'I am Brahma.' From it all this sprang. Thus, whatever Deva was awakened (so as to know Brahma), he indeed became that (Brahma); and the same with Rishis [9] and men. The Rishi Vamadeva saw and understood it, singing: 'I was Manu (moon), I was the sun.' (*Rig-Veda* 4, 26, 1.) Therefore, now also he who thus knows that he is Brahma, becomes all this, and even the Devas cannot prevent it, for he himself is their Self." [10]

In his great discourse on sleep and death Yâjñavalkya says: "But as to the man who does not desire, who, not desiring, is freed from desires, is satisfied in his desires, or desires the Self

[9] The sages and bards of antiquity.
[10] *Brihad-Āranyaka Upanishad,* I, 4, 9 f. Compare Paul Deussen: *Sechzig Upanishads des Veda,* 2nd ed., 1905, p. 395. Herm. Oldenberg: *Die Lehre der Upanishaden und die Anfänge des Buddhismus,* 1915, p. 131.

only, his vital spirits do not depart elsewhere. Being Brahma, he goes to Brahma." [11]

But this pantheistic view is still not carried through consistently. Moreover, it contains precisely the idea, which is fundamental for the mysticism of the *Upanishads,* of a tendency which leads away from or beyond pantheism. For if the highest principle of the world-view and the standard of life is designated as Ātman (self, I), then strictly speaking, *i.e.*, without contradiction, strict pantheism is impossible. [12] Thus the logic of the conception of Ātman frequently breaks through the pantheistic point of view. In the discourse of Yâjñavalkya the great Brahmin, shortly after the passage just quoted, Ātman is called "the subduer of all, the Ruler of all, the sovereign Lord of all." [13] And a more recent Upanishad concludes a discussion of the Ātman with the words: [14]

"For he makes him, whom he wishes to lead up from these worlds, do a good deed; and he makes him, whom he wishes to lead down from these worlds, do a bad deed. And he is the guardian of the world, he is the Lord of the universe." And the important doctrinal discourse of Cândilya, who, next to Yâjñavalkya, is the most important of the Upanishad sages, should be remembered as being fundamental for the identification of Ātman with Brahma. Its summarizing and concluding sentence sounds more theistic than pantheistic: "He from whom all works, all desires, all sweet odours and tastes proceed, who embraces all this, who never speaks and is never surprised, he, myself within the heart, is that Brahma. When I shall have departed from hence, I shall obtain him." [15] This explains why there is a masculine form of the conception of Brahmā, parallel to the neuter form (Brahmă), which is used in an entirely anthropomorphic manner. For example, the previously quoted *Kaushītaki Upanishad* contains in its beginning sections the so-called doctrine of the couch. [16] After enumerating the various stages through which the departed souls must pass in order to

[11] *Brihad-Āranyaka Upanishad,* IV, 4, 6. Comp. Deussen, *op. cit.,* p. 477.
[12] Oldenberg quite rightly remarks that, properly speaking, the Ātman is not a person but the principle of personality. *Op. cit.,* p. 101.
[13] *Brihad-Āranyaka Upanishad,* IV, 4, 22. Comp. Deussen, *op. cit.,* p. 479.
[14] *Kaushītaki-Upanishad,* III, 8. Comp. P. Deussen, *op. cit.,* p. 50 f.
[15] *Chāndogya Upanishad,* III, 14, 4. Comp. P. Deussen, *op. cit.,* p. 110.
[16] Comp. P. Deussen, *op. cit.,* pp. 23 ff.

attain Brahma it is stated: Finally it comes to the couch upon which Brahma is seated. "And he who knows this mounts it first with one foot only. Brahma says to him: 'Who art thou?' and he will answer: 'Thou art the Self of all living things. Thou art the Self. What thou art, that am I.' "

However, still more important than this definitely mythologizing description of the Brahma-world is another form of Upanishad mysticism. We see it most clearly in the *Svetâsvatara Upanishad.*[17] Here mysticism involves an outspoken monotheistic tendency. Of course the reasoning is confused and varies in its details. Nevertheless, on the whole the expression of monotheistic faith is strongly and unmistakably predominant.

This Upanishad begins with the question of the original basis and underlying power of all existence. The answer, which is given in the name of the sages who practice meditation and contemplation, is as follows:

> "God's autonomy is hidden by his own Gunas;[18]
> He it is who precedes all powers to be named,
> Along with time and the soul, as the One."

This Upanishad further appeals to the famous hymn of the *Rig-Veda*[19] dedicated to the "unknown God," whose ten verses conclude uniformly with the question: "What God shall we adore with our oblation?"[20]

As if in answer to this question it is then stated in the following verses of the Upanishad:

[17] Comp. Paul Deussen, *op. cit.,* pp. 291 ff.

[18] The Guṇas are the individual elements of a whole, its constituents. The idea plays an important rôle—in a different interpretation—in the Sāṃkya philosophy. Comp. Richard Garbe: *Die Sāṃkya-Philosophie. Eine Darstellung des indischen Rationalismus,* Leipsic, 1894, pp. 209 ff.

[19] *Rig-Veda,* X, 121. Comp. Paul Deussen: *Allgemeine Geschichte der Philosophie,* etc., Vol. I, part 1, pp. 128 ff. Alfred Hillebrandt: *Lieder des Rigveda,* p. 132. Hillebrandt gives the hymn the title: "To the Unknown God," which quite correctly refers to its analogy with the narrative in Acts 17.

[20] The Upanishad quotes the second half of the third verse. The whole verse reads: "Who by his grandeur hath become sole ruler of all the moving world that breathes and slumbers; He who is Lord of men and Lord of cattle. What God shall we adore with our oblation?"

"Yea, this all-creating God of noble mind
Is ever to be found in the hearts of creatures.
Only they who are made ready in heart and mind
        and spirit—
Immortal shall they be who thus do know him."

"His form is not to be perceived,
No man has seen him with his eyes,
Him, who dwells in hearts, with heart and mind—
Immortal shall they be who thus do know him."

This "sovereign ruler" and "lord of all" is then invoked in other verses of this Upanishad as the powerful and awful God Rudra, of ancient Vedic belief, and then by the name of Shiva who is so prominent in later Hinduism.

The fundamental idea, which is predominant over all the diverse forms of thought, is summarized in the following verse in the last section:

"In Him, whom the God Brahma created at the
        beginning,
And delivered also the Vedas to Him,
The God, who by grace maketh himself known,
In Him, seeking salvation, do I take refuge."

We have here, then, a pre-Christian Hindu mysticism which, in spite of intimate acquaintance with pantheistic speculation, is based upon the conviction that its goal—the unio mystica—can only be attained by a belief in a personal God. Such reflections as to the historical conditions of the origin of this conviction, as are advanced by Oldenberg,[21] valuable and justifiable though they are, change the facts just as little as Deussen's condemnatory opinion,[22] which is based primarily upon a previously adopted metaphysical speculation. The main problem implicit in the facts *per se* can be grasped only by the religio-psychological method. When Deussen excludes religious experience as the criterion of judgment for his position, he gets involved in

---

[21] Herm. Oldenberg: *Die Lehre der Upanishaden und die Anfänge des Buddhismus*, pp. 273 ff.

[22] Paul Deussen: *Sechzig Upanishads des Veda*, 2nd ed., pp. 288 ff.

an argument which can not even avoid the appearance of violence and prejudice. For when he expressly states that the author of the Upanishad otherwise appears as a splendid and productive thinker, then Deussen should not be satisfied in calling this preference for the theistic conception of the divine "difficult to understand," and he should not attribute it to personal bias or to an unworthy accommodation to the dominant tendencies of the time. In any case this "unworthy accommodation" would only apply to such forms of thought of the author's system of ideas as are taken from popular religion. However, the distinctive religious conviction itself is not only independent of each one of these forms of thought, as the change of forms proves, but it is also independent of them when they are taken as a whole. For in the logical expression of his conviction, the author is able entirely to disregard them and intentionally to transcend them.

Hence Deussen's argument fails completely. It only remains for us to interpret the facts in question in the light of the religious motives of the author. His religious experience must have compelled him thoroughly to strip the speculative mysticism, which was cultivated in his surroundings, of its pantheistic element, and to bring it into harmony with a faith in God of a basically personalistic nature.

This opens up to us another vista, that is of the greatest importance in a religio-historical, as well as in a religio-psychological sense. The *Svetasvatara Upanishad* is closely related to the *Saṃkya* and to the *Yoga* philosophy, as is shown, not only by its manner of thought, but also by its terminology. And this relationship then extends beyond the *Saṃkya* and *Yoga* systems to the *Bhagavad-Gita*. The significance of this "Song of the Adorable" for the religious life of India since about the time of Jesus, can hardly be overestimated. No matter what one may think of the actual value of the *Bhagavad-Gita,* no matter how sceptical one may be of the opinion of Wilhelm von Humboldt, who was so carried away in his first enthusiasm that he declared that this song was the most profound and lofty thing which the world has seen, at any rate the extraordinary influence of the *Bhagavad-Gita* upon the religious life of India throughout the whole period of the last two thousand years is beyond doubt. Moritz Winternitz, the historian of Hindu literature who is universally recognized because of his strict objectivity, declares that there is hardly any book in India which is more widely read and more highly regarded than the *Bhagavad-Gita*. He writes: "It is the sacred book of the Bhagavatas, one of the Vishnuite sects, but it is also a devotional and prayer book for every Hindu, no matter what his sect. There are still many educated Hindus today who know the entire poem by heart. A countless number of manuscripts of it have been preserved. And since it was first printed in Calcutta in the year 1809, hardly a year has passed in which a new printing of the work has not appeared in India. The translations into modern Indian dialects are also numerous.[23] And from the religio-psychological point of view it is also especially noteworthy that the *Bhagavad-Gita* even today enjoys the greatest popularity in the most varied schools, so that "the most orthodox Brahmin is just as much edified by it as the adherents of the Brahma Samaj [24] or the theosophist who is a follower of Annie Besant." (Winternitz, p. 376.)

From the point of view of the history of literature the *Bhagavad-Gita* is a fragment of the great epic, the *Mahabharata*. It is added to the sixth book at the beginning of the account of the great decisive battle between the Kurus and the Pandavas. Arjuna, the most renowned archer of the Pandavas, is alarmed to see so many of his relatives, teachers, and friends on the opposite side, and he is uncertain whether it would not be better to be conquered rather than to conquer by killing them. But Krishna, appearing in human form as the charioteer in the chariot of Arjuna, instructs him in his duty as a warrior, that is, as a member of the Kshatriya caste. This didactic discourse of Krishna, who is also an incarnation of Vishnu, as it proceeds, considers the deepest and highest questions of a worldview and philosophy of life, the nature of deity and the relationship between deity and humanity. Krishna first reveals

[23] Moritz Winternitz: *Geschichte der Indischen Literatur,* Vol. I, Leipsic, 1909, pp. 365 ff. For the view of von Humboldt above see publications of Fr. v. Gentz, 1840, Vol. V, p. 29.

[24] The Brahma-Samāj was founded in the year 1830 by the Brahmin Rām Mohan Rai as a Hinduistic reform sect with a Christian coloring. It split into three parties. Today Rabindranath Tagore is very sympathetic with it.

himself to Arjuna as the one God, the Lord of all worlds, and finally in his super-mundane, omnipresent, flaming form.

In its religious character, as we have already stated, the *Bhagavad-Gita* is closely related to the *Svetasvatara Upanishad*. The concluding verse of the latter reads: "To the high-minded man, who has an absolute reliance (or love) (bhakti) toward God, and as toward God, so also toward the teacher, the meanings declared in this Upanishad are self-explanatory."

Oldenberg quite rightly remarks concerning this verse [25] that one still feels here the pedantic atmosphere of the Vedas, that love to God being a school lesson which is carried out according to the directions of an equally beloved teacher, but that even so it is a significant fact that in these words we see bhakti (love) enter upon its great career. The "great career" of bhakti to which the great Indologist here refers is primarily due to the influence of the *Bhagavad-Gita*. For the "Divine Song" of bhakti is precisely an ardent sacrificial love toward God.

The *Bhagavad-Gita* teaches that two paths lead to salvation: the way of knowledge reached by contemplation, and the way of dutiful action determined only by moral obligation. But both ways attain constancy and certainty only through wholehearted love toward God. For true knowledge of God first originates in the love toward God. And on the other hand, dutiful action also first attains its chief value by means of such love toward God. "No man who loves me is lost," says Krishna. And again: "Of all Yogis, I respect him as the most devout who hath faith in me, and who serveth me with his self stayed on me."

Accordingly the commentators treat the closing verse of the 11th discourse as the "key verse":

"He cometh unto me whose works are done for me; who esteemeth me supreme; who is my servant only; who is free from attachment, and who liveth amongst all men without hatred."

Yet the requirement of such love to God is grounded in the love of God to men:

[25] Hermann Oldenberg: *Die Lehre der Upanishaden und die Anfänge des Buddhismus,* p. 281.

"I am alike to all beings; to me none is hateful, and to me none is dear; but those who worship me devoutly dwell in me and I in them."

In these words we have the closest parallel in the *Bhagavad-Gita* to the New Testament, especially to the Johannine literature. (John XIV, 20.) Due to this and similar sayings, it is not surprising it has been assumed that the *Bhagavad-Gita* has been influenced by the New Testament and shows a literary dependence upon it. Hence it has been stated that this much revered monument of the ancient Hindu spirit is indebted "for the most part to Christian sources for its purest and most widely praised teachings." [26]

In the opinion of the most unprejudiced and expert modern Indologists, this position is absolutely untenable. Richard Garbe, especially, deserves the credit for having clarified the historical relationship of the *Bhagavad-Gita* to early Christianity by considering all of the subsidiary problems in question. In his discriminating and comprehensive investigation he reaches the conclusion that the seemingly Christian coloring of the *Gita* must be regarded as a genuine expression of Hindu piety. The religious meaning of bhakti was already a quite current conception in India around 400 B.C., and the possibility of a Christian influence upon the latest redaction of the *Bhagavad-Gita* is practically excluded.[27] *This brings us to the most important problem of the Bhagavad-Gita.*

For this *monotheistic personalistic mysticism* which we have been discussing does not dominate the *Bhagavad-Gita* exclusively. On the contrary, we find alongside of it the pantheistic element of the Brahma-Ātman doctrine of the *Upanishads*. And the most striking fact is that no effort whatever is made to harmonize these two trains of thought with each other. This contradiction runs throughout the whole poem. As Winternitz

[26] F. Lorinser in the introduction to his translation (Breslau, 1869), comp. Mor. Winternitz, *op. cit.*, p. 370.

[27] The final redaction of the transmitted text must be attributed to the second, or at the latest, to the third century A.D. Comp. Richard Garbe in the introduction to his translation (*Die Bhagavadgita, aus dem Sanskrit übersetzt. Mit einer Einleitung über ihre ursprüngliche Gestalt, ihre Lehren und ihr Alter*, Leipsic, 1905), pp. 58 ff.; Moritz Winternitz, *op. cit.*, p. 374.

correctly states, it must impress every reader who is not a believing Hindu or a zealous theosophist.

How is this fact to be interpreted? From the point of
view of literary criticism it would be natural to explain it as
a welding together of two different elements. It could also
be explained either by assuming a pantheistic basis with a
theistic revision, or conversely, by assuming a theistic basis
with pantheistic accretions. The first of these assumptions was
formerly often advocated, especially emphatically by Adolf
Holtzmann. The *Bhagavad-Gita* was originally a purely pantheistic poem and it was later revised by the devotees of
Vishnu-Krishna to accord with theism.

In recent times, however, this opinion has been more and
more abandoned because it does not explain the completely
predominant theistic attitude and intention of the *Bhagavad-
Gita*. Richard Garbe has made much more plausible the opposite assumption that the *Bhagavad-Gita* was originally a
purely theistic. poem and then was revised to accord with
pantheism. Garbe has even attempted to reconstruct the original form of the poem by subtracting the additions of the
brahmanistic pantheistic revision. His reconstruction has
been accepted by such prominent Indologists as George Grier-
son and Moritz Winternitz.[28]

This is a question on which we cannot venture an opinion
of our own. But it must be stated that, from the religio-
psychological point of view, even this reconstruction does not
solve the problem of the *Bhavagad-Gita*. *Indeed, the problem
even becomes more acute as a result of Garbe's critical literary
differentiation. For the tremendous religio-historical influence, which the Bhagavad-Gita has had for nearly two thousand
years and still has today, is due to its present form. This fact
must be religio-psychologically explained.* And for this purpose Garbe's investigations do make a significant contribution.

First of all it should be noted that the Tübingen Indologist,
on the basis of his comprehensive research, reaches the conclusion that the *Bhagavad-Gita* presents a remarkable mixture
of philosophical thought and unadulterated and deeply religious

---

[28] See p. 285, note 2, in the book by Winternitz cited above.

belief in God.[29]   The philosophical thought involved is naturally
conditioned by the classic tradition of Hindu philosophy.   It is
precisely the classic philosophy of Brahmanism.   To be sure
this dogmatic-scholastic philosophy contains a strong religious
element.   This complicates the problem.   But it is still of fundamental importance to realize that two components of the
Bhagavad-Gita must be differentiated: the scholastic thought of
a particular scholastic tradition, on the one hand, and the
pure and deeply religious belief in God on the other hand.
The main defect in the position of scholars such as Paul Deussen and Leopold von Schröder is that they have not realized
this.   Moreover, this same defect is present in the most exaggerated form in all schools of modern theosophy.   In the last
analysis theosophy is based upon the fact that these two component parts are confused at the very beginning, instead of
being first kept separate, so that they might then be brought
into the proper relationship to each other.   This is most evident in the theosophy of Madame Blavatsky and Mrs. Besant.
But it is equally true of Rudolf Steiner's anthroposophy.

Having established this much, the question next arises as
to where, in the development of Hindu religion, the beginnings
of bhakti piety are to be found.   On this point we must first
reject two absolutely opposite extreme views.   The claim made
by members of the Brahma Samaj and also by some representatives of theosophy, that the bhakti religion has always existed
in India, cannot be given serious historical consideration at all.
But on the other hand, the historically observable development
of religious life in India completely refutes the supposition
that bhakti spontaneously appeared, like a flash and without
any cause, as something absolutely new.   Even the more cau-
tiously framed thesis of the American Indologist Hopkins, that
bhaki cannot be much older than the *Bhagavad-Gita* itself,[30] is
refuted by historical, and certainly by psychological probability.
Everywhere in the *Bhagavad-Gita* bhakti, as ardent loving devotion to God, is demanded as something taken for granted.
But, as Garbe correctly emphasizes, a new doctrine would have
been presented in an entirely different way.

[29] Richard Garbe: *Indien und das Christentum,* 1914, p. 230.
[30] E. Washburn Hopkins: *Religions of India,* p. 429.

At this point we also find another insight in Garbe's interpretation which is religio-psychologically very noteworthy. He points out that certain elementary beginnings and faint stirrings of bhakti can be traced back to ancient Vedic times. He finds these in those hymns of the *Rig-Veda* in which the gods are called father, brother, friend, etc., and in which the relationship to the gods reveals an attitude of child-like trust. He thinks that this original feeling of naïve attachment was then gradually elevated, under the influence of monotheistic tendencies, to bhakti, the sacrificial love toward God. In the light of religio-psychological method Garbe's conjecture has the highest possible degree of probability. And once it has been clarified and defined by religio-psychological elucidation, it might possibly be partly established historically. Without forcing the issue, the previously discussed *Svetasvatara Upanishad* may be regarded as a phase of this development, since its varied elements are just as understandable under such an interpretation. And we may even refer to the group of the older Upanishads. For in the reply of Maitreyī to Yâjñavalkya we find that the personalistic tendency of religion is retained along with a complete acceptance of the monistic tendency of the Brahman-Ātman doctrine. But reading between the lines, we see that Maitreyī objects to the scholasticism of the doctrine only because it fails to do justice to her religious feelings, while Yâjñavalkya disregards the demand of his religious consciousness and uses scholastic dialectic.

New light is also thrown upon the *Bhagavad-Gita* by these conjectures. We could regard the co-existence of its two views precisely as a synthesis of the positiosn of Yâjñavalkya and Maitreyī. The supposition then arises that many readers and devotees of the *Bhagavad-Gita* must have remained comparatively indifferent to the scholasticism of the Brahma doctrine, whereas they were easily able to bring its monistic element into harmony with its completely personalistically directed faith in God.

If this view of the *Bhagavad-Gita* is accepted, it solves the religio-historical puzzle which has been presented. But this view is also proven from another approach.

We rejected the view which attributes the bhakti-piety of

the *Bhagavad-Gita* to Christian influences, to the influence of early Christian writings. But the fact remains that it contains striking similarities, not only to the Christian belief in God in general, but also particularly to the sayings of the New Testament. Insofar Hopkins, who has especially called attention to the relation of the *Bhagavad-Gita* to the Gospel of John, is absolutely correct.[31] However, in this connection the following peculiar circumstance must be noted. Two of those sentences of the *Bhagavad-Gita* which, either directly or indirectly are unmistakably analogous to Johannine sayings, are regarded by the best students of the *Gita* as formulations of the strictly pantheistic Brahma doctrine. They are: 1. "Having known this, thou shalt not again fall into this delusion; for thou wilt see all things first in thyself and then in me." (IV, 35.) 2. "He who beholdeth me in all things, and beholdeth all things is me, I forsake not him, and he forsaketh not me." (VI, 30.) These sayings of the *Bhagavad-Gita* should be put with one which we have already quoted in another connection: "Those who worship me devoutly dwell in me and I in them." (IX, 29.) Here the analogy to John XIV, 20: "In that day ye shall know that I am in my Father, and ye in me and I in you," is quite indisputable. Hence an analogy to the first two quotations must also be acknowledged, at least indirectly. Yet it is clear, as Garbe says, that in them the well-known basic view of Brahmanism is expressed.[32]

Thus, according to the judgment of this Indologist, who is usually very cautious on parallels between the *Bhagavad-Gita* and the *New Testament,* there exists an inner relationship between statements of the pantheistic Brahma doctrine and a saying of the Gospel of John, which is of fundamental importance for the whole religious attitude of that Gospel.

Yet the Gospel of John is in no wise pantheistic. Whence the relationship then, be it real or only apparent? Now it might be explained by the fact that the idea of immanence in the Christian conception of God is strongly developed in the Gospel of John. For this idea of immanence is in turn also

---

[31] E. Washburn Hopkins: *India Old and New,* New York, 1901, pp. 148 ff.
[32] Richard Garbe: *Indien und das Christentum,* 1914, p. 248.

related to the monistic direction of the 4th Gospel's philosophy
of life. *But neither the idea of immanence nor the monistic
tendency in themselves necessarily lead to pantheism.* Both
may just as well be expressed, and in the end perhaps more
adequately, unifiedly, and consistently, by a purely theistic-
personalistic belief in God. The really distinguishing characteristic of pantheism is seen first in the conception of a divine
but impersonal world-order. But in contrast to the naïve an-
thropomorphism which frequently dominates the forms of
thought and even the thought-world of the monotheistic belief
in God, the idea of immanence and also the monistic tendency
may come to be regarded as characteristic features of the pantheistic conception of God and may be treated as such. Then
the conception of the divine world-order as impersonal retreats
into the background.

*That this religio-psychologically comprehensible process has
also been active in the history of the Bhagavad-Gita and has
concealed the gap between its two divergent components is,
then, the assumption which we think solves the religio-historical
problem of the Bhagavad-Gita. To be sure, this assumption
does not alter the fact that the Bhagavad-Gita is in itself dis-
united and inconsistent.* And objectively considered, this inner
disruption is undoubtedly a very important defect in this
highly praised document of pre-Christian Indian mysticism.
It also involves the continual possibility and danger of a return to the scholasticism of Brahmanistic speculation.

4

Reviewing the previous discussions we come to these conclusions. Pantheism, mysticism, and Johannine Christianity
all share the idea of immanence and the monistic tendency.
However, in pantheism the monistic tendency is dominant and
is directed toward the whole universe, whereas in mysticism the
idea of immanence is dominant and is directed toward the
spiritual life of man. But in the Gospel of John both elements
are harmonized with the Logos concept, as is shown even in
the first sentences of the prologue. And in all three the idea
of immanence serves as a basis for the endeavour to come

into the highest possible intimate contact with the over-world and to achieve the most direct fellowship with it.

Disregarding for the present Johannine Christianity, to which we referred merely for supplementary purposes, we are here concerned with the relationship between pantheism and mysticism. As we have seen, they are not completely and necessarily identical. *And it is just for this reason that mysticism is not necessarily pantheistic.* But in accordance with the insight we have already attained, the distinguishing characteristic of mysticism must be sought within the frame-work of the idea of immanence. As we have already pointed out, the interest of mysticism's idea of immanence is directed toward the spiritual life of man. To attain a direct relationship to the over-world is the goal of the mystic's quest. And since this quest stands alone as the completely dominant and central point of the entire attitude of consciousness and mode of life of the mystic, his aim is to attain such a relationship to the over-world as is free from all intermediaries. *The immediateness of the relationship is to be enhanced and transformed into mediatorlessness.* All intermediaries are to be abandoned and excluded.

In those passages in which its most characteristic mysticism is expressed, this fact is clearly apparent in the *Bhagavad-Gita.* Even though from a literary point of view the ethical ideal of the poem is that of a dutiful conduct free from all desires, within the confines of the traditional caste system, the peculiar and actual tendency of its mysticism aims at the greatest possible negation of the world, the complete renunciation of all worldly cares and activities.[33] Precisely because of this equivocation in the *Bhagavad-Gita,* it is quite obvious that its mysticism restricts the positive ethical activity at every point where mysticism itself has the floor. The true Yogi, who is praised by the *Bhagavad-Gita,* preserves his peace of mind not only amidst cold and heat, and joy and sorrow, but

[33] That the validity of the caste system is pre-supposed in the *Bhagavad-Gita* should not be overlooked in the evaluation of its demand of dutiful conduct. Its oft-mentioned similarity to the Kantian theory of duty must accordingly be strictly qualified.—Recently Max Weber has quite correctly elucidated this fact very emphatically: *Gesammelte Aufsätze zur Religionssoziologie;* Vol. II, *Hinduismus und Buddhismus,* 1921, pp. 191 ff.

also in honor and dishonor. He is the same not only to friend and to foe, to relative and to stranger, but also to the good and to the evil (6th song, verse 7 ff.). And Krishna praises that devotee who is not concerned about this world, who is insensible to pain, who is wise and indifferent, and who has renounced every enterprise (12th song, verse 16 ff.).

To reach the goal of life, the blessing of salvation, fellowship with the divinity, by the denial of all intermediaries, even by the conscious exclusion of all intermediaries, is the practical ideal of this mysticism. Along with this practical ideal is the speculative theory that men are able to commune with this divinity in the innermost depth of the soul, in the "spark" of the soul.

Precisely this same mixture may also be found in the German Christian Mystic, of whom we are reminded by the term *spark* which has just been used to characterize the speculative theory of the *Bhagavad-Gita*.[34] To be sure Eckhart shows a critical reserve toward the mystic state of ecstasy. He frequently emphasizes and reminds us that if anyone be in such an ecstasy and learns of a sick man who is in need of a little broth, it would be much better to abandon his ecstasy and serve the needy one in love.[35] However, one should not overestimate the significance of this and similar occasional sayings. In reality they do not alter the fact that Eckhart's mysticism involves a basic quietistic tendency which does not promote, but rather restricts, does not encourage, but rather hinders an optimistic attitude and energetic work in and for the world.

In itself the desire to exclude all intermediaries belonging to this world, that is, to space-time reality, from the relationship to the over-world leads directly to an aversion to the reality conditioned by space and time.

At the same time another characteristic feature of all mysticism is explained by this fact. Since this desire, and the quest which it involves, is in conflict with the conditions of finite earthly human life, the goal which the mystic seeks can never be completely attained. The rebound is inevitable. This

[34] That Eckhart borrowed this term from Hugo of St. Victor, need not be considered here.
[35] In the *Tischgesprächen*, edition of Pfeiffer, pp. 553 f.

explains why mystics often complain of a continually recurring condition of exhaustion, and disappointment, and of being forsaken by God. When this cycle of "shouting to heaven" and "sorrowing unto death" becomes a standing rule in religion and directly determines the religious relationship, it is a sign of an abnormal and pathological condition. Religion then devours itself. Instead of strengthening and fortifying, it exhausts the energies of men. Religio-psychologically considered, this is an anomaly in religious life. For the basic religious feeling of absolute dependence is thereby impaired and finally is even destroyed. If the feeling of absolute dependence is to retain its dominant position in the religious consciousness, then man must conduct his earthly life so that it is dependent upon and consecrated to the services of the over-world of higher value. And especially within the sphere of monotheistic belief, the feeling of absolute dependence demands that man should be not merely an enjoyer of God but that he should feel himself to be and conduct himself as a co-worker with God. By treating the enjoyment of God as the goal of religious life, mysticism endangers the feeling of absolute dependence and in the end destroys it. This fact is best illustrated by a few of the epigrams of Angelus Silesius: (Book I, Verses 8, 10, 14, 100.)

"I know that without me God cannot live for a moment,
If I become naught, he must needs give up the spirit"—

"I am as great as God, he is as small as I
He cannot be above me, or I under him—"

"I am as rich as God, no speck of dust can be
Which I, O man, believe—do not share with him.—"

"God is as much in need of me as I of him,
I help to sustain his being as much as he helps me"—

And even in those sayings which apparently do justice to the feeling of absolute dependence, the effect is often enough subsequently cancelled. For example:

"God is that which he is; I, what I am through him;
But if thou knowest one, thou knowest me and him." (I, 212.)

It hardly needs to be specifically mentioned that modern mysticism is also, and especially, included in the judgment just expressed. Referring to the verses of Angelus Silesius, Wilhelm Bölsche says that it is no exaggeration to state that human mysticism has never had a clearer poetical expression, nor attained such a crystal-clear form.[36] And undoubtedly he had especially in mind the fact which has just been considered.

And just as mysticism endangers and minimizes the feeling of dependence, it produces the same effect to a still greater extent on the religious sense of duty. In the *Bhagavad-Gita*, to be sure, dutiful conduct is most emphatically demanded, indeed, so much so that some have thought that this hymn anticipates Kant's doctrine of the categorical imperative.[37] However, it is only artificially and superficially that this demand is harmonized with the mysticism of the *Gita*. Not to be concerned about this world, and to abandon all activity is the advice of its mysticism. (See XII, 16.) And we here leave entirely out of consideration its recommendation of actual Yogi practices: to sit in contemplation in some lonely spot, unmoved, holding one's body steady and looking at the tip of one's nose. (See IV, 13.)

In Eckhart we find excellent discussions of the subordination of the will to God. The question of when the will is good is thus answered: the will is perfect and good when it is unselfish, self-denying, and is trained and formed according to the will of God: the more this is true, the more steadfast and reliable the will is, and with such a will one can love or do anything else.[38] The religious sense of duty could not be formulated more excellently or fittingly. However, Eckhart himself fails to carry to its conclusion the insight which he here so clearly and definitely states. On the contrary he diverts it so that in the end it again merges with the enjoyment of God. *The consequence of this insight evidently ought to be*

---

[36] Wilhelm Bölsche in the introduction to his edition of the *Cherubinische Wandersmann*, Verlag Diederichs, 1905.

[37] Comp. Leopold v. Schröder in the introduction to his German translation of the *Bhagavad-Gita*, p. IV: "An ethical theory which is truly impressive in its earnestness and purity, and truly deserves to be ranked with Kant's categorical imperative." Concerning the exaggeration involved in this opinion, see above.

[38] In the *Tischgesprächen*, edition of F. Pfeiffer, p. 553.

for the religious man to take these higher values coming to him from the over-world, and to realize them as far as it is at all possible also in this world in which he finds himself placed as a creature, and to put at the service of this task the entire strength which grows out of the binding of his will to the will of God.

What prevents Eckhart from drawing this conclusion? Only his desire to win an immediate relationship to deity, and to exclude from this relationship all intermediaries. Whenever this desire is added to the demand, previously quoted, that man's will should be trained and formed according to the will of God, the relation to man's work in the world which this demand implies retreats into the background, thereby emptying the religious sense of duty of its ethical content.

Thus, in this respect also, the conversion of the tendency toward the greatest possible immediate fellowship with the over-world or deity into a completely unmediated relationship to it, is the deciding characteristic of the unique nature of mysticism.

And finally, this also explains mysticism's leaning toward pantheism, in the strict form in which the impersonality of the world-structure is the important factor. For when all intermediaries from ethical and historical life are excluded from the relationship to deity, deity becomes so indefinite that any idea of the personality of God then seems unfitting. Think of the words of Eckhart: "Thou shalt love him as he is, a non-God, a non-spirit, a non-person, a non-formed: rather only clear, pure, unadulterated, one-ness, far from all duality. And in this One we should eternally sink from existence into nothingness." [39] However, mysticism is not necessarily pantheistic. Pantheism is not one of its essential characteristics.

Even some of the most characteristic verses of Angelus Silesius are oriented entirely to the personal, and not to the impersonal conception of God:

"There is nothing but I and Thou, and if we two no longer be,
Then God can no longer be God, and heaven has fallen down."

[39] In the sermon on *Ephesians*, IV, 23. Edition of F. Pfeiffer, p. 320.

"God loveth me alone, he fears so much for me,
He even dies of fear because I do not cling to Him." [40]

The nature of mysticism must rather be found in its desire so to formulate the relationship to the over-world as to exclude all intermediaries from temporal finite life. Its essential characteristic is the conversion of the tendency toward the utmost possible immediate contact and fellowship with the over-world into an entirely intimate relationship which is free from all intermediaries.

The starting-point for mysticism, then, is furnished by the tendency toward the utmost possible immediate contact with the over-world. Mysticism aims at nothing else than the perfect and clear fulfilment of this tendency. And it thinks that it can reach this goal only by denying all intermediaries of a finite and temporal character. It forgets that this undertaking contradicts the conditions of finite human life. It would conjure away this contradiction by means of speculations concerning the nature of the human soul which are in their intentions deeply religious, but which are fantastic and untenable in practice. The *unio mystica* becomes an identity of the soul and "God," a suspension of the subject-object relation *per se:* [41] Tat tvam asi.[42]

The basic tendency of mysticism, the utmost possible immediate contact with the over-world, is best called the mystical tendency of the religious consciousness. Instinctively we have employed this terminology, and now our analysis has proven its correctness.

A further clarification of this terminology is now possible. For considering this mystical tendency of religion there are two ways of formulating the concept of mysticism. Every religion in which this tendency is strongly developed and dominates the religious life may be called mysticism. In this sense then, mysticism may be found, for example, in primitive Christianity

[40] *Der Cherubinische Wandersmann,* II, 178; III, 37.
[41] Karl Jaspers has described this point of view very clearly and definitely in his *"Psychologie der Weltanschauungen"* (Berlin, 1919, p. 387 ff.).
[42] Most impressively in the *Chandogya Upanishad* VI in the story of Svetaketu (Deussen, *Sechzig Upanishads,* 2nd ed., p. 159 ff.).

as well as in the Reformation, and not least in Luther himself.

But one may also restrict the concept of mysticism to that form of religion which attempts to carry out the mystical tendency in the one-sided radical fashion expounded above. For historical reasons this definition of the term is preferable. Only it must then be remembered that the concepts "mystical" and "mysticism" are to be distinguished because the former is much more general and far-reaching than the latter.[43] *And it is just this distinction that is closest to common usage.* It merely makes common usage precise by not restricting the concept of the mystical to the one-sided radical forms, while, on the other hand, it still retains, for these forms, the concept of mysticism.

5

However, the concept of "consistent mysticism," which Heiler has recently used to summarize his otherwise extraordinarily profitable researches on the problem of mysticism, must be rejected as misleading. *"Radical" mysticism is certainly not a consistent application of the mystical tendency to the religious life.*

Heiler's own discussions also show that his conception of consistent mysticism does not help to clarify, but only confuses, the situation.[44] For in the first place Heiler's definition of the concept is ambiguous. Sometimes he formulates it so that it is exemplified completely only in atheistic Hinayana Buddhism. But at other times he gives it a considerably wider connotation, even adopting a pantheistic interpretation.

How are these various definitions to be harmonized with each other? Is consistent mysticism at once atheistic and pantheistic? Or does Heiler mean that all pantheism logically leads to atheism? Either of these positions leads to the greatest difficulties. Moreover Heiler's full discussion of mysticism as a whole contradicts his definition of "consistent" mysticism. If his definition is accepted, none of the elements of mysticism

[43] The view which Wilhelm Koepp espouses in his treatise on Johann Arndt (J. A.: *Eine Untersuchung über die Mystik im Luthertum,* 1911) closely approaches our position at this point.

[44] Friedrich Heiler: *Das Gebet. Eine religionsgeschichtliche und religionspsychologische Untersuchung,* 2nd ed., 1920, pp. 248 ff.

which he recognizes and praises could be attributed to mysticism itself, but on the contrary all would have to be attributed to alien influences which change the nature of mysticism. The rôle which Heiler ascribes to so-called "personalistic" mysticism, as represented by Söderblom, is especially irreconcilable with the evaluation implied in the conception of "consistent mysticism." Thus he points out, *e.g.* that in personalistic mysticism the idea of God is more concrete and graphic: that here God is not the impersonal and vague unity beyond the realm of reality and of values, but the highest value conceived in terms of personality, the living "Lord" and loving "Saviour," who descends to finite human beings in order to lift them to himself,—the "true friend in need" who neither can nor will desert anyone, as Heiler finally adds, quoting Margaret Ebner (p. 260). But even within the limits of Heiler's own point of view, the question may be raised whether it is right to connect such phenomena with the characterization of mysticism. These critical objections apply still more to Heiler's discussion of his own subject, namely to his investigations of the phenomena of prayer within mysticism. What right has he to base, emphatically and as a matter of methodological principle, his entire treatment of this subject "primarily" upon the documents of a clear personalistic God-mysticism? [45]

Heiler's position here contains inconsistencies and contradictions which can be eliminated only by a treatment based upon such a religio-psychological method as we have advocated. However, such a treatment really can eliminate them. Insofar Heiler's attitude to the problem of mysticism confirms our own position.

And how about the relation of mysticism to Buddhism? The fact that both of them belong to the class of contemplative religions of salvation proves that they are related. But can this relationship be more precisely defined by saying, as Heiler does, that Buddhism is the most consistent (more pre-

---

[45] Comp. *op. cit.*, pp. 284 ff., p. 285. "Therefore we will attempt to give a general description of the mystical method of prayer, which is based primarily upon the documents of a clear personalistic God-mysticism, but which also takes the other expressions of mystical thought into consideration. We will show how, in the forms of mystical piety which deviate from the normal type, certain elements appear which can be found in all mysticism."

cisely: the only consistent) form of mysticism? From the religio-psychological point of view, we must answer no. And we must answer no when the question refers to the general mystical tendency of religion as well as when it refers to mysticism in the narrower sense. In the light of our previous discussion, the former is self-evident and requires no special proof.

However, Buddhism does not even represent the logical culmination of the one-sided radical mysticism. To be sure, over and above the relationship already mentioned, there is an especially close formal analogy between the two phenomena, due to the fact that the Nirvana of Buddhism represents the negative form of the "highest good" of mysticism. This explains the similarities of the contemplative exercises and of their various stages in mysticism and Buddhism. Heiler deserves credit for having pointed out these similarities in detail.[46] However, these formal analogies should not make us overlook the material differences between the corresponding states of feeling, and even of the entire state of consciousness, in these two kinds of religion.

The mystical state of consciousness is based upon two presuppositions: (1) a strong and deep religiosity, which, however, overexerts itself and then loses its balance; and (2) a strong speculative leaning, which makes possible and justifies this over-exertion and loss of balance. Buddhism shares neither of these presuppositions. Its religiosity is neither strong nor deep; it is rather so weak and shallow that one is justified in doubting whether it can even be called religion. Nor is Buddhism built upon a speculative leaning. There is no leaning toward metaphysical speculation in Buddhism and that is what is here under consideration.[47] In its inclination to rational dialectics it purposely avoids all speculative metaphysics and "metapsychics." When Mālunkyāputta tries to lead Buddha into a discussion of this nature, Buddha asks him: "What have I previously told you, Mālunkyāputta? Did I say: Come,

[46] Friedrich Heiler: *Die buddhistische Versenkung. Eine religionsgeschichtliche Untersuchung,* 1918

[47] Oldenberg remarks incidentally that an especially characteristic trait of Buddhism is a disinclination to base its view of reality on ultimate principles. Herm. Oldenberg, *Buddha,* etc., 6th ed., 1914, p. 234.

Mālunkyāputta, and be my disciple; I will teach you whether the world is eternal or not eternal, whether the world is finite or infinite, whether the living being is identical with the body or different from it, whether the perfect one lives or does not live beyond death, or whether the perfect one at the same time lives and does not live beyond death, or whether he neither lives nor does not live?" [48]   This question is put with pædagogical irony and of course the answer is no.

Therefore we must conclude that Buddhism, mysticism, and pantheism are to be treated as special forms of contemplative religions of salvation.

We must continue to reserve our opinion of Christianity. But another question forces itself upon us at this time. What about Christian Science and Theosophy? Should not these two phenomena be regarded as modern forms of contemplative religions of salvation? Undoubtedly both belong to this class of religions insofar as, and to the extent to which they can be classified as religions at all. Therefore, we must consider them here just because we must decide whether they are religious or non-religious in character.

The fact that both of them claim to be religions cannot be absolutely decisive for us. Consequently no decisive significance can be attached to the fact that Mrs. Eddy called her organization of 1879 "The Church of Christ, Scientist," and made its goal the restoration of the primitive Christian Church with its lost gift of healing the sick. And similarly the other circumstance that Mrs. Eddy appended to her major work on Christian Science, *"Science and Health,"* a "Key to the Scriptures" is just as little decisive. This key contains an exposition of the first four chapters of Genesis and of portions of the 12th and 21st chapters of the Book of Revelation. We are not here concerned with the arbitrariness of the exposition. At any rate such facts only show the opinion of the author concerning her relation to the Christian religion. Now to be sure this opinion needs to be taken into account. Mrs. Eddy attributed a religious character to Christian Science and claimed that it is a religion. Christian Science does not reject religion and does not place itself alongside of other religions. It wants to present

[48] Majjhima-Nikāya, Vol. I, p. 426. Comp. Oldenberg, *op. cit.,* p. 316.

religion, and to be religion.   Yet the general point of view is emphatically called "Science."   Hence it regards as ideal that attitude of mind which insists that the doctrines must not only be believed but they must be understood.   For example, the great fact that God is the only Spirit (or Mind) is called the foundation of all health and recovery, and it is added that this Spirit must not only be believed but must be understood. (*Science and Health,* pp. 339 ff.)   There lurks here at least an uncertainty as to the character of religious faith, which perforce points in the direction of its rationalization.   *However, this rationalization then evades the standards of rational science.* According to its own tendency it is a completely irrational rationalization.   And here again there is presented a very false analogy to religion.   It is completely false, for religion rejects rationalization, whereas Christian Science demands it and then converts it into the irrational.   Thus the irrational which is thereby produced is the pseudo-rational.   Now to be sure, the pseudo-rational is sometimes identified with the irrational.   But objectively considered, the irrational is just as different from the pseudo-rational as from the rational.

It might be asked whether a consideration of Christian Science's desire for salvation can lead us any further.   We took Buddhism's peculiar striving for salvation as the criterion for determining its religious character.   Buddhism strives to save men by lifting them out of the restrictions of space-time earthly existence.   This at least offers an indication of an overworldly goal.   But what is the nature of the salvation which Christian Science desires and promises?   It is primarily salvation from disease.   Such a doctrine of salvation has no direct connection with religion.   It is religiously neutral.   Yet the sacred scripture of Christian Science nearly always puts sin and death alongside of disease.   Hence, its salvation is directed toward sin and death, as well as toward disease, and accordingly it defines the goal of its mental healing or spiritual cure to be: health, sinlessness, and immortality.   This presents the religious element much more clearly and tangibly.   However, precisely this judgment again has to be immediately qualified. For just as is disease, so sin and death are considered to be mere illusion and error.   Therefore, in regard to all three phenomena, the advice is: conquer error by denying its reality. The one God must be regarded as the only real Being. Hence whatever exists, is God. Outside of God nothing exists, not even other spirits. This assumption excludes the possibility of a relationship to the over-worldly God-spirit, and that means that it excludes religion in the full sense of that term. And least of all is there any relationship which is basically expressed in a feeling of dependence.

So the general point of view is incoherent and ambiguous. And this incoherence is really much greater than has been pointed out so far. Hitherto our account has entirely disregarded a factor which must necessarily be considered in any complete exposition of the whole theory. The Christian Scientist also claims to be able directly to influence in a radical fashion the laws and powers of nature. For example, a sailor, who is a Christian Scientist should be able to rule the air and the great deeps, as well as the fish of the sea and the birds of the air. (*Science and Health*, p. 125.) And to this influence must also be added the further influence over the evil effects of demonic powers, which powers might harm Christian Scientists.

Here undoubtedly factors are operating which belong to the realm of magic, and they will be discussed in greater detail when we take up magic.

And the estimate of Theosophy concerning its own relation to religion cannot simply be left to its own judgment. And besides, not even its own estimate in the matter is uniform. Of the founders of modern Theosophy, Madame Blavatsky approached very closely to Buddhism in the last stage of her activity. The second edition of her book *"Isis Unveiled"* (1887) she called esoteric Buddhism. Colonel Olcott, the co-founder and second president of the Theosophical Society, became a Buddhist and remained so until his death in 1907. But Mrs. Besant, the ablest disciple of Madame Blavatsky, turned to Hinduism. Rudolf Steiner, after separating himself from Mrs. Besant, called his theosophic doctrine *Anthroposophy,* and he especially stresses the absolute independence of his anthroposophic Theosophy. The anthroposophic movement claims the right to be regarded as completely independent.[49]   But Steiner of course owes us an objective proof of this claim.   An unprejudiced examination of the actual historical connections, and the unmistakable similarities in content, emphatically argue against such independence.

However, for our religio-psychological approach we can nevertheless restrict ourselves to the present form of Steiner's Theosophy, since it is closer to German culture, and has also been more carefully and coherently formulated on the whole than other forms of theosophy.

According to Steiner, Theosophy is the completion of the religious development of humanity.   For today Theosophy is the correct way of showing the wisdom of religion so much needed by modern men.   Instead of being a new religion Theosophy furnishes the precise proofs for the validity of the old religion and consequently it is a staunch supporter of it.[50]   And Steiner attempts to place Theosophy in an especially intimate relationship to Christianity by making the theosophically comprehended Christ-drama determine the future of the development of humanity.   Moreover, the Christ-drama is not only to determine the future of the development of the earth as such but in the end that of the entire universe.   Steiner thinks that Golgotha is not only a human, but is also a cosmic event.   The Christ-self, which previously existed only as a "lofty solar being" in the sun, came down to the earth.   After the crucifixion this Christ-self was united with the earth and it can now be recognized as the central spirit of the earth.[51]

However, we are not here concerned in detail with this theosophical interpretation of Christology.   For the time being we are interested in the attitude of Theosophy to religion *per se*. And we are more especially concerned now with Steiner's thesis that Theosophy is today the correct way of revealing the wisdom of religion.   The meaning of this thesis is that Theosophy can state the higher truths at the basis of religion in such a way that the most critical thought will have to regard them as valid.   And Steiner supports this with the further thesis that

[49] Especially emphatic, e.g., in Steiner's work, *"Die Aufgabe der Geisteswissenschaft und deren Bau in Dornach,"* 1919, p. 10.
[50] Rud. Steiner: *Lebensfragen der theosophischen Bewegung,* pp. 25 ff.
[51] Rud. Steiner: *Weihnacht: Eine Betrachtung aus der Lebensweisheit.*

while the religions are true, nevertheless for many people the time is past when most people can understand religion by means of mere "faith." [52]

For Theosophy "mere faith" is, then, the real defect of traditional religion. The theosophists would overcome this defect with their spiritual-scientific (geisteswissenschaftliche) knowledge. For Theosophy considers its own basic character to be precisely scientific, that is, spiritual-scientific knowledge. *Here also the danger of a complete rationalization of religious faith, and with it of religion as a whole, becomes threatening.* And here again the rationalization is directed toward the irrational. For the conception of a spiritual-scientific knowledge of Theosophy is not the same as the distinction made in the philosophy of science between "Naturwissenschaft" and "Geisteswissenschaft," but it means occult esoteric or clairvoyant "research." It is knowledge immediately obtained by higher perception. Although concentration and meditation prepare the mind for such knowledge, it is itself a knowing which is revealed directly to the Theosophist in the vision of contemplation.

Are we dealing here with the purely irrational element in religion, or is what seems to be irrational in Theosophy merely pseudo-rational? In trying to answer this question one has to admit that the situation is here much more complicated than it is in Christian Science. Undoubtedly the unprejudiced reader is strongly impressed, on first reading Steiner's published writings, by the pseudo-rational character of his anthropological and cosmological speculations. However, after closer study of these writings, the religio-psychologically trained mind still gets the impression that in and behind all of its pseudo-rational metaphysics, factors are operative which point in the direction of the religious irrational. I cannot better describe the duality of my total impression, the more I have studied Steiner's writings, than to refer to the systems of the ancient Gnostics. Whoever studies the systems of ancient Christian Gnosticism, or rather the actual writings of the Gnostics which have come down to us, gets exactly the same inherently dual impression which is

[52] Rud. Steiner: *Wie erlangt man Erkenntnis höherer Welten?* 7th ed., 1914, pp. 25 ff.

made by Steiner's writings.[53]   *The pseudo-rational attitude com-*
pletely dominates, not only the thought-pattern which is pre-
sented, but also the whole of the reasoning.   And yet the belief
which is concealed in these wrappings is by no means merely of
a pseudo-rational nature.

On the contrary it is a belief which frequently approaches
closely to the basic belief of religion.   That the world of the
senses in which man passes his earthly life does not exhaust
reality, that it is a part of a higher order, and that man is
destined to achieve a relationship to this over-world, this content
is shared in common both by religious belief and by Steiner's
Theosophy.   Moreover Steiner sometimes remarks that such a
belief is justified only when it grows out of personal experience.

Therefore, our religio-psychological evaluation cannot agree
with such a criticism as Johannes Müller makes of Steiner's
Theosophy,[54] or at least can agree with it only with strict
reservations.   He finds the fateful error of Theosophy in the
fact that it fails to find the source of all becoming and of all
reality.   Instead of seeking this source in the divine, it seeks it
in the occult.   By placing the entire emphasis upon the stirrings
of the occult powers of the mind, which are of course something
essentially human, Theosophy fails to recognize the importance
of the metaphysical in us, the activity and stimulation of which
is to be regarded as religious receptivity.   This criticism sticks
too closely to the terminology and thought-forms of Theosophy
to do justice to its underlying attitude.   The conceptions of the
occult and of the metaphysical may in a broad sense be names for
the same tendencies of belief, and in fact they undoubtedly are
percisely in the system of Theosophy.   Hence to this extent
Rittelmeyer is correct when he says that Müller's criticism of
Theosophy is misleading.[55]   There are unmistakable connecting
links between theosophical occultism and the religious sense of
mystery.   We may assume that this is shown more clearly and
emphatically in the courses, which are open only to Steiner's

[53] The same opinion is expressed by Kurt Leese: *Moderne Theosophie,*
Berlin, 1921, pp. 145 ff.
[54] Joh. Müller: *Theosophie; zehntes Kriegsheft der Grünen Blätter,*
Elmau, 1918.
[55] Friedr. Rittelmeyer: *Joh. Müller und Rud. Steiner.*   (Die Christliche
Welt, 1918, Nos. 20-21, 22-23.)

adherents, than in his published writings.[56] Only in this way can one understand the influence which Steiner has had upon men like Rittelmeyer and Geyer.[57] But in his polemic against Johannes Müller Rittelmeyer neglects the other side of the matter. In attempting, with its "occult research," to reveal the ultimate mysteries of the development of the world and of humanity in a fantastic Gnostic mythology, and in drawing the relationship of deity and humanity into this mythological revelation, Theosophy runs the risk of severing the vital nerve of genuine religiosity which is conditioned by the feeling of dependence. And when we consider its claim to be able to create the ability for such mythological constructions through Yogi practices of concentration and meditation, we see that it builds its theoretical and speculative mythology upon a cult which is, in its whole intent, of a magical character.

[56] What I have been able to gather from those who are familiar with these courses confirms the above statement.

[57] Christian Geyer: *Theosophie und Religion,* 1919.

PART TWO

The Question of the Truth of Religion in the Light of the
Question of Its Nature

Das Wahre war schon längst gefunden,
Hat edle Geisterschaft verbunden,
Das alte Wahre fass es an.

The understanding cannot reach deity. Man must be able to transcend even the highest reason in order to rest in God. Deity reveals itself in primitive phenomena, physical as well as moral. Deity supports such phenomena and they emerge out of deity.

—GOETHE

CHAPTER VIII

THE PROOFS FOR THE EXISTENCE OF GOD

I

The indispensable demand of the religio-psychological method is that the question of the truth of religion must be approached fundamentally in the light of the question of its nature. This demand seems to be purely self-evident. And looking solely at the fact itself it really is ultimately self-evident, but looked at from the point of view of the usual methods of study it is far from being self-evident.

The demand means that in dealing with the question of the truth of religion our foremost interest must be concentrated upon uncovering and making clear the basis of validity which religion itself contains. The truth of religion cannot be proved from without but it must be established from within. However it really must be established from within and the attempt so to establish it must in any case be made.

This demand includes both a negative and a positive factor. For the truth-interest, which the religio-psychological method has taught us belongs to the very essence of the religious consciousness, works itself out in this dual way. It is just because the truth-interest belongs to the essence of the religious consciousness that it can neither be satisfied with a rationalistic apologetic nor with a basic agnosticism and relativism. On the one hand, the question of truth must be put in its full strength and inexorableness, but, on the other hand, in dealing with this question we must restrict ourselves to the really religious question of truth, that is to say, to that question of truth which arises from the truth-interest inherent in religious experience.

This excludes all orthodox apologetics, as well as all agnosticisms and every construction resulting from a purely pragmatic interpretation of religion. For the pragmatist defense of religion is a defense that is shot through with contradictions. Although it seeks to establish the truth of religion, it is a different truth from that towards which the truth-interest of religion is itself directed. To the same extent that the religio-psychological method owes gratitude to William James for his contribution to it, to the same extent must it definitely and without any reservation reject his pragmatism. And, to be sure, precisely on religio-psychological grounds. It is just that truth-interest which emerges from the religious consciousness which necessitates this decision. But this decision applies not only to the pragmatism of James, but also to every kind of pragmatic argument which either more or less perverts the truth-interest of religion or else replaces it with a mere life-interest. It applies especially to Vaihinger's theory of "as if" (fictionalism), but it also applies to Eucken's theory, in so far as he allows the truth-content of religion to be diverted to the establishment of an Absolute Spiritual Life. The truth-interest of religion rather arises from reality in the most unique sense of that word. It arises from the reality of the over-world of religious belief. For a vital relation to the over-world is possible only under the presupposition of its reality. And since the religio-psychological viewpoint, in the final analysis, makes the nature of religion consist in a vital relation of man to the over-world, on which he feels himself to be dependent, in whose value he knows himself to be secure, and which is the goal of his longing, it follows that the question of truth for this religio-psychological viewpoint is a question of the reality of this over-world. Only this way of putting the question does justice to religious conviction; only it expresses the meaning of that which religion takes to be the truth of religion. Every other way of putting the question falsifies the unique meaning of the religious truth-interest and truth-promise. Living religion, the kind which rests upon religious experience, always and without any exception whatsoever means by "the truth of religion" the reality of the over-world of the vital religious relationship.

It is concerned, therefore, with the "that," with the existence of the over-world. And for the present in our discussion we are concerned only with this existence of the over-world, and not yet with the "how" or inner essence of that over-world. Or at least, to express it more accurately, we are concerned with the inner essence of the over-world only to the extent that it is given to us in the meaning, already explained, of the idea of the over-world itself. The over-world differentiates itself according to the standards of the different forms of religious belief, and therefore has to be explained in the discussion of those separate forms, and for us that means especially in the discussion of Christianity. But referring to the over-world in general, as the objective content of all religious faith, we have now to raise the question of whether it is real, whether it actually exists. The question of the truth of religion loses its religious meaning, (and precisely this religious meaning must nevertheless be decisive for the whole problem), when it is not identified with the question of the reality of the over-world of the vital religious relationship. *Reality or illusion: these are the alternatives of the question of the truth of religion.* With the utmost insistence the religio-psychological method must stick to these alternatives, absolutely repudiating every evasion and attenuation of this disjunction.

This is the statement of the problem made by Feuerbach, which we must again take up. For Feuerbach was certainly right in his statement of the problem *per se*. And it is not an accident that the principle of the religio-psychological method fully agrees with that of Feuerbach at this point. On the contrary, it was the undeniable religio-psychological insight of Feuerbach which caused him to recognize that this statement of the problem is final. Here we must simply return to Feuerbach. It cannot be otherwise. All efforts are fruitless which, evading his statement of the problem, try to make the truth of religion scientific. They cannot accomplish their purpose, because they are falsely oriented at the very beginning, in so far as they cannot permit the truth-interest of the religious consciousness, in its specifically religious form, to come into its own. Reality or illusion: these are and remain the alternatives for the question of the truth of religion.[1]

[1] At this point the statement of the problem of the religio-psychological method comes very close to that of the philosophical and religio-theological theory of Karl Heim. (*Das Weltbild der Zukunft*, 1904; *Glaubensgewissheit. Eine Untersuchung über die Lebensfrage der Religion*, 3rd ed., 1923;

The hope of deciding between these two alternatives on the basis of the socalled proofs for the existence of God is well known. And just this is the kernel of truth in these "proofs," and the kernel of truth in the whole method of reasoning which is active in them. Although those of us who take the position of the critical philosophy of Kant must reject these proofs as uncritical and untenable, it is just as essential that we recognize the justifiable tendency which is nevertheless implicit in them.[2] Accordingly we must also accept the task of validating in some other way this justifiable tendency. This is not done by those who simply reject the proofs for the existence of God. For what these proofs intended to offer, moreover what they did give to wide circles of men of earlier times, but can, however, no longer supply today, must be replaced. But in replacing it we must be especially careful to avoid the double error which is implied in the very idea of such an undertaking. In the first place, as we have already seen, in general nothing can be proved in religion from without. And secondly, it is not the existence of God but the existence of the over-world which is in question. In general the discussion of these proofs, with which in this respect the popular treatment still coincides, does not distinguish the two parts of the task which we have already differentiated, following the religio-psychological method; but, on the contrary, so mixes them together that the very possibility of distinguishing them is at once out of the question. The objective content of the religious consciousness in its universality, the over-world, is formulated at the start to conform to monotheistic belief; indeed, the monotheistic conception of God is ordinarily accepted in its specifically Christian form. This treatment perforce leads to a premature apologetic,

---

Glaube und Denken, 1931.) However, it differs fundamentally from Heim's statement of the problem in two respects. He orients his investigation of the problem entirely to Christianity, without considering the nature of religion as such. Then, too, in dealing with the question of the nature of Christianity itself, he fails to state his problem clearly; and hence he gives no criterion to distinguish the essential from the unessential, the primary from the secondary. And in the evaluation of the question of the nature of religion in relation to that of the truth of religion lies the most significant difference between the position of Heim and our entire theory.

[2] See Georg Wobbermin: *Christian Belief in God,* translated by D. S. Robinson (Yale University Press), where the author examines each of the classic proofs for the existence of God from this point of view.—Translators' note.

whose arguments really prove nothing. When too much is taken for granted at the beginning, failure to reach a goal that is in itself attainable inevitably results. The religio-psychological method makes it perfectly clear that the distinction between the question of the specifically religious and the question of the specifically Christian must also agree with the gradual development of thought on the question of the truth of religion. But in both cases we are unquestionably concerned with the reality of the content of the religious object. So far the basic tendency of the proofs for the existenec of God is justifiable. For this basic tendency a substitute must be found.

2

This position toward the question of the truth of religion, which has been reached by the religio-psychological method, can again rest, to a considerable extent, on Schleiermacher. He himself prepared the way for this position. Moreover, he prepared the way for it precisely to the extent that he initiated the religio-psychological method. But the dialectical and speculative coloring which he mixed with this view hindered its logical development.

In paragraph 33 of the *Glaubenslehre* (2nd edition) Schleiermacher said that the recognition that the feeling of absolute dependence is a universal element in human life entirely replaces for Christian doctrine all socalled proofs for the existence of God. Schleiermacher also expressly spoke of a substitute for the traditional way of putting the problem. He held such a substitute to be necessary and he intended to offer it. The theory of a feeling of absolute dependence constitutes this substitute. Since religion has the theory of a feeling of absolute dependence as its basis, Schleiermacher's thesis also carries with it the demand that the grounds of validity of the religious conviction, which is itself rooted in religious experience, be made the decisive fact for the discussion of the question of the truth of religion. And that is just the demand which we found that we had to make, purely on the basis of the facts themselves, according to the standard of the principle of the religio-psychological method.

To be sure, Schleiermacher did not always stick consistently to this position, and still less did he consistently develop it. It was crossed and in the end made ineffective by him by the dialectical and speculative twist which he gave to his valuable insight. Because of this speculative twist Schleiermacher asserted that the feeling of absolute dependence is a universal element in human life which rests upon the absolutely universal nature of mankind. But with Schleiermacher himself this assertion remains in mid-air, and it really is not grounded in the nature of the facts in the formulation which he defended. It is a purely a priori assertion without any real validity.

It is a mistaken and an unsuitable undertaking to want to prove the existence of God or even that of the over-world of general religious belief. Yet the reality of the over-world, in the sense of religious conviction, is the presupposition and condition of all religious belief. If these two theses, which the religio-psychological viewpoint presents as equally essential, are put alongside of each other, then it follows that the truth of religion can in general be scientifically represented only in an indirect and not in a direct way. Every attempt to give a direct proof harks back to the traditional scholastic proofs for the existence of God. Schleiermacher's own position shows exactly this. His discussion of the feeling of absolute dependence as a universal element in human life which rests upon the absolutely universal nature of humanity, methodically considered, is completely analogous to the socalled ontological argument for God. It is nothing more than a special form of this ontological argument. His own demand that a substitute for all socalled proofs for God be found, Schleiermacher did not meet. In the end he remained in that self-same sphere which he desired to transcend and above which he wanted to rise. When the reasoning in question remains within the type of method of the classic proofs, there is no use talking about a substitute for these proofs in the strict sense of the word substitute. But it is just the chief strength of Schleiermacher's demand that it is rooted in his profound religio-psychological insight. We must take this demand most seriously. Since it is not merely a question of varying the traditional proofs by adding slight modifications which are like them, it is all the more necessary to consider the problem on an entirely different level of thought, and to seek on this level for a substitute for the old undertaking in methodical principles of another kind. Direct proof must be abandoned. It must be replaced by indirect arguments.

Three types of reasoning must be advanced. In the first place we must examine the usual objections to the truth of religion and, as far as possible, refute them. Then we must put to the test theories which try to comprehend the fact of religion on the assumption that it has no truth, and ask whether such theories do not themselves work with false assumptions, with distortions of the facts, and with erroneous concepts. And finally we must raise the question whether there are not in other regions and functions of human spiritual life factors which also point in the direction of the religious interpretation of the world, and which are first made intelligible by this religious interpretation and which then in turn make it understandable. All of these types of argument are in the end centered in the one question : Does not the religious interpretation of the world as a whole have more right than any other to claim validity and truth?

For this line of reasoning, however, two basic problem-complexes are implicit in all of these types of argument and are ultimately decisive for each of them. These problem-complexes are first, the relation of religion, magic, and mythology, and secondly, the relation of faith and knowledge. Accordingly our most important and primary task is to discuss fully these two problem-complexes. For the usual objections to religion in their deepest form can be refuted only in this way, and only by clarifying these relations is it possible to bring to light the grounds of validity of the truth-claim of religion which are inherent in religion itself.

CHAPTER IX

RELIGION, MAGIC, AND MYTHOLOGY

I

From various angles of approach the question of how magic and mythology are related to religion has already been thrust upon us. We will deal with magic and mythology together. For that the relation of magic to religion is analogous to the relation of mythology to religion, at least to a considerable extent, our previous discussions have already made evident. But this analogy is due to the fact that whereas both phenomena are related to religion, yet this relation is such that their method of reasoning and moreover their store of ideas are either not at all, or at least are not decisively, determined by motives originating out of the religious experience which is the basis of religious conviction, they are rather determined by motives of an entirely different nature. *We are now concerned with these motives of a different nature.* And since they specifically condition the growth of magical and mythological in contrast to religious modes of behavior, these must be motives of a magical-mythological character. Here, however, this is only a terminological description. The task which now confronts us is the giving to this terminological description a real content.

It will be appropriate to begin with mythology. *For the idea of mythology can be used as the general idea which includes the whole field of magic.* Magic is then that practice which belongs to, or is at least connected in some way with mythology.

Of course the very conception of mythology constitutes an initial difficulty. This is implied in the dual meaning of the word *mythology*. In its common usage this word signifies the material of mythological science as well as the science itself, it means myths as well as the study of myths. In order to avoid this ambiguity the use of "study of myths," a term we have previously employed, has recently been advocated as a substitute for the word mythology. In itself it would be more appropriate simply to restrict the term mythology to the work of scientific research. However, a further complication is involved in the situation. For the idea of myth is also not necessarily unambiguous. It may designate the *general mythical thought* in question, or on the other hand, the *particular mythical concepts.* And for every treatment which is at all psychologically orientated, *mythical thought* as such must finally be the main consideration. But this mythical thought in itself cannot in turn be called myth. Here one must rather fall back upon the conception of the mythological in the most general sense.

Accordingly we shall employ the term mythology to designate the totality of mythical thought. That mythology in this sense plays a very important rôle in the whole history of religion cannot be disputed. But what is the nature of that rôle?

Among contemporary philosophers, Deussen, who has given most serious consideration to the religious life of humanity in his treatment of the history of philosophy, traces all religion back to a fusion of two completely heterogeneous elements: the mythological and the moral.[1] In his opinion all religion is based upon a synthesis of these two entirely discrete elements which were originally entirely unrelated. And he goes so far as to argue that every religion is better to the extent to which the moral element emerges, and on the other hand, worse to the extent to which the moral element is stifled or over-shadowed by mythological conceptions. But Deussen finds the essence of the mythological in the personification of natural phenomena and natural forces, as when the wind is regarded as a wild charioteer or as a hunter who pursues the clouds with bow and arrow, or the sun is thought of as an untiring wanderer who knows and finds his way, or the storm is taken to be a battle of opposing armies which fight each other in the sky. Now the mythological side of religion is also found

---

[1] Paul Deussen: *Allgemeine Geschichte der Philosophie.* Mit besonderer Berücksichtigung der Religionen, Vol. I, 2nd ed., 1906, pp. 77 ff.

in the fact that man's æsthetic imagination endows with will and personality the forces of nature which surround him. Yet genuine religion does not arise until this mythology is fused with the inner experience of the absolutely binding consciousness of an ethical standard. And the criterion for determining whether religion is genuine is to be found in the degree to which the moral or the mythological element is preponderant.

It cannot be doubted that Deussen has here attempted to develop strictly scientifically, and thereby at the same time to prove, a theory of the nature of religion which enjoys the greatest popularity in wide circles of intellectuals, although it is usually not so precisely formulated. However, it is just this precise formulation by the philosopher which reveals the basic nature of the whole theory. It is obvious that this theory intends to designate as mythology all of the content of religion which does not consist of morality, or which cannot at least be directly converted into morality, so that it can reject it. *On this theory the value of religion and therewith its truth are exclusively determined by its moral content.* Now this principle involves Deussen in difficulties insofar as the existence of a religion is supposed to be dependent upon the fusion of the moral with the mythological element in his theory. For this normative principle, which the logic of the theory involves so far as it is not already present as a *petitio principii,* would demand as its ideal the conversion of religion into morality. And this inner contradiction becomes all the greater in the case of the follower of Schopenhauer, who was not only a philosopher like his teacher but was like him also an ardent student of religion, because he attempts to bring this philosophical value-judgment which his whole theory presupposes, into harmony with the scientific conscience of the student of religion. To accomplish this he is not content merely to assert that every religion is better to the degree in which the moral element emerges, and worse to the degree in which it is contaminated by mythological conceptions. But he proceeds to the other assertion that the more the former is the case, the more the religion in question becomes genuine "religion," whereas the more the latter occurs, the less such religion corresponds to the "real nature" of religion. For how can the real nature of religion consist exclusively of its moral element, if this real nature can only come into existence at all as a result of a fusion of the moral with the mythological element?

Yet the root defect of this so self-contradictory a view lies still deeper. Precisely taken, this theory excludes entirely from the determination of the nature of religion, religion per se, the specifically and uniquely religious element. Deussen includes mythology and morality in the essence of religion : but the piety developing out of religious experience he does not consider. And since morality *per se* is admittedly not religion, the theory demands that the specifically religious element be found in mythology. Now this is exactly what this theory, especially in its popular form, means. And the dominating connecting thought is that the personification of natural forces produces the conceptions of the gods, and that the religious content of religion, taken in its more restricted sense, is concentrated in this. But such reasoning is false and does not touch the heart of the matter. We have already seen that the nature of religion cannot be found in gods or in conceptions of the gods. And here this judgment is again confirmed. Conceptions of the gods may be of a purely mythological nature, and this is equally true of some monotheistic conceptions. Such conceptions are not necessarily, or at least not directly religious. The personal relationship, which is revealed by the feeling of dependence and the feelings of security and yearning and without which there can be no legitimate reference to religion, is lacking. In itself mythology is precisely not religion. And Deussen admits this when he traces religion to the fusion of mythology and morality. And then this assumption involves him in the self-contradiction which we have already indicated.

Subject to this correction we can accept the essentials of Deussen's discussions of mythology as such. In our opinion these need only to be supplemented and to be more accurately expounded. Mythical thought is not restricted to the nature myth, with which Deussen's argument is exclusively concerned. All of the content of human perception and knowledge (in the pre-scientific sense of the term) may become the subject-matter of mythical thinking. To be sure the nature myth shows most significantly the uniqueness of mythical thinking.

That this uniqueness of the thinking that produces myths consists in the "personifying" process has long been recognized by discerning mythologists.[2] And in the great work of the last years of his life Wilhelm Wundt also described in detail the psychological conditions of this personifying or apperceptive process.

And yet, the idea of a mythological personification must be protected against misunderstanding and misuse. Mythological personification tends to think of processes of every possible sort—in nature myths they are the events of external nature—in terms of human behavior, and to interpret all of them as being analogous to human conditions and to human activities. And since men and animals are frequently confused with or converted into each other in a myth, to the conception of human we must here add that of animal behavior. Mythological personification, then, tends toward an anthropomorphic or zomorphic formulation of objects or events. However, mythological personification is not conditioned by the thought of spiritual and ethical personality. Strictly speaking this is self-evident because this type of thought cannot be grasped at the level of mythical thought. And yet it is very imperative to call attention to this fact. *For not only popular thought, but even scientific research, is continually in danger of reading spiritual and ethical factors into the idea of mythological personification, even though they do not rightly belong there.* Wherever the expression personification is used to designate myth-producing personification, this danger is at least immanent. For the interest of mythical thought is not directed toward personification in the sense of spiritual and ethical persons. A recognition of this fact is of great importance for the understanding of the relation of religion to mythology.[3]

[2] We refer in particular to A. Böckh: *Enzyklopædie u. Methodologie der philologischen Wissenschaften,* 2nd ed., edited by E. Bratuscheck, 1886, p. 561.

[3] In the German edition the author included here a long digression, printed mostly in smaller type than the rest of the text, in which he gives an illuminating discussion of primitive monotheism and its relation to mythology and to magic. Since it summarizes much original research, some of which is not available in English, we have translated this material in full and the reader will find it exceptionally informative. However, it seemed best to put it in Appendix II, which we have entitled "Primitive Monotheism and Mythology" (see below, pp. 356 ff.), and in Appendix III,

2

How, now, is the close relationship between magic and religion to be interpreted? What is the inner relationship of magic and religion to each other? *Obviously this question is of the greatest importance for the evaluation of the problem of the truth of religion.* And recently it has been discussed with great interest. Among the various attempted solutions two may especially lay claim to the most careful consideration: The theory of Frazer, because he has studied all of the material most thoroughly; and the theory of Leuba, because he has tried especially to clarify the psychological conditions of the relationship between religion and magic. A criticism of these two theories will enable us to define our own position.

We will only remark in passing that we consider a third much-discussed theory, which attempts to determine the relation of religion and magic in a purely sociological manner, to be a failure. The chief representative of this attempt is Emile Durkheim.[4] On this view the decisive difference between religion and magic consists solely in the fact that religion has a social and magic an anti-social tendency. The relation to an assumed mystical power is common both to religion and to magic, but in the one case religious rites and in the other case magical practices try to make this power act. For the religious rites the social tendency is essential, as is shown in the formulation of religious groups, but the magical practices express themselves in anti-social practices. However, this distinction does not go to the heart of the matter. It makes the mistake of putting a secondary factor into the foreground, and this diverts attention from the more basic fundamental factor. Hence this theory turns out to be a construction which perverts the facts.[5] Magic is not always nor is it necessarily anti-social. To place totemistic cults entirely on the side of religion is a perversion of the facts. Moreover, there are also other forms of magic which are not only not anti-social, but

which we have entitled "Religion and Magic." (See below, pp. 371 ff.)— Translators' note.

[4] See Emile Durkheim: *Elementary Forms of the Religious Life,* translated by Joseph Ward Swain.

[5] At this point Karl Beth also opposes Durkheim.

which have a positive social purpose. All magical healing has a social purpose, and so does all magical activity that aims to bring benefits to the whole tribe.

The merely sociological formulation of the relation of religion and magic does not, therefore, do justice to the facts. The discussion of the theories advanced by Frazer and Leuba will take us farther.

Frazer finds the nature of magic in a certain type of association of ideas.[6] He thinks that magic is the wrong application of the principle of the association of ideas. Accordingly Frazer traces all magic back to the basic categories of association—association by spatial or temporal contiguity, and association by similarity. This enables him to distinguish between two main groups of magical practices : *contagious magic,* which is based upon association by contiguity, and *imitative magic,* which is based upon association by similarity. Thus the structure of magic corresponds exactly to that of the association of ideas. Magic is based upon the principle of the association of ideas, but of course upon a false, naïve, and unjustified application of this principle.

Thus Frazer characterizes the nature of magic. But he defines its relation to religion in the following way. Magic precedes religion. It is the earlier stage of the development of human thought. Religion first came into being when man recognized and understood the futility of magic. The failure of magic made possible the rise of religion, which was an attempt to obtain, with the help of the gods, what magical practices proved unable to secure.

Thus the relation which Frazer finds between magic and religion is a purely negative relation. The insufficiency of magic was first realized, then its efficacy began to be doubted, and finally an entirely different method, in fact, the direct opposite, was devised; man no longer attempted to realize his desires and purposes by his own magical practices, but by recognizing higher powers and by praying to them for protection and aid. This process was, of course, only very slow and

[6] J. G. Frazer: *The Golden Bough,* A Study in Magic and Religion, 2nd ed., Vol. I (London, 1900, especially pp. 7-128), 3rd ed., Part I, Vols. I and II: *The Magic Art and the Evolution of Kings* (1911, especially Vol. I, pp. 52-243).

gradual. At first there were only a few individuals who attained this insight, and then gradually others followed them. That is the way Frazer accounts for the fact that at times magic and religion exist alongside of each other. But otherwise the two phenomena are alike only in the goal which they seek to attain.

Magic has for Frazer, on the other hand, a positive relation to science. He thinks that both lie along the same line, but at opposite ends of it. And here, again, the principle of the association of ideas is supposed to furnish the inner connection. For Frazer thinks that science is also based upon and always uses this principle, the difference merely being that science tests the association of ideas in a critical way by an appeal to experience, whereas magic fails to apply this critical test. Therefore science works with valid associations, whereas magic works with false associations. This explains why Frazer calls magic "the bastard sister of science." He thinks that there is an inner relationship between magic and science, while magic and religion have only a negative and external relationship to each other.

One might think that this theory of the famous English scholar is highly favorable to religion. On the one hand, it frees religion from any inner connection with such a questionable phenomenon as magic. And its difference from magic seems all the more assured and clear because, on the other hand, science, and all rational scientific knowledge, is put in relationship to magic.

However, there is another side of the matter. For in the last analysis this theory is hostile to religion—perhaps not according to Frazer's purpose, but certainly in its actual consequences. To be sure, magic and science are inter-related phenomena; and of course religion is in complete contrast to magic. However, in the first place, this contrast between magic and religion logically implies a contrast between religion and science, in the sense that they are treated as mutually exclusive phenomena. And secondly, the road which magic and science here share with each other is the natural path of development of mental life. It is the normal basic principle of human mental evolution which is here revealed: in magic, to be sure, it is still very inadequate and faulty; only science can emancipate it from these deficiencies and faults. Yet it is the normal principle of all mental development and of all human culture.

In contrast to this line of evolution, religion is on a totally wrong path. It seeks to overcome and to supplant magic, but it does this in an entirely capricious manner by means of arbitrary speculation. Religion now appears in this new light as capricious speculation. To be sure, it is in contrast with magic, but instead of going back to the normal and legitimate motives of human mental life and applying them properly, religion is in contrast with them too. For the only normal basic motives of mental life are the principles of the association of ideas. Religion is, therefore, entirely upon the wrong track. Science alone can provide the correct and normal way of overcoming magic. Religion has to be excluded from the normal development of human mental life. In the end, this is the logic of Frazer's whole position.

How is this theory to be evaluated? Upon close examination it proves to be a construction which does violence to the actual facts. Let us prove this evaluation from various points of approach.

It is incorrect and a mere construction to identify the principle of magic with the association of ideas and to treat the association of ideas as constituting the real essence of magic. It is true that idea-associations are present in magic, but they certainly do not constitute its actual basic principle. The nature of magic cannot be understood from this approach.

In order to carry out his interpretation Frazer has arbitrarily to narrow down the field of magic. For a dual division underlies the principle of the association of ideas: association by contiguity (spatial or temporal contiguity) and association by similarity. Now if the decisive principle of magic is to be traced back to the association of ideas, then magic has to be classified this way. So Frazer has contagious magic corresponding to association by contiguity, and imitative magic corresponding to association by similarity. And he thinks that magic not only does but must exhaust itself in these two forms. But precisely this does violence to the facts. Alongside of contagious magic and imitative magic there is another form of magic, which may be briefly designated as magic of the will: magical effects produced by a mere assertion of the will. This form of magic cannot be reduced to either of the other two forms without doing violence to the facts.

Furthermore, Frazer's statement of the relation between magic and science is incorrect. For that the association of ideas constitutes the principle of science is even less true than that it constitutes the principle of magic. Associations of ideas of course often enough play a rôle in science. But they do not constitute its actual principle. Moreover, identifying the nature of science with the association of ideas, and nothing but the association of ideas, would mean the abrogation of science as science. For in the last analysis associations of ideas are always subject to coincidence and caprice. Here Frazer is still following completely in the footsteps of Hume, who attempted to explain completely causality and the perception of cause in terms of mere idea-associations. The principle of causality is merely the sequence of two events, and accordingly, the sequence of two impressions. But Hume's conception of causality has since been completely disproven by Kant's criticism. Mere temporal sequence does not in itself constitute the nature of the causal relation. For the vital factor in any causal connection is the necessity which is expressed therein; and in itself mere sequence does not involve necessity. The same holds of Frazer's theory. Mere association of ideas so little constitutes the nature of science that, taken by itself, it cannot even make possible scientific work and scientific thinking. Scientific thinking is thinking according to the principle of sufficient reason, and a mere association of ideas is never a sufficient reason.

Frazer's conception of the relation of magic and religion presupposes a different basis for religion than for magic and science. But on its own grounds this presupposition can also be proven to be absolutely false. According to Frazer's theory, magic first preceded religion and was then supplanted by religion. This implies that the two main stages must have been: magic without religion and religion without magic. Magic combined with religion would have to be an exception and a merely temporary condition. But the actual situation is quite different. All the evidence we have from savage life reveals magic and religion always existing side by side. Magic without religion cannot be proven historically. And we can only find religion without magic in Christianity, and here also this is not at all completely realized. However, it is at least set up as an ideal.

And so the relation between magic and religion must still be of a different nature. In order to determine this relation more correctly and less one-sidedly we have to keep clearly in mind two facts which, just because they are somewhat contradictory to each other, permit us to see the problem in its full depth: 1. Magic extends throughout nearly the whole history of religion and permeates all religions. 2. However, in the Biblical, and especially in the Christian religion, there is a sharp cleavage between magic and religion, which is emphatically applied as a matter of principle, although in practice it is not always completely carried through. For their separation is demanded by the New Testament. We need only think of the Lord's Prayer which, according to the synoptic tradition, presents the most concentrated summary of the whole religious attitude of Jesus. The very context in which it is expressly placed, where it is contrasted with babbling and "much speaking," implies also a contrast to magic. But the contrast to all magic is most clearly expressed in the petition which is central to the whole prayer: "Thy will be done on earth as it is in heaven."

What is the result of this dual consideration? It proves that magic and religion, in spite of their differences, are nevertheless in close contact at one point. This one conviction is shared by both of them: namely, that there are powers which lie beyond the natural sphere of human energies: powers of a super-human, super-sensual, super-natural kind. In the end the basic conviction which is shared by both magic and religion is just this: that there exists a reality of a higher type and of a higher order, a higher reality which lies beyond the whole of mundane existence, and that man is able to get into contact with this higher reality.

The difference between them is that, whereas magic wishes

to force this over-world into the service of man, and would command these super-sensual powers by coercion, religion is convinced, and becomes all the more convinced as it becomes clear concerning its own nature, that the very presupposition in regard to the super-sensual world is that of man's subordination and obedience to it, and accordingly, that a relationship to the over-world can only be won by an attitude of subordination and trusting surrender.

That we must so state the relation between magic and religion, and that this is the only way to do justice to the facts, can be shown by a critical elucidation of the other theory, which we said had recently become widely held along with Frazer's theory. It is the theory developed by the American psychologist and student of religion, Leuba.[7]

Leuba begins, just as Frazer did, with the attempt to clarify, first of all, the relation between magic and religion, and then that between magic and science. But Leuba aims to base his conception upon an extensive psychological foundation, which is in many respects noteworthy and instructive.

Leuba says that in general there are three main forms or types of human attitudes which must be differentiated. These three attitudes may be seen in all of human life. They express the various methods by which man attempts to get along with the powers which surround and influence him. For man seeks to do this in three different ways, which indicate three different types of attitudes. Leuba names these three types of attitudes *the mechanical, the coercive,* and *the anthropopathic.* What he means by these terms is graphically illustrated by the following example. He imagines a fireman on a steamer, shoveling coal down in the hold of the ship. In his judgment and understanding of the power of heat this fireman is a typical representative of the mechanical attitude. He knows by experience that the functioning of the engine and, consequently, that the motion of the ship is conditioned by the shoveling of coal. But when that evening this same fireman has a succession of bad luck in a card game, and in trying to bring about a change

[7] James H. Leuba, *The Psychological Origin and the Nature of Religion,* London, 1909; *A Psychological Study of Religion, its Origin, Function and Future,* New York, 1912, pp. 57-191.

of luck, jumps up and walks around the table backwards, his behavior indicates a coercive attitude. And if, finally, in a moment of the greatest danger, he falls to his knees and in passionate terms petitions an invisible power for help, he exemplifies the anthropopathic type of attitude.

Leuba thinks that the anthropopathic attitude includes the religious sphere of human life. To be sure, this attitude does not exhaust itself in religion, but goes farther. Religion is only a part of the sphere of the anthropopathic attitude; the other part, being constituted by the attitude of men toward each other, is the sphere of ethical and social behavior.

Leuba designates as anthropopathic that attitude of man which is based upon motives of attraction or repulsion and which employs promises or threats. And that applies (1) to the attitude of men toward each other, and (2) to the sphere of religion.

The mechanical attitude is in sharpest contrast to this anthropopathic attitude. Here everything that is personal, emotional, or volitional is excluded, here nothing can be accomplished by promises or threats; here only mechanical effects or objects or processes are involved. And precisely for this reason, Leuba says, the quantitative relationships here play a decisive rôle; indeed they constitute the standard. For example, in the illustration used above a certain quantity of coal is necessary to heat the boiler to generate steam enough to make possible the ship's motion, and just as her speed is dependent upon the quantity of coal used, so in this mechanical sphere as a whole the quantitative relationships are everywhere actually decisive. And all mechanical attitudes, Leuba declares, include some practical knowledge of the quantitative relationships involved, a practical knowledge of the quantitative relations between events that are in the causal relation to each other. Such knowledge need not always be a conceptually clear knowledge, but nevertheless in practice it must exist to some extent. And precisely for this reason, Leuba sees in this mechanical attitude the doorstep to science, indeed, both the beginning and the first stage of science. And both are concerned with the quantitative relations between causes and effects. To observe and accurately to measure these quantitative relations constitutes the nature of science. Since science is the direct continuation of the mechanical attitude, that attitude is itself the elementary stage of science.

' In between these two kinds of human attitude, the anthropopathic and the mechanical, Leuba finds the coercive, *i.e.,* the magical. For his conception of coercion is only another name for the magical. And for Leuba this stands between the other two attitudes in such a way that it is sharply separated from each of them. It is differentiated from the mechanical attitude by its indifference to everything quantitative, and from the anthropopathic by its indifference to everything personal.

In this way Leuba attempts to determine the relation of magic both to science and to religion. All three phenomena are strictly differentiated; religion has no inner relationship either to science or to magic. For neither science nor magic are anthropopathic, but religion is anthropopathic and it is just this anthropopathic element that constitutes its real nature and its active principle.

At the first glance this theory also appears to be comparatively favorable to religion. To be sure, religion is placed in fundamental contrast to science; but there seems to be a compensation for this in the fact that it is likewise placed in an equally fundamental contrast to magic. However, in the end this theory also turns against religion, since it is ultimately decisive that religion is subsumed under the anthropopathic attitude. For, as the name itself signifies, the anthropopathic attitude is normally and justifiably the attitude of men to each other, it is the emotional and volitional behavior of men toward each other. Now it is unjustifiable to transfer religion from its original sphere to another realm, as this theory does. Judged by the presupposed basic principle, that is unjustifiable and arbitrary. *In this theory, too, religion carries, from the very beginning, its own death-warrant.* In the formulation of this scheme of three attitudes a value-judgment is implied, which presupposes a negative answer to the question of the truth of religion. First of all, the coercive attitude is unjustified; for it has no real existence. For in the psychological structure of man's mental life, the coercive or magical attitude cannot exist alongside of the mechanical and the anthropopathic attitudes. And insofar as this magical attitude is exclusively defined and evaluated from the viewpoint of coercive action, it is based entirely upon capricious and egoistic motives. Coercive action, the action which aims to force all non-human powers into the service of man, is nothing but egoistic caprice. To the extent that magic is a coercive attitude it actually is pure caprice, and nothing but caprice and it could include no aspect which would not be pure caprice from the very beginning.

The question, then, is whether magic is adequately and completely explained by the conception of the coercive attitude. Certainly the coercive motive is active in it, but is it the only motive that is active? We will take up this question later. Here let us return to the consideration that in Leuba's theory as a whole religion also has no real basis in the mental life of man. If, as a matter of principle, religion can be subsumed under the anthropopathic attitude, then it thereby stands condemned. For the legitimate sphere of the anthropopathic is just the anthropopathic, that is—the sphere of human relationships, of the relationships of men to each other. This makes religion also a product of caprice. Normally and correctly there is only the mechanical-scientific attitude on the one side in Leuba's theory, and the anthropopathic attitude as ethical-social action on the other side. The religious, as well as the coercive-magical attitude, is unjustified. In spite of the sharp psychological differentiation between magic and religion, the evaluation of both of them is the same and it is equally negative.

However, Leuba's whole theory is just as incorrect and misleading as is Frazer's. The scheme of three types of attitudes is very cleverly formulated and it contains some valid ideas, but on the whole and as a whole it is objectionable, more precisely, it is psychologically objectionable. This criticism applies first of all to the mechanical attitude as the elementary stage of science. It is a very daring statement, that all purely mechanical action involves a practical knowledge of quantitative relationships, at least if this expression is to be anything more than an empty tautology. For unless Leuba's statement is merely an empty tautology reflection upon this mechanical action can have no content. And since mechanical action is found even among animals, this judgment would also have to apply to them, and the statement that a practical knowledge of quantitative relationships is involved in the mechanical actions of animals would be nonsense. However, the other side of the matter is even more important. As Leuba uses the term, mechanical action cannot be taken as the elementary stage of science. Leuba wants to have it so in order to make quantitative relationships decisive for both. But that is not correct. The decisive principle of science is not that of quantitative relationships. This is indisputable in the case of the mental or the cultural sciences (Geisteswissenschaften), since for them the quantitative relationships are often quite secondary. In the natural sciences the quantitative relationships of course play a very significant rôle and are not secondary, but even there quantity is not so important as to be called the actually decisive principle. However, this fact may be left out of consideration, since, in any case, Leuba's theory implies a one-sided restriction of science to the natural sciences. His theory is applicable only to one sphere of science, namely to physical science. When applied to science as a whole it is absolutely false. But his scheme of three attitudes does involve the whole of science, and this must necessarily be the case since there is no other place in it than the mechanical attitude for any other department of science. Consequently the structure of his scheme is faulty at this point. But with this the whole theory falls. For the mechanical and the anthropopathic attitudes are correlative conceptions, and correlated phenomena. If the category of the mechanical attitude is untenable as Leuba has formulated it, then this holds also of the anthropopathic attitude and accordingly, also of the evaluation of religion implicit in it. And so the third element in his scheme also involves an unjustified and false construction.

And, at least to a certain extent, the same thing applies again to the remaining second part of his scheme. To designate magic as a coercive attitude is one-sided, if thereby one aims to give an exhaustive description of its real nature. For such a description leaves the intimate relationship between magic and religion, which history reveals to us, completely unfathomable. This intimate relationship only becomes understandable when we take into consideration the belief which underlies both magic and religion. That belief is that there are powers of a higher type which transcend the whole sphere of the world of nature and of the senses; and that means that there is a reality of another type and of another order than that of empirical existence, and a reality of another type and of another order in turn means of a higher type and of a higher order.

Upon this common basis the specific essence of magic is its aim to force these powers of a higher sphere of existence into its own sphere and to subordinate them to it. It aims to force them into its service, and hence it tries with its natural powers to elevate itself above these higher powers. According to its form of activity magic is coercive. Leuba is quite right in thinking that this coercive tendency is essential to magic. But this factor alone does not constitute the essence of magic, since it presupposes another factor which is common both to magic and to religion. Now religion applies this common basic belief in precisely the opposite direction from that of magic; it emphasizes the necessity of subordination and of surrender to the higher super-sensuous reality. And religion regards this subordination and surrender as the prerequisite to any possibility of gaining a share in the powers of the super-sensuous world. Obviously this form of that basic belief is the only normal one, the only one which is really consistent with that belief, and which does justice to its innermost tendency. Magic, however, is an abnormal form or expression of that belief; abnormal because it is self-contradictory.

And so the peculiar relationship between magic and religion which history reveals, becomes understandable. For history reveals the most numerous contacts between these two phenomena throughout the whole course of human development. But it also shows us, on the other hand, that a sharp conflict ensues, especially in Christianity. The rejection of all magic is the necessary outcome of the religious position which is adopted in the New Testament.   It is true that in the history of the Christian Churches magical elements have repeatedly regained entrance, but the Protestant Reformation deliberately waged war upon all magic.   When Luther declared that God is that power from whom we obtain all good things and in whom we take refuge in every need, and that to have a God means therefore to believe and to trust in him with one's whole heart, then he most emphatically rejected every form of magic.

And likewise, with the conception of the nature of religion expressed in this declaration of Luther, every connection between religion and mythology, and every introduction of mythological elements into religion, is in principle unconditionally rejected.   And herewith our discussion, completing its circuit, returns again to its starting-point.

As we have indicated above, we can formulate the idea of mythology in the general and most inclusive sense so that it includes magic within itself as its associated practice.   And when this is done the conclusion of our investigation must be formulated in such a way that religion and magic are in essence radically differentiated even though they are in close contact at one point.   This one point of contact explains the ever-recurring inroads of mythological thinking upon the sphere of religious belief in human history.   But in the nature of the case the other just mentioned fact must be ultimately decisive for the essential determination of the relation of religion and mythology.   And therefore, in spite of his remarkable command of the facts, the theory which Wilhelm Wundt attempts to prove in the three weighty volumes of the second part of his *Völkerpsychologie* entitled *Religion und Mythus,* is on the whole, fundamentally false.   He tries to prove that, in human culture, religion emerged from the myth, and also to exhibit the definite factors in this process, thereby explaining the origin and structure of the religious consciousness.   And his final judgment is that the religious idea of God is a synthesis of the conceptions of demons and of mythical heroes.

However, all of Wundt's arguments are vitiated by the

root defect that he failed to see the duality of the relation of religion and mythology, which was discussed above, and this caused him to fail completely to give an unequivocal and methodically controllable norm for a specific characterization of the nature of religion.

CHAPTER X

I

It was Kant, the founder of critical philosophy, who said:
"I have found it necessary to deny knowledge in order to
make room for faith."

This statement is found in this form in the preface to the
second edition of the *Critique of Pure Reason,* and that means
that it occupies the especially important place of safeguarding
Kant's basic and fundamental position against mis-understand-
ings and mis-interpretations on the occasion of the second
issuance of his *magnum opus.* Yet this statement of Kant has
itself very often been misunderstood and misused, and it is
still today all too often misapplied. It is misunderstood and
abused when it is used to minimize in any way the significance
and the value of knowledge, to depreciate scientific investigation and even science itself. No one could evaluate science,
scientific research and knowledge, any higher than Kant did.
On the other hand, it is primarily a genuine misunderstanding
and misuse of Kant's statement to interpret it to mean that
the belief, of which he speaks, is to be identified with a completely definite and fixed set of ecclesiastical dogmas. For it
is simply out of the question seriously to interpret Kant this
way.

What, then, does this statement really mean? Now this
will become clear if we place the sentence in the context in
which Kant himself wrote it, and simply take with it the
sentence which immediately precedes it. For just before this
statement stands the sentence: "The assumption—as made on
behalf of the necessary practical employment of my reason—
of *God, freedom, and immortality* is not permissible unless at

the same time speculative reason be deprived of its pretensions to transcendent insight." [1]

Thus Kant turned himself against every attempt to answer the ultimate and most significant questions which men can ask—the questions of God, freedom, and immortality he took to be such—by the way of an assumed purely theoretical knowledge. All such efforts, Kant said, are in truth rationalistic presumptions, arrogant, unjustifiable, and untenable speculations, and they are also a presumptuous over-stepping of the boundaries of purely theoretical knowledge in the name of this knowledge itself. They are metaphysical speculations, or, conversely, speculative metaphysics. And such speculative metaphysics is fallacious in two respects: It infringes both upon the interest of science, of scientific research and knowledge, and upon the interest of the belief, or the conviction of belief of religion.

It was in this sense that Kant said: I must deny knowledge in order to make room for faith. Knowledge means here the popular and presumptuous knowledge of ultimate issues, popular solutions of the riddle of the universe, and Kant is saying that he had to destroy this kind of knowledge in order to make room for faith, and to show how religious belief can exist along side of knowledge, the strictest kind of knowledge, the profoundest scientific research and knowledge. However, Kant repudiated purely speculative metaphysics, and he repudiated it without any qualification whatsoever. And since traditional metaphysics always deals with the problem of a philosophy of life, we can express Kant's thought as follows: Kant repudiated purely rationalistic solutions of the problem of a philosophy of life, and accordingly he repudiated in general every purely theoretical quest for and defense of a philosophy of life. Hence we may conclude that a philosophy of life is neither to be attained nor defended by means of theoretical knowledge alone. A philosophy of life is not a scientific and theoretical type of knowledge purely as such. And the proof for this is that, when scientific knowledge tries to attain such

[1] From Norman Kemp Smith's translation of Kant's *Critique of Pure Reason*, p. 29 (Macmillan and Co., Ltd.).—Translators' note.

a goal, it always ends in empty speculations and day-dreams.

This conclusion, however, at once places us in the very thick of the struggle for a philosophy of life for our own day. For exactly what Kant denied, and what we, following him, have denied, modern monism asserts, indeed, modern monism regards this as the central issue of the present day struggle for a philosophy of life.

In the years immediately preceding the world-war this monism engaged in the widest kind of propaganda, and since the war it has entered the arena with renewed energy. This propaganda has been and still is especially promulgated by the members of the *Society of Monists,* which Haeckel founded.

This monism asserts exactly what we denied in our summary of Kant's position above. And it makes this assertion in such a way as to treat it as quite the most decisive and portentous principle of the entire monistic system, and accordingly of the entire monistic propaganda.

This is made especially clear by the systematic platform of the two famous leaders of the *Society of Monists.* Haeckel and Ostwald (died in 1932) are these two well known leaders, and both men are unquestionably eminent and distinguished scholars within their own special field. It can only be deeply deplored that this fact has often been questioned and denied in the midst of the struggle for a philosophy of life. The publication of Haeckel's popular *Riddle of the Universe,* which appeared at the turn of the 19th century and numberless editions and translations of which soon spread to almost all languages, was what in particular led to the founding of the *Society of Monists.* The socalled monistic philosophy of life, which Haeckel advanced in this book as the alleged necessary conclusion of scientific knowledge, desires and aims to bring the Society of Monists to the masses. Indeed, the very title of the book, the *Riddle of the Universe,* which means, indeed, the solution, yes, the finally valid solution of the riddle of the universe, also contains this aim, which is really the basis of the whole undertaking.

During the world-war Haeckel published a book under the title *Eternity.* The sub-title runs: "World-war reflections on

life and death, religion and the theory of evolution." [2] Here
quite expressly the author claims that all of the questions of a
philosophy of life that are implied in the concept of eternity,
can be conclusively answered only on the basis of the theory of
evolution.   Indeed, their answers follow at once from a special
application of the theory of evolution to humanity.   He thinks
that the problem of the original source of mankind is the
cardinal problem of all philosophies of life.   In the preface
Haeckel writes: "From the viewpoint of my special field I
regard this question of all questions as definitely answered,
and I also find in this special field the surest . . . way of
rightly evaluating eternity!"

In a pamphlet of the *German Society of Monists,* which appeared just before the outbreak of the world-war, Ostwald
hailed Haeckel as "the founder of a scientific philosophy of
life" or, as he puts it more exactly, as the "founder of a natural scientific philosophy of life." [3]   The use of these two
ideas is extraordinarily characteristic of the whole manner of
thinking of Ostwald, Haeckel, and their followers.   However,
both ideas are ambiguous.   Each by itself can be interpreted
and used so that it is free from objections.   One can rightly
speak of a *scientific philosophy of life,* in the sense that a
philosophy of life must also defend itself before the forum of
science.   But Ostwald does not so understand the idea, rather
for him a scientific philosophy of life is only such a philosophy
of life as is exclusively, *i.e.,* apparently exclusively, built upon
scientific knowledge.   And this conception of a philosophy of
life Ostwald then forthwith substitutes for the other idea of
a natural scientific philosophy of life.   A philosophy of life
must be built solely upon the natural sciences.   So interpreted,
however, the demand for a natural scientific philosophy of life
is entirely unjustifiable, indeed it is in itself shot through with
contradictions.   A philosophy of life should take into account
the whole of reality, and it should never be built only upon
that section of reality which constitutes the field of the natural sciences.

[2] Berlin, G. Reimer, 1915.   Translated into English by Thomas Seltzer
(Truthseeker Press).
[3] Number 30, Leipsic, 1914, pp. 5, 7, and 43.

On the other hand, one can also connect with the expression *natural scientific philosophy of life* a valid meaning, as for example when one thinks of a philosophy of life which takes its departure from the natural sciences, and accordingly lays special weight upon the conclusions of these sciences.

However, to Ostwald and Haeckel it is truly self-evident, or it should at least be self-evident that natural scientific knowledge in general, must, and to be sure in an all-inclusive way, acknowledge a philosophy of life which can pass as scientific. Of course this does not always happen, and the defenders of the religious and ecclesiastical philosophy of life have often taken such a scientific philosophy of life too lightly. That is the serious reproach the monists make from which we certainly cannot exempt religious leaders. But nevertheless it remains true that the idea of a natural scientific philosophy of life, as this is understood by Ostwald and Haeckel, is false and inconsistent. Moreover, the general idea of a scientific philosophy of life, at least as soon as it is interpreted to mean that scientific knowledge is itself able to reach a philosophy of life, is false and inconsistent too.

No, this program is erroneous. A philosophy of life can only be grounded in knowledge and belief, in belief and knowledge. Apart from any belief (ohne allen Glauben), or still better, apart from any believing (ohne alles Glauben) a philosophy of life can neither be attained nor defended. But we here stand at a point where a misunderstanding and misuse of truths that are not comprehended lurks to a greater extent than almost anywhere else. Consequently we must do everything possible to reach full clarity in our discussion, thereby correcting every misunderstanding and excluding every misuse of these truths.

Just for this reason I have already proposed expressing the idea of belief, which is here in question, not primarily in the masculine but rather in the neuter gender. Apart from any believing (ohne alles Glauben), we shall say, a philosophy of life can neither be won nor be defended.

Believing is the presupposition of a philosophy of life, of every philosophy of life, yes, of the very possibility of a philosophy of life. It is the condition and, to be sure, the indispens-

able condition for reaching a philosophy of life, and, as we have
said, of absolutely any philosophy of life, regardless of the kind
it is.　Believing (Das Glauben)—I purposely formulate it so
and not in the masculine gender (Der Glaube).　Of course the
statement would not be false in itself, if the masculine gender
were used, but it would be misunderstood.　For no particular
kind of belief is here under consideration, but on the contrary
believing only as a psychical and spiritual function.　Therefore,
we are not here considering any belief that has a definite content, and we are also not necessarily considering religious belief,
that is to say, a belief having a religious content.　No, the
problem of belief does not simply coincide with the religious
problem, even though believing finds its fullest and profoundest
expression in religion.　But we must grasp the idea of belief as
a universal idea, so that it will neither exclude nor yet be restricted to religious belief.

That believing, which underlies religious belief as a psychical and spiritual function, but which is not restricted to religious
belief, is what is the presupposition of every philosophy of life.
But here now a new misunderstanding usually begins.　What
is belief in this universal sense of the word?　Popular common-
sense usage of everyday life likes to think of this belief as a
mere opinion or supposition, that is to say, as opinion in the
sense of what is not-yet-knowledge, or of knowledge that is not
yet satisfying or not yet completed, and that means as a mere
step toward knowledge or as imperfect or incomplete knowledge.　For in this sense opinion, is, indeed, simply the lower
degree of knowledge, and it differs from knowledge not in quality but only in quantity, not in essence and in principle, but on
the contrary only in degree.　Such opinion contains the desire
and the demand of being raised to the level of knowledge.　It
is only its elevation to knowledge which brings the inner
tendency of opinion to its completion.

If one identifies belief with this popular conception of
opinion, then all that we have just said about opinion will also
hold of belief.　Then belief will also appear to be only a stage
of knowledge, which would develop as soon as possible into
genuine and real knowledge.　But this popular conception mis-
takes the inner nature of that which is rightly called belief.

Kant has already made it absolutely clear that belief cannot be simply identified with, but on the contrary must be strictly and sharply distinguished from opinion. An entire section of the *Critique of Pure Reason* bears the heading: "Of Opinion, Knowledge, and Belief." [4] There belief is distinguished not only from knowledge but from opinion; and opinion, knowledge, and belief are dealt wth as three separate things and in definite differentiation from each other. I will not explain the way in which Kant makes this differentiation. His position here is ingenious and instructive, but yet it does not quite do justice to the facts.

Recently this question has been discussed from the philosophical approach especially by William James, Friedrich Paulsen, Rudolf Eucken, Heinrich Rickert, Richard Hönigswald, Hermann Count Keyserling, Hermann Schwarz, Max Scheler, and August Messer; and from the theological approach by Wilhelm Herrmann, Julius Kaftan, Arthur Titius, Reinhold Seeberg, Rudolf Otto, Karl Heim, and Karl Stange; while Ernst Troeltsch and Heinrich Scholz may both be equally well included in either group.

2

In order to define our own attitude toward this issue, let us return to the point which we had already reached.

Opinion, we saw, is a stage of knowledge; it lies in the same line with knowledge, only it lies at the beginning of this line, or still better, if we think of the line as perpendicular, it lies at the lowest end of the line. Opinion can always be more and more elevated to knowledge. Accordingly the hypothesis also belongs with opinion. An hypothesis is the technical and theoretical form of an opinion. Therefore the hypothesis serves knowledge, scientific knowledge. Indeed, accurately expressed, all scientific knowledge is hypothetical, in varying degrees and stages up to that of the highest degree of probability, which is usually regarded simply as certain knowledge. But the fact is

---

[4] It is the third section of the second chapter of the Transcendental Doctrine of Method, 2nd ed., pp. 848 ff. See Norman Kemp Smith's translation, p. 645.

that scientific knowledge can never extend beyond the highest degree of probability.   At least, if we disregard logic and pure mathematics, it is true that, accurately expressed, all scientific knowledge is hypothetical.   This fact is not altered by Newton's famous warning against an unjustifiable use of hypotheses, nor by Ostwald's recent claim to have established a natural science that is free from hypotheses.   Newton's well-known statement: *"hypotheses non fingo,"* "I do not use hypotheses," with which he declined to concern himself about the basis of universal gravitation, is expressly directed against imaginative and also against pseudo-hypotheses.   Such arbitrary and imaginative hypotheses Newton rightly repudiated.   They have no proper place in physics nor in science generally.

Yet Newton's statement is not directed against the ultimate hypothetical character of all scientific knowledge.   On the contrary it presupposes this.   For when Newton, in the same sense in which he repudiated the forming of arbitrary suppositions about the ultimate basis of universal gravitation, at another time said that he knew that the planets are related to each other *as if* they are attracting each other, but that he did not know whether they really are attracting each other, we have indeed in this fundamental assertion an admirable example of the scientific use of hypotheses.   This assertion of Newton is completely in accord with the famous statements of the great physicists, Gustav Robert Kirchoff and Heinrich Hertz.   Kirchoff's well known definition, which has also been misinterpreted number-less times, runs (see his *Lehrbuch der Mechanik*) : "The task of natural science is to describe, as fully as possible and in the simplest possible manner, the phenomena appearing in nature," and note that he says to describe, not to explain.   Kirchoff thereby restricts the task of natural science as a matter of principle to description, that is to the most complete and the simplest description possible.   And it is also implied that we will gradually succeed in finding a still more complete and a still simpler description by a classification of the collection of known natural laws.   Such a classification is often referred to as an explanation.   This type of explanation Kirchoff's description does not exclude; on the contrary it demands it; but at the same time it emphasizes that this "explanation" is itself, in turn, ultimately a description, and is not an explanation in the sense of a definite solution of the riddle of the universe, nor in the sense of an exhibition of the ultimate basis or of the *veræ causæ* of the processes of the universe.

And Hertz, in the introduction to his mechanics,[5] says directly that hypotheses are pictures or models which man makes out of the phenomena of nature. It is aside from the point that many misinterpretations of this statement have been made. For it remains true that all progress in scientific knowledge depends upon progress in the forming of hypotheses, and upon reaching progressively better established and more comprehensive hypotheses.

Ostwald's claim to have established with his *energetics* a natural science that is free from hypotheses does not in the least alter this fact.[6] For Ostwald's energetics is not free from hypotheses. On the contrary it is so little free from hypotheses that the idea of energy, as it is used in Ostwald's energetics, even contains an hypothetical element. It is only from a quite restricted point of view, and only in an hypothetical way, that such diverse entities as warmth, light, sound, vibration, electricity, elasticity, and chemical affinity can be brought together under a common universal concept of energy. Hence it remains true that scientific knowledge rests upon the formulation of hypotheses. Yet the hypothesis is the methodical form of an opinion. Consequently, in this respect also, the inner relationship of opinion and knowledge is revealed. On the other hand, it is entirely different with belief!—Belief in the narrower and unique sense,—not yet in the specifically religious sense, but in the narrower sense in which belief differs from opinion—, such belief is not a stage of knowledge, it is not a not-yet-knowledge, which can be and wants to become elevated to the level of knowledge, but it is inherently and qualitatively and by its own intrinsic nature different from knowledge. For in the last analysis such belief is a decision of the will which is not an

[5] Heinrich Hertz: *Die Prinzipien der Mechanik in neuem Zusammenhang dargestellt,* Leipsic, 1894.

[6] Wilhelm Ostwald: *Vorlesungen über Naturphilosophie,* 3rd edition, 1905. Also in many smaller monographs (for example: *Die Energie*) and in many essays in his *Annalen der Naturphilosophie.* See also his *Lebenslinien,* 1927.

affair to be determined in a purely theoretical way. Belief is
such a decision of the will, or expressed still better and more
accurately: belief rests upon such a decision of the will, that is
to say, it is a conviction resting upon such a decision of the
will: a volitional conviction in a sense which withdraws it from
purely theoretical judgment, and consequently from strict scientific knowledge. And indeed—for this must also be especially
stressed—a decision of the will and a conviction which is so
little founded upon cognition and scientific knowledge that it is
on the contrary determined more by an instinctive element. In
other words we can speak exactly of an instinctive decision of
the will and of an instinctive volitional conviction.

Yet in human life such belief undoubtedly has its justification and also the greatest significance. So we must conclude
even when we ignore religious belief, and here at the beginning
leave the religious problem entirely out of consideration.

Howsoever it may be with religion and with religious belief,
belief in general, in the sense already defined, undoubtedly has
a justification and also an enormous significance.

For example, such belief is active in every important decision of great statesmen and generals. But further, it is also
rooted in our common everyday life. For such belief is also
active in all friendship and in all love; and, to be sure, the more
it is active the deeper is the friendship or the love in question.
Apart from such belief true friendship and true love are impossible. For true friendship and true love are not established
purely theoretically, at many a point, yes and exactly at the
most decisive point, they withdraw themselves from the purely
theoretical type of knowledge and also from a strictly scientific
scrutiny.

The belief that is active in friendship and love and which is
their very taproot, cannot be raised to the level of knowledge;
but it absolutely does not want to be raised to and to be transformed into knowledge. And if this could be done it would
not be an exaltation but a suppression of true friendship and
of true love; it would not result in a higher but in a lower
degree of friendship and of love.

Now religious belief lies exactly along this line, only it lies
in an extension of this line. In it, too, we are concerned with

a volitional conviction.—But let us ignore religion a little longer. What now specifically interests us in this analysis is this, that such belief as instinctive volitional decision and instinctive volitional conviction is an element in every philosophy of life. Apart from such belief no philosophy of life can exist and apart from such belief no philosophy of life can be defended. Select any of the philosophies of life which have played a rôle in the history of philosophy that you wish, and you will always find that instinctive rational conviction forms an important element in them. And that is not merely an historical fact, but on the contrary it is an indispensable fact. Apart from every belief a philosophy of life is, generally speaking, impossible. Apart from every belief a naturalistic philosophy of life is just as impossible as an idealistic one, and again, apart from every belief a pessimistic philosophy of life is just as impossible as an optimistic one.

He who, in building his philosophy of life, would repudiate all belief will find only one way out: that of a basic and radical scepticism. Only the thorough-going and consistent sceptic comes out of his reflections upon the problem of a philosophy of life without any belief, and the words *thorough-going* and *consistent* must here be taken in their strictest sense.

And consistent scepticism means, to state it accurately, not a definite form or type of philosophy of life, but on the contrary the denial of every philosophy of life.

If this is true, must not this final alternative of denying every philosophy of life perhaps be put forward as a demand? At least is this not the wisest policy for all who would think scientifically? Now we could just as well demand that friendship and love be denied. For we never attain these by mere cognition and purely theoretical knowledge, but just as we never reach a philosophy of life without belief so we can never attain friendship or love without belief. Radical and consistent scepticism on the problem of a philosophy of life is, then, exceptionally rare, even among those who pretend to be sceptics. When one looks closer he will discover that the scepticism is often broken through here and there. And exactly that makes the whole attitude of the sceptic inconsistent.

Yet mere neutrality is absolutely impossible on this matter

of a philosophy of life. In the struggle for a philosophy of life he who would remain completely neutral and would take no stand on this issue, he who would take no stand on the great basic questions of a philosophy of life is self-deceived. For such assumed neutrality in practice always amounts to a definite decision. Whoever tries not to decide between an idealistic and a naturalistic philosophy of life, and who seeks to remain neutral on this issue, thereby already represents and defends in practice a naturalistic philosophy of life. For an idealistic philosophy of life does not permit such a neutrality, it demands one's active defense of the idealistic way of thinking. And the same holds of pessimism and optimism. Whoever claims to take no position here, but tries to withhold his decision, he thereby already throws his will to the one side, namely to the side of pessimism, for the optimistic philosophy of life never tolerates such neutrality, but demands an optimistic type of activity. Such activity is a *conditio sine qua non* of the optimistic way of thinking itself.

Indeed, if we disregard all scholarly distinctions of separate forms and if we leave religion out of account for the moment, these are the great chief types of a philosophy of life. These four, in two pairs, one of which we may call a *theoretical* type of philosophy of life and the other pair a *practical* type of philosophy of life—an *idealistic* and a *naturalistic* type on the one hand and an *optimistic* and a *pessimistic* type on the other hand—these are the four great chief types of a philosophy of life.

Now it at once follows that a union of the idealistic and the optimistic types produces a tendency toward religion; whereas a union of the naturalistic and the pessimistic types gives a tendency against religion. What we said above about both of these pairs of philosophies of life, namely, that mere neutrality is here not really possible, also holds of the alternative between the religious and the anti-religious type of philosophy of life. For the assumed neutrality, the intention to remain neutral to the religious problem in practice already means the taking of a position against religion and in opposition to the religious philosophy of life. The religious philosophy of life does not tolerate this neutrality; it demands of its adherents practical activity in the sense of the religious way of thinking (worship), and it is just this activity that is the indispensable condition of the religious philosophy of life itself.

However that may be, a philosophy of life, generally speaking, is not possible apart from belief, apart from every belief in the sense explained above, neither the idealistic nor the naturalistic, neither the optimistic nor the pessimistic philosophy of life can be reached or defended purely rationally. For purely rationally and with the help of nothing but strict scientific knowledge, one cannot decide whether or not the spiritual principle permeates the world; and in the end that is the controversy between idealism and naturalism. And it is equally true that purely rationally one cannot decide whether or not life is worth living. And this is the question which determines the controversy between optimism and pessimism. No, apart from every belief a philosophy of life, generally speaking, is not possible. Only the consistent representative of radical scepticism dispenses with all belief, or would dispense with all belief, if there really were such a consistent sceptic.

Thus is stands so far as the question of a philosophy of life in general is concerned. In every philosophy of life a belief, in the sense of a volitionally determined conviction, is active; and in the religious philosophy of life this is the case in the most concrete and most emphatic way. But on this point and in this respect the religious philosophy of life does not differ in principle, but only in degree, from other philosophies of life. Indeed the religious philosophy of life can claim the credit for allowing the basic problem of a philosophy of life, of any philosophy of life, to come to clearest expression. For the basic problem of any philosophy of life is the relation of belief to knowledge, the relation of the conviction of belief to scientific knowledge. And it is just in the religious philosophy of life that this is clearest, since in it belief, which is a part of every philosophy of life, enters most strictly and emphatically into the phenomenon.

Yet the religious philosophy of life, if it is to appeal generally to scientifically trained men, must also be defended before the forum of science. It ought not to be turned into knowledge. No philosophy of life can be completely transformed into knowledge, and least of all the religious. Nevertheless the religious philosophy of life must maintain its position alongside of the justifiable claims of scientific knowledge, and it must also be defended before the forum of science. Otherwise we shall reach the position that there are two kinds of truth, essentially as the schoolmen of the Middle Ages worked out that theory. But that is a dilemmatic situation in which neither scientific knowledge nor religious belief is established, in which neither the interest of science nor the interest of religious belief is satisfied. For the very conception of truth demands unity. Dual truth is at the same time a twofold annulment of truth and a double contradiction of truth. Hence not only must science insist that the religious philosophy of life be scientifically established, but this demand also belongs absolutely to the strictest interest of the religious philosophy of life itself.

3

Thus every philosophy of life is concerned with the relation of belief to knowledge and of knowledge to belief. The French philosopher Bergson attempts in a unique way to evade this fact, which alone represents the actual situation.[7]

As a means of reaching a philosophy of life Bergson recommends *intuition,* that is to say, the process which he describes by the word *intuition,* a word which is itself by no means unambiguous. By the aid of such intuition he wants to gain an insight into the ultimate relations of all things, to give an answer to the questions of the whence and the whither, and to learn what reality contains in its innermost essence.

Hence Bergson would set aside both knowledge and belief, scientific knowledge as well as religious conviction. A philosophy of life ought not to be determined by belief and knowledge, in the way that was explained above, so that the belief to which we are referred in the highest and most ultimate questions of life is put into relation to knowledge, to the most exact scientific knowledge, and is thereby controlled and safeguarded

---

[7] Two important works of Bergson are: *Creative Evolution,* translated by Arthur Mitchell (Henry Holt & Co.) and *An Introduction to Metaphysics,* translated by T. E. Hulme (G. P. Putnam's Sons).

against arbitrary speculation. Not that, but on the contrary Bergson will point and open a third way of reaching truth, a way which is independent of both science and belief, and which will supplant both. This way is the one mentioned, the assumed intuition, the intuition of the ultimate basis and constitution of all being and becoming. Now this use of intuition, with its varieties of meaning, certainly contains an element of truth. Intuition as the immediate grasping of truths is active both in scientific knowledge and in the conviction of belief— it is active in different ways both in science and in belief. The only question is whether intuition can do what Bergson wants it to do, namely, offer a way of grasping the truth which is independent of knowledge and belief.

Does this intuition, coming out with such a claim, not rather lead again to arbitrary speculation, and thus to a metaphysics which is nothing less than an empty construction? Does it not lead to exactly that kind of speculative metaphysics against which Kant so impressively warned?

The philosophy of life which Bergson would win by this method, with its doctrine of a vital impetus (*élan vital*), certainly stands in a somewhat analogous relation to the religious philosophy of life, yet exactly at the decisive point it nevertheless stands in the sharpest contrast to the religious philosophy of life. For it does not look upon the over-world or "God" as the original source of all being and of all life, of all formation and development of life, but, on the contrary, this formation and development of life is itself put first, and then later the conception of God, in a disfigured form, is misinterpreted so that God is taken to be a product of the spatio-temporal universe. To build this metaphysics Bergson turns to intuition.

How is one to regard this whole undertaking? In order to come to a decision on this matter we must turn our attention to the relation in which Bergson places instinct and intuition. For it is just this relation which serves to justify his use of intuition. The way in which Bergson uses intuition to answer the question of a philosophy of life, shoving aside both science and belief, he attempts to justify by his estimation of the relation between intuition and instinct. The intuition of his metaphysics is to be the utilization for the sphere of a philosophy of life of the grasp of truth that is instinctive. The methodical principle of intuition he takes to be the principle of instinct. This principle of the instincts is to be developed into the methodical principle of intuition, and then likewise into the methodical principle of metaphysics and of a philosophy of life.

Now what is to be said about this? Bergson would develop instinct into intuition by letting instinct reflect upon itself and by allowing it to reach a knowledge of itself. Intuition is thus taken to be instinct that is self-conscious, the instinct that reflects upon itself, the instinct which turns inward to consciousness instead of that which, as is usually the case, turns outward to things.

And to the extent that he can teach his own instinct, which has become conscious, to reflect upon itself Bergson aims to extend this reflection to the infinite. Accordingly intuition can unveil for us the ultimate secrets of all life, and, in general, of all being, it can reveal to us what the inner nature of reality is. Thus Bergson's intuition transcends scientific knowledge and at the same time it makes belief superfluous. This is the claim which Bergson makes for intuition and he makes it on the basis of the relationship in which he places intuition and instinct. But precisely this estimate of the relationship between intuition and instinct is certainly nothing less than an arbitrary construction, which, being itself arbitrary, can only culminate in arbitrary speculation.

It is an arbitrary construction, yes, and at the same time it is a construction that is shot through with contradictions. For an instinct which is conscious of itself, and which reflects upon itself is an inherently contradictory conception of an instinct. The instincts which we know do not reflect, either about themselves or about the secrets of reality. On the contrary, it is precisely the lack of the ability to reflect which constitutes the essence of instinct and of all instinctive action. If instinct should begin to reflect, it would cease to be instinct. Only intelligence reflects.

But Bergson has to leave intelligence out of account, since his intuition is to have nothing to do with intelligence and is to be as different from intelligent scientific knowledge as it is different, on the other side, from belief and the conviction of belief.

That is the trick of Bergson and of his philosophy. At least with reference to the relation of belief and knowledge it is a mere trick. A philosophy of life can only be established by belief and knowledge, by knowledge and belief. Belief and knowledge must be brought into a unity in a philosophy of life.

CHAPTER XI

ILLUSIONISM AND THE PROBLEM OF TRUTH

I

Historically, the most significant and influential champion of the illusionistic theory of religion is Ludwig Feuerbach. The extraordinary service which he rendered by his uncompromisingly clear statement of the problem of truth in religion was discussed sufficiently above. But Feuerbach arrived at this clear and precise statement of the problem of truth from his conception of the nature of religion. And the significance of his conception of the nature of religion is in turn conditioned by his deeply penetrative insight into the psychological structure of the religious consciousness.

So far, then, from the religio-psychological point of view, we entirely agree in a formal way with Feuerbach's position. Further on, of course, our ways part and lead in entirely opposite directions. What is the reason for this parting into opposite directions? The reason is that Feuerbach, in spite of very significant beginnings toward a genuine religio-psychological understanding of religion, finally succumbed to the error which he at first combated and sought to avoid. As he himself frequently stated, he sought to do nothing else to religion but to open her eyes, *i.e.* in contrast to Hegel's rationalization of religion, he wanted to show how to understand religion and to grasp its inner meaning. But instead of doing this his own theory of religion is likewise an arbitrary construction which, although it differed from Hegel's in form, is just as complete a rationalization of religion. For as we have already seen, from a religio-psychological point of view it must be stated that Feuerbach's idea of religion is "man's instinct for happiness which is satisfied in the imagination." And the same thing is true of the theory, which more accurately defines this main thesis; that man believes in gods because he has the desire to be happy; that the gods are the wishes of men thought of as already realized; that they were created by man in order to satisfy his needs, namely, to protect his interests and realize his ideals; that religion is concerned with the attitude of man toward himself, more precisely, with the attitude of the individual human being to humanity as such, to the human species.

That in the last analysis we have in this completely unified view of religion a purely a priori construction, is especially evident at those points in Feuerbach's discussion where he defends his attitude toward the problem of truth. Thus in summarizing his argument in the final criticism of *Das Wesen des Christentums,* he says: "The necessary turning point of the whole matter is this frank confession and admission that the consciousness of God is nothing else but the consciousness of the species, that man can and should only lift himself above the limitations of his individuality but not above the laws, the positive actual nature of humanity, that man can think, surmise, imagine, feel, believe, desire, love, and worship no other being as an absolute being except the phenomenon of the nature of man."

This twice-repeated "can," which here bears the whole burden of proof, is a verbal expression of the completely unfounded and—at least within the bounds of Feuerbach's theory—unprovable comprehensive judgment with which the whole theory stands or falls.

Feuerbach himself expressly emphasized the fact that he originated his philosophy of religion only because of his opposition to Hegel and that this fact is essential to an understanding and an evaluation of it.[1] This judgment is so entirely correct that it really constitutes the final criticism of his own position. Although Feuerbach's position is the exact opposite of Hegel's in method, nevertheless both theories are upon the same level.

Feuerbach also combined with his polemic against Hegel an

[1] *Sämtliche Werke,* edition of Wilh. Bolin and Friedr. Jodl, Vol. VII, pp. 265 f. (*"Zur Beurteilung der Schrift: das Wesen des Christentums";* 1824). Kurt Leese (*Die Prinzipienlehre der neueren systemmatischen Theologie im Lichte der Kritik Ludwig Feuerbachs,* Leipzic, 1912) has quite correctly strongly emphasized Feuerbach's opposition to Hegel.—See also Leese's book: *Philosophie und Theologie in Spätidealismus.* Feuerbach's *Das Wesen des Christentums* has been translated by Marian Evans with the title: *The Essence of Christianity.*

equally keen criticism of Schleiermacher, not realizing that it was precisely Schleiermacher, with his radical return to the religious states of feeling or to religious experience, who could have shown him how actually to conquer and to surmount Hegel.

Yet Feuerbach learned much from Schleiermacher, indeed one is even forced to say that he is indebted to Schleiermacher for his best insights.[2] In the *Vorlesungen über das Wesen der Religion,* which are highly important for his philosophy of religion, this is especially evident. Here Feuerbach consciously and admittedly goes back to Schleiermacher's formulation of the religious feeling of dependence. The feeling of dependence, he says in so many words, is the only correct universal concept with which to describe and to explain the psychological or subjective basis of religion. But this valuable insight which he took from Schleiermacher is then spoiled by Feuerbach's a priori construction, which he set up in an entirely Hegelian manner and with which he subordinates the religious feeling of dependence to the instinct of self-preservation. The religious feeling of dependence, Feuerbach argues, is not a new phenomenon which evidences itself alongside of the will to live of the instinct of self-preservation, but it is only this will to live as such, in a restricted form. It is an indirect or negative self-feeling.

This obscures Schleiermacher's basic insight and ultimately even converts it into its opposite. For, on the testimony of religious experience, the feeling of dependence is undoubtedly not self-feeling in Feuerbach's sense, but a feeling of being conditioned, or of being determined by a higher reality.

Feuerbach overlooks this ultimately decisive character of the religious feeling of dependence. It is only because of this oversight that it is possible for him to treat the "egoism" of the instinct of self-preservation as the *subjective* basis of religion

[2] And in later life Feuerbach expressed his indebtedness to Schleiermacher. Standing before the Dreifaltigkeits-Kirche, during a visit to Berlin in 1864, he recalled the "happiness of his youthful period in Berlin" and the impression which Schleiermacher's sermons made upon him. "There was nothing of argument about him, but he only spoke out of the fullest conviction, raising and solving problems so as to leave his listeners to consider them for themselves. Because of these experiences Berlin is unforgettable to me and this place upon which we stand is holy ground." Comp. Adolf Kohut; *Ludwig Feuerbach; sein Leben und seine Werke,* 1909, p. 336.

and then to make this "subjective" basis ultimate and the only real basis. As a result of this speculative twist and this misinterpretation of the facts, religion is made to appear a mere illusion; concretely stated, religion appears to be magic and mythology. For, as the detailed discussions unmistakably show, Feuerbach's pet idea of "anthropology," involves both of these elements. And just for this reason Feuerbach's statement summarizing the whole of his argument, that all theology must be converted back into anthropology, also ultimately rests upon a mere a priori construction.

Feuerbach facilitated this construction for himself, and at the same time he made it difficult for his readers to discern the speculative character of his theory, by his method of first orienting the whole elaboration and proof of his position to the question of the nature of Christianity, and only later to the question of the universal nature of religion *per se*.[3]

As a result of this method of treatment, which really is a methodological reversal of the facts, two things follow which must be kept constantly in mind in any accurate evaluation of Feuerbach's argument. First, Feuerbach's position is too exclusively based upon a criticism of traditional conceptions of God. He did not realize that religion *per se* cannot be defined just with the conception of God and without any other differentiae. The tautology involved in such a definition of religion serves him as a very effective means for misinterpretations and unfounded judgments. Secondly, the real strength of Feuerbach's criticism of religion applies to the traditional forms of thought in which religious convictions are expressed, and especially to those of ecclesiastical dogmas. Among these criticisms found in his writings there are insights of a genuinely religio-psychological nature and even today they are very noteworthy. But even the most valuable of such insights do not prove his conception of the nature of religion as such. Due to its metaphysical and speculative character, Feuerbach's theory

---

[3] *"Das Wesen des Christentums"* appeared in 1841. Feuerbach said that his aim was to bring together his "widely scattered, occasional, aphoristic, and polemical ideas on Religion and Christianity, on theology and the philosophy of religion, in a concentrated, developed, applied, proven, conserved and reformed, restricted and expanded form." He delivered the *"Vorlesungen über das Wesen der Religion"* in the winter of 1848-49 in Heidelberg and published them in 1851.

that religion is a mere illusion cannot maintain itself in the face of careful examination.

2

During the last fifty years, however, several different attempts have been made to correct this defect in Feuerbach and to base the illusionistic theory upon demonstrable facts.

Foremost among these new forms of the illusionistic theory is socalled *medical materialism*. Looking for the genetic cause of religion in sexuality, it finds the nature of religion to be an aberration of the sex instinct. William James criticized this theory with such strict objectivity and his criticism is so convincing that we need only to call attention to it and to say that we regard it as final.[4] The fact that all mental functions are in some way related to organic processes is so very general as to exclude such an interpretation just of the function of the religious life. And the fact that the importance of the age of puberty is by no means restricted to the religious sphere makes this still more true. Moreover, as James remarks with justifiable irony, one might just as well attribute the nature of religion to a disturbance of the digestive or of the respiratory functions.

However, today medical materialism's theory of religion is being re-formulated so as to make an impression by connecting the most recent medical theories with the latest research into the history of religion. The psycho-analysts who follow Freud are so formulating it. And the segment of the history of religion which they employ for this expressed purpose is totemism. Consequently, in order to state our attitude to the psycho-analytic theory of religion, we must first determine the nature of totemism, at least as far as that is at all possible in the present stage of our knowledge in this field.

In totemism, religion and magic meet. As Strehlow's great work (See Appendix III) has recently especially shown us, totemistic cults are magical cults, that is to say, cults with the unmistakable magical purpose of strengthening and multiplying the

---

[4] *Varieties of Religious Experience,* p. 12.

totem animals (or, more generally speaking, the totem objects), but at the same time they are religious cults, since they awaken attitudes and convictions which are closely analogous to religious attitudes and convictions. Strehlow has given special attention precisely to the clarification of this point. And the Australian natives, even those who have become converts to Christianity, leave no doubt on this matter. For the Christian natives have expressly and repeatedly affirmed that, as far as they can recall, their former totemistic celebrations are similar to their present Christian religious celebrations, attitudes, and convictions.

In general there are two types of totemism: animal and tribal totemism. To be sure, there are important exceptions to this rule, but in all probability these actually are exceptions which only prove the rule, that is to say, they are exceptions which constitute derivative and secondary phenomena. Thus we occasionally find plant totemism in addition to animal totemism. However, plant totemism is so comparatively rare and occurs within such narrow geographical limits that it must appear, over against the great bulk of totemism, either as a derived or as a borrowed form, and therefore in either case as a secondary phenomenon.

On the other hand totemism is not everywhere purely tribal. Rather, we frequently find alongside of tribal totemism, individual totemism also, and in addition, a socalled sex totemism. Individual totemism means that each individual has his own totem which then becomes, to a certain extent, his genius or protector, and sex totemism means that the sexes have separate totems; the men have a male totem and the women a female totem. Sex totemism also occurs so rarely and is so geographically limited, that for these reasons alone it must be regarded as a secondary and derivative form. Individual totemism occurs more frequently, but it not only does not exclude but is frequently found in combination with tribal totemism, or in other words, it is based upon tribal totemism. This is especially true, for example, in Australia where otherwise tribal totemism quite manifestly constitutes the actually basic type of totemism. Hence we must conclude that individual totemism is also a secondary phenomenon, that it presupposes tribal totemism as its basis and represents a more unique development of this basic form.

In connection with individual totemism the socalled "conception totemism" should be mentioned, that is, the peculiar idea that either at certain totem places, or else due to totems, the "seeds" of babies gain entrance into those women who happen to be present at the time, and that this predetermines the children who thus come into the world for that particular totem. Now in the first place this idea already presupposes individual totemism. And besides, it is so rare, its prevalence is geographically so restricted, and finally it stands in such a merely indirect relation to the basic principle of totemism that for these three reasons this idea of "conception" totemism is especially and absolutely merely a secondary phenomenon. Nevertheless the attempt has been made to explain all of the phenomena by "conception" totemism. Indeed no less a person than Frazer himself, the famous English ethnologist and student of religion, defended the theory that the whole totemistic world-view, and likewise also the whole totemistic cult practice, is ultimately derived from the idea of "conception" totemism, which makes him think that all totemism is due to primitive man's ignorance of physiology.[5]

This theory of Frazer does so little justice to the whole phenomenon of totemism and to its total significance in the development of human culture, and above all it reveals so little or rather such an absolute lack of understanding of the religious importance of totemism, that it cannot even claim serious consideration. And merely from the point of view of ethnology it is untenable for the reasons mentioned above. It is, then, a theory or hypothesis advanced only as a way out of a dilemma.

To be sure, all the other theories of totemism which have been offered are also more or less completely hypotheses which, for want of a better, have been brought forth as ways out of a dilemma. Briefly to mention the most important theories, this is true, for example, of those theories which derive totemism from the custom of using nick-names. Names of animals are said to be the original fact, that is, names of animals applied either in derision or in fun to certain persons. And then, in the memory of the next generation, the respective animals were themselves substituted for the names of the animals; and thus these animals came to be regarded and ceremonially worshiped as the ancestors of certain families. But it is naturally a ridiculous procedure to try to trace back so widely prevalent a phenomenon as totemism, which enters so deeply into the ultimate and deepest problems, and which has had such an influence upon the whole world-view and the entire social life, to a mere misunderstanding of epithets and nick-names. And were this theory revised so that, omitting

[5] J. G. Frazer, *Totemism and Exogamy,* 4 vols., London, 1910. The concluding theory in Vol. IV, pp. 1-169.

epithets or nick-names, the cause of totemism is nevertheless held to be the misunderstanding of the original names of animals, this criticism would also apply equally well to this revision of the theory.

Another theory seeks to explain the origin of totemism by the conditions and circumstances of the hunter's life. The determining motive is said to be the hunter's desire to insure the greatest possible amount of game. But this theory is also false. It mentions a factor which has entered into the total picture but which cannot of itself explain the whole phenomenon of totemism, and this means that it cannot in itself be regarded as the really basic factor. Moreover, it is even directly contradicted, and therefore frequently eliminated in practice, by the opposite tendency of sparing the totem animals.

Finally there remains the theory of Wilhelm Wundt. He tried to explain totemism entirely by animism, that is, with the animistic theory which dominates his whole attitude towards the science of religion. In totemism we are concerned with a definite individual form of the belief in the soul. The original totem animals were soul-animals, the reincarnations of departed souls. However, in the first place this theory is based upon Wundt's general animistic theory which unjustifiably exaggerates the importance and the extent of animism. And secondly, this theory also fails to clarify precisely the real distinguishing character of totemism, namely, the religious evaluation of the animal cult and the intimate relation of the worship of totem animals to the social views, customs, and practices of the worshipers.

How, then, can we gain a better understanding of this phenomenon which is of such great importance in the science of religion? This can be accomplished by placing totemism in the frame-work which was worked out in our treatment of the relation between magic and religion. (See Chap. IX and Appendix III.)

For magical and religious motives are quite often intermingled, and they are so intermingled in totemism. The desire for game, for the strengthening and the increase of the animals of the chase, explains the magical motives. And precisely these magical motives may then be converted into religious motives, or to put it into better and factual terms: they may receive a religious colouring. However, this is only a later, a secondary turning of totemism in the direction of the religious. But totemism also contains genuinely religious motives, and that means original religious motives. How are these original religious aspects of totemism to be explained and interpreted? To answer this question we must first ascertain what for primitive man is the relation between human beings and animals. This is revealed to us by the most original stories, which have been preserved for us, and which are also embedded in our own fairy stories. Here men and animals have mutual fellowship with each other. Inter-marriage between human beings and animals, as well as the transformation of people into animals or vice versa, are the usual thing. But more than that: frequently animals even appear as the benefactors and saviours of humanity. Thus not only are they made equal to men, but they are to a large extent even regarded as superior to men. Such an evaluation and opinion of animals is apparently explained by the fact that they actually are superior to men in some ways and especially in the possession of manifold mysterious powers and abilities. That explains why the transformation of a man into an animal in these folk-stories is not regarded as bad but as good, not as a degradation but as an elevation of man. It is not until a later period that the relation is gradually transposed so that the changing of a man into an animal comes to be regarded as a limitation or degradation. But originally it frequently meant a privilege and an advancement.

Consequently it cannot be doubted that because of their mysterious powers and abilities the animals appear to primitive people —not always, but nevertheless frequently, or at least in part (logical consistency is not at all vital to primitive man)—to be the representatives of a higher and mysterious kind of power, and thus they seem somehow to represent a higher reality. Primitive people are in relation to this higher reality and therefore they desire and seek all the more to have a closer relation to it.

This means that it is the impression of the overwhelming and the mysterious, of that which inspires awe and reverence that underlies totemism and explains its religious character. And this also explains the social aspect of totemism or the complex of social phenomena and customs embedded in totemism. For that same impression of the mysterious and the overwhelming to which awe and reverence are due is also combined with the idea of the spirits of departed ancestors. Hence, under this view-point, which apparently constitutes the *tertium comparationis,* these two different phenomena—animals and ancestral spirits, are brought into relation to each other and are finally even put on an equality and substituted for each other. *In this way both factors are subordinated to a more inclusive point of view and this results in a unified total phenomenon of a religious character.* For these impressions of the overwhelming and the mysterious, and the holy awe and reverence which accompany them, are the same in totemism and in ancestor-worship and they are also precisely the basic motives and factors of the religious attitude, of all religious consciousness and of all religious life. They are the motives and elements which produce in the religious consciousness the certainty of a higher reality or over-world, that higher reality upon which one feels dependent, in whose protection one hopes for security, and which is accordingly regarded as the goal of one's striving. This certainty of a higher world is of course in no way restricted to the totemistic conception. On the contrary, within and solely by means of totemism it cannot reach a pure and complete development. Nevertheless even within the totemistic conception this certainty does find expression, or more precisely stated, it gropes for an expression even though that expression is still a halting and a distorted one.

In my opinion this is the correct interpretation and evaluation of totemism.

However, an entirely different conception of totemism is being defended today, and one which claims to make possible at the same time an entirely new presentation and a conclusive answer to the *questions of the nature and the truth of religion.*

It is the psychoanalysts who make this claim. Psychoanalysis was founded by the Viennese neuropathologist Sigmund Freud. Originally it was a purely medical method or rather a purely medical technique. The principle of this medical psychoanalysis was and is, to gain influence over the unconscious substructure of human psychic life, over the instinctive forces of this unconscious substructure or psychic under-world. For psychoanalysts assumed that these elementary instinctive wishes are of an organic origin, and that they have been pushed back or "repressed" in the course of the conscious development of the psychic life, that they are still latently active and that they seek in various ways and by many disguises to assert their claims, to force their way into the conscious life and to find satisfaction. And hence the idea of psychoanalysis means that by analysis, that is, by the analysis of the hidden wishes of psychic life, these repressed instinctive stirrings and forces can be uncovered and that then they may be influenced and may even be given a harmless expression.[6]

To this summary of the general idea of psychoanalysis, it must also be immediately added that Freud and his disciples seek and find, or claim to seek and find these repressed instincts exclusively, or at any rate almost exclusively, in the sphere of the sexual, more exactly, in sexual abnormality, in the sphere of sexual irregularity and pathology. A complete definition of the idea of psychoanalysis as taught by Freud and his school must include this fact. It is of course not included in the original idea *per se* but from the very beginning it is so read into this idea as to make it the ultimately decisive characteristic. Now psychoanalysis taken in this sense, the psychoanalytic viewpoint and the method used by Freud and his followers, has recently been extended far beyond the medical sphere in which it originated. The psychoanalysts have deliberately applied it to the mental and cultural sciences in the most comprehensive way. Their own journal *Image* is directly devoted to the application of psychoanalysis to the social sciences (Geisteswissenschaften). And in addition the publications of the *Internationale psychoanalytische Bibliothek* frequently discuss problems or themes from the sphere of the mental and cultural sciences (Geistes- und Kulturwissenschaften). Furthermore, in the sphere of the mental sciences, to which the psychoanalytic method lays special claim, it is precisely the science of religion, along with that of art, which stands in the forefront. Not to mention a large number of short articles and essays, Freud himself has discussed the fundamental problems of the science of religion in his book *Totem and Tabu* (1912), and upon this foundation his follower Theodore Reik has recently published a comprehensive treatise entitled *"Probleme der Religionspsychologie"* (1919). [*Totem and Tabu* has been translated by A. A. Brill.]

Freud and Reik both begin with totemism, but their formulations are of the most far-reaching importance for the whole science of religion, for these formulations *claim to be decisive answers to the questions of the nature and the truth of religion.*

---

[6] The terms *unconscious, wish, repression, expression* used here, as well as the terms *suppression, sublimation, libido, psyche,* et cetera, are technical terms of the Freudian psychology. See E. B. Holt: *The Freudian Wish,* Henry Holt & Co. Translators' note.

In order to understand the nature of totemism the psychoanalysts think that we must proceed from what happened in
the primitive horde of men. From this point we may then soon
gain a correct understanding of religion in general, for precisely those events which happened in the primitive horde are
still occurring today, and especially are the instinctive impulses
and desires which caused them still operative. Now it is just
these instinctive impulses that they say are still today the actual
motives of religion, and hence they alone are able to give us
information about the questions of the nature and the truth of
religion.

What are these events in the primitive horde? They have
to do with the relation of the growing children, especially the
growing sons, to their parents, to the father and the mother of
the primitive horde. The psychoanalysts say that our knowledge of the emotions of the psyche of the young, which has been
given to us by psychoanalysis, makes it absolutely necessary for
us to assume that jealousy developed in the growing sons of the
primitive horde against the father who had appropriated their
mother for himself alone. The psychoanalysts call this the
Oedipus complex in the emotional life of youth; it is directed
against the father in hatred and envy and seeks to possess the
mother to satisfy its libido. In the primitive horde the inevitable result was that the father became increasingly harsh
and brutal, and drove away one son after another. And now
again it became inevitable that the sons should unite and accomplish together that which they would not have been able to do
as individuals: together they put the father out of the way and,
following the tendency of their instinctive impulses, they did
this as thoroughly as possible by murdering and devouring him.
This primeval experience of humanity: the murdering and devouring of the father of the primitive horde by the growing
sons who were jealous of him on account of their mother, although an event which happened in primitive times, has had
significant and consequential effects down to our own day.
This event was fundamental to the whole cultural development
of humanity, and equally so to the origin and the evolution of
religion.

However, the incestuous desires of the sons toward their

mother were not satisfied. Although the way was open to each of them after the murder and devouring of the father, there were so many brothers that each one was prevented from attaining the goal of his desires. Since each one wanted to take the place of his father, but was kept from so doing by the desire of the others to do the same thing, they all finally desisted. Of their own accord, and with better success than their father, they proceeded to prohibit incest and to federate men into a fraternal clan, thus establishing the law of marriage and creating the basis for all further social institutions. Then too, another effect of this crime upon the psyche of the sons was the awakening of remorse, shame, and longing. Ashamed of their rash act, they were seized by remorse. And now they remembered their father with a sense of longing and of love, and this was increased by a sort of reaction. Hence they sought for a substitute for their father so that they might give expression to these feelings of remorse, love, and reverence, and make amends, as far as possible, for what they had so rashly done. The nearest substitute for their father available was an animal. This animal now became the recipient of the filial love of belated obedience which in reality should have been bestowed upon the father. Thus totemism began. Since love and reverence were strengthened by reaction and were given to the animal as the substitute for the father, the feeling which arose toward the totem animal as the representative of the father was so heightened and enhanced that the idea of God arose.

And now the father, who of course had unfortunately been killed and devoured, was exalted and deified in their memory. He was deified: and this is at once both the origin and the actual meaning of the idea of God. For the reasoning of the phychoanalysts here is this: Deification includes the idea of the divinity or the deity. Consequently, if the process of deification is clarified, then *ipso facto* the origin and the actual meaning of the idea of God is also explained. Not just its origin, but also at the same time its actual significance. For the very motives which originally led to the creation of the idea of God are the same motives that are ultimately decisive for all religion later on down to the present day, both for all religious feeling and for all religious thought. Unconscious and hidden though they be, the desire to violate the mother and consequently the desire to dispose of the father repeatedly arise.   But then in consequence remorse and shame also always arise and produce by their reaction, a heightening of love, respect, and reverence. Thus the same duality or polarity of feelings is just as decisive now as it was in the past and it will always remain decisive. The psychoanalysts call this *ambivalence of feelings,* and in general the deepest nature of the psychic life of man is to be found in such ambivalence of feelings.   Everywhere this ambivalence, this dualism, this alternation between opposing states of feeling, between feelings of aversion and of inclination, of hate and of love, is operative.   And so this ambivalence of feelings is supposed to explain the origin and the meaning of religion, and the "belief in God."

Now so far as the problem of the origin of religion is concerned, the theory which we have just sketched must be supplemented as follows: even in the very first act which gave rise to the whole development and which was predominantly an act of hatred, the ambivalence of feelings was working itself out.   For the sons devoured their murdered father, not only because that was the most radical method of getting him out of the way, but because it was at the same time the most primitive way of identifying themselves with him.   Consumption seemed to them to be the most radical way of identifying themselves with the man whom they simultaneously loved and hated.   And then this method of identification was continued when the father was replaced by the totem animal, and even later when, as a result of external cultural influences, the idea of God had become separated from the totem animal and from totemism.

This same ambivalence of feelings was again operative in their attitude toward the totem animal, regarded as the substitute for the father.   To be sure the sons showered their evidences of love and reverence upon the animal in a manner which signified deification or which at least led to deification; but immediately the rebellion and hatred of the sons was again awakened.   This tendency toward continued rebellion and hatred had to be satisfied and so there arose the occasional ceremony of the totem feast, at which—even though under the disguise of formal rites—the slaughtered totem animal was again devoured.

In the above summary I have purposely employed Freud's own terminology, and the outcome of it all is that the father God once walked bodily upon the earth, and used his ruling power as the chief of the primitive horde, until his sons banded themselves together and killed and devoured him; further, that as a result of this act of elimination and the reaction which it caused, the first social institutions arose, consisting of the basic moral laws and the oldest form of religion, totemism; consequently, that the later religions also have the same content and attempt to remove the traces of and to atone for this crime, while they cannot help repeating again and again the elimination of the father. That is the theory of religion of the psychoanalysts. What is to be said of it?

The misleading factor in the whole theory is already implied in the conceptions of psychoanalysis. Psychoanalysis as such only demands an analytical investigation of the psychic life, in itself it involves nothing like what is made vital in this concrete application. It does not even imply the necessity of always tracing back everything ultimately and exclusively to sexual motives, and besides, that is done in such an unnatural fashion that finally everything is actually attributed to sexual perversion or pathology.

How psychoanalysis is to be evaluated when it is restricted to the field of medicine and is employed solely as a medical technique, that must and should here remain an open question. On this matter the opinions of medical authorities are widely divergent. We cannot venture an opinion. Nevertheless this statement of the problem is in general understandable and justified for the sphere of medicine because medicine is concerned with the cure of morbid states and conditions, and presupposes the existence and the effects of such morbid states and conditions. And the same would similarly apply to the fields of pedagogy and pastoral ministration.[7]

On the other hand when this psychoanalytic method is used to explain human spiritual and cultural life in its entirety, then this means using the abnormal and the morbid as a principle to

[7] In this connection I refer to the works of Osk. Pfister: *Die psychoanalytische Methode*, 1913, *Was bietet die Psychoanalyse dem Erzieher?* 1917. *Analytische Seelsorge*, 1927.

explain the normal and the healthy.   But that is itself directly abnormal, and in the end it becomes even senseless and ridiculous.   The situation can best be illustrated by the expression *"Oedipus Complex"* which is so popular among he psychoanalysts.   This expression is supposed to designate that original experience of humanity, that is, that the growing sons, driven by their sexual libido for the mother, murder and devour the father.   And this expression at the same time also means that the whole Oedipus saga and poetry is based upon the after-effects of these instinctive desires.   For if in this saga the tragic fate of Oedipus is brought about because he unwittingly killed his father Laius and married his mother Jocasta, then behind this tragical motivation the real motives are clearly enough discernible for a psychoanalytic interpretation.   And that should also especially mean, as the psychoanalysts expressly point out, that Sophocles' occupation with the material which he put into writing in his Oedipus dramas, proves how strong these motives of murder and incest were in him.   In such an assertion it is quite apparent that exactly what appears as the result of psychoanalysis is arbitrarily read into the phenomena under consideration, and that therefore the whole socalled interpretation is based upon a mere *petitio principii.*

Moreover, the psychoanalytic view proves in the highest degree arbitrary and meaningless when it is applied to the field of religion, when it is used to interpret the phenomena of the history of religion.   An understanding of religious phenomena is possible only on the basis of religious experience and with the aid of one's own religious experience.   We have previously discussed this extensively.   But in psychoanalysis religious experience is not taken into account, it is simply completely excluded. What religion is in the sense of religious experience, and of the religious conviction which is based upon it, is not taken into account and of course cannot be taken into account, if the psychoanalytic interpretation is not immediately and without any qualification to be rejected.   For what in the world has religious experience and religious conviction to do with incestuous instincts and with desires which aim at the violation of the mother, and which, therefore, impel the elimination, the murder, and the devouring of the father?

This socalled original experience of humanity is at any rate not the beginning of man's religious development and therefore it cannot in any case constitute its permanent vital content. It cannot be its beginning, not even its most primitive beginning. It has simply and absolutely nothing to do with religion at all. More than that: it is not even the original experience of humanity, and cannot justly be so called, nor could it even be justly called such if the fact itself could legitimately be asserted. For there is nothing specifically human about it at all, it is entirely animalistic. But even the fact as such, the mere assertion of such a fact, is open to the most serious doubts and objections. For to an increasingly universal extent recent ethnological research has established the fact that cannibalism does not belong to the most primitive level of mankind, and therefore that it does not characterize the prehistoric age of humanity.

Suppose, however, that this event, this crime, really did constitute the beginning and even the vital content of religion, then how could the piety of woman be understood? Since the motives of religion assumed by the psychoanalysts are exclusively the motives of the male psyche, religion would really have to be restricted to men. At least the piety of women could only be of a quite secondary nature, taken over from men and experienced in imitation of them. But that undoubtedly contradicts the real psychological state of affairs.

And finally the whole theory fails tragically just at the most critical point. The most critical point is where the idea of God, the origin and lasting validity of the idea of God, is to be explained, that is, made understandable. How is that done? It is done by referring to the process of deifying the totem animal. The totem animal as the representative of the father, as a substitute for the murdered and devoured father, is deified. But the deification involves the idea of deity, the idea of God.

So the deification of the totem animal explains the God-concept of humanity, the origin and permanent validity of this God-concept. Marvelous! The deification explains the idea of God! That is an explanation like that of Uncle Bräsig in Reuter's story: why is there so much poverty? Well—that is because people are so poor! So the idea of God comes from the deification of the totem animal!

Thus, in the end, the psychoanalytic interpretation of the religious problem ends in absurdity.[8]

3

The impression which Feuerbach's *Das Wesen des Christentums* made upon Karl Marx and his school is described by Friedrich Engels in his work, *Ludwig Feuerbach und der Ausgang der klassischen deutschen Philosophie.*[9] One must himself have experienced the emancipating effect of Feuerbach in order to understand this impression. The enthusiasm was universal: "At that time we were all Feuerbachians."

The fact of the matter is that Feuerbach's theory of religion is closely related to economic socialism. If religion is man's instinct of happiness which is satisfied in his imagination, then the conclusion is only too near at hand that man invented religion precisely in order to deceive himself or others about the happiness which is denied to him in this world. In a few remarks Marx himself had already more closely characterized the connecting line which leads from Feuerbach to his own theory.[10] In the most detailed and scholarly manner Friedrich Engels has so clarified this connection as to place the very idea which again connects Feuerbach with Schleiermacher into the foreground, namely, the idea of the feeling of dependence.[11] Religion is nothing but the fancied reflection of those outward forces which dominate man's everyday life. Among these forces the social become increasingly more important with time. And not until human society, by the confiscation of property and by a planned operation of all production, has freed itself and every one of its members from the present slavery, will the last alien power vanish which is now still reflected in religion; and

[8] This fact is also shown in Freud's more recent publications. See his *Die Zukunft einer Illusion,* 1928, and *Das Unbehagen in der Kultur,* Vienna, 1930.

[9] Reprint from the "Neue Zeit," 1886, 5th ed. Stuttgart, 1910.

[10] In the discussion of the *"Kritik der Hegelschen Rechtsphilosophie,"* 1884, and in his guiding principles which Engels, *op. cit.,* has reprinted.

[11] In addition to the treatise already mentioned, compare his polemic against Dühring: *Herm. Eugen Dührings Umwälzung der Wissenschaft,* 1878.

then religious reflection will also vanish because there will be nothing more upon which it can reflect.

To one using the religio-psychological method it is apparent that this adaptation of Feuerbach's illusionistic theory to support the Marxian philosophy of life still retains Feuerbach's basic error. The whole argument here rests upon a complete misunderstanding of the essential nature of the religious feeling of dependence. The reasoning of Marx and Engels applies to the misuse of the religious feeling of dependence only, and not to that feeling itself. For the dependence which is denoted by religion exists also in the highest conceivable stage of economic independence, and it may even be increased and intensified by such economic independence.

However, this hurried rejection of the socialistic form of Feuerbach's illusionistic theory does not suffice. For we must now examine a noteworthy attempt to support this basic theory by placing it in the broad framework of the general history of religion. Otto Gruppe has made such an attempt in a study of the history of religion which is carried out with vast erudition.[12] The main points of his theory may be summarized as follows.

In the history of mankind religion was invented at a definite time and under very specific circumstances; and it then reached the remaining sections and portions of humanity only by communication. Gruppe definitely denies a general inclination of the human soul to religion. Man has no active natural impulse to religion; he has only a passive potentiality for acquiring religion from others. Therefore the whole phenomenon of religion must finally be traced back to one single invention of religion which occurred at a particular time, under particular circumstances, and for a particular purpose. Gruppe calls this view *adaptionism,* the theory of adaptation. The wide prevalence of religion is the result of an adaptation or accommodation of the whole to a single invention which occurred but once. He supposes the territory of western Asia to be the home of this invention. The time cannot be precisely stated; but for Gruppe it probably does not coincide with the beginning of

---

[12] Otto Gruppe, *"Die griechischen Kulte und Mythen in ihren Beziehungen zu den orientalischen Religionen,"* Leipsic, 1887. Comp. also his *"Griechische Mythologie und Religionsgeschichte,"* 2 vols, Munich, 1906.

human history. It rather presupposes certain results of the development of human history, especially in the field of social organization.

According to Gruppe religion was established in the interest of the rulers of society in conscious violation of the laws of logic. It was established in the interest of the "rulers" insofar, namely, as religion offered to the disinherited elements in society, that is, to the poor and the outcasts, an apparent satisfaction of the instincts of self-preservation and self-enhancement. And so the masses are soothed by religion, and prevented from rebelling against the social system.

Therefore, on this view, the establishment or invention of religion presupposes that the distinctions of property and enjoyment had become so great that the envy of the property-less was a menace to those holding property. Gruppe expressly states that as long as the differences were slight, there was no incentive for the invention of religion. And inversely, he adds, in case a social upheaval should at some time blot out the distinction between the propertied and the property-less, the religious inclination would also cease to function. Like certain organs of the body which have become superfluous, religion would gradually atrophy and would finally disappear entirely. For then the very incentive for the preservation of religion would be lacking. Correspondingly Gruppe argues, religion also could only have arisen, or more precisely, could only have been invented, after the incentive for it was given by social conditions, that is, by social maladjustments. On this view, then, the invention of religion must have been preceded in history by a period during which there was no religion. To prove this assumption Gruppe appeals to the alleged absence of religion among many primitive peoples. For he holds that there is a not inconsiderable number of primitive groups who must be denied every semblance of religion.

Stated briefly, this is the socalled adaptionism theory of the first beginnings of religion *per se* in the evolution of mankind. The theory of an actual "invention" of religion has never had such a consistent, comprehensive, and erudite representative as Gruppe.

Now for this very reason adaptionism proves conclusively

the untenability of every invention theory. For adaptionism breaks down as soon as we apply the test of religio-psychological empathy, and the point where it breaks down is its thesis that man has no active impulse toward religion, but has only a passive potentiality in the form of the capacity for acquiring religion from others. This thesis is not merely an incidental assumption but it is the basic and decisive assumption for the formulation and application of the whole theory. Hence the theory itself stands or falls with this thesis. But this thesis is, in the first place, a clear begging of the question. Gruppe has not really established it in any way. Moreover, it is self-contradictory. The distinction between an active impulse and a passive potentiality is, at least in the manner in which Gruppe posits it, psychologically unjustifiable. A potentiality of the psychical and spiritual life is never merely passive; insofar as it is an actual potentiality, it contains within itself an element of activity. Then, too, upon closer examination the argument with which Gruppe seeks to justify this distinction turns out to be false and illogical. Experience, says Gruppe, teaches everyone who is willing to be taught, that in contrast to the needs and impulses which arise of their own accord, the religious feeling is not inherited but is acquired by training and is communicated from without. As examples of the needs and impulses which arise of their own accord, Gruppe mentions the need for food and rest, as well as the instinct of reproduction. Now in contrast to these "active impulses" religion is merely a passive potentiality. However, such a comparison between religion and psycho-physiological instincts proves nothing, except what needs no demonstration, namely, that religion does not belong to these psycho-physiological instincts. But what about such things as morality, art, and science? Has man an active impulse toward them, or merely a passive potentiality? Here the disjunction is apparently just as false as in the case of religion. The conception of a merely "passive" potentiality is psychologically impossible, and is at the same time the basic error of the whole theory.

However, the theory is also shown to be unjustified and untenable by the supplementary hypothesis which it necessitates. For Gruppe has to assume an original lack of religion in human life and history. He writes: "The undivided human race accordingly possessed no religion, and no religious impulse." Yet real history knows no such lack of religion. As far back as we are able to trace history, we find religion everywhere. And even in "pre-history," where all direct historical communication by means of writings and records ceases and where the excavations and discoveries alone give us any information concerning the life of man, archeological discoveries still show the traces of some—no matter how primitive—religious ideas and practices. And that even holds, especially in the light of the discoveries of the very latest research, to an extent which was formerly not even surmised. The cave drawings of the ice age which have been recently discovered, especially in Northern Spain and Southern France, seem also to portray in part religious ideas and practices. At least scholars who are otherwise as divergent in their religious and philosophical views as the French Abbé Breuil and the German anthropologist Herm. Klaatsch agree in this opinion.[13]

However that may be, at any rate this theory turns out to be a capricious hypothesis at the only point where a real test of its validity can be made. The analogy to living savages, to which Gruppe expressly appeals, fails him; for this supposed analogy is a mere fiction. There are no existing races or tribes which are completely without religion. The reports which assert the contrary cannot bear critical examination.

The statement that there are a number of races and tribes which lack religion of course plays an important rôle in the anti-religious literature of our day. The scientific compendium of all of the attempts which have been made in this direction is the famous book of the English scholar Lubbock (Lord Avebury): *The Origin of Civilization and the Primitive Conditions of Man.* In this work Lubbock undertook to describe the evolution of religion in history and he abruptly labeled its first stage atheism. He took atheism in the strict sense of the word to mean an absolute lack of all religious elements. In Lub-

[13] Comp. Hugo Obermaier: *Der Mensch der Vorzeit* (Der Mensch aller Zeiten, Vol. I), Berlin-Munich, 1913; especially pp. 413 ff. Obermaier follows very closely the investigations and views of Abbé Breuil. Herm. Klaatsch: *Die Anfänge von Kunst und Religion in der Urmenschheit*, Leipsic, 1913, pp. 19 f.

bock's opinion such a purely negative stage constitutes the elementary stage of religious evolution; and then come fetishism, nature worship, shamanism, idolatry, belief in creation and finally a union of religion with morality. But the elementary stage of the whole evolutionary process is atheism in the broad sense. And Lubbock especially emphasized this very thesis, and attempted to establish it by the use of comprehensive data, such as the reports of missionaries, of travelers, and of scientific explorers. Using this material he claimed that he could prove that many tribes have been discovered that are lacking in every trace of religion.

That practically all of Lubbock's argument is open to attack is of course no longer questioned in serious scientific circles. However, a criticism of the whole material from a specifically religio-psychological point of view has heretofore never been attempted. And yet precisely the religio-psychological clarification and testing of this material is of the greatest interest, since it is of decisive importance in determining whether that answer to the question, which is today still customary, is true.

In order to give such a religio-psychological clarification I shall select as examples two of Lubbock's especially reliable and credible authorities, upon whose evidence he himself placed special emphasis. These examples are at the same time perfectly typical of the way in which reports of travelers are still being used today.

For the absence of religion among the Kaffir tribes Lubbock refers to the account of his travels of Burchell, a recognized and dependable scholar.[14] Referring to the tribe of the Bachapins, Burchell writes: "I saw no trace of religion." But along with this statement from his report there is another referring to the numerous superstitions and superstitious fables of the same tribe. Superstitions of all kinds are found among them in prodigious numbers. Now at once the question arises whether there are not religious elements in these superstitions. For applying the religio-psychological method it cannot be doubted that the conception of superstition is not unequivocal but is an

[14] Comp. *Wilh. Burchells Reise in das Innere Afrikas.* Neue Bibliothek der wichtigsten Reisebeschreibungen 32, 39. Comp. especially, Vol. 39, p. 538 and pp. 545 ff.

entirely relative conception. It is found wherever belief is
found, and the boundary line between belief and superstition is
very dfficult to determine. It shifts in the most varied ways.
From the point of view of monotheism, all polytheism could
be called superstition, and from the Biblical point of view, all
extra-Biblical religion might be regarded as superstition. But
even within both points of view very significant differences may
be found. With varying degrees of belief, the determination
and evaluation of superstition also varies.

It is therefore unjustifiable to assert the absence of religion
in a tribe when at the same time superstition is attributed to it,
and when no attempt is made to distinguish superstition from
religious belief. That this conclusion is correct can even be
emphatically proven in the case under consideration. For Lubbock's witness adds: "They seem to believe that a highest being
rules the world; but they mix so much superstition with this
belief that their morality, or even their religious feeling, hardly
seems to be involved in it." (*Ibid.*, 39, p. 421.) Here then this
same witness admits the presence of religious belief, merely
censuring its being mixed with so much superstition. Now that
absolutely is not an absence of religion. And besides, how
indefinite, how unprovable, and how false is the assertion upon
which everything here depends, that religious feeling *hardly
seems* to be involved at all?

Here is another example which is no less typical. In this
case, too, an especially important witness of Lubbock is the
source, the famous natural scientist Wallace. Lubbock refers
to Wallace to prove the absence of religion among the inhabitants of some of the Melanesian Islands. For in his
voluminous work on his travels in the Malay Peninsula Wallace
says of a group of natives that he found no sign of religion
among them. Yet further on he reports that the belief in magic
is indigenous to these islands, and then adds:[15] "So I was
thought to be a magician and I was not able to overcome this
impression; I have no doubt that I shall be converted, by the
next generation or perhaps even sooner, into a magician or
semi-god, into a wonder-worker and a being possessing super-
natural knowledge." Many other cases are known of Euro-

[15] A. R. Wallace, *The Malay Archipelago*, Vol. II, pp. 229, and 243.

peans having been regarded as creatures of a higher realm by savages. But this naturally implies a belief in the existence of higher creatures. Hence, for the religio-psychological evaluation of the matter, this witness himself disproves the statement of the absence of religion.

At the same time both examples show how great are the psychological difficulties involved in making a report on the question whether socalled primitive people have a religion. The Berlin ethnologist K. Th. Preuss quite correctly writes in the preface to his masterly treatise on the religion of the Kora Indians, in which he has recorded the results for the field of religion of his Nayarit expedition: "Today no ethnologist can still think that a native, no matter how well he is trained, can explain the characteristics of his religious beliefs to an investigator; what he believes must rather be deduced from a mosaic of reports of various authorities and from numerous observations which throw light upon the beliefs in question from the most varied angles." [16]

Lubbock's material does not stand being tested by this standard, and yet, for the religio-psychological treatment, this standard must be regarded as the only valid one.

Nor does the only example which is today being cited with conviction by serious ethnologists as proof of an absence of religion, stand the test of this standard either. Recently professional ethnologists have claimed actual absence of religion only in the case of one tribe, the Kubu in southern Sumatra. The ethnologist W. Volz has asserted that there is a complete lack of religion among the Kubu, and he has also expressed this opinion in the widely circulated encyclopaedia, edited by G. Buschan, entitled *"Illustrierte Völkerkunde."* Among other things he there says: "The socalled 'savage' Kubu are a small tribe confined to the most inaccessible primeval forest of southern Sumatra. They live together in families and wander about in small family hordes without any permanent residence, spending the night under very simple shelters made of branches or in available crevices, and consuming their entire time in the search for food—Transcendental ideas of every kind, and even

[16] K. Th. Preuss; *Die Nayarit-Expedition,* Textaufnahmen und Beobachtungen unter mexikanischen Indianern, Vol. I, Teubner, 1912, p. III.

the most simple superstitions, are beyond the Kubu; accordingly, every idea of magic is absent, and the presence of medicine men is unknown. They feel powerless in the face of sickness and death, and if someone dies they simply leave him lie and go their way. So we actually have in these savage Kubu a nation without any trace of religion, a nation which is culturally hardly more advanced than the animals of the jungle." [17]

From the point of view of the religio-psychological evaluation it must first of all be noted here that Volz admits that this is the only example of a tribe which is actually devoid of religion. This in itself should counsel the greatest caution, and it raises strong doubts as to the correctness of his statement. For it is absolutely out of harmony with the otherwise general unanimity which we find everywhere in the psychic life of savages. Then too, this assertion is emphatically challenged by very expert students of this tribe. Dutchmen, for example, who have lived among these Kubu and have observed them carefully for years report that even though they do live on a very low cultural plane, they are in no wise devoid of religion. Like the other tribes of Indonesia they are animists. In the first place they have a very elaborate and varied belief in magic, in addition to a belief in souls and spirits, and in the second place, they worship the dead with sacrifices of rice and fruits. There is also found among them the belief in a highest god (Radja Njawa), who administers punishments and rewards to the dead, even though he has little importance for ordinary life. [18]

Thus when we apply Preuss's standard in the evaluation of the whole question, which we have recognized as the only standard that is religio-psychologically adequate, it must be concluded that in this case of the Kubu tribe also there is not, in all probability, an absence of religion.

Gruppe's attempt to build the socialistic form of the illusionistic theory upon the foundation of the general history of re-

[17] *Op. cit.,* p. 248.—Compare B. Hagen, *Die Orang Kubu auf Sumatra,* Publications of the Municipal Museum, Frankfurt, a.M. Vol. II, 1908, pp. 159 ff.: "No transcendental ideas of any kind," "—without any religious conceptions."
[18] Compare G. J. van Dongen in the *Bidragen tot de Taal-land-en* volken Kunde van Nederl. Indie, 1910, pp. 54 ff,

ligion must then be regarded as a failure. Even with the most comprehensive scholarship and the keenest penetration this socialistic form of the illusionistic theory cannot be made tenable. It contradicts the actual facts of history as we are taught to understand them by the religio-psychological method.

4

The efforts of the American psychologist Leuba have as their goal the central idea of Feuerbach's theory. He has attempted to formulate this central idea more exactly than was possible for Feuerbach, and thereby to free it from all objectionable features.

In criticizing Leuba we had best begin again with the three theses summarizing his view. They are:

1. Belief in the gods of religion rests upon inductions drawn from the inner life.
2. Religious experience, as inner experience, belongs entirely to the jurisdiction of empirical psychology.
3. Since the gods of religion are empirical gods, they belong to the jurisdiction of science (especially to empirical psychology, which shows the religious belief in the gods to be an untenable illusion).[19]

This series of theses is intended as a logical syllogism, so that the third as the conclusion necessarily follows from the first and the second as major and minor premises. But as interpreted by Leuba, both premises are either ambiguous or false, and this invalidates the conclusion. Leuba interprets the first thesis to mean that the character of the religious relationship does not belong to the primary nature of religious experi-

[19] James H. Leuba, *A Psychological Study of Religion*, New York, 1912, p. 212. See especially pp. 207-277. I have purposely stated these theses in briefer form in order to emphasize the decisive points. Leuba's own formulation is as follows: 1. That belief in the gods of religion and indirectly, certain other fundamental doctrines, rest as a matter of fact upon inductions drawn from the inner life. 2. That religious experience (inner experience) belongs entirely to psychology—entirely being used in the same sense as when it is claimed that the non-religious portions of conscious life belong entirely to science. 3. That, since the gods of religion are empirical gods, they belong to science.

ence, but is of a secondary nature, and rests upon a later reflective interpretation. But in reality it is just the opposite. The conception which Leuba advances and which he puts into his first thesis, rests upon an interpretation, or to be more exact, upon a re-interpretation of the basic religious experience. At least this must be said insofar as religious experience is understood as it really is. When such a reversal of the facts, which must be regarded as a methodological source of error of primary importance, is avoided as a matter of principle, then no one can doubt that a religious relationship belongs to the basic structure of the religious consciousness. An attitude of consciousness, in which there is no relation to the objective content (idea of the object) of religious belief, cannot correctly be called religious.

This also indicates our attitude toward Leuba's second thesis, that religious experience, as inner experience, belongs entirely to the jurisdiction of empirical psychology. Religious experience in its entirety may rightly be subjected to an empirical psychological examination. But it is incorrect to say that such an empirical psychological investigation is the only methodologically valid method for religio-psychological research (and then for the whole science of religion). For to religious belief *per se* religious experience is not empirical experience, involving as it certainly does, a relationship to the religious idea of the object. And it is only this relationship to the religious idea of the object which gives it its specifically religious character. However, the religious idea of the object is for religious belief not of an empirical but of an absolutely super-empirical nature.

With these two theses the third, which follows from them, necessarily falls also. But at the same time this third thesis, that the gods of religion are empirical gods, throws light upon the relation in which Leuba puts the previous theses. What is involved here is the determination of the relation of belief to knowledge in general, and then, specifically, of the relation of religious belief in God to the metaphysical hypothesis of the Absolute. In the treatment of this problem Leuba is influenced in the strongest way by positivistic philosophy, primarily by the views of Comte himself, and in addition, particularly by Herbert Spencer. And here also he again uses modern empirical psychology to overcome the weaknesses in the positions of these philosophers, and to give greater firmness and certainty to their general theory. In my opinion it must be unconditionally denied that he has really succeeded in this, no matter how noteworthy and instructive his discussions are in some details,[20] and even though they show a greater consistency and unity in their empirical-psychological manner of thinking than do the systems of Comte and Spencer.

In dealing with the relation of belief to knowledge, Leuba, as a matter of principle, regards all belief as a mere preliminary stage of real knowledge, which he identifies with scientific perception. Therefore scientific perception, on its part, must furnish the ultimate criteria for the evaluation of belief. According to this view the certainty of belief cannot legitimately be regarded as having intrinsic value. Here Leuba follows all the positivists in ignoring the insight which was gained by Kant. But he seeks to justify psychologically this return to a pre-Kantian position. His argument is based upon the idea that in scientific research also, belief as a hypothetical anticipation of scientific knowledge, plays a rôle which is in itself psychologically justified, a rôle which is of course justified only on the assumption that belief is ultimately absolutely subordinate to strictly rational perception. But precisely this demand must also, as a matter of principle, be applied to all belief. Just as in the sphere of science, so in that of religion also, statements of belief are indications of incomplete knowledge. Consequently such statements of belief must also be supplanted and replaced by more and more complete statements, that is, by strictly rational knowledge.

This argument of Leuba is invalid. For the comparison of religious statements of belief with scientific hypotheses is unjustified, it is false and misleading. This seems to have a semblance of justification because, by "statements of belief," Leuba always means definite patterns of ideas and often he even means traditional ecclesiastical "dogmas." It is true that these contain

---

[20] In this connection see the careful discussions of Maria Heinsius, *Der Streit über theozentrische und anthropozentrische Theologie*. Tübingen, 1918.

factors which are quite similar to the hypotheses of science. However, this does not apply to the religious convictions which underlie these dogmas. In a religio-psychological respect, Leuba's psychologically oriented thinking still lacks the necessary clarity and precision at this point.

This criticism also applies to Leuba's discussion of the question of the relation of the religious belief in God to the metaphysical theory of the Absolute. At first he places all emphasis upon the differences between these two phenomena, and in this part of his discussion we can only agree with him absolutely. For that these two phenomena are not simply identical, and that they must therefore be differentiated in scientific thought, is a self-evident conclusion from the religio-psychological method, since the basic principle of the metaphysics, which accepts the Absolute, does not rest upon religious experience. On the other hand Leuba is also quite right in his contention that orthodox theology and traditional philosophy of religion still lack the necessary strictness and clarity. However, even Schleiermacher energetically insisted upon this, of course without carrying it through completely, and Albrecht Ritschl rendered a lasting service in this very respect, of course without himself avoiding exaggeration and one-sidedness. But in Leuba's theory, too, even though in a different fashion, exaggeration and one-sidedness are evident.

For Leuba asserts that we are dealing with two absolutely different ideas of God which have nothing to do with each other and which, rather, stand in sharp contrast to each other. The metaphysical idea of the Absolute is a product of philosophical speculation, and as such it is removed from the control of science. But, on the other hand, it must also be strictly separated from the religious idea of God and it must not be brought into any relation to that idea at all. According to Leuba, then, these two ideas of God have absolutely nothing in common except the name. But what is the reason for this identity of names?

"The theologians," Leuba answers, "use the expression 'God' in two entirely different senses. Therefore the confusion." In this answer Leuba neglected to place the philosophers alongside of the theologians, and this is absolutely necessary in

view of the historical facts. For this reason alone his answer
is inadequate. And it would be just as inadequate if it included
this addition, except that its inadequacy would then be immediately apparent. Does not this very usage, which persists
throughout the whole history of human thought, show that
these two conceptions of God, let them be as different as they
may be, still have an inherent relationship to each other?

Leuba answers "No!" and he claims to be able to establish
his denial by actual facts. From a psychological point of view
he shows that only philosophical speculation tries to conceive of
an infinite object, but that the religious consciousness requires
a finite object. Although Leuba develops this argument, his
discussion really does not amount to any more than the statement just expressed, and it is absolutely invalid. So far as the
religious consciousness is concerned, we must first seek, not
what it requires, but the fact which constitutes it. Even in a
formal way Leuba's thesis must therefore be challenged from
a religio-psychological point of view. His way of stating the
problem does not correspond either with the psychological or
with the logical structure of the religious consciousness. Then,
too, his thesis must be especially rejected as false in content.
In the sense of religious belief, (and Leuba too aims to speak
in its name) the object or content of the religious consciousness is not a finite entity. It is rather an entity which extends
beyond the whole realm of finite reality, or at least, insofar
as its primitive beginnings are to be included, an entity which
points beyond this finite realm. Nor is this insight affected
by Leuba's assertion that the religious idea of God is necessarily anthropomorphic, on the ground that religious persons
require a personality of a finite-empirical kind as the object of
their religious relationship. For in addition to the fact that an
unjustified reference to "requirement" or "demand" again re-
curs here, the statement itself is false. And again the error
lies in the fact that Leuba does not, or at least does not sufficiently distinguish between belief *per se,* belief which is based
upon religious experience, and its rational formulations, and the
conceptual forms in which it is expressed. The anthropo-
morphism of religious thinking cannot be forthwith attributed
to the basic religious belief.

Going back still farther, it must be emphasized again that Leuba's criticism of the religious consciousness is too exclusively and one-sidedly bound to the belief in God, or more precisely, to the idea of God. That explains why he takes monotheism to be only a sub-form of polytheism. He completely disregards the enormous importance of the difference between plural religions and single religions for the religious consciousness *per se*. And that is why he leaves entirely out of consideration the basic religious idea of the over-world, which, in spite of all their differences, is common to both kinds of religion. *As soon as this is taken into consideration, as the facts demand, Leuba's assertion that religious belief and the metaphysics of the Absolute constitute an exclusive contrast to each other, collapses entirely.* A sharp differentiation between these two entities is of course very necessary. For in the first place, as has already been stated, they are not simply identical. The religious conviction goes considerably beyond the metaphysical Absolute in its conception of an over-world determined by the feelings of dependence, security, and longing. Besides, the conscious intention in the two cases is absolutely different. Metaphysics aims to reach a complete understanding of the universe, religion lives in a personal relationship to the over-world. But the more this difference is recognized and the clearer it is defined, the clearer becomes their common characteristics. Both agree in accepting a transcendental reality, (transcendental being here used in the broadest sense of the term to mean a reality which transcends the whole world conceived as a natural entity).[21] And by and to the extent of their mutual agreement they confirm each other.

5

At this point in our discussion we must return again to the theory of religion of the neo-Kantian, Paul Natorp. With the greatest emphasis he also rejects the transcendental claim of religion. This is due to his conceiving of religious feeling as a

[21] This statement is not intended to involve the socalled problem of transcendence and immanence, which will be considered when we discuss the Christian idea of God. Comp. also above, pp. 207 f. See the author's *Christian Belief in God* (Yale Press), Chapter V.

pure subjectivity which excludes every relation to an object and consequently also every objective content. We have already seen that this thory, as a determination of the nature of religion, is a mere construction whose a priori principle distorts religious belief. And we have also previously pointed out that an answer to the problem of the truth of religion is anticipated in this theory inasmuch as such an answer plays an important part in Natorp's determination of the nature of religion. Here it is instructive to note his special treatment of the problem of truth. He reasons as follows. Insofar as the concept of objective validity is retained, its meaning, and consequently the claim to such validity are both ineradicable parts of the concept of the existential transcendent. But in the nature of the case the validity of religious belief cannot be established with strict objectivity. For critical thought in the Kantian sense, objectively valid knowledge is restricted to the sphere of sense experience and rational knowledge. Consequently the objectivity of religious belief and its trancendental claim must be abandoned.[22]

What shall we say about this argument? Is it convincing? Certainly it is not. It is rather an empty, sham argument. The concepts of "objective" and "objectivity" are ambiguous, since they are first used to mean rational demonstration and then phenomenality. The validity of religious belief certainly is not objective in the first sense, that is to say, this validity cannot, like rational knowledge, be established by rational demonstration. But it does not at all follow from this that for religious belief there is no object involved in the religious relationship. It only follows that this object cannot be grasped by theoretical and rational knowledge. The objectivity of this object as such is not in the least affected by this limitation of rational knowledge.

Much like Natorp, Georg Simmel has also advocated a purely subjectivistic interpretation of religion which involves an emphatic rejection of its transcendental claims.[23] But it is even

[22] See Paul Natorp: *Die Religion innerhalb der Grenzen der Humanität,* 2nd ed., pp. 46 ff., pp. 99 ff.
[23] In this connection the following writings of Simmel are especially important: 1. *Beiträge zur Erkenntnistheorie der Religion* (in the Zeitschrift für Philosophie and philosophische Kritik, Vol. 119, 1901). 2. *Die*

more apparent than with Natorp that Simmel's subjectivistic theory of religion is so constructed as to accord with the previously established tenets of his philosophical system, or rather, of his whole manner of philosophical thinking, since we can only speak of Simmel having a system in a very qualified sense. However, he has not dealt with the actual phenomenon of religious life in any such comprehensive way as Natorp has done. Neither has he taken the trouble to orient his view to the study of the science of religion. He always presents merely an interpretation of the religious problem which accords with the principles of his philosophy as a whole, but which, generally speaking, is formulated without taking religious belief into consideration. And since his philosophical thought as a whole is entirely subjective, either absolutely excluding all objectivity, or at least shoving it aside as being unimportant, the subjectivistic interpretation of religion at once follows as a necessary consequence of these presuppositions. Simmel thinks that meaning and value always reside only in the process of life itself, and not in any objective entities. Hence, as a matter of principle, he also regards religion only from the point of view of its psychic function. And just because it is self-evident to him that this theory of religion is the only possible or adequate view, not only does he fail to give any evidence for it, he does not even make a serious attempt to prove it.

Of course the occupation of such a keen and versatile thinker with the problem of religion has resulted in many contributions to the problem which are gratefully acknowledged. Yet Simmel's way of treating the problem of religion, and especially the problem of religious truth, does not begin to do justice to the full seriousness of it.

The ultimate significance of religion for Simmel's philosophy consists in the fact that it is a category, one of many

Religion (in the collection: Die Gesellschaft; 1906). 3. *Das Problem der Religiösen Lage* (in the compendium edited by Max Frischeisen-Köhler: Weltanschauung, 1911; reprinted in: Philosophische Kultur, gesammelte Essays, 1911, 2nd ed., 1918). 4. *Lebensanschauung*, 1919 (published posthumously).—In addition, Simmel's other writings are of course also to be considered, especially: *Kant; Probleme der Geschichtsphilosophie; Hauptprobleme der Philosophie (Göschen); Rembrandt, ein kunstphilosophischer Versuch—*. Of the literature dealing with Simmel the following have already been mentioned: Wilhelm Knevels: *Simmel's Religionstheorie* and Friedrich Karl Schumann: *Religion und Wirklichkeit*.

categories with which man, from various points of view, constructs his philosophy of life. His total view concludes that in principle all categories may be applied to every content, and conversely, that all contents may be brought into a relation to every category. But to the religious man himself, religion is concerned only with that ultimate and highest reality which transcends the entire phenomenal world, from which then, of course, this whole sense world must for this very reason get its meaning.

In Simmel's philosophy, however, this reality also appears as a category just like any of the other categories of the possible spheres of consciousness. Hence he robs that transcendental reality, toward which religious belief is directed, of its objectivity.

"The transcendental world" so Simmel tells us, "is that point at which the religiously perceived category is converted into objects." [24] Although this thesis reduces Simmel's theory of religion to a very precise, brief formula, it nevertheless proves it to be an arbitrary philosophical construction. And when we also consider the comparison with which he himself amplifies this thesis, then the weakness of this philosophical construction as such at once becomes apparent. For he adds to the above statement the following: "Just as the three-dimensional sphere of perception is that point at which those things which are perceived by the senses become objects." Thus Simmel's subjectivistic interpretation of religion rests upon a purely subjectivistic and phenomenalistic theory of knowledge and is a part of his general subjectivistic and phenomenalistic philosophy of life. But even under this presupposition the above comparison is false, and does not illustrate what it is supposed to illustrate. It shows rather that religion itself stands opposed to all perceptual thought. For even though the three-dimensional sphere could be called that point at which sense-perceptions attain objectivity, there is nothing corresponding to this in the case of religion. Here Simmel has to treat the transcendental world as the point of objective-becoming, but the real issue is precisely the objectivity of this transcendental world itself; and this compels him to add the new and entirely

[24] Georg Simmel: *Die Religion,* p. 51.

fantastic interpretation that the religiously perceived category itself is "converted into objects."

"Into objects": in conclusion attention must also be directed to this phrase. For religious belief, as we have already said, the issue at stake is ultimately only whether the over-world is objective, no matter how it may be more closely defined. But Simmel here speaks of objects in the plural sense, and that can only mean that he attributes to the secondary concrete ideas of religious belief the same value that he attaches to the basic religious belief. That this interpretation is correct is confirmed by a number of Simmel's own statements elsewhere. For example, he writes that the religious meaning "distils itself, so to speak, from life, and builds for itself its own exclusive world, the world of the transcendental, of ecclesiastical dogmas, and of the means of salvation." [25] No matter how valuable his other philosophical achievements may be, from the religio-psychological point of view anyone who puts these three phenomena on the same plane has forfeited the right to be regarded as an important authority on the question of the truth of religion.

Let us now consider another type of illusionism, namely, Vaihinger's philosophy of "as if" with its strict *fictionalism*.[26] Fictionalism claims to make the basic tendency of Kant's whole philosophical labors consistent, but it has a special interest precisely in the *problem of religious truth*. Vaihinger himself admits this and the whole plan of his monumental work is enough proof of it. To be sure, he failed to formulate the problem of religious truth clearly from the point of view of its generality for all religions. On the contrary both his statement of the problem and his religio-philosophical discussions, are oriented exclusively to Christianity. This explains why Vaihinger, in stating his religio-philosophical position, nearly always has the theistic or deistic idea of God immediately in mind, and it also explains why he put the belief in immortality upon the same level with this idea of God. However, when we

---

[25] In the essay, *Uber das Problem der religiösen Lage: Philosophische Kultur*, p. 236.

[26] Hans Vaihinger: *Die Philosophie des Als Ob*. System der theoretischen, praktischen und religiösen Fiktionen der Menschheit auf Grund eines idealistischen Positivismus. Berlin (1911), 1927. Translated by C. K. Ogden.

take the basic religious belief in its universality, this is a very radical restriction of the problem, and for the religio-scientific and especially for the religio-psychological treatment, it is a restriction which must, at the very outset, be regarded as a fundamental defect in fictionalism. Then, too, there can be no doubt but what Vaihinger also wishes, throughout his discussion, to subordinate the basic religious belief *per se* to the point of view of his fictionalism.

And now as we begin to criticize fictionalism, it must be explicitly stated in advance that our criticism does not aim to minimize in any way the services which Vaihinger has rendered to the interpretation of Kant, to logic, and finally to philosophy in general.[27]

Vaihinger undertakes to prove that the expression "as if," so often used by Kant, must, in view of the basic tendency of his philosophy, be interpreted as an actual fiction, that is, as a consciously false assumption which has practical utility but which does not possess truth and is unreal. The relation of such a fiction to an hypothesis completely clarifies the character of the fiction as Vaihinger conceives it. An hypothesis, according to its purpose, aims at reality; it seeks to be, and as far as possible, it should be established, that is, "verified." A fiction, on the other hand, is "false from the very beginning" and it can only be "justified" by its usefulness. The theory of evolution is an hypothesis, but Goethe's protozoon, or a "legal party" are fictions. Two characteristics, or rather, two groups of characteristics are then ultimately decisive for a fiction: (1) violence of the assumption, inner contradiction, and logical impossibility, and (2) usefulness, expediency, and even indispensability for a particular realm of reality or thought.

Here we are interested only in Vaihinger's application of this "as if" point of view to the sphere of religion. But precisely in this sphere, as he expressly asserts, it achieves its

[27] Heinrich Scholz presents a treatment of the "as if" philosophy of religion, that is as detailed as it is penetrating, in his book *Die Religionsphilosophie des Als Ob,* 1921.—Of the remaining literature I select as being especially noteworthy: Kurt Kesseler, *Das Problem der Religion in der Gegenwartsphilosophie,* 2nd ed., 1920, p. 43 ff.; Arthur Liebert, *Das Problem der Geltung,* 1914, p. 62 ff.; Herm. Hegenwald, *Gegenwartsphilosophie und Christliche Religion,* 1913; Otto Ritschl, *Die doppelte Wahrheit im der Philosophie des Als Ob,* 1925.

greatest triumphs. For it shows us that all religious beliefs are to be treated as fictions, and that means as assumptions, characterized by the two criteria just mentioned. On the one hand, religious beliefs are arbitrary and false assumptions which do not correspond to reality and, on the other hand, in a practical way, that is, for ethical conduct, they are useful and even indispensable. To live as if an over-world exists, even though one knows that it does not actually exist, is the religion of the "as if," and Vaihinger thinks that it is the only religion worthy of philosophers and of the philosophically enlightened.

The decisive validation of the criteria of utility and practicality makes this philosophy of the "as if" quite like pragmatism. But its emphasis upon the known falsity of the assumption in question differentiates it from pragmatism. In the sphere of religion especially this difference entirely out-weighs the formal similarity. From personal acquaintance with William James I know that his own attitude toward religion, and his whole way of thinking on religious matters was totally different from that of the philosophy of the "as if." To be sure, James claimed that pragmatism, which weighs everything by its practical value, can scientifically defend the truth of religion. But we have already found that pragmatism, due to the exclusiveness of its statement of the problem and due to its not being able to point to any unequivocal criterion, shifts and superficially interprets the problem of religious truth. But much more violently does fictionalism shift this problem.

Since Vaihinger has so definitely placed his appeal to Kant into the foreground, we can best state our own attitude toward fictionalism by discussing his evaluation of Kant's philosophy of religion.

It is true that Kant's language frequently leaves open a purely fictional interpretation. Vaihinger explains this by differentiating between a "critical" and a "dogmatic" Kant. The critical Kant recognizes and teaches that religious belief is a "mere idea" in the sense of a pure fiction, but the dogmatic Kant frequently reverts to the pre-critical position and holds fast to the reality of the deity (more generally: the over-world), although formally subordinating it to a fictional and

symbolical evaluation.[28]   In my opinion this interpretation is
not applicable to a thinker such as Kant.   It ascribes to him a
degree of confusion and a continual change of opinion that is
absolutely unthinkable in his case.   For in order for this interpretation to be true Kant must not only have neglected to state
his view with absolute clarity in every one of his many writings,
but he would also have had to waver continually in his views
from one writing to another.   We shall restrict our survey to
his chief works.   While in his *"Kritik der reinen Vernunft"*
(1781) he would have had to espouse a strict fictionalism, at
least in a very considerable number of passages, in the *Prolegomena* (1783) he would have had to make his teaching so
crude as to presuppose as self-evident the actual existence of a
highest being, merely applying the character of "as if" to his
attributes.   But in the *Grundlegung zur Metaphysik der Sitten*
(1785) he would have allowed the strictly critical (fictional)
point of view to dominate again, while in the *Kritik der praktischen Vernunft* (1788), striking a different note once more,
he would have replaced the daring radicalism of the preceding
work by a growing "dogmatism" (acceptance of reality).   In
the *"Kritik der Urteilskraft"* (1790) he would, at least at the
conclusion, practically have given up his critical "as if" doctrine whereas the work which belongs to a later period, *Über
die Fortschritte der Metaphysik* would have again presented a
more daring, frank, and consistent interpretation of this doctrine, while the *Religion innerhalb der Grenzen der blossen Vernunft* would have remained only in part upon the same level.[29]
    The necessary conclusion of such an evaluation of Kant's
writings would be the assumption that on the most fundamental point of his entire philosophy of religion and ethics,
Kant himself was not absolutely clear as to how the problem

    [28] The idea of the symbolical in Vaihinger's category of "symbolical
fictions" (*op. cit.,* pp. 39 ff.) contains an element of truth which is important for the psychology of religion, but he is entirely unjustified in
combining it with the idea of fiction.   And the statement that Schleiermacher converted all dogmas from hypotheses into fictions indicates an
absolute misunderstanding of Schleiermacher's purpose and point of view.
    [29] Vaihinger's expectation that Kant's posthumous works would sub-
stantiate the "as if" doctrine (*op. cit.,* p. 733) has since been shown to be
false by the editor, Erich Adickes: *Kant's Opus posthumum, dargestellt
und beurteilt von Erich Adickes,* Berlin, 1920.   Comp. especially pp. 827 ff.
and the concluding discussion, pp. 846 ff.

should be stated, to say nothing of his being clear as to his own attitude. But in my opinion this necessary conclusion proves that such an evaluation is absurd.

How then is the fact under consideration to be explained? An approach to a satisfactory explanation can be made by referring to several passages in the face of which Vaihinger's theory obviously collapses. Thus in the "transcendental dialectic" of the *Critique of Pure Reason,* the work that is especially important for our whole problem, the following sentence is found: "We are free to derive the appearances of the world and their existence from other appearances, with unfailing confidence, just as if there were no necessary being, while yet we are also free to strive unceasingly toward the completeness of that derivation, just as if such a being were presupposed as an ultimate ground." [30] Both of the possible attitudes mentioned here are introduced with "as if," yet both cannot be fictions in Vaihinger's sense, that is, consciously false assumptions. For if one were false then the other would have to be true. Using this approach to explain the fact under consideration, two things must be said.

1. The ambiguity in this statement is due to Kant's frequent failure to express himself precisely. Yet in other passages he does give quite exact statements as is shown by their very laboriousness. And these statements are absolutely unequivocal. The ambiguous passages must be interpreted in the light of these precise statements. But Vaihinger's interpretation does not do justice to these very passages. In the work *Über die Fortschritte der Metaphysik,* which Vaihinger himself praises for its frank and daring presentation of the "as if" doctrine, we read: *"Theoretically considered,* the argument for the correctness of a belief is no argument for the truth of what it asserts, and therefore such an argument constitutes no objective information as to the reality of the objects of the belief, since that is impossible in respect to the supersensual, but such an argument is only subjectively and practically valid, and for practical purposes it is sufficient information to act *as if we*

[30] Book II, part 3, section 5, appendix, 2nd ed., p. 646. See Norman Kemp Smith's translation, p. 517.

knew that these objects were real." [31]   Thus, in this painstakingly precise statement "as if" refers not to the existence of the supersensual as such, but to our "knowing" of it, that is, to our theoretical and rational knowledge of it.   To be sure, this can only be called fictional knowledge.   We can and should recognize that we do not possess rational knowledge of the supersensual and that we cannot comprehend it by the theoretical reason.

2. In addition to this it must be remembered that Kant's philosophy of religion, basing religious belief exclusively upon morality, does deprive it of that independence which it gets from religious experience.   This involves him in an actual incomplete disjunction.   He contrasts theoretical speculation with that kind of practical-moral belief which expresses itself only in moral action.   *The specifically religious attitude is therefore entirely excluded.*   It is not excluded for any particular reasons but it is left out of consideration.   The consequence of this is that the problem of the reality of the supersensual often has to be entirely, or at least almost entirely, disregarded.

Now this second fact, which we must take into account if we want to understand Kant's philosophy of religion, brings us at once to the real defect in fictionalism.   For Vaihinger makes no effort whatever to remedy this evident defect in the Kantian theory.   On the contrary he dogmatically accepts Kant's position and here again without offering any proof, yes, without even making any attempt to prove it.   Thus his whole discussion of the problem of the nature of religion accords with his previously established (negative) decision on the problem of its truth.   We can only thank Vaihinger for allowing this circle, which dominates his "as if" philosophy of religion, to be so unmistakably recognized.

However, this vicious circle in his reasoning reaches out still further.   It is not only of a methodological but also of an epistemological nature.   Inasmuch as he regards all religious beliefs as fictions, he presupposes a criterion which justifies this verdict.   Yet he does not give such a criterion and he cannot so long as he is unwilling completely to abandon the Kantian basis of criticism upon which he so decidedly stands.   For according

[31] Philosophische Bibliothek, *Kleine Schriften,* III, p. 129.

to the principles of Kant the fact that rational knowledge is in and of itself unable to prove the reality of the religious over-world, absolutely does not justify the assertion of its non-existence in an inclusive and conclusive statement of a philosophy of life.

This leads us to the deepest source of error of the fictional-istic philosophy of religion. It lies in the fact that Vaihinger completely tears asunder the two main realms of all human existence. The realities of every-day life and those of rational reflection are not synthesized into a higher unity. No attempt is even made to bring them into harmony and to make them consistent. They are and remain radically divorced from each other. In the inclusive sense which stands out so clearly in Kant's terminology (theoretical reason—practical reason) rea-son does not play any rôle at all. Consequently the whole theory ends in absurdity. For if that which is consciously false, that which is "untrue at the very beginning" is at the same time designated as not only useful and practical but also as indis-pensable—that is, as indispensable not only in the sense of a heuristic principle of rational knowledge but also for one's en-tire world-view and philosophy of life, is not that absurdity? To conduct one's life as if a supersensual world exists, although one knows positively and definitely that it does not exist, is not that absurdity?

In the concluding presentation of his position Vaihinger is forced to admit that whoever follows this philosophy of "as if" will act "unreasonably, taken strictly theoretically." But the fact is this admission does not go far enough. Such conduct would not only be theoretically unreasonable, it would also be especially and absolutely practically unreasonable. Real life protests against such an absurdity. In this respect William James, with his keen sense for the realities of life, saw much more clearly than Vaihinger, and although in his *Pragmatism* he defended a view which is theoretically disputable because it is one-sided, in a practical way it is a much more significant position than that of the founder of the philosophy of "as if." Fictionalism was devised at a desk, it is a purely conceptual creation born in the study room of the scholar, and lacking the contact with and the reality of life. But that is why it ultimately also fails theoretically. It reverts to scholasticism, for it leads to a dualistic conception of truth. Vaihinger himself is honest enough openly to acknowledge this, but this does not alter the fact that the doctrine of dualistic truth is basically scholastic, and that it is an open affront to Kantian "criticism."

And so the most modern, ingenious, and radical attempt to dispute the truth of religion ends in practical absurdity and in a theoretical retreat into scholasticism.

6

Let us summarize what we have said. If all attempts which try to prove that the claims of religious belief to truth and to transcendence are illusions fail, then we may see in this fact an indirect proof of the reasonableness of religion. And to substantiate this, it may be added that it is only religious belief which makes possible a uniting into a higher synthesis the actuality of experience and the reflection of rational knowledge.

Moreover, since religious experience stands in a most intimate relation to the most profound and consequently to the most positive certainty of reality which is or can be at all possible for men, it cannot be treated as essentially illusory. For it stands in the closest relationship to the certainty of reality indicated by Descartes' *cogito, ergo sum* argument, and upon which the whole modern theory of knowledge rests. When this statement is freed from the intellectualistic and rationalistic limitation which the word *cogito* usually involves, and which Descartes also, in spite of his own superior insight, favored, when *cogito* is understood purely in the sense of the experience of the self, then the validity of his statement is unshakable.

For in personal reflection upon the particular empirical phenomena of self-consciousness the identity of the self which pervades all of these phenomena is grasped as a reality, and this same reality underlies all other experiences and all reflection upon all the contents of consciousness that are given. The experience of the self confirms the most positive certainty of reality which man can at all conceive. It is the presupposition for every "belief in the existence of the external world," to use Dilthey's characteristic, even though not entirely unobjectionable, phrase,[32] and that means that it is the presupposition for the validity of the reality of the external world as a whole. For the reality of the external world arises from that opposite which stands in contrast to and restricts the self.

But we have already seen that the relation to the self or the category of the self by its very nature belongs to the structure of the religious consciousness. In the fundamental religious experience there is involved, then, a relationship in which the self, the prime reality and source of all certainty and validity of every other reality, constitutes one pole. Hence we are actually forced to accept as reasonable the assumption that the other pole does not lie in an illusion or fiction of human thought, but that it does and must lie in the ultimate and highest reality itself. And this is what the determining religious belief asserts on the basis of religious experience. For on the one hand, this prime reality of human certainty, the self, cannot itself yet claim to be the ultimate and highest reality, since that would not only exclude religious experience in advance and without proof, but in addition (regarded merely epistemologically) it would lead to solipsism. But solipsism, the view that the individual thinker is the only certain reality, must undoubtedly appear to common-sense to be a perfect absurdity since it mocks all of the realities of life. And it actually is universally regarded as an absurdity, if we disregard the few cranks who try to make an impression by sacrificing the realities of life to their own theories. On the other hand, however, the alternative already mentioned must be taken as the only other alternative. If the counter-pole of the religious relationship does not constitute the ultimate and highest reality, then religion really is based upon a fiction or an illusion. There is no third alternative. For any other conceivable object of religious belief would in religion's own estimation itself be a fiction or an illusion.

Therefore the choice of this alternative by religious belief must be taken to be reasonable. For to question the validity of the basic religious experience would mean that any attempt to give the final necessary proof for the prime reality of man's cer-

---

[32] Wilh. Dilthey, *Beiträge zur Lösung der Frage vom Ursprung unseres Glaubens an die Realität der Aussenwelt und seinem Recht*, Berlin, 1890. Comp. also Max Frischeisen-Köhler, *Wissenschaft und Wirklichkeit*, Leipsic, 1912, pp. 273 ff.

tainty of reality would end in illusionism. But in that case the illusionism of every complete philosophy of life would logically be the inescapable consequence. The very natural objection that if the prime reality of man's certainty of reality does not include within itself the necessary proof, then the return to a supposedly ultimate and highest reality would be of no avail, since that would signify a *regressus in infinitum,* loses its justification upon more careful consideration. For there is neither any justified occasion nor, precisely taken, even any possibility of going back still farther. The supposed return would be a mere duplication.

There is no reasonable way of going back farther behind that fact which the prime reality of man's certainty of reality is able to establish by its two basic functions—the direct practical conduct of life, and the logical-rational reflective activity of the mind. The essential content of religion must therefore be regarded as reasonable by human judgment as a whole, even though for the individual it occasionally and repeatedly signifies a completely irrational fact.

And this conviction is also the justifiable element of truth in mysticism, which claims that within the depths of the human soul the deity is present as the final and highest reality. Of course, contrary to its own purpose, mysticism thereby runs the risk of simply identifying the ground of the soul with deity. "That is the spark which is so near to God that it constitutes a single undifferentiated 'one' with him."—Tat tvam asi : "That is the primeval being, that is the self, that art thou, O Svetaketu !"

But in rejecting this unjustly asserted identity we must be careful not to overlook the element of truth in the under-lying idea of mysticism.

And the remaining objection, that is, that the validity of the belief in the existence of the ultimate highest reality is impaired, or even completely abrogated, by that relationship which is believed in and is realized by religious faith, insofar as this relationship makes the human self a condition of that existence, is disposed of precisely by the fact, so strongly emphasized in mysticism, that the religious relationship can only be induced by pure passivity on the part of man. This fact is self-evident when the nature of religion is rightly understood. For if the feeling of dependence is made the basic religious feeling, and if the feelings of security and yearning are subordinated to it, then pure passivity on the part of man must be the basic condition for the realization of the religious relationship. And so the religious relationship does not endanger either the uniqueness of the ultimate and highest reality or the value which is mediated by that reality. On the contrary, despite all of its irrationality, the religious assurance unquestionably can be made reasonable. To be sure we must avoid the error of translating this reasonableness into a rational necessity. That would be an unjustifiable exaggeration of a position which is in itself justifiable. And at the same time it would mean the rationalization of religion. But it cannot be too strongly emphasized that to rationalize religion is to destroy religion as religion. Although we must abandon every attempt to prove that the truth-value of religion is a rational necessity, we must just as emphatically stress the reasonableness of religion.

The question now arises as to whether, from the religio-psychological standpoint, we can carry further the discussion of the thesis which is based upon the opposite interpretation of the rationality of the religious assurance of truth.

CHAPTER XII

THE RELIGIOUS PHILOSOPHY OF LIFE AND MODERN NATURAL SCIENCE

I

In accordance with the nature of religion the religious philosophy of life has as its most important ingredient the belief in an over-world. For it is just the basic conviction of the religious philosophy of life that the temporal and spatial sense-world does not have the basis and the meaning of its existence in itself, but, on the contrary, in a reality of a higher order—in "God."

This basic conviction of the religious philosophy of life is most clearly and definitely expressed in the idea of creation. Hence the denial of creation originating in modern natural science stands in the sharpest opposition to the religious philosophy of life. But since the idea of creation gets its purest and most logical development in the belief in creation of Christianity, the opposition is usually especially directed against the christian form of the idea of creation. Yet the opposition is by no means exhausted in the polemic against the specifically christian form of the idea of creation. The basic argument reaches much further and applies much more generally. Here, then, we must deal especially with this basic argument.

Moreover, we shall stick to the chief form of the anti-religious argument. Haeckel has named it "the natural history of creation." [1] Therewith he has set the religious idea of creation in opposition to the socalled natural history of creation, in order to prove that the former is antiquated and unacceptable to present-day scientific thought. But the whole idea of a

[1] Ernst Haeckel: *Natürliche Schöpfungsgeschichte,* 1868. The later editions are in two volumes (10th edition, Berlin, 1902). English translation: *History of Creation,* translated by E. Ray Lankester (Appleton).

natural history of creation is combined with the idea of evolution.

Now is the natural history of creation really what it claims to be? No! we dare to answer; it absolutely is not what it claims to be; it breaks down completely and it breaks down just at the most decisive point.

For what is the content of the idea of creation? More definitely: What is its object? Now its object is just creation, that is to say, the universe as creation, and thus the universe itself, the universe as such, the universe as a whole.

That a universe exists at all, this universe in which we live, to which with our bodily existence we belong, that, says religious belief, is to be understood as the creation of God. Just this: that is, this fact of the universe as a whole the socalled natural history of creation must explain *naturalistically,* it must treat it as a necessary product of nature, if it really wants to refute the idea of creation and the philosophy of life of the belief in creation. Now does it do that? No, it does not, but on the contrary, it evades this whole issue and substitutes for the original problem that is in question, an entirely different problem.

For it substitutes for the universe itself, the universe as a whole, the *present-day condition* of the universe. This present-day condition of the universe it seeks to explain naturalistically, that is, as the outcome of necessary processes of nature. Its entire argument applies to the present-day condition of the world, but not to the existence of the universe in general. The natural history of creation, however, has to assume this general existence of the universe, and has to take that existence as self-evident, but that means that it has to assume the unique object of the belief in creation and to take it as self-evident.

The representatives of the natural history of creation, however, cover up this evasion of the issue by simply identifying the belief in creation with the naïve ideas of the story of creation as it is told in the Old Testament.

And it is just the failure to distinguish between conceptual forms and intellectual expressions of religion and the inner essence of religious conviction, or, differently expressed, it is just the failure to attend to the psychological structure of the religious consciousness that makes this evasion possible.

Just as soon as one makes this unavoidable religio-psychological distinction, there can no longer be any doubt over what is the kernel of religious conviction in the Old Testament story, or, perhaps it would be more exact to say, stories of creation. The Old Testament concerns itself with two aspects of creation: the universe as a whole, the entire actuality of the universe, on the one hand, and humanity, the life of mankind in the universe, on the other hand. To refer the universe as a whole, and then, in particular, to refer men, human life, back to God; that is the meaning of the Old Testament story of creation, and, we may add, that is also the meaning of the belief in creation in general.

The particular concepts of the Old Testament story of creation are of no significance.

Now for this very reason we must not make it our business to bring the details of the Old Testament story of creation into harmony with present-day scientific knowledge. That kind of procedure is doomed to failure from the beginning, and therefore it is to be absolutely rejected, regardless of whether it is attempted from the side of theology or from that of natural science.

For example, this holds even of such a relatively cautious attempt as has repeatedly been made by the botanist and natural philosopher, Reinke.[2]

As is customary in all such attempts at a comparison, Reinke thinks of the days of creation of the Genesis story as creation cycles, but although he does not, to be sure, attempt to correlate each creation cycle with a particular stage of evolution in modern science,—a correlation which is only possible with the worst kind of subterfuge, yet he does especially stress the fact that many different periods or acts of creation have to be distinguished, and have to be sharply differentiated from each other. Thus the process of formation must be sharply distinguished from the genetic process, not only because they differ in content or actuality, but, on the contrary, just in relation to the process

[2] Johannes Reinke: *Die Welt als Tat,* 6th edition, Berlin, 1915. See also his book *Naturwissenschaft, Weltanschauung, Religion,* 1925.

of formation. Reinke means that the process of formation of the universe cannot be thought of, as present-day natural science so often does think of it, as a single process. For he thinks that at least two, if not three, independent acts of formation must be assumed and must be contrasted with one another: the formation of the inorganic world; the formation of the organic world; and perhaps also the formation of mankind. And to support this theory he then appeals to the story of creation in Genesis.

Now this is a misuse of this story of creation, and also, generally speaking, a misuse of religious ideas. If Reinke holds his theory to be justifiable and necessary on the basis of his study of natural science, then he should defend it with arguments drawn from natural science. But he should never consider a religious tradition competent to deal with questions of natural science. And above all, he should not drag the religious belief in creation into a controversy in natural science, and he should not use it as an argument in this controversy. The religious belief in creation is independent of whether the process of formation of the universe is single or plural and of whether it is to be conceived as single or as plural. Speaking concretely, this also means that the socalled question of spontaneous generation, whether life evolved out of matter or arose by spontaneous generation in matter is true or not, and the other question of whether man was created or descended from a lower form of life—such questions are for the religious philosophy of life, and also for the christian philosophy of life, of no significance. Let this or that process of formation be conceived and affirmed, as always the religious belief only lays emphasis upon the fact, and of course it also actually does stress the fact, that in every case the process of formation is due to the over-world, to "God."

However that belief is independent of the alternative: either spontaneous generation or not spontanous generation; it is likewise independent of how in the evolutionary process man is related to the higher vertebrates. No matter whether we accept the pure Darwinian theory of Haeckel, or the theory of the anthropologist Klaatsch, who died during the world war and whose theory almost reverses the usual form of the Darwinian theory, or finally, whether we accept any other theory; in every case the process of formation in question can itself be brought under the idea of creation.

The question of "the origin of the primates of men" is so little the unique and the cardinal problem for a philosophy of life, in spite of Haeckel's assertion in his last published work that it is, that, on the contrary, a philosophy of life, strictly and generally speaking, has only a historical and by no means a factual interest in this question.

The basic conviction of the religious philosophy of life is, then, not to be refuted by the natural history of creation. But we can say more. The world picture of scientific research itself makes accessible to us an insight into and an outlook upon the religious position. For this world picture of scientific research remains essentially in the sphere of the relative and of relativity, and thereby refers to an Absolute which lies beyond it. Indeed, this world picture of scientific research expresses in the clearest possible way the immeasurableness and the inconclusiveness of our apprehension of the spatio-temporal universe.

Let me give two examples of the extent to which this is true.

The modern physicist Chwolson has incidentally raised the question of whether physical laws—the laws on which all physical science depends—can be applied to the universe. "Can we," so his question runs, "apply the laws of physics to the universe?" [3]

To answer this question in accordance with the postulates of science Chwolson offers two analogies, and first this one:

He calls the space which surrounds us astronomical space A. This astronomical space A is the space accurately measured by our best instruments, by our largest telescopes and our most sensitive photographic plates. Chwolson then assumes a space Z, which is one billion (N 1,000,000,000) times larger than space A and which encloses space A. And now Chwolson asks: how is space Z related to infinite space, using infinity in the

[3] In the Zeitschrift *Unsere Welt,* February 1911. Additional references are: Erich Becher: *Philosophische Voraussetzungen der exakten Naturwissenschaften,* Leipsic, 1907; *Naturphilosophie* in Kultur der Gegenwart III, VII, 1914; and *Weltgebäude, Weltgesetze, Weltentwicklung,* Berlin, 1915: Bernhard Bavink, *Ergebnisse und Probleme der Naturwissenschaft,* Leipsic (1914), 1930.

mathematical sense of the word? Over against such an infinite space, Chwolson answers, and this answer is obviously unavoidable, space Z is only a needle point, only a grain of dust.

This physicist then places a second analogy alongside of this first one, but one which points in the opposite direction. He assumes a tiny universe. He imagines a rational being of ultramicroscopic size inhabiting an atom of copper, a being whose physical universe is an atom of copper. This being, so he assumes, discovers its universe; it learns that its universe is a complete system of electrons, and with its optical instruments it discovers other universes, the neighboring atoms of copper. On the basis of its observations it concludes that these other universes are of the same constitution as is its own universe. The totality of all these universes this being can reach we may call its astronomical space A. For us that would be a tiny sliver of copper. If now, says Chwolson, this being should draw the conclusion: "The universe is made out of copper," then that would be analogous to our assuming that our known physical laws hold of the universe in its entirety. And conversely: when we apply the laws of physics, the laws of our exact science of physics, to the universe, to all reality, then we are like that being who thought that the universe is made of copper.

These two analogies of the famous physicist are certainly not entirely free from error from an epistemological point of view. In the first place the assumption of a rational being, who is restricted to the realm of a single chemical element, is an arbitrary assumption. But even though this assumption is granted, we could not say that such a being could in any way succeed in gaining a knowledge of other elements and of their laws, and thus finally in winning a knowledge of the whole table of elements and of their laws, that is to say, of just the physico-chemical world which we know, the world of our physical and chemical science. This reservation must be made and therefore Chwolson's argument is not wholly free from objections.

Nevertheless the very mentioning of this defect makes this argument very clear in a respect that is irrefutable and that goes to the heart of the matter: for it shows to what an extent our research remains in the relative and in the realms of relativity.

And for this same purpose I wish now to refer to the so-called theory of relativity in the special present-day sense of the word, that is to say, to the modern theory of relativity of Einstein and Minkowski, which stands in contrast to the older principle of relativity of the dynamics of Galileo and Newton.

For its basic postulate Einstein's theory of relativity assumes that time and distance measurements are dependent upon the position of observers, and that they vary with this position: (the clocks on the sun and on the earth run differently, and also the distances measured by the inhabitants of the earth differ from the distances measured by the inhabitants of the sun); and it also assumes a unique view of the relation of space to time and of the relation of spatio-temporal events.[4]   Indeed, it places time in complete analogy with the three dimensions of space.   The three dimensions of space and the one of time thus appear as interchangeable dimensions of the physical world picture.   Howsoever this theory may be judged scientifically, in any case it brings to sharp expression the fact that the spatio-temporal universe, which our research is able to grasp, is no absolute and final reality that is self-contained and self-sufficient. Rather it is and remains within the sphere of the relative.   To be sure Minkowski describes the four dimensional spatio-temporal universe with the phrase "absolute universe."   However, as here used, the word *absolute* itself is only thought of as relative.   It is not even absolute for epistemological reflection, which rests upon psychical and spiritual life, with its time-span. And still less is it absolute for the religious attitude, which completely transcends the whole spatio-temporal universe.   But precisely for that reason the expression "absolute universe" proves that scientific research here opens the way to a vista and a prospect of the religious position.   For again the question must here be raised of whether the theory of relativity can

[4] From the rich literature I recommend especially the following: H. A. Lorentz, A. Einstein and H. Minkowski: *Das Relativitätsprinzip, Abhandlungen*, Leipsic, 1915; A. Einstein: *Über die spezielle und allegmeine Relativitätstheorie* (for the general reader, Sammlung Vieweg); and M. Schlick: *Raum und Zeit in der gegenwärtigen Physik*, Berlin, 3rd edition, 1920, *Vorlesungen über Relativitätstheorie*, 1922; Herm. Weyl, *Raum, Zeit, Materie*, 1925.

apply to the whole of reality, of whether it can pass as the final and the whole truth, or whether it does not much more presuppose another kind, a non-relative and an absolute truth, the reality of Absolute Truth. And this question gives an outlook upon religion.

2

Another essential characteristic of the religious philosophy of life is its teleological character. The religious philosophy of life, and to an even greater extent, the Christian philosophy of life, is teleological. It knows about an ultimate purpose and it knows the goal of the world as a whole and of human life in particular. It sees the meaning, purpose, and goal of the world in its relation to the transcendent reality, to "God."

From this point of view the chief opponent of the religious philosophy of life during the last fifty years has been Darwinism, with its theory of selection or natural selection. The theory of natural selection is not exactly the same in the biological theory of evolution as the theory of descent. It is rather a very definite development of the theory of descent. It aims to explain the kind of descent and the way descent takes place, and it also aims to explain biological evolution as a whole. In fact, it would explain these facts according to the following scheme: without any selectivity and without any purpose, nature offers a wealth of possibilities for the production of life; the selection of these is determined entirely by the struggle for existence, that is to say, exclusively by the principle of utility. Chance and utility: these two factors or principles are the uniquely determining ones for the interpretation of the theory of natural selection.

If in Germany Haeckel ranks as the most popular defender of the Darwinian theory of natural selection, nevertheless it was not he, but rather the earlier zoologist Weismann, of Freiburg, who developed this theory most profoundly and logically.[5] His pregnant characterization of the theory is the "omnipotence" of natural selection. And this word *omnipotence* (Allmacht) best directs attention to the decisive and underlying

---

[5] August Weismann: *Vorträge über die Deszendenztheorie*, 2 vols., 3rd edition, Jena, 1913.

principle of the theory. But the active factor in the evolution
of life is just this natural selection and this alone. No other
forces and no other factors are of equal importance for evolution, and least of all are any forces and factors of a teleological
(purposive) character of equal importance. "The essence of
natural selection," says Weismann, "rests upon an accumula-
tion of tiny useful deviations in the direction of their utility.
Thus utility is formed and grows, and great effects first come
into existence slowly through a summing up of numerous tiny
advances." This, in fact, is the omnipotence of natural selection. Yet the theory is not thus necessarily put into absolute
contradiction with the teleological and religious philosophy of
life. As long as it stays within its own realm, it can be subordinated to a teleological philosophy of life, as, for example,
when this whole sequence of natural selection is looked upon
as a system of means to the higher development of life as the
end, and which end is then thought of as being dependent upon
a supreme Will.

Now the theory of natural selection itself cannot rightly
object to such an interpretation, since it is itself only a theory
of the way in which evolution has proceeded.

However, today the situation is like this. Only under very
definite restrictions and with significant modifications is Darwinism any longer accepted by a large number of the younger
scientists.[6] This attitude began with the mutations theory,
which was originated by the botanist de Vries. It does not
regard evolution as proceeding by tiny gliding transitions, but
as developing by leaps from one stage of development to another. This implies such a great shift in the strict Darwinian
theory as to break down its extreme anti-teleological position
and to weaken its usual anti-teleological argumentative strength.
For this argumentative strength lies exactly in the fact that the
evolution was conceived as proceeding quite generally and necessarily by gliding transitions.

Far more important, however, is the fact that the most
recent biological research, in its own field of investigation, turns
more and more in a direction which, instead of excluding, actu-

[6] See Oscar Hertwig: *Das Werden der Organismen,* 2nd ed., 1918.
See also Richard Hertwig, *Abstammungslehre und neuere Biologie,* 1927.

ally requires the teleological interpretation. The controversy over the socalled *neo-vitalism* we shall here leave entirely out of account. Whether this neo-vitalism is to be judged right or wrong—and to us it seems extraordinarily worthy of attention, especially in the form in which it is defended by Hans Driesch in his numerous works which are as scientifically exact as they are philosophically profound—may be left to exact science and natural philosophy. But certain considerations, which are independent of all special theories and which rest upon the narrowest teleological form of the question, are of the widest significance.

The investigations which we have in mind here relate to the processes of growth, regeneration, and reproduction in living beings. Just the more exact investigation of these processes, carried on during the last twenty years, has revealed the thorough-going teleological structure of the phenomena of life. That just these processes in all of their peculiarities can be brought under a purely mechanical interpretation is, to be sure, not excluded by this fact. Yet these processes themselves in their entirety exhibit a decided teleological character.

That the processes of growth and of regeneration demand an inclusive teleological interpretation is made clear even by the most elementary forms of life. All higher organisms go back to the one celled organisms. They are made up of single cells, but they grow just from a particular cell, the original germ-cell. This happens by the original cell, with its primary unified nucleus, partitioning itself again and again until, finally, by such multiple divisions, it creates a complicated structure that then further develops itself. Out of the original unified cell there is first formed an organism with two cells, out of this organism one with four cells is formed, then one with eight, then one with sixteen cells, and so on in this way.

The totality of these cells normally forms a unified organism. But if, now, in the second stage, that of the two-celled organism, one cell dies, then, at least under favorable conditions, a complete organism will develop out of the remaining cell. Both halves, which together ordinarily produce the whole organism, also possess the ability, the potency, each by itself alone, to produce the whole organism. Indeed this peculiarity is by no means restricted to the stage where there are two cells, but it is also true of the later stages of embryonic development and true, too, in a much different way. A complete organism can also be formed out of two-fourths, but also out of three-fourths of the constituent parts; and again, if we take the stage of eight cells, out of four-eighths of the constituents, but also out of three-eighths, and likewise out of five-eighths, six-eighths and seven-eighths of these constituents.

Driesch, who has himself had a very important part in this research, has invented a name for these facts which we have just sketched, the name "equi-potential systems." [7] This means: every element of the embryo has the capacity to produce that definite whole, which, under usual conditions, is produced by the totality of the parts.

The first stage of growth of living organisms—and partly also even the much more complicated later stages—actually are such harmonious equi-potential systems. Hence they greatly excel what can be done by machines constructed by human intelligence and skill, and, to be sure, exactly in a teleological respect, that is, in respect to their purposive structure. No man-made machine constitutes a harmonious equi-potential system of this kind. But the innermost essence of a harmonious equi-potential system is purposiveness; and it remains purposiveness no matter to what extent all particular factors may be brought under a purely mechanical interpretation.

Now let us consider the research into hybridism and chromosomes.

The investigation of the phenomenon of hybridism in plants led to the Mendelian rule, which was named after the Augustinian Father Mendel. Its basic principle runs: If one crosses two forms that are not too unlike, the newly produced generation bifurcates, with further inbreeding, into the different aspects of the parent forms in quite definite percentages. With the crossing of two plants with red and white blossoms, which are closely related forms, under certain conditions the first generation yields only pink flowers. But the third generation will consist of twenty-five per cent of white, twenty-five per cent of

---

[7] Hans Driesch: *Philosophie des Organischen,* 2 vols., Leipzig, 1909, Vol. I, pp. 119 ff. Driesch's work is in English.

red and fifty per cent of pink flowers. And this proportion always holds even to the last generation of that kind of pink flowered plant.

This is the very simplest case where only one different characteristic for each plant is involved. When a greater number of characteristics, for example, three, eight, ten, or even more, are involved the situation becomes extraordinarily complicated, yet fixed percentages are always found for wide ranges of plants.

In all probability the phenomena of hybridism are connected with those of chromosome research. Chromosomes are especially important parts of the nucleus which determine reproduction. The socalled chromatin arranges itself in the nucleus in a rod-shaped form of chromatin filaments, called chromosomes. And it has been found that the chromatin of an impregnated egg cell lies alongside of that of the sperm cell, and that the resulting cell division takes place as a splitting first of the separate chromosomes, then of the two nuclei, then of the two cells, and that each part of the divided cell contains the same amount of chromatin from the father as from the mother, and that, in the partition of the chromatin received from the two parents, this precise distribution is carried through all further cell divisions.

Taking both the theory of hybridism and the theory of chromosomes together we may say: Research into hybridism and chromosomes proves that the Darwinian postulate of non-selectivity and purposelessness must here be absolutely denied. On the contrary these investigations show that an orderliness of the most marvelous kind rules in inheritance, an orderliness such as no one ever before held to be possible and yet which is purposive in its innermost essence.

Finally let us mention the "serviceableness to the stranger" type of purposiveness, whose importance to the question of a philosophy of life has been rightly stressed by Erich Becher.[8] Gall worts exhibit this kind of purposiveness in a typical way. Here the host plant cares for the gall guest by growing a plant nest at the place where it is stung by the parent insect and by

[8] Erich Becher: *Die fremddienliche Zweckmässigkeit der Pflanzengallen*, Leipsic, 1917.

providing many other protective arrangements, whereas the gall larva during its parasitic life only injures the plant in question. Becher thinks that the only satisfactory explanation of this remarkable phenomenon is the assumption of an over-individual psychical life which, in its ramifications, penetrates into the individual living organism, Becher's assertion goes too far. This definite type of speculative and metaphysical interpretation, which he defends, cannot be regarded as the only possible explanation. But he is entirely right in the general assumption which underlies his theory, that these phenomena demand an interpretation that is throughout and essentially teleologically oriented.

Thus from various angles of approach the most recent research of natural science itself points in the direction of a teleological interpretation of nature. And such a teleological interpretation is then necessarily accompanied by a teleological philosophy of life. But the most logical and comprehensive form of a teleological philosophy of life is the religious philosophy of life.

CHAPTER XIII

THE PRIMACY OF RELIGION IN THE SPIRITUAL LIFE

I

The complex problem to which we now have to turn is usually expressed by the phrase "Religion and Culture." Hence it is concerned with the relation of religion and culture, and especially with the relation in which religion on its side stands to culture. Thus the word culture is here used to include the totality of the purposes and ideals of the inner life. This way of speaking undoubtedly has its justification and it is especially fitted to bring to clear expression the problem that is here involved. Yet it cannot claim to be the only possible or even the only justifiable way of speaking. For such a claim would carry with it the temptation to take a definite position to the problem in advance. And when such an evident fallacy of *petitio principii* is committed, then the question usually implied is: "Is religion hostile or friendly to culture?" And this is thought of as a valid disjunction. But just this disjunctive proposition is incomplete, since it does not do justice to the actual situation. This is the first universal and inclusive insight which the religiopsychological method yields and establishes in this field of investigation. For as soon as one seriously considers the problem the incompleteness of this disjunction at once follows. In history we find both hostility and friendliness of religion to culture. And on this point there are also important differences between different religions and between different sects of the same religion. But when we make that total set of conditions in history that is specifically religious in the sense of religious experience the decisive fact, then there can be no question whatever but that religion in its essence is neither hostile nor friendly to culture. On the contrary, over against culture religion is essentially critical, that is to say, it asks the direction in which culture is going and what the ultimate aim of culture is. In the historical process of development, and under the influence of definite historical phenomena, religion becomes either hostile or friendly to culture. But in its essence religion is critical of culture.

Thus the question of the relation of religion to culture cannot be answered when we take the point of view that religion must be either hostile or friendly to culture.

Moreover, still another much liked approach to this question fails to achieve its purpose. We have in mind the attempt to answer the question by the historical and genetic method. One calls attention to the fact that everywhere the beginning of culture goes back to religion. The fact expressed in this statement is indeed not to be denied. Moreover it is important to call attention to it. Science and art have evolved out of religion, in the sense that originally they were built up out of the incentives to worship which were inherent in religious interests. Hence in the history of mankind it is always among representatives of religion that the beginnings of culture are to be found. Nevertheless the fact that religion has very often displayed the strongest energy in the building up of communal life is of special importance. Indeed communal life is the presupposition of every evolution of history and therefore of all true culture. In fact the religious idea has been taken to be the organizing principle of all social development. Fustel de Coulanges has expounded this idea in an especially ingenious and scholarly way.[1] To be sure such a construction cannot be developed without doing violence to the facts. Yet the historical material showing that the most primitive human societies are strengthened and established by religion actually supports this theory.

Hence religion has rightly been called the mother of all culture. Yet, starting from this fact we are also unable to reach a decision as to the place of religion in human cultural and spiritual life. For on the other side of the argument it so happens that in history itself a gradual differentiation and an increasing independence of the different functions of life takes place, and this process of increasing independence has the greatest significance for all these functions. The fact that science, art, and technics separate from each other, while retaining at

[1] Fustel de Coulanges: *La cité antique*, Paris, 1870. Translated into English by Willard Small under the title: *The Ancient City*.

the same time an apparently inseparable connection with religion, is what enables religion to accomplish the great services for which we have to thank her. He who objects to making these external realms of spiritual and cultural life independent and unique, and who will only concede to them value and possibly the right to exist to the extent that they remain in direct dependence upon religion, must treat the evolution of human history as such as abnormal, in fact, he must consider this evolution to be absolutely reversed. Such a view, however, is not only not in any way scientifically defensible, but it must also be decisively rejected from the viewpoint of religion itself.[2] For it conflicts with the feeling of absolute dependence as the basic religious feeling. The religious conviction must recognize and accept the whole course of history as "willed by God." As we have seen even radical Buddhism, in spite of its rejection of the idea of God, does this in its basic doctrine of Buddha.

Under this same judgment, which we have just validated for the fields of science, art, and technics, the field of morality must also be brought. To be sure this is true only with a definite restriction. For the insight which we have already won, that a moral element is a part of religion itself, remains true. But even though religion does include an essential ingredient of morality, it does not follow as the converse of this proposition that morality is also in a direct relation of dependence upon religion. And we must be on our guard against making such an assertion. For then we could not justify precisely the most exact and the most critical unfolding of the moral consciousness which is revealed to us by history. Kant's ethics, which we must regard as the most exact and most critical unfolding of the moral consciousness, with its idea of autonomy, claims complete independence and a unique validity, and indeed, in such a way that it stands and falls with this claim. Now it is true that Kant's idea of autonomy is itself not free from objection. If this idea is interpreted to mean that the human will gave the

[2] It is to me an especially great satisfaction that I am in full agreement on this point with Theophil Steinmann, the philosopher of religion of the Moravian Brethren. Compare his important contributions to the Bericht des theologischen Seminars der Brüdergemeinde, Leipsic, 1899.—Among the other literature I would especially mention: Joh. Wendland *Die Stellung der Religion im Geistesleben* (Beiträge zur Förderung christlicher Theologie, Vol. XXV, Part II, 1920).

moral law to itself and that it is the original source of that law, then this is an exaggeration which the nature of the moral consciousness will not substantiate. But nevertheless the demand for the autonomy of the moral will, in the sense that its establishment on a purely external authority is abandoned and the unique validity of the moral norms is defended against all external authorities, is actually defensible and indispensable. We must accept these moral norms because of their inherent value, and we must recognize them as the expression of our own mind. For obedience to a purely external authority does not constitute true morality. It is true that such obedience does constitute the essence of legality, of juridical thought and procedure. The difference between legality and morality would disappear if obedience to an external authority really did constitute the essence of morality. But our moral consciousness rebels against this. To obey laws which are forced upon us from without and only because they do come to us from without, can never be truly moral behavior. No, we must distinguish as sharply as possible mere legality from genuine morality. Therefore, we must emphatically and absolutely reject heteronomy of the moral will, in the sense of its being founded upon a mere external authority, and we must insist that the moral law be recognized and affirmed for its own inherent worth. So far as Kant's idea of autonomy aims to stress this demand it is right and it will always remain right. But this very fact proves that the independence of morality from religion also has to be conceded.

Now it is to be further noted that the other cultural functions must also be subordinated to morality when they themselves become incumbent upon anyone. To the extent that these functions are experienced as being incumbent upon one and as having to be fulfilled they acquire the character of moral activities. Here, however, there is the important difference between morality in the strict sense and these other activities that whereas everybody is obligated to be moral yet not everyone is obligated to be a scientist, an artist, or a technician. Yet for those who do devote themselves to science, art, or technics, these types of work can and do become incumbent upon them.

Thus these activities can be subordinated to the idea of a moral task. And in this subordination they receive what morality itself has—independence and unique validity over against religion. That this independence and unique validity must also be adjudged right when the subordination of these activities to morality does not exist and is not even possible, is generally taken to be self-evident.

2

Now in view of this state of affairs is it not altogether hopeless to claim for religion a definite significance for the whole of human cultural and spiritual life? Must we not much more draw the only other conclusion which states the relation of religion to other aspects of culture after the fashion of the well-known saying of Goethe: "He who possesses science and art also has religion"? In view of the position taken above no objection can be made to the extension of this saying of Goethe to include morality. And then it would follow as the rational, if not even the necessary conclusion that religion is to be regarded as having only an entirely secondary significance for the cultural life, howsoever one may more closely define the nuance of meaning of the term cultural life. According to the usual view two possible interpretations of Goethe's saying are to be distinguished: either that the possession of science and art offers at the same time a satisfactory substitute for religion, so that he who possesses science and art no longer needs religion, or the possession of science and art includes the legitimate content of religion, so that he who fulfills the demands of both thereby fulfills also the unique purpose of religion. For the first of these interpretations the opposite of Goethe's saying seems to hold: "He who does not possess science and art, has religion." But for the second of these interpretations the categorical proposition "also has religion" holds.

However, in both cases the conclusion is actually untenable and fallacious.

As soon as the essential meaning of the question of the specifically religious is acknowledged for all judgments on religious problems, one can no longer think that the possession of science and art can be substituted for the possession of religion. For naturally no other aspects of culture can serve as a substitute for the specifically religious. Should even the possibility of a substitute be considered, the indispensable presupposition of that would be the rationalizing or the æsthetizing of religion, but in the end that would mean the transformation of religion into science or into art. And exactly the same would hold on the other interpretation. Science and art could in any case only include the rational or the æsthetic constituent parts of religion, leaving its non-rational core unjustified.

Perhaps though the saying of Goethe contains a third nuance of meaning, and it may well be that this third sense is exactly the one which best expresses the actual situation. Later we shall raise this question again, but for the present let us stick to the actual situation itself.

Let us repeat our question: as a result of our previous discussion is not the very possibility of claiming that religion has a meaning for the whole of cultural and spiritual life excluded? Certainly every such attempt is excluded which obtains such a meaning at the sacrifice of the independence of the other spiritual functions. But the religio-psychological method makes accessible to us the possibility, along with the recognition of the independence of these functions, of coming nearer to this goal, to the extent that it directs us to penetrate into the depths, to lay bare the ultimate motive and tendency of the psychical and spiritual functions of life, and thus to ferret out the hidden tunnel which closely connects together these different spheres of culture.

Accordingly, to accomplish this purpose we shall begin with the ethical sphere, the sphere of moral conduct in the narrower sense. For this sphere of the moral is in any case relatively nearest to religion, since religion itself includes an ethical element in its consciousness of obligation.

Now in the sphere of the moral we at once find a point of contact with the religious way of speaking and thinking in the sense of humility as that is evoked by the subordination of the moral agent to his duty. As Kant said, duty sets up a law that itself evokes veneration even against the agent's will: and that is why Kant characterized the idea of duty as "holy." [3] But the sense of humility also essentially belongs to the religious sphere, since it necessarily follows from the relation of man to the over-world. Those whom religion calls to speak can never be proud, said Schleiermacher, for they are always filled with humility. But the analogy implied here is not restricted to the relation of religion to morality. There also grows out of the other spheres of spiritual life, if not a lasting humility, then at least a passing disposition toward humility, as soon as the task changes from the little and the trivial into the noble and becomes a striving after an ideal. Think, for example, of such sayings of Goethe as these: "The most beautiful happiness of thinking men comes from fathoming the fathomable and from quietly reverencing the unfathomable." "He who knowingly declares himself to be limited is nearest to perfection." "The reason why I like to commune with Nature is that she is always right and the error can only be my own."

If one analyzes this disposition and feeling of humility more carefully he will find that in the end it rests upon the longing for the transcendence of the ideal that is in question. Such a longing for transcendence is primarily expressed in the idea of an infinite task. Every cultural activity arouses the feeling of an infinite task, and all the more the more seriously it is taken. And thus there comes to be increasingly united with such activity the consciousness of the infinity of the task in question. But when it is so used what does the word infinity mean? It means that one's task, notwithstanding the mightiest exertion and the greatest efforts, nevertheless always lies beyond what he has already accomplished. And that means, speaking exactly, the endlessness of our task, its endless progress. Yet this endless progress—this, too, we must add to make the actual situation quite clear—is a progress within the finite world. When one carries through generally the description of this fact which we have expressed in terms of an endless task, then two other things have to be noted. In the first place, this terminology, when taken by itself, is not unequivocal; its sense of endlessness must

[3] On this point see what from a religio-psychological point of view are the very excellent remarks of Söderblom about Kant's use of the word "holy" in *Das Werden des Gottesglaubens,* 1926, pp. 212 ff.

be more clearly defined. But in the second place, this terminology nevertheless indicates that, even with such a clearer determination, the problem itself is not solved. That problem goes beyond endlessness as such, and merges with the question of an infinity which has to be described as being without end in the strictest sense. For the truth is that an infinity which remains within the finite is a finite infinity, to express the matter quite sharply. But that is a contradictory idea which refers to something beyond itself.

Actually, then, at certain high levels of spiritual and cultural life the longing for transcendence rises above the level of which we have been speaking, and thereby comes much closer to the specifically religious conviction of transcendence. This is the case when the ideal in question is no longer thought of as an endlessly remote goal, but on the contrary as an ideal that is by nature unattainable in finite existence and as exalted above the whole sphere of finite reality.

This especially holds of the high levels of morality and of the quest for truth. The complete actualization of the moral ideal appears to be a thing that is actually excluded by the limitations of finitude. Kant referred to moral perfection as a "holiness" which is unattainable for man in this finite life and yet which stands clearly before his eyes as an ideal. What the striving after truth means Socrates had already discovered when he praised as the highest knowledge the knowledge that we actually know nothing; and Goethe has Faust proclaim: "And see, that we can know nothing, that will almost consume my heart." Thus within the non-religious spheres of spiritual life longing leads to that transcendental which lies beyond the level of finite existence and beyond endless progress in the finite world, and finally to that truer infinite which is exalted above everything finite.

That this judgment is indispensable, and expresses the cardinal truth of the actual situation, is best shown by the attempts to deny it. Natorp can again claim to represent these attempts most profoundly. For this purpose he emphasizes with great weight and in itself quite rightly, that the idea of an endless task means that the work in question must always be conceived as progressing, it means, then, an endless progress of work.

Alongside of this thesis that it means a progress without end, Natorp then equally stresses the other thesis that it is nevertheless not a progress without definite direction, but, on the contrary, that the permanent direction of progress is that positive meaning constituted by the idea of infinity in its technical meaning and significance. In itself this reasoning is also justifiable. But it at once makes it necessary to raise the wider question: "How is this permanent direction to be guaranteed if it does not lead to a definite goal?" Natorp does not consider this question at all. Yet, on the other hand, he thinks that the striving of man to anchor his life in its eternal depths is justifiable. But must we not again ask: "Where is this eternal depth?" In general where does Natorp get the right to talk about this eternal depth at all? For the fact is that "endless progress" in the finite offers no such eternal depth. Natorp even admits this. But to this admission he adds the assertion that in so far as the direction of progress can be recognized as unswervingly fixed a certainty of eternity accompanies this recognition. We have already seen that this assertion is not really established by Natorp's reasoning. All the more valuable is it as evidence that Natorp sees himself forced by the actual facts to contradict his own reasoning. That this really is so is abundantly proven by the statement which he appends. For he says that this eternity in fact has only a critical and not a definitive value for the pure understanding. But he who turns his will in the direction of its eternal purpose gets the very positive and rich experience that his will thereby becomes one with that holy will, which eternally lives when the human will falters. For the idea of the "holy will which lives eternally" means, if it has an unambiguous meaning at all, a transcendental reality over against everything finite, an over-world in the strict sense of the word, which is authoritative for religious conviction.

Now, in conclusion, it is correct to speak of the primacy of religion in the spiritual life. For since matters stand as we have now made it clear that they do stand, religion occupies the supreme place in the realm of spiritual life, holding all the other aspects and functions of that life together and referring them to the ultimate goal.

From this position let us once more consider the saying of Goethe: "He who possesses science and art, also has religion."

This saying gets a factual and a valid meaning, when it is interpreted to mean that with which Goethe would, of course, to the highest extent have agreed, namely, that science and art, understood in their deepest sense, refer beyond themselves and beyond the whole condition of finite existence, and point in the direction of the religious conviction.[4]

It is just as Schleiermacher said that religion necessarily springs of itself from every good soul, that its own peculiar province is the human heart where it holds absolute sway, and that it is worthy, because of its inner power, to move the noblest and most superior people. And this is so because religion, in its deepest and most unique essence, does not leave man to himself alone and does not keep him bound to himself, but, on the contrary, it brings him into relation to and into communion with the ultimate and highest reality—the "absolute world" in the strict sense of the word, the world of absolute value.

The further-reaching question can not here be discussed but can only be thrown out: "May not the belief in God of Christianity as the objective content of religion be so grasped that a balance is established, not just between contemplative redemptive religiosity and moralistic legal religiosity, between pantheism and deism, between mysticism and morality, but in addition, that a balance is also established between the validity of transcendence and immanence in the idea of God itself?"

The decisive question which the religio-psychological method has to put is this: "Can christian belief inwardly and essentially unite the conviction that all things are of God, through God, and unto God (Romans XI, 36) with the conviction that "in Him we live and move, and have our being" (Acts XVII, 28)?

[4] In my opinion the justifiable kernel of truth in the position of Rud. Eucken, as he has attempted to establish it with his "noological method" lies here. See especially his book: *Der Wahrheitsgehalt der Religion*, 3rd ed., 1912 (English translation). See also Kurt Kesseler: *Das Problem der Religion in der Gegenwartsphilosophie*, 2nd ed., Leipsic, 1920. The same is true of the position of Ernst Troeltsch, which is oriented to the question of the a priori of religion. We will return to this question in our discussion of the nature of Christianity. (See Georg Wobbermin: *Das Wesen und die Wahrheit des Christentums, Systematische Theologie*, Vol. III.) Compare also: *Richtlinien evangelischer Theologie zur Überwindung der gegenwärtigen Krisis*, Chs. I-III, Göttingen, 1929.

For then that belief would be justified which finds its classic expression in the Lord's prayer, and which has received from Augustine the well-known form: "O God, Thou hast made us for Thyself, and our souls are restless until they find their rest in Thee."

APPENDICES

APPENDIX I

THE SIGNIFICANCE OF SCHLEIERMACHER'S HERMENEUTICS FOR HIS WORK IN THE SCIENCE OF RELIGION

A controversy over the significance of Schleiermacher has raged in German theology ever since the close of the world-war. In the period just before the war Schleiermacher was almost universally treated as the founder of a new epoch of theological work that was in harmony with modern culture, even though reservations were made with regard to his various positions toward all special questions. Today, among the representatives of the so-called *dialectical theology*, such as Karl Barth, Emil Brunner, and Friedrich Gogarten, Schleiermacher's significance is either generally denied or it is treated as being wholly of a negative value; he is not to be acknowledged as a true leader, but, on the contrary, he must be opposed as a false leader and repudiated. This fact is primarily due to Schleiermacher's having himself thought, and of having taught others to think of theological work as basically identical with work in the science of religion. He rejected the old definition of theology which sprung from scholasticism, namely, that it is the science of God—the *doctrina de deo*. For critical thought, and that means for scientific thought, there is and can be no "science of God." Theological work can only be judged scientific when it is the "science of religion"—religion being understood in its historical and psychical nature, that is to say, as the history and psychology of religion.

In contrast to this viewpoint dialectical theology returns to the old scholastic definition and to the manner of thinking implied in that definition. Indeed this is connected with a general inclination toward scholasticism which is today variously expressed within the field of philosophy. Thus the polemic against Schleiermacher is in the main built up as follows. It is asked whether Schleiermacher's own position as a whole is determined by a

TRANSLATORS' NOTE: This is a paper presented to the *Gesellschaft der Wissenschaften* at Göttingen by Professor Wobbermin on the sixth of June, 1930, and it is included here with his permission to supplement his discussion of Schleiermacher in Chapters III-V.

genuinely religious motive and whether it was his intention to
bring this specifically religious motive to the clearest possible
expression, or, if this is not the case, whether, on the contrary,
his position as a whole is not ultimately an expression of a speculative construction, and, indeed, actually is a speculative construction
that is essentially built upon the philosophy of identity in the sense
of Schelling. If this latter alternative is true, Schleiermacher's
position would be nothing more than a particular form or a
definite type of the philosophy of identity of Schelling, which
holds the ultimate and highest original principle of being, underlying all particular kinds and stages of existence, to be a supreme
but as yet undifferentiated unity of opposites, an as yet undifferentiated union of matter and spirit.

It is this last mentioned interpretation of Schleiermacher that
is today defended by the representatives of the socalled dialectical
theology. In his *Die Mystik und das Wort,* which first appeared
in 1924 and the second edition of which came out in 1929, Emil
Brunner has especially attempted to establish most thoroughly and
consequentially this interpretation of Schleiermacher.[1]

That such an interpretation can be made at all is due to the
fact that Schleiermacher was unquestionably influenced by the
philosophy of identity, and that he—if I may first try to formulate
the problem in as objective and as inclusive a way as possible—
attempted to connect his position on the science of religion with
the philosophy of identity. Especially did he do this in his own
critical and epistemological undertaking, in his attempt to reach a
critical and epistemological metaphysics as this is found in his
Dialektik, a work published posthumously on the basis of lecture
notes. Only the question arises of just how we are to evaluate
this connecting of his position with the philosophy of identity,
of what is primary and what is secondary, of whether this connection was itself Schleiermacher's original and basic intention,
or whether it was an afterthought which, above all, has to be
treated as secondary, the original basic purpose being independent
of it.

Two important facts especially bear witness that this last
alternative is to be judged true, and not the former as Barth,

[1] Tübingen, J. C. B. Mohr. The sub-title runs: *Der Gegensatz zwischen
moderner Religionsauffasung und christlichem Glauben, dargestellt an der
Theologie Schleiermachers.* In English dialectical theology is more often
referred to as *Barthian theology,* after its founder, Karl Barth. (See his
The Word of God and the Word of Man, translated by Douglas Horton).
It is also sometimes called *crisis theology.* Translators' note.

Brunner, and their friends think. (1) In this attempt Schleiermacher did not reach a unified conclusion. On the contrary every new sketch of his *Dialektik* reveals a new form of the attempt which deviates from the earlier form. (2) On the other hand, Schleiermacher, in looking back over his life work, most emphatically stated that in his own opinion his position to the science of religion should be regarded as independent of his speculative epistemological discussions.

However, the decision can first be won with respect to all of the existing material. And here we find ourselves in a fortunate situation, since Schleiermacher has himself developed for us the basic propositions with which, in his opinion, the interpretation of other authors has to be made. Strangely enough these basic propositions have hitherto not been sufficiently stressed in the present-day controversy over Schleiermacher. Indeed, those defenders of the word who at the moment claim to be modern interpreters of Schleiermacher leave them entirely unnoticed. Yet it cannot be seriously doubted that, at least for the interpretation of Schleiermacher himself, these basic propositions which he gave must be evaluated as a pertinent way of interpreting literary products, howsoever these propositions may be judged in general. And since they actually are the propositions of Schleiermacher, one not only has the right but, on the contrary, one is even obligated to use them in interpreting Schleiermacher himself.

Schleiermacher expounded these basic principles of interpretation in two discussions before the Academy of Science of Berlin under the inclusive title: *Über den Begriff der Hermeneutik.*[2] They are reprinted in volume III of the philosophy section of his complete works. Schleiermacher's posthumously published lectures, *Hermeneutik und Kritik mit besonderer Beziehung auf das Neue Testament* (in volume VII of the theological section of his complete works) may also be mentioned. In these lectures. Schleiermacher attempted to lay down his basic principles of interpretation in the exposition of the New Testament. However these basic principles themselves are more exactly and clearly worked out in his two discussions before the Berlin Academy of Science. There Schleiermacher developed them in opposition to the principles of interpretation of the philologists, Friedrich Wolf and Friedrich Ast.

In agreement with these philologists he lays the greatest em-

[2] Read in the open meetings of the Academy on August 13th and October 22nd, 1829.

phasis on the view that while every understanding of a whole is dependent upon an understanding of the parts, yet conversely that the understanding of the parts is often dependent upon an understanding of the whole to which they belong, and that a circle of alternating clarity between parts and whole and whole and parts is not only indispensable but also methodically fundamental. From this point Schleiermacher then goes beyond the philologists to his own statements. More decisive than they he makes the idea of understanding the basic concept in interpretation, and at the same time he formulates his idea of understanding more sharply than they had defined it in that he examined and more precisely determined it psychologically. Taking the psychological viewpoint he first emphasized the fact that the interpreter's task is in no way concerned only with literary productions, but that it is also concerned with every oral utterance of whatever significance. He writes: "When I am not satisfied with the usual degree of understanding, but, on the contrary, try to fathom how well in my friend's conversation the transition has been made from one thought to another, or when I trace out the views, judgments and pursuits which go best with the fact that he expresses himself exactly so and not otherwise on a given subject, I very often arrest myself in the midst of the act of interpreting familiar discourse."

Now the analogy here implied is also especially applicable in the exposition of written material. For in contrast to oral discourse the impulse is greater and therefore the task is clearer to interpret a succession of thoughts about any subject under consideration as being also an emerging of a moment of life, as an activity and accordingly as an expression of the author's whole spiritual being. Consequently the interpreter of written matter must direct attention to the inner spiritual activity of the author; he must try to grasp the entire inner course of the accompanying activity of the author, and for this purpose he must strive to comprehend the author's inner state of mind and feeling. *In this sense the psychological aspect of the problem necessarily belongs to the task of interpretation.*

Therefore Schleiermacher distinguishes two chief tasks for interpretation as a whole, which, to be sure, must be taken together, but which, owing to their methodical arrangement and tendency, are essentially different, so that interpretation is actually a question of a reciprocal supplementation of two different kinds of principles. Thus, on the one hand, interpretation demands grammatical and historical labor, and, on the other hand, it demands psychological labor. In itself the grammatical and historical task is unified. Its two chief aspects, the grammatical and the historical, are not to be set in opposition to each other as Wolf had done. But on the other hand the *psychological* task must be especially distinguished from the grammatical and historical, for otherwise the interpretative process will not succeed in penetrating into the depths of the formation of ideas and down to the ultimate motives underlying this formative process. But only thus is a real understanding of the thoughts under consideration, for example the theory of ideas of Plato, possible.

The justification and, indeed, the necessity of this duality of the task of interpretation Schleiermacher seeks to establish more exactly by connecting it with the principle of alternating between the parts and the whole. Every piece of writing, he argues, is in two respects a part in relation to a larger whole. It is first a particular, or a part in relation to the linguistic and historical group of literature to which it belongs and of which it is a fragment. It can be understood only in relation to this whole. That is the grammatical and historical task. But it is likewise a part in relation to a larger whole as the act of a creator, as Schleiermacher expresses it, which with the author's other acts forms the whole of his life; and it can be understood only in relation to this whole too; that is to say, in relation to the author's temperament and to his manner of living as a whole, in relation also to his attitude toward the problem of the meaning of life in general. This is the psychological task.

These basic principles of interpretation of Schleiermacher will not here be examined from the point of view of their general validity. Here we are interested only in applying them to the interpretation of Schleiermacher himself. For this purpose attention must first be called to one thing. When Schleiermacher so strongly emphasized the psychological aspect of interpretation, and thereby insisted that the inner condition of the thinking of the author must be uncovered, the psychical process of the formation and association of ideas, this formulation might give the impression that his whole position is subjectivistic, and hence that it is psychological in the psychologistic sense that he took the decisive task to be the comprehension of an author's state of mind as such. However Schleiermacher absolutely did not mean this. To be sure he did not reach complete theoretical clarity on this point. But what he really meant and intended to mean is obvious from

his more detailed statements. For him everything subjective is
only a means for the purpose of reaching the objective which lies
behind the subjective. To express this in modern terminology his
psychological viewpoint is through and through *intentional.* Its
intention is directed toward what the author *actually* means, toward his νόημα and not toward his νόησις, again using modern
terminology; it is directed towards the thought or meaning-content of his statements and, indeed, toward that meaning-content
which corresponds to the ultimate motives of his thinking.[3]

Now what follows from this with regard to the adjudication
of the controversy mentioned at the beginning of our discussion?
Is the thesis valid that Schleiermacher's entire position on the science of religion is only an expression of his speculative philosophy
of identity? *If this thesis is to be taken as valid then precisely the
psychological view upon which he placed so much stress must be
disregarded in interpreting Schleiermacher.*

For everything that we know about the personal manner of
thinking and living of Schleiermacher goes against this thesis. In
particular the statements which Schleiermacher made in his letters
to his friends, and in which in the usual way he gave reports of the
progress of his scientific work, would have to be eliminated in
deciding this controversy. Moreover, any real consideration of his
sermons would also have to be eliminated. In fact, in the book
already mentioned Brunner takes this position: for the decision of
the whole controversy the content of Schleiermacher's letters cannot be considered at all and just as little can the content of the
sermons be taken into account. Let us leave the sermons aside for
the present, since the problem is more complicated when they are
considered. But Brunner makes his basic demand apply with equal
weight to the content of Schleiermacher's letters. The letters of
special importance in this connection are those containing the detailed statements which Schleiermacher wrote to his pupil and
younger colleague, Dr. Lücke, who taught at Göttingen. In these
letters he expounded the basic position of his chief work exactly
in the direction of the thesis laid down with great emphasis in that
chief work itself (*Der Glaubenslehre*), that the work on the science of religion must within its own sphere be kept free from

---

[3] The technical terms referred to here as modern terminology are from
the socalled *phenomenology* founded by Edmund Husserl. See Husserl's
article entitled *phenomenology* in the last (14th) edition of the *Encyclopedia
Britannica.* See also the brief exposition in D. S. Robinson's *An Introduction to Living Philosophy,* pp. 331-335 and the references there given.
Translators' note.

every influence of philosophical and speculative theories, and that for him just this effort to carry through to a finish *this* methodical basic principle is the decisive major purpose of his whole chief work. Without any reservation or restriction he submits it to criticism under this point of view.

Brunner insists that these statements of Schleiermacher cannot be taken into consideration at all in considering his chief work, since they are epistolary remarks. For if they were taken into account the interpretation of the chief work would be pushed off on the wrong track of historical and biographical interest. Such historical and biographical interest must be left entirely out of account in the interpretation. For a church-historical investigation of Schleiermacher's development these letters have real value, but only for this. For the interpretation of his chief work itself they cannot be considered. *On the contrary this interpretation must be made by leaving out of account all temporal factors and therefore without reference to the personality of the author.*

In this demand the position of Brunner, and therewith his whole attitude toward the problem, reaches its most critical point. Interpretation of a literary work by leaving out of account all temporal factors and therefore without reference to the personality of the author! Why, that is precisely the opposite of what Schleiermacher formulated in his concept of the psychological aspect of interpretation and put forward as a demand of any actual understanding of a piece of writing. Now again we will not here ask the general question of whether an interpretation of a literary work by leaving out of account all temporal factors and without reference to the personality of the author is at all possible, and whether, if possible, it offers the ideal type of interpretation. In Brunner's interpretation of Schleiermacher the situation is in any case this: with this basic proposition he makes it possible in interpreting Schleiermacher's work to bring into the foreground, and then to make it the sole decisive principle of interpretation, the philosophical and speculative element which came into Schleiermacher's work against his own intention out of and in consequence of the time in which he lived. For Brunner shoves aside everything that does not fit into and is inconsistent with this principle. But in this case that obviously does violence to the author. For in this way precisely Schleiermacher's basic purpose is not evaluated, but, on the contrary, it is turned into its absolute opposite.

The basic leaving out of consideration of the sermons is also elucidated by this fundamental attitude of Brunner. To be sure the position taken on this question is certainly more difficult. It lies in quite another direction and has an entirely different task than is the case in work on the science of religion. For the interpretation of work on the science of religion the sermons, therefore, have only an indirect and not a direct value; moreover the indirect value can only be utilized with great caution. Yet the demand of Brunner that the sermons cannot, as a matter of principle, be taken into account at all, but, on the contrary, and as a matter of principle, must be left out of account, is actually unjustifiable, indeed, in the last analysis it is an absurdity. When an academic theologian also serves as a preacher, he must naturally keep his preaching in harmony with his work on the science of religion, if he wishes to be and ought to be taken at all seriously by others. Now Brunner does not deny that Schleiermacher wanted and ought to be taken seriously. Consequently his demand that we are here considering is unjustifiable and indefensible. And it is all the more so because just with Schleiermacher another fact has to be considered. He consciously, deliberately, and directly related his preaching to his academic activity. He thought of and practiced it as a supplement to and a correlate of his academic work. He was convinced that he could best make clear the relation of science to piety by this dual activity.[4] And that he did not err

---

[4] From Schleiermacher's *Leben. In Briefen*, Vol. II, 2nd ed., Berlin, 1860, p. 17. "Recently I also preached once more. I have a real desire to be able to speak in public again in my own parish of the most sacred things."—*Op. cit.*, pp. 17-18. "A week ago I really preached in church for the first time (not yet in my own parish, that is unfortunately still in the far distant future, but for someone else) and Steffens gave me great satisfaction when he accidentally heard of it and came to church. He showed such a lively enthusiasm afterwards and told me that I was fortunate to have such a beautiful vocation, and affirmed that it is not only the only way to get right into the heart of things, but a necessary correlate of the scientific view which is still only half completed—precisely as I had formulated the relation in my Ethics."

Op. cit., pp. 43-44. "For my part I readily understand that I cannot become so completely identified with any other congregation as I can with an academic one, but I must of course first create it, and it will always consist of only a small number. To speak from the lecture platform according to scientific principles, and, at the same time, to give myself up entirely to the pulpit, to preach to the uneducated—with the exception of courtly folk, in their case I could do it—that would be hard for me. But I can really hope, by relating my pulpit discourses to my lectures, to make very clear to the students the connection between speculation and piety and thus at the same time to enlighten and enkindle them from both directions."

Op. cit., Vol. IV, Berlin, 1863, p. 156. "For miraculously enough, my sermons find approval and are attracting Moravian families here also. No fisherman's catch can show more variety than my ecclesiastical auditorium:

in this belief not only many of his students but also other men on the faculty, such as Wilhelm von Humboldt and the philosopher Steffens, convinced him.[5]

Moreover, the positive argument with which Brunner supports his position is not sound. Schleiermacher is a symbolist; he taught the symbolical character of religious terms. In this way he justified himself for his procedure of bringing to expression by means of the traditional ecclesiastical and religious terminology an entirely different and purely speculative and philosophical meaning. Now it is true that Schleiermacher more intensively considered and more conclusively developed the understanding of the sym-

Moravian Brethren, Jews, baptized and unbaptized, young philosophers and philologists, and elegant ladies. The beautiful picture of the holy Anthony is always before my eyes. And so I hope that something must be enkindled here and there."

[5] *Op. cit.,* Vol. II, p. 18, Comp. note 1—W. V. Humboldt, *Briefe an eine Freundin,* published by Albert Lietzmann, Vol. II, Leipsic, 1909, p. 343: "The strength of his preaching and of all his spiritual activities lay in his profound heart-searching speech. It would be wrong to call it eloquence for it was free from all artifice; it was the convincing, penetrating, and overwhelming out-pouring of feeling which was not merely enlightened by a rare spirit but which seemed rather to be attuned to him, and to be a part of him. By nature Schleiermacher had a child-like, simple, believing disposition, his faith really flowed from his heart. But in addition to this he also had a decided leaning toward speculation. With the same popularity and success, he held a position at the University of Berlin as a teacher of philosophy and also as a teacher of theology; and his *Ethics,* a thoroughly philosophical work, stands in the most intimate relationship to his *Dogmatics.* Speculation and faith are frequently regarded as opposites, but it was precisely peculiar to this man that he could intimately relate them to each other without doing violence either to the freedom or depth of the one, or to the simplicity of the other." Of Schleiermacher's own students we shall mention A. Twesten who became Schleiermacher's successor at Berlin. In the memorial address which Twesten delivered at the University of Berlin upon the occasion of the 100th anniversary of Schleiermacher's birthday (*Zur Erinnerung an Friedrich Daniel Ernst Schleiermacher,* Berlin, 1869, p. 29), he said: "With his sermons he hoped primarily to make very clear to students of theology the relationship between science and piety, and to enlighten and to enthuse them in this way from both directions, from pulpit and from lecture platform. But students of all departments also constituted a larger part of the audience which his sermons attracted. They felt themselves attracted and instructed by the clarity and simplicity with which Schleiermacher knew how to expound the Scriptures, to answer difficult questions, to untangle doubts, and to develop principles of life and faith, in which the tools of critical or dialectical discussions were completely invisible, although their fruits were evident in penetrating depth and keenness."

From the more recent literature let me quote the judgment of one of the most thorough modern experts on Schleiermacher, Johannes Bauer (*Schleiermacher als patriotischer Prediger,* 1908, p. 149): "Whoever attempts to understand Schleiermacher as a theologian, without estimating him as a preacher, will never, according to Schleiermacher's own judgment and that of his students and listeners, do justice to him."

bolical character of religious terms than had hitherto been done. But in and of itself that was in the interest of the clarification of the religious conviction itself. Therefore, on this point Brunner involves himself in a peculiar contradiction with this argument. He himself admits that in the end every theologian is and must be a symbolist, indeed, he holds that all statements about deity are inadequate. But now Brunner wants to lay down a fundamental distinction between the way in which every theologian is perforce a symbolist and the way in which Schleiermacher was one. In reality the value difference of the various symbols must be set forth. But for Schleiermacher such a value difference does not exist at all, for him all symbols are equally immeasurable. He is a symbolist in the sense of complete theological agnosticism. This last assertion of Brunner is an absolute construction which not only does not fit the facts, but, on the contrary, turns them topsy turvy. For Schleiermacher's whole concern in his chief work was just this: to work out the decisive meaning of the traditional symbolical forms of expression of the religious conviction in accordance with the basic motives and tendencies of that religious conviction itself. To what extent he succeeded in this purpose in particular cases must, to be sure, be determined case by case. And a scrupulous examination shows, in my opinion, that in any case he only partly succeeded, but that, on the other hand, statements that are really worthy of attention in that direction are found in Schleiermacher's writings. Anyway—and that is what matters here—Brunner's attempt to condemn the procedure of Schleiermacher as altogether a priori lacks an unambiguous and an adequate psychological support.

And finally the same is true of the way of judging with which Brunner argues about Schleiermacher's own *Dialektik*. Here the error also lies in the direction which Schleiermacher described with the concept "psychological" in his *Hermeneutik*. For in this respect Brunner's reasoning is quite unpsychological. This judgment is even valid of Brunner's whole account of the *Dialektik* of Schleiermacher in so far as he leaves entirely unnoticed the exceptional difficulties which are present in the unfinished condition of this posthumously published work.[6] It is true that the theoretical

---

[6] Compare the preface of the editor of the *Dialektik* (*Sämtliche Werke,* Philosophy section, Volume IV, Part 2, edited by L. Jonas). See also J. Halpern: *Schleiermachers Dialektik,* mit Unterstützung der Königlichen preussischen Akademie der Wissenschaften herausgegeben, Berlin, 1903, the introduction of the editor; and Georg Wehrung: *Die Dialektik Schleiermachers,* Tübingen, 1920, introduction.

epistemological standpoint which Schleiermacher here represents can be described in the widest sense as a philosophy of identity. But this philosophy of identity position of Schleiermacher in the various drafts of the *Dialektik* comprises so many and such significant differences in the basic view and theory itself that as a result Brunner's use of the concept "philosophy of identity" is inaccurate and even unjustifiable. Here, however, that cannot be dealt with more in detail.

Yet the following has still to be considered. For the total standpoint of the *Dialektik* of Schleiermacher a view of the relation of the special sciences to philosophy is characteristic, indeed, not simply characteristic but even of overwhelming importance, yet here again it is not considered by Brunner at all and hence his interpretation of Schleiermacher miscarries. That is to say, Schleiermacher had the deepest appreciation of empirical science, of real knowledge and real science, as he expressed it in his own terminology. Accordingly he repudiated with great firmness every type of philosophy which either directly or indirectly excludes such an estimate of real science. In this respect he stood in the sharpest opposition just to Fichte and to Schelling. And that especially applies to Schelling's form of the philosophy of identity. "It is presumptuous to expound philosophy directly as science and improper to say of the sciences which part of their content is transient and which part ought to live permanently in real knowledge." So runs paragraph twenty-three of the sketch of 1814 (of the *Dialektik*). And Schleiermacher always held to this statement. He accepted it for the mental (Geisteswissenschaften) just as much as he did for the natural sciences. In relation to the latter he emphasized "how weak all speculative theories of nature are and what progress the knowledge of nature had made by the opposite experimental method." [7] Hence he demanded as a *conditio sine qua non* of a normal cultivation of philosophy that philosophical reflection must absolutely cling to and conscientiously consider the relation between philosophy and real science. Real science and philosophy must be developed together toward a goal that is continually being approached. Precisely for this reason an absolute completion of philosophy is in general excluded.[8] And what in Schleiermacher's view is true of the relation between real science and philosophy in general is likewise true of the relation

---

[7] *Loco citato,* p. 559 (Sketch E according to Jonas, note after the lecture).

[8] *Loco citato,* pp. 13 ff. (paragraphs 29 ff., the sketch of 1814).

between the science of religion and the philosophy of religion. *Starting from different points of departure and working with different principles each ought to strive for a common goal.* But the possibility of a far-reaching agreement and union belongs at the end and not at the beginning.

The relation of Schleiermacher's work on the science of religion to the philosophy of identity of his contemporaries, as well as to his own philosophy of identity, must be brought under this point of view. But this gives an entirely different principle of evaluation than that employed by Brunner and his friends, and from such a principle, which is alone consistent with Schleiermacher's purpose, there follows the possibility of an unprejudiced estimation of the theological and religio-scientific position of Schleiermacher, whereas Brunner, Barth, and Gogarten do this violence in an extremely one-sided way in accordance with a prior misunderstanding.

However, what overwhelming significance for his whole life work Schleiermacher's conception of the relation between real science and philosophy has is shown still further by the fact that he also defended it elsewhere on an especially significant occasion with the strongest emphasis. I refer especially to the preparatory article on the founding of Berlin University entitled *Gelegentliche Gedanken über Universitäten in deutschem Sinn.*[9] Here he attempted to throw light on the relation which actually exists between higher institutions of learning, universities, and academies of science.

Apart from their pedagogical task, the higher institutions of learning should promulgate knowledge (Kenntnis), that is to say, they ought to spread the most important knowledge that has hitherto been won and train the mental powers on this knowledge. The academies of science ought to purify and increase knowledge (Wissen) by unique scientific research. Between the two stand the universities. They have some of the tasks of both the others, on the one hand to increase and on the other hand to prepare and to introduce knowledge. Yet the specific task of the universities is another. It is to awaken and to train the scientific spirit as such, the spirit of scientific thinking and research; the spirit of science which in the higher schools cannot yet be awakened, or, at least, only in a quite elementary way, whereas in the academies science is presupposed as a working necessity.

[9] Friedrich Schleiermacher's *Sämtliche Werke.* On philosophy, Volume I, pp. 535 ff.

In concluding this line of thought Schleiermacher here also speaks of the relation between science and philosophy. And here also he defends with great emphasis the view already expounded. Although he mentions no names he is obviously directing against Fichte and Schelling the warning against every philosophy in the form of empty speculation and vigorously emphasizing the necessity and the significance of all real knowledge. Agreement and union, however, also come in here only as a distant goal of work and not as its beginning.[10]

In the light of this point of view, therefore, the much abused statement, which we have received as one of the last of Schleiermacher's death-bed sayings is made clearer: "He had to think the deepest speculative thoughts and for him they were completely identical with his innermost religious experience."[11] For the evaluation of Schleiermacher's methodical, scientific, working procedure this death statement cannot rightly be employed as an unequivocal criterion.

[10] On this point see the pertinent discussion of Georg Wehring: *Die Dialektik Schleiermachers*, 1920, p. 58.

[11] From *Schleiermacher's Leben. In Briefen,* Volume II, p. 511.

APPENDIX II

In order to gain a better and a more adequate understanding of the relation between religion and mythology than the customary treatment, which Deussen has formulated into a strictly applied theory (see above, pp. 235 ff.), is able to give us, let us clarify the whole problem by discussing one definite part of it. In the present state of religio-historical research *a consideration of so-called primitive monotheism* is especially adapted to this purpose. But in order to take a position to primitive monotheism that is in accord with the principles of the religio-psychological method, it is necessary to reach out somewhat farther.[12]

The theory of primitive monotheism has had a long preliminary history. Although we must here entirely disregard the dogmatic theory of degeneration of the schoolmen, it must at least be mentioned that in certain rudimentary beginnings even David Hume, and then in the 19th century Creuzer, Schelling, and Max Müller, advocated a theory of primitive monotheism. As the original form of religion, Schelling assumed a relative monotheism which preceded all polytheistic differentiations, but which, just for this reason, did not yet stand in conscious and exclusive contrast to polytheism. Max Müller took up this view of Schelling and attempted to apply it concretely. Considering certain hymns and prayers of the *Rig-Veda,* he showed that although the existence of various divinities is assumed in them, nevertheless at times some one individual divinity is regarded as independent of the others, and that the highest power or even a complete omnipotence which is not shared with any other being, is ascribed to it. For this naïve form of monotheism Müller coined the term *henotheism,* for which he occasionally substituted the still more precise term *kathenotheism.* These expressions aim to designate that form of religion in which the worshiper at times turns to one God as if there were no other gods, without, however, denying the existence of others.

---

[12] Comp. my treatise *Die Frage nach den Anfängen der Religion in religionspsychologischer Beleuchtung* in the Zeitschrift für angewandte Psychologie, IX, 1915, pp. 333 ff.

And upon this basis Müller set up the theory that this henotheism lies at the basis of all historically developed religions, and consequently that it also precedes all actual polytheisms. Man's original belief in deity was neither strictly polytheistic nor strictly monotheistic, but rather henotheistic in the above-mentioned sense of that term. And from such henotheism the line of evolution then led through polytheism to actual monotheism.

Müller's henotheistic theory no doubt contains a significant element of truth. To begin with, in its first purely historical part, that is, in application to the religion of the *Rig-Veda,* it is partially justified. And that is also fairly generally recognized. Recently, however, this recognition has usually also been restricted to this historical part of Müller's theory. But the religio-psychological method must go farther than this. It must also attribute to this theory an element of truth of a general nature. The tendency toward concentration is natural to religious feeling. This tendency is expressed above all in ritual, as the conscious expression of religious feeling. Accordingly, even in the realm of pure polytheism, the ritual not infrequently bears a strongly henotheistic character. On the other hand, the need of concentration inherent in religious feeling is also frequently satisfied in the realm of monotheistic religion, especially in cases where there is a lack of conciseness of thinking and where the logic of monotheistic faith is not really universally applied or retained. These two facts correspond to the basic idea of the henotheistic theory. And the recognition of them precisely in their duality, then leads to the further realization that a form of religious consciousness, at least closely approaching a state of neutrality between the monotheistic and polytheistic forms, is possible and probable.

However, Max Müller's claim to have discovered in Vedic henotheism the original form of all religion and of all religious life was an entirely unjustified hypothesis. For to try to treat the religion of the *Rig-Veda* as the elementary and original stage of all religious life is completely arbitrary, and is contradicted by the most weighty evidence. The very fact that the *Rig-Veda* presupposes such an advanced stage of general cultural development makes this assumption extremely improbable at the very start. At any rate, Müller's hypothesis that naïve monotheism constituted the universal original form of religion, even hangs in mid-air in his own theory. For he did not verify this hypothesis for genuinely primitive religion. But the aim of those scholars who today advocate a new form of the theory of universal primitive monotheism, is to accomplish just this, and they claim to have succeeded. They are the followers of the Scotchman Andrew Lang, who died shortly before the war, the Viennese Indologist Leopold von Schröder, who died in 1920, and especially the ethnologist P. Wilhelm Schmidt. These scholars even go farther than Max Müller, for they speak of an actual (in the strict sense) primitive monotheism as the source and the original form of the religious consciousness.

The originator of this modern form of the theory of primitive monotheism was the versatile Scotch scholar, Andrew Lang. He published his theory for the first time in the year 1898 in his book, *The Making of Religion*.[13] But in order correctly to evaluate and to appreciate the significance of Lang's whole undertaking, it must be remembered that in the period immediately preceding, that is, during the last decade of the nineteenth century, Tylor's and Lubbock's epoch-making studies of man's early history and the beginnings of human culture were carried out, and that these studies, along with other labors of these scholars, led to a complete rejection of the old theory of degeneration. And in connection with this new evaluation of the entire historical development of human cultural life the overwhelming majority of theologians at the same time also rejected genuine primitive monotheism in the field of Old Testament religion, and attempted to show that, even in Israel, strict monotheism had not been the dominant religious conception at least at the beginning. At any rate it was no longer seriously disputed that, if the unique development in Israel were disregarded, in the strict sense there could be no thought of a universal primitive monotheism, as the first stage of the general evolution of the religion of man.

It was just then that Lang began to assert and to attempt to prove what all of recent science, including the specifically theological, had opposed and rejected, and what he himself had attacked and rejected in many of his earlier publications. For he had stood in the first ranks in the attack upon Max Müller.

Lang now espoused the theory that everywhere monotheistic belief in God had been the beginning of religious development, that it is the primary and in this sense the primitive form of religion. He argued that even today monotheism can be proven to be the religion of primitive peoples, at least to a large extent.

---

[13] 3rd ed., 1909, London. Of the other publications of Lang compare: *Magic and Religion, Custom and Myth, Ritual and Religion, The Secret of Totem.*

And he thought of monotheism in the strict, yes, even in the very strictest sense of the word, both in the religious and in the ethical respect. To state it concisely, he thought of ethical monotheism in the full sense of that word, in the sense which differentiates it from Biblical monotheism only by its lack of conceptual clarity.

Lang attempted to substantiate this view by an appeal to ethnology. He argued that the material which recent ethnology presents, when rightly evaluated, compels us to adopt this view. In passing we cannot refrain from recalling that a short time previously an attempt had been made, in the name of this same ethnology, to prove the absence of religion among the lower races. So the suspicion at once arises that Lang's theory is an opposite type of one-sidedness, which is based upon an exaggeration and a stretching of the actual facts.

In reply to such general conclusions Lang points very insistently to the concrete material. Everything depends upon the facts. We must simply bow before the facts. All conjectures must be subordinated to the facts. And here he is insofar quite right, of course. It is self-evident that everything finally depends upon the facts, but the facts must be understood and interpreted. And even in his preliminary methodological discussion Lang fails to take this sufficiently into account.

What are the facts to which he appeals? The material which he primarily considered and which should ultimately be of decisive importance, is taken from the natives of Australia, especially from those of the southeast portion. And the same thing applies also to Schmidt. Compared to the material from Australia the remaining material, no matter from how widely it is drawn by both of these scholars, is only of secondary value, so we will restrict our discussion to the Australian data.

That the native Australians live upon one of the lowest cultural planes is indisputable. They are still in the socalled hunting and gathering stage, that is to say, they make their living exclusively by hunting and by gathering fruits and herbs. They do as little gardening and farming as cattle-raising, and they are acquainted neither with pottery nor with metals. And that is why the study of the cultural life of these Australians is most interesting and valuable precisely for the science of religion.

The beginning of a study of the Australians, which would measure up to the standards of modern research, was made by the Englishman, Howitt. For years he lived among and studied the tribes of Southeast Australia. He learned the languages of a number of tribes and finally he obtained frequent permission to participate in their secret rites. The data which he gathered in this way he first of all published in separated articles in British journals, but later these were brought together in a single volume: *The Native Tribes of Southeast Australia,* London, 1904.

Lang based his theory upon this material, but in his ethnological treatment of it he reached very different conclusions than Howitt himself. He thought that Howitt's material proves that definite traces of a pure ethical monotheism are unmistakably present among the backward natives of Australia. For among them is found the belief in a highest being who is regarded as the heavenly father and who, as father, is God in heaven, and who serves at the same time as the guardian, rewarder or punisher of moral conduct, not only in this life but in a life beyond. However, we must briefly summarize the essential material as a basis for reaching our own conclusions.[14]

Among the Narrinyeri tribe the highest being is called Nurrundere and Martummere. He is supposed to have created all things on earth, to have given weapons of war and the chase to men, and to have established all the rites and ceremonies relating to birth and death. Nurrundere then went to Wyirrawarre, *i.e.* to heaven, and he took his children with him. His name is always mentioned with reverence by the Narrinyeri.

The Wiimbaio tribe also speak with great reverence of their Nurelli. He is supposed to have created the whole country with its rivers, trees, and animals. He gave the black men their laws, and then ascended into heaven, where he is represented by a constellation. He had two wives, and carried two spears. His ascent to heaven took place near Lake Victoria.

Among the tribes of Southwest Victoria the highest being is called Pirnmeheeal (our father). He is portrayed as a gigantic man who lives above the clouds. He is kind and never harms anyone. He is seldom mentioned, but always with respect.

In a number of other tribes the highest being is called Bunjil. Most of them say that he has two wives and some that he also has a brother. He is also called Mami-ngata; *i.e.* "our father" and Mami-ngorak, which also means "our father." He taught men all of the crafts and gave them laws. Then he rose to heaven in a whirlwind.

[14] We find the material in Howitt in Chapter VIII (Beliefs and Burial Practices) especially in the section entitled: The Tribal All-Father. Mrs. Langdon Parker's book, *The Euahlayi Tribe,* London, 1905, should be used for supplementary purposes.

Among the Kurnai the highest being is known only by the name of Mungan-ngaua, "our father." In olden times he lived on the earth and taught the Kurnai all skills. He had one son Tundun, who married and became the tribal father of the Kurnai.

Among still other tribes the name of the highest being is Daramulun. He lived on earth a long time ago with his mother Ngalalbal. Daramulun planted the trees, gave laws, and taught the mysteries. Later he ascended into heaven where he now lives and from whence he watches the actions of men. After death the shadows (souls) of men go to him. The women also know of his existence, but they only call him Papang, *i.e.* "father."

Other tribes call their highest being Baiame. He came from afar and changed the already existent animals into men, and made new men out of clay. In addition, he gave men laws, taught them all kinds of crafts, and then went back to the place from which he came. He has a totem for every part of his body and he gave to each tribe its totem. He has two wives. After death everyone must appear before him for judgment. Three sins cannot be forgiven: murder, lying to the elders of the tribe, and stealing a woman with whom marriage is not permitted by the marriage laws of the tribe. On the other hand, kindness to old and weak persons is emphasized as a commandment of Baiame. Women do not use the name of Baiame but only the name Boyjerh, *i.e.* father.

The mysteries, which have been mentioned several times, are the secret ceremonies with which the boys, at about the age of fourteen, are taken from the supervision of the mother and the company of their sisters, and are initiated into the circle of the men as full-fledged members of the tribe. In connection with these initiation ceremonies, images of the respective God, cut into the bark of a tree or moulded out of clay, are employed, but these are destroyed again immediately after the ceremonies are completed.

Immediately after these ceremonies the laws of the tribe are impressed upon the boys. According to Howitt's statement they are the following: 1. To listen to the old men and obey them. 2. To share all possessions with friends. 3. To live in peace with one's friends. 4. To have nothing to do with girls or married women. 5. To keep the dietary tabus until they are repealed by the old men.

Even at the first perusal of this material two things are at once noticeable. Firstly, that here among primitive people we undoubtedly find in a very noteworthy way, the belief in a highest being which,—to formulate it at once from the standpoint of the religio-psychological method—shows a certain monotheistic tendency. But it must be added that a crass mythology of the lowest type is so closely interwoven with this belief that there can be absolutely no thought of a monotheism which is in any sense genuine. And the religio-psychological method must at the same time distinctly emphasize this second fact. Every serious attempt to understand the ideas contained in this belief will inevitably result in the practically complete disappearance of the monotheistic tendency behind the motives with which it is intertwined. We must call attention to this fact with the greatest emphasis since P. Wilh. Schmidt does not even mention it in his discussions.

Lang places special emphasis upon two facts. First, that these highest beings, who are thought of as living in heaven, are frequently designated as "father," and even as "our father." This, he thinks, is a perfect analogy to the Biblical belief in God. And secondly, Lang strongly emphasizes the connection of this belief with moral regulations. These moral regulations present a perfect analogy, not only to the Old Testament decalogue, but also to the commandment of love to one's neighbor.

What position shall we now take, in a general and summary way, toward Lang's conception? From two starting points the attempt has been made briefly to dispose of the whole question by rejecting as insufficient all of the material to which Lang appeals. On the one hand, it has been said that all of this material, insofar as it proves a belief in a highest being, originated in Christianity. It has been borrowed from Christianity, especially from the missionaries. Tylor especially tried to defend this estimation of the situation. These highest beings, which Lang delights in calling *high gods,* are in reality *loan-gods.* However, this position is not plausible. It is contradicted by the wide prevalence of primitive monotheism, which is by no means restricted to Australia, but is also very frequently found in similar, although in less certain and less clear forms, among other primitive tribes. In view of this fact a general rejection of the belief cannot be considered, at least not from a religio-psychological point of view. And this argument is greatly strengthened by the fact that this belief is often intimately connected with ancient traditions and institutions, and especially with secret religious rites and ceremonies.

However, the attempt has been made to dispose of the whole

dispute in another very simple way. Without any questioning of the material as such, it has been said that we are confronted here simply with a mythology, which has had nothing whatever to do with religion. This point of view is taken, *e. g.* by Paul Ehrenreich in his valuable book, *Die Allgemeine Mythologie und ihre ethnologischen Grundlagen.*[15] The "highest beings," the high gods, are of a purely mythical nature and have nothing to do with religion. But this solution is also inadequate for the religiopsychological method, for it presupposes such a strict separation of religion and mythology (or myth) as to beg the question. The problem, then, is more profound, and necessitates a more thorough-going treatment.

So far as Lang is concerned we must first of all add to what has been said that he undoubtedly makes great exaggerations in his evaluation of the monotheistic and ethical character of these conceptions. He thinks that the Australian belief in high gods is a perfect analogy to the Biblical belief in a father-God. Just because the term father is also used to refer to these Australian high gods, Lang thinks that the same intensification of the religious relationship is implied in them as in the corresponding Biblical view. But this reasoning is entirely misleading and absolutely false. Calling these high gods "father" is comparable only in a very restricted sense to the Biblical belief in a father-God. For it has been expressly shown that the members of all of these tribes use the word "father" quite generally for the older men and especially for the chiefs. Moreover, it is very noteworthy and decisive for a religio-psychological evaluation, that often it is just the women alone who are allowed to use the term "father" instead of the specific name for the god. Yet according to the unanimous testimony of all reports and according to the evidence of the traditions of the cults, the women are themselves not initiated into the depths of the religious faith. And so the name of father does not take us very deeply into their religious belief. Hence from the religio-psychological viewpoint Lang's argument, which is based upon the use of this name, must be expressly branded as fallacious.

And the situation is not much better with reference to Lang's emphasis upon the ethical content of this belief. That primitive monotheism presents a perfect analogy, not only to the decalogue as a whole, but also to the specific requirement of love to one's

[15] Leipsic, 1910 (Mythologische Bibliothek, published by the Gesellschaft für vergleichende Mythenforschung IV, 1), pp. 18 ff.

neighbor, is a terrific exaggeration which again entirely lacks religio-psychological insight. In any case this opinion contains only the most elementary beginnings in the direction of the requirements of the religio-psychological method. It is clear enough to every psychologically oriented judgment that even the most important of the regulations to which Lang refers, and which we have previously quoted, are determined by the interests of the elders of the tribe. They want to be sure that their authority is secure, they do not want their claim to the women, and likewise their rights in regard to the marriage of their daughters, to be tampered with, and they wish to reserve the best food supplies for themselves. Thus, here there can be no idea of neighborly love in the Christian sense. Even the requirements of sharing with friends, and of living in peace with them, are emphatically restricted to the members of one's own tribe. And so, even as a matter of principle, the morality is only tribal morality.

This, then, is the first thing that must be said: Lang exaggerates tremendously in evaluating the ethical and monotheistic character of primitive monotheism. And then this must also be added: Even though all of these phenomena cannot be regarded as simply having been borrowed from Christianity, it is still entirely possible that in their present form they are under the influence of Christianity, and hence that they contain a partly Christian or Biblical colouring. Not only is this possible, it is also probable. The very fact that this belief is most prevalent just in Southeast Australia supports this view. The territory of the Southeast Australia high gods is the hinter-land of the large cities of Sidney, Melbourne, and Adelaide, and mission work has been directly carried on among the tribes residing here since the beginning of the 19th century. Since Howitt's reports belong to the period after 1870, and since they can only be supported very occasionally and fragmentarily by earlier witnesses from the first half of the 19th century, the assumption that Christian influences have played a part cannot be rejected. And in view of this fact Lang's theory must be considerably modified in any case. The ethical and monotheistic character of the belief in a highest being, as it is found among the Southeast Australians, cannot be forced in the way in which Lang forces it. Moreover, with regard to the situation at present, we must still reckon with a partial Biblical colouring and influence.

But in direct opposition to this evaluation of the situation P. Wilh. Schmidt has recently made the attempt to formulate more precisely and to carry out Lang's idea even more radically than he did himself.[16]

For this purpose, and also in order to prove his own theory which asserts a primitive monotheism in the strictest sense, Schmidt takes two paths. He attempts (1) to increase Lang's evidence; and (2) by means of critical study to formulate more convincingly that evidence. A discussion of this dual undertaking of Schmidt from the point of view of the religio-psychological method should bring the whole problem nearer to a satisfactory solution.

Of the new material which Schmidt presents, that portion which refers to Australia is again of the greatest importance. It is drawn especially from Central Australia. Formerly no belief like the Southeast Australian belief in a highest being was known among the Central Australians. Until recently we were dependent upon the works of Baldwin Spencer and Gillen: *The Native Tribes of Australia* (London, 1899), and *The Northern Tribes of Central Australia* (London, 1904), for a knowledge of these tribes. These works contain exact descriptions and photographic reproductions of many of the ritualistic ceremonies of the Central Australian tribes. But they mention no belief like primitive monotheism. And even in their supplementary volume, *Across Australia* (London, 1913), these authors took the same purely negative point of view on this matter.

However, the reliability of the statements of Spencer and Gillen has recently been seriously questioned. Almost without exception the ceremonies in question take place at night only. By request Spencer and Gillen had them performed during the day, which must have given many occasions for differences. I know from personal correspondence that Hermann Klaatsch, who has made extensive expeditions in Australia, took a very skeptical view of the reliability of the books of these two English scholars. But recently a German work has appeared which is parallel to that of Spencer and Gillen.

The German missionary Strehlow, who has been working in Central Australia since 1892, has published penetrating studies of the chief tribes, the Aranda and Loritja. This publication has

---

[16] Wilh. Schmidt began his in any case very fruitful studies with a number of treatises published in the Zeitschrift für Völker- und Sprachenkunde *"Anthropos"*; he later continued and summarized them in the voluminous work, *Der Ursprung der Gottesidee*, Vol. I (1912), 1926, Vol. II, 1928, Vol. III, 1931.

appeared in the *Veröffentlichungen des Frankfurter Städtischen Völkermuseums* (Vols. I-IV, 1907-1915).

From Strehlow we learn of a belief of the Central Australians, which apparently stands in analogy to that of the Southeast Australians, but which, on the other hand, nevertheless takes a quite unique, and especially in a religio-psychological respect, very illuminating form. But here again we must first briefly present the material.

According to the tradition of the Aranda there is a highest good being, Altjira. He is eternal and is depicted as a great strong man of ruddy complexion, whose long blond hair falls down over his shoulders. Altjira has legs like those of an emu and is therefore called *iliinka* (ilia = emu, inka = feet). He has many wives, called tnéera (the beautiful ones) who have dog legs and are also red in color. He has many sons and daughters, the former having emu legs; the latter, dog legs. Handsome young men and beautiful young women frequent his environs.—He lives in heaven which is eternal and which is imagined as a continent. Altjira is the good God of the Aranda who is known not only by the men, but also by the women. But his domain is restricted to heaven. He did not create, nor is he interested in man. The Aranda neither fear nor love him.

The earth, which is likewise eternal, was originally covered by the sea, except that several mountains projected out of this great mass of water. On the side of one of these mountains there were many undeveloped human beings, whose limbs were grown together and who were also grown fast to each other. Other undeveloped people lived in the water.

When the water had drained from the land the *Altjira-Ngamitjina* (*i.e.* the eternally uncreated, totem gods, according to Strehlow's terminology) appeared everywhere out of the earth, having lived previously in subterranean caves. Most of them appeared in human form, but they were endowed with super-human powers and they possessed the ability to reproduce those animals whose names they bore. Many of them also wandered about permanently as animals. Among all these totem gods the characteristic habits or peculiarities of the respective animal are in evidence. These totem gods possess certain places where they have lived and where they gave birth to their totem animals. Some of these totem gods remained where their tribes now dwell. On the other hand, other Altjira made long journeys and later returned to their homes with several young men. On these journeys they instructed the young novices and nearly every day staged ceremonial acts which had the purpose of initiating (intitjiuma) them into the secrets of the men, and of bringing about the thriving and the increase of their totem. After the earth had become dry, the people who were grown together lived on for a long time in their helpless condition, until a totem god came to their aid. First he separated the individual creatures from each other with a stone knife and then he separated their limbs. He taught these people to make fire and to prepare food; he gave them weapons and implements and established their marriage castes.—After death the souls of men go to the island of the dead in the north, and there, after various blind excursions, they are annihilated by a stroke of lightning.

Closely akin to these traditions of the Aranda (Strehlow, Vol. I) are those of the Loritja (Strehlow, Vol. II); they differ only in the detailed shadings of the conceptions.

The analogy of these "traditions" to the Southeast Australian belief in the high gods is unmistakable. But on the other hand there are the following important differences.

1. The high god stands here in a definite connection with totemistic conceptions and ceremonial practices. Totemism is that phenomenon, widely prevalent among primitive races, which regards individual tribes as standing in an intimate relationship to certain animals (or less frequently to certain plants), a relationship having a religious character, or at least a character analogous to the religious relationship. The members of the particular tribal group are frequently either prohibited from killing the totem animal at all, or at least from eating it themselves, or at least definite restrictions about eating it are imposed upon them. They frequently regard the totem animal as the ancestor of their clan or tribe. A peculiar social arrangement often goes with totemism, namely, that the members of a totem group are not allowed to intermarry. This is the socalled institution of exogamy. If the tribe has two totem groups, such as the hawk and the crow groups, then the hawk men can marry only crow women, and the crow men can marry only hawk women. But this classification is often elaborated still farther. In the place of a division into two totem groups, very often there is a division into four or even eight groups. When the latter holds, one-eighth of the tribe is restricted in its marital possibilities to another definite eighth.

Now among the Central Australian tribes the idea of the high god is also a part of this totemism. He of course stands above the other totem gods,[17] but only in a socalled abstract fashion. Here the practically dominant basic attitude is polytheistic, except that the high god projects above the others. The fact that among the Aranda the name of the high god is at the same time a generic term for the totem gods (Altjira—Altjira-Ngamitjina) is very enlightening in this connection.

2. The ranking of the high god above the totem gods is due, however, to his practical unimportance. According to the statements of the natives themselves he is not considered in practical religious life ("they neither fear nor love him"). Now of course such statements must be taken with great caution by anyone using the religio-psychological method. For even under circumstances which are quite different from those of primitive peoples the danger of self-deception in such a statement is very great. In all probability, then, it must be qualified by saying that the high god is only of slight importance in a practical way. Only after this careful evaluation of the situation can it be understood that, nevertheless, the belief in the existence of the high god is still expressly emphasized and consciously retained. Nevertheless, to these people this being is and remains at an unapproachable distance.

3. But the connection with the totem gods also makes possible a more definite contentual determination of the character of the high god. For these tribes the totem gods are at the same time the tribal ancestors and the givers of culture. To them are attributed the more important cultural values and institutions. Among these cultural institutions, and even primary among them, is the cultus, or sacred ceremonies. But in its essence this cultus is essentially magical. In addition to the initiation of new members it is concerned with the magical increase and strengthening of the totem objects, primarily the totem animals or totem plants. This proves that it is a magical cultus, but as such it has at the same time, as has been expressly shown,[18] a religious significance.

Accordingly the high god must be conceived as the supreme and the over-towering god among all of the totem gods. He is the common tribal ancestor of all of the individual tribes, upon whom all individual totems are dependent and from whom likewise

[17] I have purposely retained the expression "totem gods" which Strehlow employs. It is not entirely unobjectionable, but it well expresses the polytheistic or polydæmonistic background of the conception.

[18] Comp. Strehlow, *op. cit.*, III, 1st part, p. 8.

all of the various totemistic powers, the magical powers of the various totem cults, are derived. And this figure is connected with the mythology of heaven. He is localized in the sphere of heaven, whether the identification with the sun or moon is carried out or not. This evaluation of the Central Australian belief in a highest being should of course not be taken in the genetic, but exclusively in the religio-psychological sense. It must be said, then, that perhaps the acceptance of such a highest being had already preceded the totemistic culture in a genetic-historical fashion. Even then the qualification would have to be made that the magical and polytheistic (or polydaemonistic) factors, which have attained their specific and peculiar expression in totemism, were here combined with this belief in a highest being.

However, this conclusion at once takes us back to the high gods of the Southeast Australians. And now the question arises: Are the high gods of the Southeast Australians to be treated as being like those of the Central Australians? Or conversely: Are the high gods of the Central Australians like those of the Southeast? On the first alternative we would have a higher development which might be essentially attributed to Christian influence. In the other case we would have in Australia a deformation and obscuration of an originally pure monotheistic belief. P. Wilh. Schmidt advocates the latter alternative. Our own evaluation, presented from the religio-psychological point of view, apparently commits us to the first-mentioned and contrasting view, that is, to the view that the Southeast Australian material is to be understood in analogy to the Central Australian. Accordingly, it too must be denied the character of real primitive monotheism.

The correctness of this conclusion can also be proven by the material from Southeast Australia. In a larger number of cases it is expressly reported concerning the Southeast Australian high gods that in the traditions of the cult the magical powers are derived from them.[19] And concerning one of the most important of the gods, Baiame, it is expressly stated that, according to the traditions of the cult, he unites all totems within himself, in other words, that he himself stands above all individual totems.

Therefore we have here the connection, not only with mythology, which was proven at the start, but also with totemism and with magic. It is for this reason that we interpret the Southeast Australian tradition of the highest being entirely in analogy to

---

[19] Comp. A. W. Howitt, *The Native Tribes of Southeast Australia.* London 1904, p. 410.

the Central Australian, and conversely, the Central Australian according to the Southeast Australian.[20]

So we must let the matter rest with the following statement: the Southeast Australian tradition concerning the "highest being," as it exists today, is in all probability partly influenced by Christianity. And in any case it must be taken together with the tradition of the Central Australian tribes. There can be no thought of genuine monotheism. Nevertheless, there is a noteworthy monotheistic tendency. However, this tendency is inseparably connected with those mythological, magical, and polydaemonistic motives which have attained a unique form in the totemistic conceptions, without being materially dependent upon these motives.

From the point of view of this religio-psychologically orientated position to the new theory of primitive monotheism, the following general observation follows for the solution of our whole problem.

Originally religion, magic, and mythology seem to have been inextricably interwoven. Schelling and Max Müller were on the right track when they assumed a still undifferentiated stage prior to later differentiated forms of belief. But this view must be carried back much farther, and it must be carried through in a much more detailed way, than Schelling and Max Müller attempted to do. It is not, as they assumed, only the still undifferentiated condition prior to monotheism and polytheism, but much more universally the still undifferentiated condition prior to the distinction between religion, magic, and mythology with which we are concerned. Yet just for this reason religious belief may at the same time occasionally emerge out of this background with a strong monotheistic colouring. For the magical and mythological elements do not belong to the essential nature of religion as such, no matter how great a rôle they may play in the historical process of religious development, because of their common background.

But in order to establish this general view more firmly, we must try to delve still deeper, and therefore it is necessary to discuss the relations between religion and magic more at length.

---

[20] I have taken up in greater detail further questions belonging to this whole problem in my treatise already mentioned: *Die Frage nach den Anfängen der Religion in religionspsychologischer Beleuchtung,* pp. 385 ff. Here it is only necessary to add that I do not, from a religio-psychological approach, reject the ethnological "method of cultural spheres," which P. Wilh. Schmidt employs, but only the particular argument for his religioscientific theory which he attempts to deduce from this method.

APPENDIX III

RELIGION AND MAGIC

For this purpose let us begin again with the totemistic cults of the Australians of which we have already spoken. For these cults bear an unmistakable magical character. The natives say that their aim is to produce by cult practices an increase or a strengthening of the totem—usually this refers to animal but less frequently to plant totems. In the great majority of cases the cult practice consists in an imitative representation of the respective totem animal's habits of living. Carl Strehlow has inimitably described a large number of such totem cults.[21] He has also published the texts of a variety of cult songs in the original language, with an accurate German translation.

The magical character of these cults is unmistakable. And yet the religious tinge cannot be denied. Strehlow, who as a missionary, is very cautious in just this respect, and who always has the tendency to regard all pagan religious elements as non-religious, summarizes his judgment in the following fashion: "The natives regard this ceremony as a kind of divine worship, just as the Christians regard their religious practices." And Strehlow expressly adds that this evaluation of the practices has been confirmed by Christian as well as by pagan natives. Thus one cannot entirely deny that there is a real religious significance to these cults. Moreover, the purpose of strengthening or of multiplying the totem objects does not absolutely exclude such a specifically religious significance. This is shown by the fact that this aim apparently does not exhaust the basic tendency of the cult, indeed, it may perhaps even be regarded as secondary. Strehlow reports that the natives themselves place the most emphasis upon the traditional commandments of the totem ancestors. To the question of why these cults are celebrated, they repeatedly answered that the ancestors had commanded it, and that is also

---

[21] *Op. cit.*, Vol. III, *Die totemistischen Kulte der Aranda-und Loritja-Stämme* (the first and second parts, 1910 and 1911). Supplementary material in Vol. IV, *Das soziale Leben der Aranda und Loritja*, 1913 and 1915.

the reason why they are celebrated just as they are and in no other way. The consciousness of dependence, which this statement reveals, seems of course to rest purely upon human authority. But in reality this is not true. In the first place, the totem ancestors are not purely human authorities for the Australians. And then it must also be considered that while such cults are perhaps dominantly celebrated to increase the useful animals and plants, still this is not always the case, for they are also sometimes celebrated to conserve completely useless and even harmful totem objects.[22] And it is also an especially noteworthy fact that specific places where, according to tradition, some totem ancestor had once rested or dressed himself, are also regarded as totems.[23]

All of these facts force us to assume that these cults are ultimately directed toward that mysterious power which is active in all totems and which is likewise assumed in the *churingas* (the "bull-roarers" of the cult ceremonies). The aim of strengthening this power is conditioned by the belief that man is dependent upon and obligated to it; and therefore it is of a religious nature.[24]

Yet the magical character of these cults certainly cannot be disputed. That becomes even more evident when we take into consideration the fact that alongside of and analogous to the animal and plant cults are other cults whose magical nature is absolutely unmistakable. For example, we find a moon cult whose express purpose is to make the moon shine more brightly so that hunting can be carried on better at night; a fire cult which is celebrated in winter to give the fire more power to warm; and a rain cult which is supposed to frighten away rain that is not needed.

Now these last-named cults take us completely into the realm of genuine magic. To what extent? What is magic after all? What is its real essence?

The German word for magic is the same as the word for sorcery. However, we should not call magic sorcery because that would imply a premature value-judgment. And to an even greater extent this is true of the distinction between white and black magic. It will be better to survey the whole field of magic, and to distinguish its chief types, of which there are three.

---

[22] Comp. the lists in Strehlow, Vol. II, pp. 61 ff.

[23] Strehlow, *op. cit.,* p. 72, note 5.

[24] At this point my view coincides with the opinion advanced by Emile Durkheim (*Les formes élémentaires de la vie religieuse,* 1912). Although I do not accept his theory as a whole, Karl Beth also (*Religion und Magie bei den Naturvölkern,* 1914, 2nd ed., 1927) espouses a similar position with careful and convincing arguments, but he is in closer agreement with Durkheim than the facts seem to me to justify.

1. *Imitative magic.* The cult practices of the Australians already discussed belong here. And the following especially frequent phenomena also belong here: an image of a man is made and the image is treated as one would wish to treat that man. Nails are driven into the image in order to injure the person it represents, or the image is burned or thrown into the water to bring about that person's death. Or a weapon is pointed or hurled in the direction of an enemy one wishes to destroy.

2. *Contagious magic.* Anything that has been in any kind of contact with another thing may influence it. The main point of this idea is that any effect produced upon a single part of an object or of a person, will also affect the whole object or the whole person. For example, the possession of a wisp of hair or even of a single hair of another man will give one power over him. And the same is also especially true of the nails or nail-clippings, but occasionally also of every other part or organ of the body. And the same is true of clothing. Any article of clothing is thought to contain the vital energy of its present or previous wearer and consequently it may be used accordingly.

3. *Magic by the simple assertion of the will.* All spells and charms are of this type. For example, living beings, men or animals, or even movable objects are held fast to a particular spot by a word of command. And the attempts to injure an enemy by the simple recitation or singing of a magical spell also belong here.

All three types of magic are found in the most intimate connection with primitive religions. But not merely that. They are also found to the greatest extent in connection with the higher and even with the very advanced forms of religion. Even in the Old Testament such magic is not absent, in spite of the attack of the religion of Jahweh upon this heathenish "abomination." For example, the story of how Jacob acquired his stock of cattle (Genesis 30) is magic. The background of the account of the battle of Gibeon, where Joshua made the sun stand still upon Gibeon and the moon in the valley of Aijalon (Joshua 10) is magic.

Magic is frequently encountered in the stories of Elijah and Elisha. When Elijah calls Elisha to be his successor he throws his cloak over him, and the narrator indicated that thereby the lot of Elisha's destiny is cast. (I Kings, 19.) Shortly before his death Elisha reassures King Joash concerning the future. He tells him to shoot an arrow toward the east, saying: "Jahweh's arrow of victory, the arrow of victory over Syria." The first phrase places the magical act (which is clearly expressed in the second phrase) under the authority of the belief in Jahweh. Then Elisha commands the king to strike the ground with the arrows, and when the king stops after striking the ground three times Elisha scolds him: "Thou shouldst have smitten five or six times; then hadst thou smitten Syria till thou hadst consumed it; whereas now thou shalt smite Syria but thrice." (II Kings, 13.)

Even among the great writing prophets magic is present. Their socalled symbolic actions are often not of a merely symbolical nature. Yet they are certainly not purely magical acts. Nevertheless the magical conception still lurks in the background and remains an active factor. For example, when Jeremiah comes before the people with a yoke upon his shoulders in order to impress upon them that for the time being they must remain under the yoke of Babylon, his opponent Hananiah tears the yoke from his shoulders and breaks it. Then Jeremiah makes a yoke of iron and comes again to Hananiah, saying: "Thou hast broken the bars of wood. But Jehovah has put a yoke of iron upon the neck of all these nations that they may serve the King of Babylon, and they shall serve him." (Jeremiah 27 and 28.) Here the magical background is obvious.

INDEX

375

Index

377

Legalistic religion, 190 f.
Lehmann, 31, 127.
Lehman-Tessel, 70 n.
Leibniz, 25.
LeRoy, 61 n.
Leuba, 12 ff., 81 ff., 239 ff., 296 ff.
Liebert, 306 n.
Life, eternal; see also Immortality; in Buddhism, 64 ff., 105.
Lipps, 52 f.
Longing, 157 ff.
Lorentz, 322 n.
Lorinser, 202 n.
Lubbock (Lord Avebury), 291 ff., 358.
Lücke, 80 f., 348.
Luther, ii, 5 ff., 24 ff., 54, 57, 147 f., 251.

Macintosh, viii, xvi.
Magic, 30, 54, 72, 123 f., 132 f., 172 f., 178 f., 189 f., 219 ff., 234 ff., 274 ff., 368 f., Appendix III.
Maier, 16 f., 52.
Mana, 30, 123 f., 134, 189.
Mannhardt, 134.
Marett, 172.
Markham, 161 n.
Marx, 287.
Materialism, 255 ff., 274 f., 316 ff.
Mehlis, 156 n.
Meinhof, 62.
Mendel, 326 f.
Miracle, 145.
Monism (materialistic), 255 ff., 316 ff.
Monotheism, 119, 186 ff., 202 ff., 301; primitive, Appendix II.
Morality and religion, 148 f., 167 ff., 235 ff., Ch. XIII; Kant, on, 310.
Müller, Johannes, 222.
Müller, Max, 60, 140, 356 f., 370.
Mutations, theory of, 324 f.
Mystical tendency of religion, 186 ff.
Mysticism, 105 ff., 186 ff., 314.
Mythology, 72, 95, 131 f., 234 ff., 370.

National religions, 189 f.
Natorp, 75, 81, 95 ff., 146 ff., 301 ff., 336 f.
Naturalistic philosophy, Ch. X.
Natural religion, 25.
Negation of the self, 106 ff.
Neo-Buddhism, 143 f., 167, 178.
Newton, 260.
Nietzsche, 119 n., 166 n.
Nirvana, 103 f., 137 ff., 162 ff., 216.
Normative standard, method of, 33, 38.

Obermeier, 291 n.
Obligation, sense of, 165, 167 ff.
Oedipus complex, 281, 285.
Olcott, 70, 219.
Oldenberg, 55 n., 63 n., 64 n., 65 n., 66, 102 ff., 114 n., 125 n., 132 n., 135 n., 138 ff., 164, 177, 180 n., 195 n. ff., 216 n. f.
Opinion, in relation to knowledge and belief, 258 f.
Optimism, 263 ff.
Origin of religion; Freudian theory, 279 ff.; Adaptionist (Gruppe), 288 ff.
Ostwald, 255 ff.
Otto, Rudolph, x, 74, 81, 91 ff., 100 n., 145 n., 168 ff., 259.
Over-world, 100, 118 ff., 133 ff., 181 f., 288 ff.

Pantheism, 75, 120, 192 ff.
Parker, 360 n.
Pessimism, 263 ff.
Pfeiffer, 112.
Pfister, 284 n.
Pfleiderer, 121.
Plotinus, 57, 111.
Polytheism, 119, 186 ff., 356.
Positivism, 298.
Poussin, 66.
Pragmatism, 11, 18, 227 f., 307, 311.
Prayer, 57 ff., 67 ff., 100 ff., 159 ff., 171 ff.
Pre-historic religion, 291.
Preuss, 61, 160 n., 294.
Primitive religion, 58 ff., 121 ff., 134 ff., 158 ff., 189, Ch. IX, Appendix II.
Propitiation, 178 ff.
Protestantism, 54.
Psalms, 62, 156 ff.
Psycho-analysis, 29 f., 274, 279 ff.
Psychology, empirical, vi, 8 ff., 48, 85 n., 297 f.

Rationalization of religion, 170, 218, 221 f., 253 ff., 270 ff., 315.
Reden; see also Addresses on Religion.
Reformation, 54; see also Luther.
Reik, 280.
Reinke, 318 f.
Reischle, 35, 37 f.
Relationship, the religious, 100 ff., 116 ff., 131, 313 f.
Relativity, theory of, 322.
Religio-historical method, 7, 31 ff., 34, 38.

BUNKER HILL COMMUNITY COLLEGE

3 6189 00008 6636

GV 721.2 .B78 G87 1984
Guttmann, Allen.
The games must go on

DATE DUE	BORROWER'S NAME

GV 721.2 .B78 G87 1984
Guttmann, Allen.
The games must go on

BUNKER HILL

BHCC

COMMUNITY COLLEGE
CHARLESTOWN, MASS.

#9411983